The House of God

The House of God

A Book of Meditations on the First Epistle of Paul to Timothy for Students of the Gospel Ministry

John Peter Bodner

RESOURCE *Publications* • Eugene, Oregon

THE HOUSE OF GOD
A Book of Meditations on the First Epistle of Paul to Timothy for Students of the Gospel Ministry

Copyright © 2013 John Peter Bodner. All rights reserved. Except for brief quotations in critical publications or reviews, no part of this book may be reproduced in any manner without prior written permission from the publisher. Write: Permissions, Wipf and Stock Publishers, 199 W. 8th Ave., Suite 3, Eugene, OR 97401.

Resource Publications
An Imprint of Wipf and Stock Publishers
199 W. 8th Ave., Suite 3
Eugene, OR 97401
www.wipfandstock.com

ISBN 13: 978-1-62032-687-9
Manufactured in the U.S.A.

Extracts from the Authorized Version of the Bible (The King James Bible), the rights in which are vested in the Crown, are reproduced by permission of the Crown's Patentee, Cambridge University Press.

to
the Glory of God Triune
and
In Affectionate Remembrance
of
my Devoted, Godly Wife
Dorothy Hazel Crellin
and
my loving parents
John and Victoria Bodner

Foreword

CHRISTIANS SPEAK OF "EXPERIENTIAL religion." Especially this phrase is on the lips of pastors.

It means having a more than cerebral acquaintance with Jesus Christ. There is a belief in the Lord that acknowledges truly that He was a Man in space-and-time history, but the devils themselves possess such historical faith, and they tremble. More than such faith is required to have any assurance one is a true disciple of Jesus Christ.

To have any usefulness in the kingdom of God, especially as a servant of the Word of God, and a servant of the Lord of the Word, an experience of conviction of one's great need and the Lord's great mercy is essential. But more than that, an awareness of God's personal dealings with you in testing, in the providences of life, in teaching you lessons to strengthen your faith and deepen your appreciation of His love in Jesus Christ, that love which passes knowledge. All that is needed: growingly so.

To speak and preach helpfully to others, then, your own inner personality, your heart and soul must know the steady and variegated operations of the Word and the Spirit upon your inner man. We are talking of an increasing, growing relationship with a living and loving Person, your Master, Jesus Christ the Son of God, who reigns over the entire universe, so that you cry, "Oh, that I might know Him better! To love and serve Him much better than I have!" These are the longings that manifest true piety.

It is Jonathan Edwards' sustained emphasis that the heart of true religion is found in the affections. The greatest of all the Commandments is to love the Lord our God with our entire being. The stress is not on man's mind simply to understand God—though our intellect is to be devoted to the fascinating contemplation of the living God. Supremely, it is an *experiential knowledge* that we yearn for, not mere "experiential feelings"—that is a mere tautology. Knowledge—yes, let us have knowledge: knowledge of the Bible, knowledge of God as Creator, Sustainer and Judge, knowledge of Jesus Christ in His two natures as God and Man, in His three offices as Prophet, Priest and King, in His three states—eternal, humiliated and exalted. Let us know more of the Holy Spirit as a divine Person, equal to God in power and glory. Let us know the way of redemption accomplished and applied in Christ. We must know all the counsel of God. We must have more than vague feelings about religion, mere notions of what is the one true revealed religion. Knowledge of the true God we must have, but it must be *experiential knowledge*. Joseph Hart the hymn-writer famously wrote:

> Vain is all our best devotion,
> If on false foundations built;
> True religion's more than notion,
> Something must be known and felt.

Here is the usefulness of the book that lies in your hand. There are fine commentaries on the Pastoral Epistles. Many can be commended and should be studied carefully. These brief chapters are aimed at stirring up our affections by the impact of what the simple text so vividly shows of Paul's concern for Timothy and for all servants of God. If only we possessed all that we profess, and believed all that we believe!

John Peter Bodner has been a Canadian friend of mine for many years, spending one happy summer with me in Aberystwyth at the end of his studies at Westminster Theological Seminary in Philadelphia. We share the same *alma mater*; we love the same truths, we both desire to preach with the Holy Spirit sent down from heaven. I am convinced that the simple devotional reading of this book on First Timothy, its exhortations and hymns, while letting its truths do their own work in our entire personalities, cannot but serve the end of reviving "experimental religion" in all who read it.

There is no greater need than that the doctrines that have been re-discovered in the past decades through the Protestant world should be vitally known, felt, and loved, moving preachers and congregations alike in the service of our great God. May the fruit of the revived Christianity that we pray for be one great end of reading these pages.

Rev. Geoffrey B. Thomas,
Minister, Alfred Place Baptist Church, Aberystwyth, Wales

Foreword

The Holy Spirit directed the apostle Paul to write the body of literature commonly labeled "the Pastoral Epistles" (1, 2 Timothy, and Titus). This designation is appropriate, since these letters were addressed by the veteran missionary to his two younger co-laborers in the Gospel. They required precise instructions about maintaining order in the Churches under their charge. There were false teachers to refute, Church leaders to appoint, gender roles to clarify, and moral conduct to define.

Although the distinct pastoral thrust of these epistles cannot be seriously denied, we also recognize their considerable value for the entire Body of Christ. These devotionals, in most cases, reflecting upon the text of 1 Timothy, contain numerous theological insights that will prove fruitful for Christians generally and particularly for pastors and seminary students.

As I gaze across at a bookshelf laden with volumes on the New Testament, I can see larger treatments on Paul's epistles to Timothy. Many of them address matters related to dating, authorship, and complex textual issues. Admittedly, it is not the design of this book to tackle the finer details which fall within the purview of major commentaries. Nonetheless, the author has placed in our hands a theological gem. This is a magnificently constructed work that proceeds methodically and competently through the biblical text. It is marked by that admirable lucidity, brevity, refreshing saneness, and pastoral fervor that is inimitably associated with the author.

Readers will feel the weight of the biblical text and taste its sweetness as they peruse the material before them. They will be sharpened, blessed, and challenged to relish the grace of the Lord Jesus Christ and to carry out their calling to spread the fame of the blessed Savior.

Rev. Dr. Glendon G. Thompson,
Pastor, Jarvis Street Baptist Church, Toronto, Ontario, Canada

Preface

IN THE COURSE OF examining my own life and labor as a Minister of the Gospel, I was greatly challenged by hearing Dr. A.N. Martin of New Jersey expounding and applying 1 Timothy 4:11–16 during a one day conference for pastors at Canton, Michigan, in the United States. It seemed to me that the Spirit of grace had led the preacher into applications of particularly pertinent personal and practical help for my soul and service.

As I later reviewed my notes and the passage so expounded, I noted this directive from the Apostle:

Meditate upon these things; give thyself wholly to them; that thy profiting may appear to all. (1 Timothy 4:15).

It was thus laid upon my heart that I should give myself to extended, prayerful reflection and rumination upon this Epistle in light of the whole counsel of God in Holy Scripture, as the Holy Ghost might grant me light and leading.

The exercises of devotional meditation which followed this course began on 1 January 2006 and closed on 25 May 2008. They are here presented in a form slightly edited to allow for weekly reading by my brethren in the ministry and by students seeking to prepare for the good work of a bishop, elder, pastor, and teacher in the house of God.

Each section supplies *an original hymn*. A course of *select Bible readings* covers the words and works of leading men of God in the Old Testament, many of the richest portions of the New Testament, and the whole Psalter. Finally, there is a *meditation* on a portion of 1 Timothy. To these 145 devotions have been added 12 short devotional pieces written for magazines and local church bulletins under the heading "From My Bible." The book can thus serve as a weekly companion to a seminarian for three years of training. In addition, I would warmly commend to any student of the ministry unfamiliar with the Heidelberg Catechism to read and reflect upon its 52 Lord's Days each year of his studies.

This is neither an exegetical commentary nor a series of expository sermons. While I have on occasion consulted lexicon and concordance to ascertain more clearly the intent of the sacred text, I have not attempted an academic work here. I have sought throughout to mull over and assimilate to my heart the words of life in their immediate import to my own soul. I invite the reader to share my experience by retaining the first person. I hope I have not strayed far from the simple truths that offer themselves at once to the devout mind, nor in any way wrested the Scriptures.

Preface

    In humble hope that reading these Meditations may accrue to others some of the profit I have experienced in writing them, I now offer them to those who labor "for the Word of God, and for the testimony of Jesus Christ." May we all know the blessedness of that man who meditates in the Law of the Lord day and night (Josh 1:8; Psalm 1).

Affectionately yours in the Lord Jesus, our faithful Savior,
Rev. John Peter Bodner M.A., M.Div.
Pastor, Hope Assembly, Mississauga, Canada

First Epistle of Paul to Timothy

Salutation—1:1-2

1:1 Paul, an apostle of Jesus Christ by the commandment of God our Saviour, and Lord Jesus Christ, *which is* our hope; 2Unto Timothy, *my* own son in the faith: Grace, mercy, *and* peace, from God our Father and Jesus Christ our Lord.

Charge to Keep Sound Doctrine: Law and Gospel—1:3-20

3As I besought thee to abide still at Ephesus, when I went into Macedonia, that thou mightest charge some that they teach no other doctrine, 4Neither give heed to fables and endless genealogies, which minister questions, rather than godly edifying which is in faith: *so do.*

5Now the end of the commandment is charity out of a pure heart, and *of* a good conscience, and *of* faith unfeigned: 6From which some having swerved have turned aside unto vain jangling; 7Desiring to be teachers of the law; understanding neither what they say, nor whereof they affirm.

8But we know that the law *is* good, if a man use it lawfully; 9Knowing this, that the law is not made for a righteous man, but for the lawless and disobedient, for the ungodly and for sinners, for unholy and profane, for murderers of fathers and murderers of mothers, for manslayers, 10For whoremongers, for them that defile themselves with mankind, for menstealers, for liars, for perjured persons, and if there be any other thing that is contrary to sound doctrine; 11According to the glorious gospel of the blessed God, which was committed to my trust.

12And I thank Christ Jesus our Lord, who hath enabled me, for that he counted me faithful, putting me into the ministry; 13Who was before a blasphemer, and a persecutor, and injurious: but I obtained mercy, because I did *it* ignorantly in unbelief. 14And the grace of our Lord was exceeding abundant with faith and love which is in Christ Jesus. 15This *is* a faithful saying, and worthy of all acceptation, that Christ Jesus came into the world to save sinners; of whom I am chief. 16Howbeit for this cause I obtained mercy, that in me first Jesus Christ might shew forth all longsuffering, for a pattern to them which should hereafter believe on him to life everlasting.

17Now unto the King eternal, immortal, invisible, the only wise God, *be* honour and glory for ever and ever. Amen.

18This charge I commit unto thee, son Timothy, according to the prophecies which went before on thee, that thou by them mightest war a good warfare; 19Holding faith, and a good conscience; which some having put away concerning faith have made shipwreck: 20Of whom is Hymenaeus and Alexander; whom I have delivered unto Satan, that they may learn not to blaspheme.

Exhortation to Prayer—2:1–7

2:1 I exhort therefore, that, first of all, supplications, prayers, intercessions, *and* giving of thanks, be made for all men; 2For kings, and *for* all that are in authority; that we may lead a quiet and peaceable life in all godliness and honesty. 3For this *is* good and acceptable in the sight of God our Saviour; 4Who will have all men to be saved, and to come unto the knowledge of the truth. 5For *there is* one God, and one mediator between God and men, the man Christ Jesus; 6Who gave himself a ransom for all, to be testified in due time. 7Whereunto I am ordained a preacher, and an apostle, (I speak the truth in Christ, *and* lie not;) a teacher of the Gentiles in faith and verity.

Men and Women at Public Worship—2:8–15

8I will therefore that men pray every where, lifting up holy hands, without wrath and doubting. 9In like manner also, that women adorn themselves in modest apparel, with shamefacedness and sobriety; not with braided hair, or gold, or pearls, or costly array; 10But (which becometh women professing godliness) with good works.

11Let the woman learn in silence with all subjection. 12But I suffer not a woman to teach, nor to usurp authority over the man, but to be in silence. 13For Adam was first formed, then Eve. 14And Adam was not deceived, but the woman being deceived was in the transgression. 15Notwithstanding she shall be saved in childbearing, if they continue in faith and charity and holiness with sobriety.

The Offices: Bishop and Deacons—3:1–13

3:1 This *is* a true saying, If a man desire the office of a bishop, he desireth a good work. 2A bishop then must be blameless, the husband of one wife, vigilant, sober, of good behaviour, given to hospitality, apt to teach; 3Not given to wine, no striker, not greedy of filthy lucre; but patient, not a brawler, not covetous; 4One that ruleth well his own house, having his children in subjection with all gravity; 5(For if a man know not how to rule his own house, how shall he take care of the church of God?) 6Not a novice, lest being lifted up with pride he fall into the condemnation of the devil. 7Moreover he must have a good report of them which are without; lest he fall into reproach and the snare of the devil.

8Likewise *must* the deacons *be* grave, not double-tongued, not given to much wine, not greedy of filthy lucre; 9Holding the mystery of the faith in a pure conscience. 10And let these also first be proved; then let them use the office of a deacon, being *found* blameless. 11Even so *must their* wives be grave, not slanderers, sober, faithful in all things. 12Let the deacons be the husbands of one wife, ruling their children and their own houses well. 13For they that have used the office of a deacon well purchase to themselves a good degree, and great boldness in the faith which is in Christ Jesus.

The House of God; The Mystery of Godliness—3:14-16

14These things write I unto thee, hoping to come unto thee shortly: 15But if I tarry long, that thou mayest know how thou oughtest to behave thyself in the house of God, which is the church of the living God, the pillar and ground of the truth. 16And without controversy great is the mystery of godliness:

>God was manifest in the flesh,
>justified in the Spirit,
>seen of angels,
>preached unto the Gentiles,
>believed on in the world,
>received up into glory.

The Latter Times; A Good Minister of Jesus Christ—4:1-10

4:1Now the Spirit speaketh expressly, that in the latter times some shall depart from the faith, giving heed to seducing spirits, and doctrines of devils; 2Speaking lies in hypocrisy; having their conscience seared with a hot iron; 3Forbidding to marry, *and commanding* to abstain from meats, which God hath created to be received with thanksgiving of them which believe and know the truth. 4For every creature of God *is* good, and nothing to be refused, if it be received with thanksgiving: 5For it is sanctified by the word of God and prayer.

6If thou put the brethren in remembrance of these things, thou shalt be a good minister of Jesus Christ, nourished up in the words of faith and of good doctrine, whereunto thou hast attained.

7But refuse profane and old wives' fables, and exercise thyself *rather* unto godliness. 8For bodily exercise profiteth little: but godliness is profitable unto all things, having promise of the life that now is, and of that which is to come.

9This *is* a faithful saying and worthy of all acceptation. 10For therefore we both labour and suffer reproach, because we trust in the living God, who is the Saviour of all men, specially of those that believe.

These Things Command and Teach—4:11-16

11These things command and teach.

12Let no man despise thy youth; but be thou an example of the believers, in word, in conversation, in charity, in spirit, in faith, in purity. 13Till I come, give attendance to reading, to exhortation, to doctrine. 14Neglect not the gift that is in thee, which was given thee by prophecy, with the laying on of the hands of the presbytery. 15Meditate upon these things; give thyself wholly to them; that thy profiting may appear to all.

16Take heed unto thyself, and unto the doctrine; continue in them: for in doing this thou shalt both save thyself, and them that hear thee.

The House of God

Father, Brethren, Mothers, Sisters—5:1-2

5:1 Rebuke not an elder, but intreat *him* as a father; *and* the younger men as brethren; 2 The elder women as mothers; the younger as sisters, with all purity.

Widows Indeed—5:3-16

3 Honour widows that are widows indeed. 4 But if any widow have children or nephews, let them learn first to shew piety at home, and to requite their parents: for that is good and acceptable before God.

5 Now she that is a widow indeed, and desolate, trusteth in God, and continueth in supplications and prayers night and day. 6 But she that liveth in pleasure is dead while she liveth.

7 And these things give in charge, that they may be blameless. 8 But if any provide not for his own, and specially for those of his own house, he hath denied the faith, and is worse than an infidel.

9 Let not a widow be taken into the number under threescore years old, having been the wife of one man, 10 Well reported of for good works; if she have brought up children, if she have lodged strangers, if she have washed the saints' feet, if she have relieved the afflicted, if she have diligently followed every good work.

11 But the younger widows refuse: for when they have begun to wax wanton against Christ, they will marry; 12 Having damnation, because they have cast off their first faith. 13 And withal they learn *to be* idle, wandering about from house to house; and not only idle, but tattlers also and busybodies, speaking things which they ought not.

14 I will therefore that the younger women marry, bear children, guide the house, give none occasion to the adversary to speak reproachfully. 15 For some are already turned aside after Satan. 16 If any man or woman that believeth have widows, let them relieve them, and let not the church be charged; that it may relieve them that are widows indeed.

The Elders—5:17-25

17 Let the elders that rule well be counted worthy of double honour, especially they who labour in the word and doctrine. 18 For the scripture saith, THOU SHALT NOT MUZZLE THE OX THAT TREADETH OUT THE CORN. And, THE LABOURER *IS* WORTHY OF HIS REWARD.

19 Against an elder receive not an accusation, but before two or three witnesses. 20 Them that sin rebuke before all, that others also may fear.

21 I charge *thee* before God, and the Lord Jesus Christ, and the elect angels, that thou observe these things without preferring one before another, doing nothing by partiality.

22 Lay hands suddenly on no man, neither be partaker of other men's sins: keep thyself pure.

23Drink no longer water, but use a little wine for thy stomach's sake and thine often infirmities.

24Some men's sins are open beforehand, going before to judgment; and some *men* they follow after. 25Likewise also the good works *of some* are manifest beforehand; and they that are otherwise cannot be hid.

Servants and Masters—6:1-2

6:1Let as many servants as are under the yoke count their own masters worthy of all honour, that the name of God and *his* doctrine be not blasphemed. 2And they that have believing masters, let them not despise *them,* because they are brethren; but rather do *them* service, because they are faithful and beloved, partakers of the benefit.

Wholesome Words: Love of Money and Contentment—6:2-12

2These things teach and exhort. 3If any man teach otherwise, and consent not to wholesome words, *even* the words of our Lord Jesus Christ, and to the doctrine which is according to godliness; 4He is proud, knowing nothing, but doting about questions and strifes of words, whereof cometh envy, strife, railings, evil surmisings, 5Perverse disputings of men of corrupt minds, and destitute of the truth, supposing that gain is godliness: from such withdraw thyself.

6But godliness with contentment is great gain. 7For we brought nothing into *this* world, *and it is* certain we can carry nothing out. 8And having food and raiment let us be therewith content.

9But they that will be rich fall into temptation and a snare, and *into* many foolish and hurtful lusts, which drown men in destruction and perdition. 10For the love of money is the root of all evil: which while some coveted after, they have erred from the faith, and pierced themselves through with many sorrows.

11But thou, O man of God, flee these things; and follow after righteousness, godliness, faith, love, patience, meekness. 12Fight the good fight of faith, lay hold on eternal life, whereunto thou art also called, and hast professed a good profession before many witnesses.

A Charge to Keep—6:13-16

13I give thee charge in the sight of God, who quickeneth all things, and *before* Christ Jesus, who before Pontius Pilate witnessed a good confession; 14That thou keep *this* commandment without spot, unrebukeable, until the appearing of our Lord Jesus Christ: 15Which in his times he shall shew, *who is* the blessed and only Potentate, the King of kings, and Lord of lords; 16Who only hath immortality, dwelling in the light which no man can approach unto; whom no man hath seen, nor can see: to whom *be* honour and power everlasting. Amen.

The Rich in this World: Rich in Good Works—6:17-19

^{17}Charge them that are rich in this world, that they be not highminded, nor trust in uncertain riches, but in the living God, who giveth us richly all things to enjoy; ^{18}That they do good, that they be rich in good works, ready to distribute, willing to communicate; ^{19}Laying up in store for themselves a good foundation against the time to come, that they may lay hold on eternal life.

Farewell: Grace—6:20

^{20}O Timothy, keep that which is committed to thy trust, avoiding profane *and* vain babblings, and oppositions of science falsely so called: ^{21}Which some professing have erred concerning the faith.

Grace *be* with thee. Amen.

1. Hallelujah! Hallelujah!

1 Hallelujah! Hallelujah!
Praise our God forevermore
Saints and angels, earth and heaven,
Worship, bless Him and adore:
O declare His glory now
Till to Him all nations bow!

2 Hallelujah! Hallelujah!
Tell the sovereign, boundless love
Of our God, th'Almighty Father
Who in mercy, from above
Gave His own beloved Son
For the sins which we had done!

3 Hallelujah! Hallelujah!
Sound the Name of Jesus Christ,
God th'incarnate Son, our Savior,
Only Prophet, King and Priest
Who to save us, once hath bled,
Died, and risen from the dead!

4 Hallelujah! Hallelujah!
Now the Holy Spirit laud
Who through prophets and apostles
Breathed the oracles of God,
Witness with the written Word
Unto Christ our risen Lord!

5 Hallelujah, Hallelujah!
One true living God proclaim,
Father, Son and Holy Spirit,
Who possess the Sacred Name
Of Jehovah: at His throne
Bow and worship Him alone!

8.7.8.7.7.7.

The House of God

> Preparatory Reading: Old Testament: Genesis 12
> New Testament: Matthew 1 Psalm: 1

1 Timothy : Reading the entire Epistle

The Book of God is in my hand—the Holy Scriptures. Let me pray that God may be pleased to give me freely the mind of Christ in these words which the Holy Ghost teaches. And let me prayerfully, slowly, thoughtfully take up and read this whole Epistle that I may give more earnest heed to the great salvation, and the great Savior it reveals.

Savior Jesus! Cleanse and purge me as a vessel fit and meet for Thy use, my Master! How can I "make full proof" of Thy call and "my ministry?" Thou hast set Thy servant and Apostle *Paul* as a "teacher of the Gentiles in faith and verity." He has written by Thy Spirit to instruct Timothy, "how to behave in the House of God, which is the Church of the living God, the ground and pillar of the truth." To him he declared, "Commit the same unto faithful men able to teach others also." And so in my hands through Thy churches' instruction, I hold my Bible, and in it hold this Epistle. Help me give myself wholly to these things, and continue in them, that my progress may be clear to all. Use this meditation, line upon line, precept upon precept, that I may take heed to myself and to the doctrine, and so to save myself and all who hear me (2 Tim 2:21; 4:5; 2 Tim 1:11)

A Prayer for Illumination

Holy, holy, holy, Lord God of hosts:
Heaven and earth is full of Thy glory!
How excellent is Thy Name in all the earth,
Who hast exalted Thy glory above the heavens.
Thou hast magnified Thy Word above all Thy Name:
Thy Word is truth:

Almighty Father, only-begotten Son, Holy Spirit of God
Thou art Jehovah, which dwelt in the bush:
Who hast given the Law by Moses,
Who spakest by the Prophets,
Who in these last days hast spoken to us
In Thy Son Jesus Christ, full of grace and truth:

No man hath seen Thee at any time;
No man can look upon Thee and live.
Thou hast spoken: we have heard only a voice.
Thou art neither in the fire, the wind or the earthquake,
But in a still, small voice.

The House of God

Yet Thou who hast commanded the light the shine out of darkness
Hast shined in our hearts to give us the knowledge of Thy glory
In the face of Jesus Christ.
That which was from the beginning, even the eternal Life
That was with Thee, O God, that with Thee is God,
Seen, heard, handled, witnessed
The Word made flesh—God manifest in the flesh
Is declared to us by the Apostles;
That we also might have fellowship with Thee
And with Thy Son Jesus:
These things are written that our joy might be full.

We have received the Gospel
How that Christ died for our sins
according to the Scriptures,
That He was buried and rose again the third day
according to the Scriptures;
For thus it is written, and thus it behooved Christ to suffer and to rise
That repentance and remission of sins be preached in His Name
To all nations,
Preaching Jesus beginning at the same Scriptures.

And we have known these Holy Scriptures
Which are able to make us wise to salvation
Through faith that is in Christ Jesus:
We, even we who once were without God
and without hope in the world
are now built together a very habitation of God by the Spirit
founded upon the Apostles and Prophets,
JESUS CHRIST Himself the chief cornerstone.

We come to Thee, O Lord Jesus,
For to whom else can we go?
Thou hast these words of eternal life!
We believe and are sure that Thou art that Christ,
The Son of the living God!
We sit and hear Thy Word now at Thy feet,
Prince and Savior
Angel of the Covenant
In whom we delight:
Show us now what is noted in the Scripture of truth!

The House of God

No Scripture has come by private interpretation;
But holy men spake as they were moved of the Holy Ghost:
We beseech Thee then, Lord Jesus,
Pray the Father, that He send us the Comforter, the Holy Ghost
To lead us into all truth,
To bring to remembrance whatsoever Thou hast said
To glorify Thee!

Come to us Thyself, in Him:
Open the Scriptures and expound in them all
The things concerning Thyself
In the Law, the Prophets and the Psalms,
In the Gospels, the Epistles and the Revelation,
Till our hearts burn within us:
Let Thy words abide in us,
That we may abide in Thee.

Open our understanding
That we may understand the Scriptures, and search the Scriptures
For in them we have eternal life, and these testify of The.
Grant us to fulfill Thy royal Law according to the Scripture
And be blessed in knowing these things as we do them.
Give us in patience and comfort of the Scriptures
To have hope
For whatsoever things were written aforetime
Were written for our learning.

Make us mighty in the Scriptures,
To know our God, and do exploits for Him:
Sanctify us by Thy truth
Leave us not to be drawn away with the errors of the wicked
Who know neither the Scriptures nor Thy power,
But grow in grace and knowledge of Thee,
Our Lord and Savior.
Leave us not a prey to the unlearned and unstable
Which wrest the Scriptures to their own destruction,
And know neither what they say nor whereof they affirm.

Open our eyes to behold wondrous things out of Thy Law,
And to see no man but Jesus only,
To believe the Scripture, and the Word which Jesus spake,
For the Spirit of prophecy is
The Word God and the testimony of Jesus Christ

Let Thy mercies come also unto us, O Lord
Even Thy salvation, according to Thy Word.

We ask all this in His Name.
May we receive, and our joy be full.
Let His Name endure as the sun,
And let the whole earth be filled with His glory!
Amen, and Amen.

2. One, Living True, Eternal God

1 One living, true, eternal God
With heart and voice do we confess
Creator of the heavens abroad
And earth around, forever blest!

2 "God is:" in all His works we see
Displayed His wisdom and His might;
By faith we own His majesty,
And seek Him, veiled beyond our sight.

3 "God is a Spirit:" worshippers
In truth and spirit now He seeks;
With image, shrine, and rite, man errs:
For by His Word alone God speaks.

4 That Word reveals that "God is light"
In Him no darkness is at all;
Our sin cannot endure His sight,
Whose light is unapproachable.

5 "Our God is a consuming fire"
The King of saints is just and true
In all His ways; in judgments dire
The wicked perish from His view.

6 Yet by the Gospel, "God is love"
Who saves the sinner, yet is just
He gave His Son from heaven above,
Upon the cross to die for us.

7 Eternal, infinite, unchanged,
In being, wisdom, and in power,
All-holy, just, most good and true,
We praise Thy glory in this hour!

8 One God, revealed in Persons Three:
The Father, Word and Holy Ghost:
Thy praise, Most Blessed Trinity,
Earth's fullness gives with Heaven's host!

L.M.

The House of God

Preparatory Reading: Old Testament: Genesis 13;
  New Testament: Matthew 2 Psalm: 2

1 Timothy 1:1

Paul, an apostle of Jesus Christ by the commandment of God our Savior, and Lord Jesus Christ, *which is* our hope;

Paul, an apostle of Jesus Christ: When he writes these lines, none can any longer challenge his title and claim. Timothy, and all the saints now know fully his "doctrine, manner of life, purpose, faith, longsuffering, charity patience, persecutions" (2 Tim 3:11–12). He has seen the risen Lord (1 Cor 9:1); he has ministered with all the signs of an apostle (2 Cor 12:12); he has suffered the great things the Savior foretold Ananias, and testified before kings, Israel and the heathen as His chosen vessel (Acts 9:15–16). We cannot doubt that he writes the Lord's commandments (1 Cor 14:37). Hearing him, I hear Christ (Luke 10:16); let me follow him as he follows Christ (1 Cor 11:1).

An apostle . . . by the commandment of God our Savior, and Lord Jesus Christ: God who separated Paul from his mother's womb, and called him by His grace, has revealed His Son in him to preach to the Gentiles (Gal 1:15–16). A stewardship of the Gospel is committed to him, necessity is laid upon him—woe if he preach not the Gospel! (1 Cor 9:16–17); For no man takes this office to himself, but he that is called (Heb. 5:4), even as the risen Lord led him captive and gave him gifts (Eph 4:7–11).

So was Paul "made a minister" (Eph 3:7)—and so must I be "made a minister" by God's Son. How can I preach, except I be sent (Rom 10:15)? Does the love of Christ constrain me? Do I persuade men knowing well the terrors of the Lord (2 Cor 5:11, 14)? To Timothy, and at last now to me, Paul says, "I give thee charge in the sight of God . . . and before Christ Jesus . . . that thou keep this commandment without spot, unrebukable" (1 Tim. 6:13–16).

Let me not forget that I too am "under authority"—authority that brings confidence for my work, and demands obedience to fulfill it. Lord Jesus, when Thou sayest "Go," let me go; "Come," let me come; "Do this," let me do (Matt 8:11)!

Lord Jesus Christ, who is our hope: He is our Hope, which makes not ashamed—for God commends His love to us in that while we were yet sinners, Christ died for us; and that love of God is shed abroad in our hearts by the Holy Ghost (Rom 5:5–10). We through the Spirit wait for the hope of righteousness by faith. For in Christ Jesus faith avails which works by love (Gal 5:5–6). The grace of God has appeared, teaching us that we should live soberly, righteously and godly in this present age, looking for that blessed hope, and the glorious appearing of the great God and our Savior Jesus Christ, who gave Himself for us, that He might redeem and purify to Himself a peculiar people, zealous of good works (Tit. 2:11–14). A present security, a certain deliverance, and glorious future—this is my hope—*Jesus Christ . . . our hope.*

3. Jesus our Lord, Walk With Us in the Way

1 Jesus our Lord, walk with us in the way;
Slow are our hearts, our holden eyes are blind:
Draw near, go with us at the close of day,
Soothe all our sadness, still our foolish mind.

2 Jesus our Lord, talk with us in the way;
Speak we too much, and reason without faith:
Looking we see not, hearing we gainsay—
Open our eyes to what the Scripture saith.

3 Jesus our Lord, in Prophets, Law and Psalms,
Thyself reveal, and of Thee let us learn;
Upbraid our hardened hearts, our doubts and qualms—
Speak, till our hearts again within us burn!

4 O pass us not, Lord Jesus, by the way;
We would constrain Thee with us to abide:
Still with us tarry, far spent is the day;
We fain would know Thee now in breaking bread.

5 Jesus our Lord, who still amidst us stands,
Open the Scriptures, all Thy glory show;
Open our eyes, display Thy feet and hands:
Open our understanding, Thee to know!

6 Here do we tarry, witnesses to Thee:
Spirit-endued, with power from on high,
Preaching repentance, and redemption free—
We bless Thee, praise Thee, ever in Thee joy!

10.10.10.10.

Preparatory Reading: Old Testament: Genesis 14;
  New Testament: Matthew 3 Psalm: 3

1 Timothy 1:1–2

Paul, an apostle of Jesus Christ by the commandment of God our Saviour, and Lord Jesus Christ, *which is* our hope; ²Unto Timothy, *my* own son in the faith: Grace, mercy, *and* peace, from God our Father and Jesus Christ our Lord.

Unto Timothy, mine own son in the faith: Paul is now about to open all his counsels, commandment, precepts, passions and life-long ambition to please Christ and win His crown from his heart, and entrust them all to Timothy: here is his legacy, here is the future of the apostolic Gospel, the apostolic Scriptures, the apostolic Churches. All are "committed" to "his own son in the faith." To the Savior Paul has committed his own soul (2 Tim. 1:14). To Timothy Paul now commits his own work (1 Tim. 6:20).

Paul, being dead, will yet speak through Timothy; and Timothy in turn will speak for Paul through us, and this Word is committed to us (2 Tim 2:2). So Paul is committing that same trust down the centuries to our day, to us, and to me.

Mine own son in the faith: Paul has "begotten" Timothy by the Gospel in Lystra and Derbe (1 Cor 4:15, Acts 14:6–21, 16:1–2). The lad, with his mother and grandmother are the travail of his soul (Gal 4:19) for whom he bears the scars of being stoned and left for dead (Gal 6:17; Acts 14:6–7, 19–22). He sees the impress of his doctrine and desires upon this young man *in the faith;* he recalls now years of faithful, routine service to Christ with him as "father and son" (Phil. 2:22), cherishing him with his interventions (1 Cor 16:10–11) and intercessions (2 Tim. 1:3). Other men now see me as a *son in the faith*—let me pray that I too may "beget" others "by the Gospel" and to others commit the faith, my charge and my "good things" (2 Tim. 1:13–14).

Paul blesses this his son and prepares him for all he must learn, by commending him to God in Christ Jesus—to His *grace,* despite all our sin and corruption; to His *mercy,* despite all our sorrow and misery; to His *peace,* despite all our trials and troubles. Enveloped in the presence and power, the favor and love of the Father and the Savior, sin cannot overcome *grace,* Satan cannot assail *mercy,* circumstance cannot perturb *peace.* The flesh, the devil and the world are shut out behind the closet door where God alone sees in secret (Matt 6:6; Isa 26: 20).

Wall my soul round; hedge me in, O Father God, in Thy *grace,* greater than my sin; in Thy *mercy,* in every time of need; in Thy *peace* which passes all understanding—keep my heart and mind by *Jesus Christ our Lord!*

The House of God

4. My Only Comfort

1 My only comfort would you know
Amid this world of sin and woe
That keeps my heart through all its strife—
The pangs of death, the pains of life?

2 In life, in death, is this alone
My comfort—I am not my own:
With soul and body I belong
To Jesus Christ, my Strength and Song.

3 My faithful Savior, with His Blood,
Full satisfaction made to God
For all my sins, and rescued me
From all the devil's tyranny.

4 He so preserves and keeps me still
That now, without my Father's will
No hair can fall from off my head
Yea, all must serve my good instead.

5 My soul He therefore doth assure
Shall to eternal life endure:
And me His Spirit willing makes
Henceforth to live for Jesu's sake.

6 My guilt, though I cannot forget
Is great, His grace surpasses yet:
My gratitude shall ever praise
His glory to eternal days!

7 Let heaven and earth acclaim abroad
JEHOVAH—one, true living God
Eternal King and LORD of hosts:
The Father, Son and Holy Ghost!

L.M.

Preparatory Reading: Old Testament: Genesis 15;
  New Testament: Matthew 4 Psalm: 4

1 Timothy 1:3-4

3As I besought thee to abide still at Ephesus, when I went into Macedonia, that thou mightest charge some that they teach no other doctrine, 4Neither give heed to fables and endless genealogies, which minister questions, rather than godly edifying which is in faith: *so do.*

Abide still . . . so do: Lord Jesus, arm me and nerve me to persevere and discharge my calling where I am; to keep on with my task and get it done—without loitering, malingering, or hesitation. What I am to do, I know; how I am to live, I know. Make me a doer and no mere hearer of Thy Word—and bless me in my deed! (1 Cor 7:20, 24; Jas 1:22, 25).

To my hearers, and all believers, I must *charge them that they teach no other doctrine*: to stick to the Scriptures, not to meddle with the Gospel message, neither to add nor take away jot nor title. This is so vital, and yet so hard. So prone are we to love novelty; to flatter ourselves with vain embellishment—as if we might enhance a rare painting with graffiti to show we were there! *No other doctrine* than the good confession of Thy Word in truth need I know, need I learn, need I heed. Such a vast treasure have I in the Bible, so unsearchable are the riches of Christ—I have a life's work even fairly to master it all or really use it. What need then of *other doctrine?* (Ps 119:72, 96; Eph 3:8).

I may and must insist that my people and hearers *give heed to no other doctrine,* for none other is divinely revealed (1 Tim.6:1), guaranteed to save (1 Thess. 2:13), effectual in power, or able to make us free (John 8:31). This is "the doctrine according to godliness" (1 Tim. 6:3), the "doctrine of God our Saviour" (Tit. 2:10), "the doctrine of Christ" (2 John 9) "good doctrine" (Prov 4:2), "sound doctrine" (Tit. 2:1)—doctrine that drops as the rain and distills as the dew (Deut 32:21).

No other doctrine has any claim or place in my life, or my hearers' lives. If I am not wise in my own conceits, and not wise above what is written, what of it? The wisdom of this world is foolishness with God; I am Christ's, and Christ is God's (Rom 12:16; 1 Cor 4:6, 3:19–23).

The world passes away, and the lusts thereof; only he who does the will of God abide for ever. (1 John 2:17). Savior, let me *abide still* and *so do.*

5. Jesus, Thou art My Shepherd

1 Jesus, Thou art My Shepherd
I shall not want, with Thee;
Green pastures, quiet waters
In these Thou feedest me:
My soul Thou soon restorest
From straying and distress,
And for Thy Name's sake leadest
In paths of righteousness.

2 Yea, though in death's dark shadow,
I walk, I will not fear
For evil, since my comfort
Thy rod and staff still are:
A Table Thou preparest
Before my very foes,
My head with oil anointest,
And my cup overflows.

3 Thy goodness and Thy mercy
Shall follow all my ways
To keep me close beside Thee
Through all my earthly days;
Till in God's House forever
In safety I will dwell:
Naught from Thy love can sever—
Thou doest all things well!

7.6.7.6.D

Preparatory Reading: Old Testament: Genesis 16;
   New Testament: Matthew 5 Psalm: 5

1 Timothy 1:3-4

3As I besought thee to abide still at Ephesus, when I went into Macedonia, that thou mightest charge some that they teach no other doctrine, 4Neither give heed to fables and endless genealogies, which minister questions, rather than godly edifying which is in faith: *so do.*

Neither give heed to fables and endless genealogies: Paul is insisting that I shun all of which *fables and endless genealogies* are but a sample. All that is alien to the Bible; all that distorts or embellishes the Bible; all that merely fascinates; all that teases mysteries out of minutiae—in a word all that glisters and is not gold. Soon the Apostle will unveil the real nature of such stuff: "doctrines of devils" (4:1), "lies in hypocrisy" (4:2), "profane and old wives' fables" (4:7), "strifes of words" (6:4), "perverse disputings" (6:5), "profane and vain babblings," "science falsely so called" (6:20).

I so need the sanctified sense to sift the precious from the vile. (Jer 15:16, 19), the wheat from the chaff (Jer 23:28). Let me prove all things, and hold fast that which is good (1Th. 5:21) with such tests as these, "What saith the Scripture?" (Rom 4:3). "Of what manner of spirit is this?" (Luke 9:55). "Where are the old paths, where is the good way, where is rest for the soul?" (Jer 6:16). "Whosoever transgresseth, and abideth not in the doctrine of Christ, hath not God" (2 John 9).

Rather than godly edifying which is in faith: Lord Christ, who wast anointed of Thy Father with the Spirit without measure to speak the words of God (John 3:34), to speak a word in season to the weary (Isa 50:4) to preach the Gospel to the poor, to heal the broken hearted, to preach deliverance to captives, and recovering of sight to the blind, to set the bruised at liberty (Luke 4:18), empower my poor preaching by the Spirit of grace so to bless my hearers.

Make my ministry *edifying*: instructing, encouraging, directing, correcting, exhorting in the truth of Thy Word; *godly edifying*: Spirit-filled, and not with fleshly wisdom; glorifying God, and not exalting self; preaching Christ Jesus the Lord and myself a servant for Jesu's sake; not tickling the itching ear, but engaging heart, mind and will to hear and obey the voice of the living, Triune God; *godly edifying in faith:* holding fast the form of sound doctrine in the faith once delivered to the saints; holding forth the Word of life with prayerful confidence of faith in the Gospel's power to save.

So do: Father of mercies, work in me by Thy Holy Spirit to will and do Thy good pleasure that I may do and teach *no other doctrine . . . than godly edifying which is in faith. So do!* Amen.

The House of God

6. Hear God's good, just, holy Law

1 Hear God's good, just, holy Law
Reverently, with fear and awe:
God's own finger traced in stone
All these Ten Commands alone!

2 "I am God the LORD alone: [Preface]
So, beside Me, worship none! [First]
Keep My Word to seek My face [Second]
Put no image in My place!"

3 "Never take My Name in vain, [Third]
Nor My holy Day profane: [Fourth]
Six days work, and one day rest ----
So thy family will be blest!"

4 " Honour parents, rulers, all; [Fifth]
Do no violence—great, or small: [Sixth]
Keep from all adultery, [Seventh]
And from all uncleanness flee!"

5 "Do not steal, but earn thy due: [Eighth]
Do not speak but what is true: [Ninth]
Do not covet; be content— [Tenth]
Let thy life for Me be spent!"
[Sum of Law & Golden Rule]

6 Love the LORD thy God with all
Heart and mind and strength and soul!
Love thy neighbor as thou would
Have him love and do thee good.

[*Christ* the end of the Law]
7 Jesus Christ, who bled and died,
Has Himself now satisfied
All the Law and so imparts
All its precepts to our hearts.

8 Weary sinner, flee to Christ!
His own Blood has paid the price
For all sins against the Law:
Turn and trust Him, joy with awe!

9 To our God, the Three in One,
Father, Holy Spirit, Son
Bring we praise eternally,
God Most Holy Trinity!

7.7.7.7.

The House of God

Preparatory Reading: Old Testament: Genesis 17;
New Testament: Matthew 6 Psalm: 6

1 Timothy 1:5

5Now the end of the commandment is charity out of a pure heart,
and *of* a good conscience, and *of* faith unfeigned

To what *end*, to what goal is the Apostle's charge to teach no other doctrine? Indeed what is the goal of the very Word of life in Law and Gospel? What then is the goal and proof of my ministry?

Now the end of the commandment is charity: What love does not move, is worthless; what love does not govern is wicked; what love does not grow and thrive from, is barren, cursed ground (1 Cor 13). So do I rightly divide the Word of truth as a pastor after God's own heart? Where is the constraining love of Christ among my motives for service? Where is the servant love of Christ for the people I minister to? Where is the fragrant love of Christ in the approach, attitude, affections and address of my preaching?

The end of the commandment is charity. Do I leave people with warmer, more enlarged hearts, open to the Gospel, if they are lost; open to the great things of God's Law if they are saved? What does all my sermon-making and pulpiteering achieve to this supreme end?

Charity out of a pure heart, and of a good conscience, and of faith unfeigned: All is not love which takes the name or makes a show of love. The divine *charity* which the Word works must come *out of* a renewed soul whose *faith* is *unfeigned; out of* a *pure heart; out of* a renewed mind with a *good conscience*—in short, *out of* the whole man as a new creature in Christ.

O God my Savior, by Thy Holy Spirit create in me a *pure heart*—clean, single, and true (Ps 51 10; Ps 86:11-12; Heb. 10:22). By the Blood of Christ purge my conscience of dead works to serve Thee, and exercise me always to have a conscience void of offense toward Thee and man—to have a *good conscience* in all things to live honestly, whose testimony is that in simplicity and godly sincerity, not with fleshly wisdom, but by Thy grace I have had my conduct in the world and toward Thy people; a *pure conscience* in which to serve Thee (Heb.9:14; Acts 24:16; Heb. 13:18; 2 Cor 1:12; 2 Tim. 1:3). Increase my *faith*; let me endure the trying of my faith that works patience, that patience may have its perfect work till I am whole, entire, lacking nothing. Grant me to hold fast Thy faithfulness, and have such faith in Thee as works by love, faith filled with love, power and a sound mind (Luke 17:5; James 1:3-4; Mark 11:22; Gal 5:6; 2 Tim. 1:7).

In me, O my covenant Triune God, work the *end of the commandment,* the end of all Thy commandments; write Thy laws upon my mind, and heart, that in me all may see that *the end of the commandment is charity out of a pure heart, and of a good conscience, and of faith unfeigned* (Ezek 36:26-27; Jer 31:33; Heb. 8:10).

7. Lord Jesus, true and living Vine

1 Lord Jesus, true and living Vine,
In Thee I ever would abide;
O let Thy grace my soul entwine!
My faith clings to Thy riven side.

2 O Father, Who as Husbandman
Hast grafted me into Thy Son,
Purge, cleanse me, as Thy love may plan,
Till precious fruit to Thee be won.

3 Come, Holy Spirit, let Thy Word
Dwell richly in my mind and heart,
That I may live in Christ the Lord,
And from His presence ne'er depart!

4 Rooted in love's most holy ground,
Built up and stablished in the faith,
With joyful thanks I would abound
And walk in all the Scripture saith.

5 As Vine and branch, let me abide
In Christ, and He abide in me!
Lord, may Thy Name be glorified
In worship, work, and witness free.

6 Hear, heed my longing, earnest prayer:
Reveal Thy glory—Christ in me!
With all Thy saints, O let me share
Thy glory when Thy face I see!

7 To Father, Son and Spirit, praise!
To God the LORD, the One in Three
Be glory all the length of days,
Now and to all eternity!

L.M.

The House of God

Preparatory Reading: Old Testament: Genesis 18;
New Testament: Matthew 7 Psalm: 7

1 Timothy 1:6–7

6From which some having swerved have turned aside unto vain jangling; 7Desiring to be teachers of the law; understanding neither what they say, nor whereof they affirm.

Here is a warning, here is a caution—will I hear it, and heed it? Those perverse men have arisen from the midst of the Church, even as Paul warned the elders of Ephesus at Miletus (Acts 20:20). The wolves raven from outside, seeking to penetrate and pillage; the perverts emerge inside, like mavericks straying and stampeding the flock to destruction. How Paul could say in all truth, "Many walk, of whom I have told you often, and now tell you even weeping, that they are the enemies of the cross of Christ" (Phil. 3:18). Enemies of Christ—enemies! Men who dare betray the Son of God with their hands upon His Table, His bread in their mouths—worse than Judas Iscariot himself! Am I so blind with conceit, so stupefied with complacency that I cannot think to ask, "Lord, is it I?" Lord Jesus, is it I? (Matt 26:20–25).

Some having swerved have turned aside: They lost their bearing *from which*—from what? from "the end of the commandment", from the whole design of Scripture and the mandate of the Gospel ministry; from "charity out of a pure heart, and of a good conscience, and of faith unfeigned" (1:5). Blind men, leading the blind into the ditch! (Matt 15:12–14). No conscience, no faith, no charity, no heart!

Now, do I really know where I am going, how, and why? No clown in the circus, no buffoon on the stage can match the tragicomedy of a preacher whose life has *swerved, turned aside* and fallen short, filled with popularity, notoriety, ingenuity: a fig tree with nothing but leaves!

Without charity, all knowledge of all mysteries, all gifts of prophecy, all is nothing (1 Cor 13:1–4) so when we *having swerved, have turned aside* all we have left, all we do is *vain jangling.*

Lord Jesus! King of glory, Head of the Church, what love and forbearance moves Thy heart and stays Thy hand not to scourge from Thy presence every mercenary, hobby-horsing knave and fool that make merchandise of Thy Word and of souls in Thy courts as a den of thieves! What patience is Thine with this poor wayfaring fool, this unprofitable servant, that Thy children should not fail to be fed with meat! Have I fed them in due season? Is their meat needful, wholesome? Forbid, Savior, that I too should *swerve and turn aside to vain jangling!*

8. Lord Jesus, take my ransomed life

1 Lord Jesus, take my ransomed life,
And use it to Thy praise
Through sorrow, suffering, strain or strife:
To Thee I yield my days.

2 Send where Thou wilt: there shall I go
In all the vast world wide,
To work, to weep, to wait, to sow
Till comes Thy harvest-tide

3 I hold not dear to live or die,
But to complete my race,
My ministry—to testify
The Gospel of Thy grace

4 "He must increase, I must decrease"
Let me my days thus spend
Till I at last depart in peace,
Enduring to the end.

C.M.

The House of God

Preparatory Reading: Old Testament: Genesis 19;
New Testament: Matthew 8 Psalm: 8

1 Timothy 1:6–7

6From which some having swerved have turned aside unto vain jangling; 7Desiring to be teachers of the law; understanding neither what they say, nor whereof they affirm.

I put out my hand, and count the fingers. For every finger, I know a name. Each name belongs to a man once active in the Gospel ministry. Every man was better, brighter, more able, more attractive, than ever I could be. I remember them, because I admired them; yes, I loved them. Everyone of them is now out of Christian service. When I think of them, I weep. When I think of myself, I shudder.

Every pastor probably knows such names—more, or less. Every seminarian can expect that one or other class-mate may fall, or depart from the faith.

Paul warned the saints "often" of "many" who had become "enemies of the cross of Christ." He warned them "even weeping" (Phil. 3:18). He must have known some of them by name, from better days. During his first prison term in Rome, he wrote happily enough about Demas, right alongside Luke (Col.4:14). At his last imprisonment in Rome, he must break the news to Timothy, "Demas hath forsaken me . . . only Luke is with me" (2 Tim. 4:10–11). The Apostle John might have felt the same sorrow of soul as he wrote his host Gaius, condemning Diotrephes, and commending Demetrius (3 John)

Why do such men of which Paul speaks here, careen from the sense and sanctity of a Scriptural ministry of the Gospel? Some, he tells us, *desire to be teachers of the law, understanding neither what they say nor whereof they affirm*. They long to strike a pose, assume airs, take a name as *teachers of the law*. Like the scribes, they yearn and "love to go in long clothing, and love salutations in the market places, and the chief seats in the synagogues, and the uppermost rooms at feasts" (Mark 12:38–39). Every age and place sees such, who in their own culture and context hanker for the privilege, purse, and prestige of the sage, and are willing to play the fool to get them.

And fools they are. They run, but have no tidings; they run when the Lord did not send them (2 Sam 18:19–32; Jer 23:21–22). They have no content; no vital grasp of Biblical theology, no sound doctrine, no aim at "godly edifying in faith" and no fruit of "charity out of a pure heart, and of a good conscience and of faith unfeigned."

Dare I dabble in passages or controversies where I *understand neither what* I *say, nor whereof* I *affirm*? Let me keep silence, Lord Jesus, rather than give out the *vain jangling* of sounding brass and clanging cymbal (1 Cor 13:1).

9. Lord Jesus Christ, our Savior King

I.
1 Lord Jesus Christ, our Savior King,
Thy praise our willing hearts would sing:
We bow the knee before Thy throne—
We glory in Thy Name alone!

2 Thou art the promised *Woman's Seed*,
Which hast our souls from bondage freed:
Who, dying, crushed the serpent's head,
And rose victorious from the dead.

3 Our King of righteousness and peace,
Thy royal priesthood ne'er shall cease:
For through Thy veil of flesh, to God
Thou hast redeemed us by Thy Blood.

4 Thou art the *Star of Jacob* bright,
Which brings to all the nations light—
Scepter of Judah, Shiloh, Sun,
To whom the people gathering come.

5 Trembling we kiss Thee, *Son of God*,
Who rules the earth with iron rod
To dash in shards of potter's clay
The wicked in Thy power's day.

6 *Thou King of glory, Lord of hosts,*
O save us to the uttermost:
Thou hast ascended up on high
Captive to lead captivity.

L.M.

The House of God

Preparatory Reading: Old Testament: Genesis 20;
New Testament: Matthew 9 Psalm: 9

1 Timothy 1:8–11

8But we know that the law *is* good, if a man use it lawfully; 9Knowing this, that the law is not made for a righteous man, but for the lawless and disobedient, for the ungodly and for sinners, for unholy and profane, for murderers of fathers and murderers of mothers, for manslayers, 10For whoremongers, for them that defile themselves with mankind, for menstealers, for liars, for perjured persons, and if there be any other thing that is contrary to sound doctrine; 11According to the glorious gospel of the blessed God, which was committed to my trust.

We know . . . knowing this: the Apostle calls me to keep every truth in the context and proportion of other truths; to make "the whole counsel of God" my aim. *The Law is good if a man use it lawfully:* Zeal for God without knowledge prompted rabbinical Jews, ignorant of God's righteousness in Christ, to go about to establish their own righteousness (Rom 10:2–3). But the works of the Law bring a curse upon us in our depravity and with it death (Rom 7:9–13; Gal 3:10). Thus *the Law is not made for a righteous man*—it does not create man's righteousness by merit of his works, but reveals his sin, to drive him to Christ.

What does the righteous standard of the holy Law reveal in all, in me? It reveals we are all the *lawless* who despise God's commandment; the *disobedient* who willfully violate it; the *ungodly* who have no fear of Him before their eyes; *sinners* enslaved to iniquity; *unholy* who are too defiled for God's sight; *profane* who actively desecrate all that reveals or represents God; *murderers of mothers, manslayers* who regard neither order nor life itself; *whoremongers* who exploit our sexual life for money; *those that defile themselves with mankind* and pervert our sexual life altogether to our confusion and damnation; *menstealers* who traffic in human life to enslave or kidnap, turning humanity to chattel like horseflesh; *liars* who love to deceive and be deceived; *perjured persons* who compound their deceit with the blasphemy of false swearing.

Is not all this heinous, horrid before my God? And is not my own heart tainted with all this, if not in open vice, then in its impulses of self-will, rebellion, uncleanness, hatred, and deceit? Yes, the Law has made me out to be what I really am before God, in *anything that is contrary to sound doctrine, according to the glorious Gospel of the blessed God*. The Law reveals my need of the Gospel's pardon. The Gospel alone can make of me what the Law shows I am not at all.

10. Lord Jesus Christ, our Savior King

II.
6 Lord Jesus Christ, our Savior King,
Thy praise our willing hearts would sing:
We bow the knee before Thy throne—
We glory in Thy Name alone !

7 O *Prince and Savior,* in Thy grace
Be Thou our Rock and Hiding place:
With judgment fill the wilderness,
The fruitful fields with righteousness.

8 Pour Thou the Spirit from on high
On us; in all our places dry
Rivers of water send, to bless
With righteous peace and quietness.

9 Light of the morning, shining clear,
Our King and God, our voice now hear:
Our worship deign with peace to bless
In beauty of Thy holiness.

10 Thy congregation's saints would sing
And Zion's children in *their King*
Be joyful; pleasure in us take,
And, Savior, beautify the meek!

11 *Lord Jesus,* grant , at Thy right hand,
That we with all Thy Church may stand
Fairer than children all of men—
Thy Bride, all glorious within !

12 In us Thy holy beauty see—
Thou art our Lord; we worship Thee,
One with the Father evermore,
And Holy Ghost, by all adored!

L.M.

The House of God

Preparatory Reading: Old Testament: Genesis 21;
New Testament: Matthew 10 Psalm: 10

1 Timothy 1:11

11 According to the glorious gospel of the blessed God,
which was committed to my trust.

The glorious Gospel of the blessed God . . . committed to my trust: This is the meaning of my life, as a Christian man, as a pastor, elder, teacher, bishop in the house of God. It is *my trust* to 'show and tell' *the glorious Gospel of the blessed God:* exhibit its power in my life; extol it to all in my witness; expound it through "godly edifying in faith" to the Church. I am a steward of the mysteries of God, and it is required that I be found faithful (1 Cor 4:1–2). A day is coming soon when my Lord Jesus will return to earth or will summons me to heaven. He will say to me "Give account of thy stewardship, for thou mayest no longer be steward" (Luke 16:2). "After a long time, the Lord of those servants cometh and reckoneth with them" (Matt 25:9). What will I have to show? Will I have profited myself and others for all the time, trouble and training of the years? How will I account for 20, 30, 40 50 years or more as a professed minister of Jesus Christ? Or dare I look ahead, as might I well look back at times, only this to say, "Lo, there Thou hast that is Thine" (Matt 25:25)? "Necessity is laid upon me; yea, woe is me, if I preach not the Gospel!" (1 Cor 9:16).

Committed to my trust is *the glorious Gospel of the blessed God. Glorious Gospel! Glorious* because it displays the glory of God in the face of Jesus Christ (2 Cor 4:4,6); *glorious* because it reveals the grace, wisdom and power of God to choose things that are not to confound things that are, that no flesh should glory in His presence (1 Cor 1:28–29); *glorious* in uniting us to Christ Jesus as our wisdom, strength, righteousness, sanctification and redemption, that, as it is written "He that glorieth, let him glory in the Lord" (1 Cor 1:30–31); *glorious* in the glad tidings of great joy it brings to all peoples in Christ the Lord, a Savior who brings "glory to God in the highest, and on earth peace, goodwill among men" (Luke 2:10–14); *glorious* in revealing "the glory, as of the Only-begotten of the Father, full of grace and truth" (John 1:14). *glorious* as that ministration of the Spirit to righteousness and life which excelled all before it (2 Cor 3:8–10).

The Gospel of the blessed God: Who will not worship this God? Paul cries, "Blessed be the God and Father of our Lord Jesus Christ, who hath blessed us with all spiritual blessings in heavenly places in Christ!" (Eph 1:1). Peter cries, "Blessed be the God and Father of our Lord Jesus Christ, which according to His abundant mercy hath begotten us again unto a lively hope by the resurrection of Jesus Christ from the dead" (1 Peter 1:1)! John hears all heaven and earth cry, "Blessing, and honour and glory and power be unto Him that sitteth upon the throne, and unto the Lamb forever and ever!" (Rev. 53–14). "Stand up and bless the LORD your God forever and ever; and blessed be Thy glorious Name, which is exalted above all blessing and praise" (Neh 9:5).

11. O Shout a Hallelujah!

1 O shout a Hallelujah!
My soul from sin is free!
My righteous Savior Jesus
Has died, and lives for me!
My tongue is filled with singing,
My heart is filled with joy,
Peace through my soul is springing
Which nothing can destroy!

Refrain: O shout a Hallelujah!
The Lamb that once was slain,
My risen Savior Jesus
Forevermore shall reign!

2 O shout of God's salvation,
And praise Him day by day:
There is no condemnation,
And nothing left to pay!
For Jesus gave the ransom
In His most precious Blood
Upon the Cross of Calvary
To bring me back to God!

3 Shout, shout of sovereign mercy,
And free, abounding grace
That gave me to the Savior
Who suffered in my place !
No, never had I loved Him,
But that He first loved me
And left His throne in heaven
To die upon the Tree!

4 O shout aloud Hosanna
And join me with the throng
Of all God's chosen people
To sing the glad new song:
All glory to the Father
All glory to the Lamb
All glory to the Spirit
One God—the great I AM!

7.6.7.6. D, Tune: God Bless the Prince of Wales

The House of God

Preparatory Reading: Old Testament: Genesis 22 ;
New Testament: Matthew 11 Psalm: 11

1 Timothy 1:12-14

12And I thank Christ Jesus our Lord, who hath enabled me, for that he counted me faithful, putting me into the ministry; 13Who was before a blasphemer, and a persecutor, and injurious: but I obtained mercy, because I did *it* ignorantly in unbelief. 14And the grace of our Lord was exceeding abundant with faith and love which is in Christ Jesus.

Who can explain or comprehend the mercy and wisdom of *Jesus Christ our Lord*? Every believer, every preacher, must find his own life story patterned in the mould of the Apostle Paul, for we are all the sinners of whom he is chief; we have hereafter believed in the pattern which the Lord made of him; we are teachers of the Gentiles as he was first and foremost as Apostle (1:15–16; 2 Tim 1:11). Paul has scrawled in his own large hand (Gal 6:11–16) what each of us scribbles after him on the pages of our lives—*mercy* (1:13), *grace* , *faith, love* (1:14).

In the great mystery of godliness, *exceeding abundant grace* bestowed *mercy* on me in my *ignorance* and *unbelief* (1:13), *counts me faithful to put me* at all *in the ministry* (1:12), *has enabled me* to hold the trust of "the glorious gospel of the blessed God" (1:11) with *faith and love* supplied *in Him* (1:14).

If without that *abundant grace*, Paul were but *a blasphemer and a persecutor, and injurious before* conversion *before* calling to the ministry of this life-giving Gospel (1:13), how much worse would I become "having swerved" and "turned aside" from "godly edifying in faith," from "charity out of a pure heart, and of a good conscience, and of faith unfeigned" (1:4–6) without that *exceeding abundant grace?* I would be worse than *a blasphemer* if all my talk amounts to "vain jangling" (1:6); worse than a *persecutor* from outside, if from within the Church I only foster "questions" (1:4) or "strifes about words" (6:4); worse than *injurious* if I cause Christ's little ones who believe to be offended (Mark 9:42–48). *Mercy* was granted me in all my sin and harm to God's people when and *because I did it ignorantly in unbelief* (1:13). Mercy will not remain for me if at the end I have run when God did not send; if I have labored in vain and be found a castaway (1:7; Jer 23:21; 1 Cor 9:27; Phil.2:15).

Savior, here is a sinner needing Thine *abundant grace with faith and love*. Without Thee I am but *injurious*, a blot of shame upon Thy cause and people, an offence to Thy children—better never to have been born, better to have been cast into the sea with a millstone hung on my neck (Matt 18:6). Keep me from falling! *Count me faithful* now, as in the day Thou didst *put me into the ministry. Enable me;* make me an able minister of the New Testament, of the Spirit that gives life. And all my days shall *I thank Jesus Christ our Lord*. Amen.

12. Come, come to Calvary!

1 Come, come to Calvary,
Look to the Lamb of God
Who bore our sins upon the Tree,
And shed His precious Blood!

2 Come to the Cross, and live!
Jesus the Crucified
Pardon and peace to all shall give
For whom He bled and died.

3 Come to the Fount of life:
Drink and be satisfied
Rivers of living water flow
From out the Savior's side.

4 Come to the feast now spread
Taste that the Lord is good:
Christ is the true and living bread
Better than angels' food.

5 Come, wine and milk now buy,
No money bring, nor price!
The gift of God, eternal life,
Is yours through Jesus Christ!

6 Come, all ye weary, rest!
Sin's burden now forsake.
Learn of our Master, and be blest!
His easy yoke now take!

7 Come, now repent, believe!
Jesus the Lord confess
Eternal life you shall receive:
Come, and you shall be blest!

S.M.

The House of God

Preparatory Reading: Old Testament: Genesis 23;
New Testament: Matthew 12 Psalm: 12

1 Timothy 1:15–16

15 This *is* a faithful saying, and worthy of all acceptation, that Christ Jesus came into the world to save sinners; of whom I am chief. 16 Howbeit for this cause I obtained mercy, that in me first Jesus Christ might shew forth all longsuffering, for a pattern to them which should hereafter believe on him to life everlasting.

O God our Father, by the Holy Spirit's grace and light bind *this saying* around my neck, write it upon the tablet of my heart; set it as a lamp to my feet shining in a dark place till Thy day break and all shadows flee away (Prov 33; Ps 119:105; 2 Pet. 1:20; Song 2:17). Thou hast given it me as a *faithful saying*, which my soul may entirely trust; that will never fail to guide me, like the pole star in the night's sky. It is suited to all my need, and to any fallen child of Adam the world over, *worthy of all acceptation*. With it I can be sure to bring blessing, to offer life and hope to any fellow sinner that ever I meet. If nothing else come out of my mouth, O God of all grace, let this come first and last: *Christ Jesus came into the world to save sinners.*

What better two words could anyone hear than *Christ Jesus?* What more could the heart of God yield or the treasure of heaven bestow, to exhaust my condemnation, to flood away my guilt, to translate me from death to life and from perdition to paradise than *Christ Jesus?*

He is my "wisdom, righteousness, sanctification, redemption;" my "all in all;" my "anchor;" "light of life;" "bread of life;" "Passover;" "Beloved;" "bridegroom" "foundation," "cornerstone"; good, great, one, chief Shepherd; "peace;" "Prince and Saviour"; "Firstborn of many brethren;" "friend of sinners;" "hope;" "life;'" "advocate;" "high priest" "mediator"—these are but the firstfruits of all His glories, and of even each of these I know but in part, nor yet the half. Pilate never knew how well he spoke when he cried, "Behold the Man!" and when he wrote "Jesus of Nazareth, King of the Jews." *Christ Jesus came into the world:* These simple words chronicle a stoop spanning infinity, whose dimensions dwarf the universe—the very length, breadth, depth and height of the love of Christ that passes knowledge. *Christ Jesus came into the world:* Eternity cradled in time; infinity swaddled in space; omniscience hidden in ignorance; omnipotence poured into weakness; the Holy One seen in that holy thing born of the virgin Mary—"God manifest in the flesh."

"Christ Jesus . . . being in the form of God, thought it not robbery to be equal with God: but made Himself of no reputation, and took upon Him the form of a servant and was made in the likeness of men: and being found in fashion as a man, He humbled Himself, and became obedient unto death, even the death of the cross." Calvary alone can tell us how "God so loved the world", and how far *Christ Jesus came into the world.*

13. No Reputation Didst Thou Make

No reputation didst Thou make
To save us from our sin,
When Thou, Lord Jesus, didst forsake
Thy throne, our flesh and blood to take:
No room was in the inn.

2 *No beauty* in Thee did we meet
As Thou on earth didst tread,
Through want and pain, in cold and heat,
No leisure so much as to eat—
No place to lay Thy head!

3 Our Guest unwelcome, gave we Thee
No water, kiss or oil?
In darkness of Gethsemane,
Throughout Thy prayers of agony,
No man cared for Thy soul!

4 Thy judges found *no fault in Thee*,
Who cam'st our souls to win:
Betrayed, deserted and denied,
For us condemned and crucified,
In Thee there is no sin!

5 *No greater love* hath any man
Than this which Thou hast shown:
No man can pluck us from Thy hand.
In no wise wilt Thou cast out him,
Who trusts in Thee alone!

6 Our sins *no more retained*, forgiven
Thy Blood hath cleansed and laved:
None other name from under heaven
To us, to any, has been given
Whereby we must be saved!

7 No man save Thee alone we see,
Jesus, our Lord, our God!
None to the Father, but by Thee,
The Life, Way, Truth that sets us free,
Can come, save through Thy Blood!

8.6.8.8.6.

The House of God

Preparatory Reading: Old Testament: Genesis 24;
New Testament: Matthew 13 Psalm: 13

1 Timothy 1:15-16

15This *is* a faithful saying, and worthy of all acceptation, that Christ Jesus came into the world to save sinners; of whom I am chief. 16Howbeit for this cause I obtained mercy, that in me first Jesus Christ might shew forth all longsuffering, for a pattern to them which should hereafter believe on him to life everlasting.

Christ Jesus came into the world: Will I not pause, think, reflect, weep over this staggering work, this strange work? "He was in the world, and the world was made by Him, and the world knew Him not." "The princes of this world crucified the Lord of glory." "Ye denied the Just One, and slew the Prince of life" (John 1:10; 1 Cor 2:8; Acts 3:14–15). He could go no further than He went at Calvary to *come into the world*—He probed its darkest pit of condemnation, He descended into the hell it deserved, and took upon Himself the eternal curse of God upon it.

And why? *To save sinners.* "He gave Himself for our sins, that He might deliver us from this present evil world, according to the will of our God and Father." "God forbid that I should glory save in the cross of our Lord Jesus Christ, by whom the world is crucified unto me, and I unto the world" (Gal 1:4; 6:14). Never was such truth spoken in jest as the mockery of the scribes, "He saved others; Himself He cannot save."

What more could He do, what more must He do, how much more must He yet suffer of my self-will, ignorance, folly and sin upon sin after sin, till I love Him as He loved me and gave Himself for me? When will the saying come to pass, that is written, "He shall see the travail of His soul, and be satisfied?"

Sinners of whom I am chief: Paul has confessed to this in writing Holy Scripture; he has spoken, moved by the Holy Ghost, and the things he writes are indeed the commandments of the Lord. The Scripture cannot be broken, so these sayings must be faithful and true. Like a man fleeing his shadow in sunlight all day, did Paul hasten through a lifetime's zealous service, aware of the shadows of his past. While he sought forget the things behind and reach out for the things before, to press toward the prize of God's high calling in Christ Jesus, he never lost the true humility of a pardoned sinner: "least of all the apostles" "less than least of all the saints," "chief of sinners." (1:15; 1 Cor 15:9; Eph 3:8). But though Paul be chief of sinners, and the Bible tells us so, yet am I a sinner, whose measure of sin cannot be far behind, who must love much because I am forgiven much. Let me then rejoice in the comfort which the Apostle's admission brings—*Howbeit for this cause I obtained mercy, that in me first Jesus Christ might shew forth all longsuffering for a pattern to them which should hereafter believe on Him to life everlasting.* Grace reigns! Grace, greater than all my sin!

14. O the Depths of All the Riches

1 O the depths of all the riches
Men and angels ne'er can sound,
Both of wisdom and of knowledge
In the God of glory found!
How unsearchable His judgments,
And His ways past finding out!"
Now, O Zion, bring the tidings,
Lift thy voice with strength, and shout!

2 "Who would dare the Lord give counsel?
Who has known Jehovah's mind?
God to none can be a Debtor,
Recompense from Him to find!
Of Him, through Him, to Him ever
Shall be, are and were all things!
Glory to Him be forever—
Amen!" All creation sings.

3 O ye heavens and earth, adore Him,
Men and angels, now extol
One true God, the Lord Jehovah,
Blest forever, over all!
Of the Father's love elected,
Through the Son's redeeming Blood,
To the Spirit's grace perfected,
Praise we now the Triune God!

8.7.8.7D

Preparatory Reading: Old Testament: Genesis 25;
New Testament: Matthew 14 Psalm: 14

1 Timothy 1:17

17Now unto the King eternal, immortal, invisible, the only wise God, *be* honour and glory for ever and ever. Amen.

Amid pressing problems, insidious errors, and anxious concerns for Timothy, the Church at Ephesus, believers at large, and the cause of Gospel truth, Paul pauses to worship. He worships *now*. His personal, lively thanks for salvation (1:12–13), the total confidence in "the glorious Gospel of the blessed God" which his experience proves and patterns (1:11,14–16) crowd upon his heart and impel him to lift up holy hands and cry *Now!* Worship is the only proper conclusion for sound doctrine, just as worship will climax and close the whole drama of redemption (Rev. 1:4–6; 5–14; 7:9–17; 11:15–18; 14:1–7; 15; 19:1–10; 21:22–26).

Now unto the King: When Paul bids us worship, he calls us to acclaim God as *King*, a "great King above all gods;" to "kneel before the Lord our Maker" (Ps 95:6) and abase ourselves before His dread, awesome sovereignty. His "exceeding abundant grace with love and faith" in Christ Jesus manifests His supreme sovereignty and royal prerogatives. His aseity, eternity, invisibility and wisdom adorn His crown as *the King* (1:17). No ignorant teacher of the Law, for all his "vain jangling" can claim the allegiance which saints owe not to Paul himself, but only to *the King*, "the blessed God" whose Gospel of grace is committed to Paul's trust (1:11). All *honor and glory* in our praises and prayers belong only *unto the King*.

Unto the King . . . God is my worship due. And all He reveals of Himself to me settles His crown rights as *the King*. Let me tremble before His presence (Ps 114:7); let me keep silence before Him (Zech 2:13; Hab 2:20); let me be still and know that He is God (Ps 46:10). Know that the LORD, He is *God* (Ps 100:3), *eternal* from everlasting to everlasting (Ps 90:2) *immortal* as the fountain of life (Ps 36:9) "I Am that I Am" (Exod 3:14) *invisible* in light to which none can approach, filling heaven and earth with His glory (6:16; Isa 6:3). He is *the only . . . God* for all the gods of the nations are idols, but the LORD made the heavens. He is in the heavens and has done whatsoever He pleased; so He is our help and our shield (Ps 96:5; 115:3,11). He is *the only wise God:* with Him is wisdom and strength; the deceived and deceiver are His, in whose hand is the breath of all mankind (Job 12:13, 16, 10). He takes the wise in their own craftiness, and knows their thoughts are vain (Job 5:5–15; Ps 94:11–15; 1 Chr 3:19–20). In praise we "give Him the glory due unto His Name" (Ps 96:8–9); we "honour Him with our substance" and service in obedience to His Word (1 Sam 2:29–39; Prov 3:5–10). His worship must endure as long as His worth, so our souls give *unto the King . . . honor and glory forever and ever*. As creatures we need to worship; as believers we delight to worship. For "Christ Jesus who came into the world to save sinners" in all His "exceeding abundant grace" constrains us to love and serve "the blessed God" as *King*. To that we can only say. *Amen*.

15. We praise Thy Name, O God most High!

1 We praise Thy Name, O God Most High!
Before Thy throne we gather;
We boldly now to Thee draw nigh
And call Thee "Abba, Father!"
Thou hast redeemed us by Thy Son;
In Jesus Christ we now are one:
For by His Blood and merit,
In us now lives Thy Spirit.

2 We now stand fast in liberty,
All bondage hence refusing,
For Christ thy Son has set us free
From sin, its fetters loosing:
Upon the Cross He bore our curse,
Thy wrath against us to disperse,
All righteousness fulfilling,
All condemnation stilling.

3 As once Thy Son in love did give
His life for us and died,
We by Thy Spirit walk and live
In Christ now crucified:
Grant us Thy name to glorify,
Our sinful flesh to mortify,
All fruits of grace displaying,
Thy holy Law obeying!

8.7.8.7.8.7.7.7.

The House of God

Preparatory Reading: Old Testament: Genesis 26;
New Testament: Matthew 15 Psalm: 15

1 Timothy 1:18-20

18This charge I commit unto thee, son Timothy, according to the prophecies which went before on thee, that thou by them mightest war a good warfare; 19Holding faith, and a good conscience; which some having put away concerning faith have made shipwreck: 20Of whom is Hymenaeus and Alexander; whom I have delivered unto Satan, that they may learn not to blaspheme.

Paul puts *this charge* into Timothy's hands—*this charge* to teach "the glorious Gospel of the blessed God"; the *charge* and "commandment" whose "end is charity out of a pure heart, and of a good conscience and of faith unfeigned", the work of "godly edifying in faith". Paul *commits this charge* to him—it is all in Timothy's hands, to carry on through all his days, and then "to commit . . . to faithful men, who shall be able to teach others also" (1:11,3–5; 2 Tim.2:2).

Timothy served his generation in the will of God and fulfilled *this charge*, as have countless other "faithful men" since, so that the Scriptures are now at my hand, the doctrines of the Gospel are known and confessed, the work of the ministry is now in my trust. Hence the apostles' *charge* is now *committed* to me. How well will I at the end fulfill *this charge*?

Paul can confide in this particular disciple and convert Timothy as *son Timothy*. Paul cherishes him for he has "served as a son with the father . . . in the Gospel" and he "naturally cares" for the saints (Phil. 2:20, 22). Timothy's deep affection for Paul brings him to tears (2 Tim.1:5). Shall I fulfill a *son's* duty to my fathers in the faith, and the faith of my forefathers?

Paul's confidence, though, does not rest in Timothy himself, rather *according to the prophecies which went before* him. God's Word marked out Timothy's gifts, and God's Church confirmed them (4:14). And that Word commissions Timothy to *war a good warfare.* It is a battle at sea amid storms, for failure means *shipwreck;* it is defensive, protective action to endure the onslaught and emerge in position *holding faith and a good conscience—*" to stand fast in the faith," "to withstand in the evil day, and, having done all things, to stand" (1 Cor 16:13; Eph 6:13). Sometimes we advance; sometimes, we retrench. (2 John 8).

Jesus my Lord, Captain of my salvation, Prince and Savior, Thou hast overcome the world: grant me good cheer that I too may overcome, endure temptation, fight the good fight, finish my course and keep the faith! (John 16:33; Jas.1:12; 2 Tim. 4:7–8). Let me overcome by the Blood of the Lamb and the word of testimony! (Rev. 12:11).

16. Lord, is it I?

1 Lord Jesus, didst Thou truly say,
"One of the Twelve shall Me betray,
That share the dish with Me" ?
Each sorrowed heart the same reply
Returned to Thee, "Lord, is it I?"
As Thou their hearts did see! (Mark 14).

2 Their strife amid the Paschal Feast,
To rank the greatest and the least,
Sank into silent shame;
For who could tell among them all
Would faithful stand or faithless fall
When powers of darkness came? (Luke 22)

3 Such treachery fell th'appointed lot
Of Judas, named Iscariot:
His heart had Satan filled (John 13, *Acts* 1)
To sell his Master as a slave
To cruel foes, who gladly gave
A pittance which he willed. (Matt 26)

4 For half the price of ointment rare
Which Mary in her loving care
Bestowed on Christ so well, (Mark 14, John 12)
This devil, called perdition's son, (John 6)
At thirty silver pieces, won (Matt 26)
His place in lowest hell! (Mark 14, John 17, *Acts* 1)

5 And yet, in vain would Peter cry,
"Though all forsake Thee, yet not I!"
In vain so all would say:
According to the Master's Word,
Thrice Simon would deny his Lord
And all would flee away. (Matt 26)

6 Once more the Savior calls us here:
The bread and cup He bids us share,
Which speak of pardoned sin: (1 Cor 11)
Yet has each guest in Christ a part
To come with clean hands and pure heart
Thus to remember Him? (Ps 15)

The House of God

> 7 Dare we presume we cannot stray,
> Should we neglect to watch and pray,
> When comes the tempter dread? (Mark 14)
> Dare we provoke our jealous Lord
> In gorging from this vile world's board,
> And touching then His bread? (1 Cor 10)
>
> 8 So now, at this our feast of love,
> Let every saint his own soul prove,
> Examination make!
> Let us at Table find a place
> Of true repentance, faith, and grace
> Before we here partake! (1 Cor 1)

8.8.6.8.8

The House of God

Preparatory Reading: Old Testament: Genesis 27
    New Testament: Matthew 16 Psalm: 16

1 Timothy 1:18-20

18This charge I commit unto thee, son Timothy, according to the prophecies which went before on thee, that thou by them mightest war a good warfare; 19Holding faith, and a good conscience; which some having put away concerning faith have made shipwreck: 20Of whom is Hymenaeus and Alexander; whom I have delivered unto Satan, that they may learn not to blaspheme.

Paul has already given Timothy ample warning against the dereliction of his duty toward *this charge. Some* have already *made shipwreck.* The entire freight of their ministry is lost on the seas of time, and their lives are shattered. "Having preached to others" they themselves are now "castaways" (1 Cor 9:27). What has run them aground is that they *have put away . . . faith and a good conscience.* By the arrogance of unbelief, by pernicious heresy, or perverse opposition to "godly edifying in faith" they have *learned to blaspheme.*

    Paul will not pass over these disgraced souls in shameful anonymity; no, he names names. The Holy Ghost who moves him to write names names. *Of whom is Hymenaeus and Alexander.* These two have ploughed their furrow, made their mark, and left their record. Their sin is engraven with an iron pen upon the sacred page. In the landscape of Scripture, they gleam as pillars of salt. Through history they stand as condemned as they shall to eternity. The Savior told His disciples to rejoice because their names were written in heaven. What is written on high, of me?

    Paul has cut short any evil influence they might have in the Churches: *whom I have delivered unto Satan, that they learn not to blaspheme.* Excommunication has sentenced them to live as "heathen or publican" (Matt 18: 17), profaned as once they professed Christ's Name in vain *that they may learn not to blaspheme.* To *put away . . . faith* and "teach any other doctrine" or "give heed to fables" to "turn aside" to "vain jangling"—this is *to blaspheme.* For to cast aside "the glorious Gospel of the blessed God" is no other than "to give heed to . . . doctrines of devils" and be fit to *be delivered unto Satan.* The prompt discipline of the congregation has placed them henceforth outside, among the incestuous, the fornicator, the covetous, the idolater, the drunkard, the railer, the extortionist and the wicked. Such hypocrites and reprobates are consigned to Satan (1 Cor 5:1–5,11,13). The devil still goes about as a roaring lion, seeking whom he may devour (1 Pet.5:8–9). He preys upon the proud , and ensnares the erring (3:6–7; 2 Tim. 2:24–26) as easy pickings. "Resist the devil and he will flee" (Jas. 4:7).

17. The Gospel of Salvation

1 The Gospel of salvation
In Christ the world shall bless:
Proclaim to every nation
The faith we now confess.
O let God's Word unhindered
Its full, free course now gain,
Till every tribe and kindred
Shall praise the Lamb once slain!

2 Declare to all the story
The Holy Scriptures tell:
God sent His Son from glory
To save our souls from hell—
One only Mediator,
The Father sanctified:
The Virgin-born Redeemer,
Christ Jesus, crucified.

3 The fullness of the Godhead
Dwells in Him bodily,
For only thus His bloodshed
Availed at Calvary:
Our nature, sinless, sharing,
He lived, thus to provide
Our righteousness, and bearing
Our sins, for us He died.

4 The Savior slain is risen!
He ever lives to plead
At God's right hand in heaven
Our cause in all our need:
No other name can save us,
None to the Father come
But by this same Lord Jesus,
Our Savior, God the Son!

5 God now commands to all men:
Repent of sin; believe
This Gospel of salvation,
And Jesus Christ receive!
He lives and pleads to save us

Unto the uttermost:
Convict, convert and call them—
Lord God, the Holy Ghost!

6 O Triune God, Jehovah,
Beside Thee there is none:
We worship, praise and bless Thee
Who hast Salvation won:
We laud the holy Father,
the co-eternal Son,
and Holy Ghost—none other,
Our God, the Three in One.

7.6.7.6. D

The House of God

Preparatory Reading: Old Testament: Genesis 28;
    New Testament: Matthew 17 Psalm: 17

1 Timothy: Reading over Chapter 1

The burden of the Word of the Lord in this first chapter of 1 Timothy has been to preserve the purity of sound doctrine, and through it the saving power of the Gospel. Let me review and reflect on this chapter, hiding God's Word in my heart, praying that my heart might be sound in His statutes.

Prayer for the defense and confirmation of the Gospel:

Glory to God in the highest
And on earth peace goodwill toward men!
Glad tidings of great joy to all people hast Thou published to us
O Lord God:
To us a Savior, which is Christ the Lord.
His Name is Jesus for He shall save His people from their sins.
Thou hast anointed Him, and the Spirit of the Lord is upon Him
To preach good tidings to the poor
Deliverance to captives, sight to the blind, liberty to the bruised!
He has come to seek and to save the lost
To give His life a ransom for many to save sinners.

And we have received this Gospel.
For our sins He has died according to the Scriptures
He was buried and rose the third day according to the Scriptures
This same Jesus Thou hast made Lord and Christ
Exalted to Thy right hand, O Father,
He has received the promised Holy Ghost
shed Him forth abundantly
with the washing of regeneration and renewing of the Spirit
to justify us by grace and make us heirs of eternal life.
In His Name
Repentance and remission of sins is now preached to all nations
As we go into all the world and preach the Gospel to every creature.

To us hast Thou entrusted the Gospel.
We are separated unto the Gospel of God
Set for the defense and confirmation of the Gospel.
How can men hear without a preacher?
How can we preach except we be sent?

The House of God

God Triune, be pleased to make our feet beautiful
who preach the Gospel of peace
Grant us to finish our course with joy
The ministry we have received of the Lord Jesus
To testify the Gospel of the grace of God!

Confirm this glorious Gospel, O blessed God, to our lives
That our daily conversation become the Gospel of Christ;
That we adorn the doctrine of God our Savior in all things:
Teach us to know nothing but Jesus Christ and Him crucified
And preach the Gospel with the Holy Ghost sent down from heaven
In demonstration of the Spirit and power.

Make us not ashamed of the Gospel
But be pleased by it to manifest Thy power to salvation
to all who believe.
Send us in the fullness of the blessing of the Gospel of Christ,
Ready if needs be to lose life itself for the Gospel's sake,
to forsake all in its service,
even to preach in regions beyond where Christ is not named.

Further the Gospel, O Lord, in all that happens to us
That Christ be magnified in us by life or death.
Forbid that we abuse our trust or authority in Thy service
In uncleanness, guile or deceit, covetousness or vainglory
But rather preach Christ Jesus the Lord
And ourselves but His servants
Not as pleasing men, but Thee, O God,
Which triest and searchest our hearts.

Strengthen us in Thy power to partake of the afflictions of the Gospel
Bless us when men revile us, persecute us
And say all manner of evil against us falsely for Thy Son's sake:
Let the Spirit of glory and of God rest upon us
When we are reproached for the Name of Christ
And get to Thy Name the glory in us
As partakers of Christ's sufferings
That the Gospel of God be spoken boldly
In power, in the Holy Ghost and in much assurance.

And defend, O Lord, we pray, Thy Gospel
From all that would corrupt us from the simplicity of Christ
with another "Jesus", another "spirit," or "another gospel"

The House of God

    Which is not another, but would pervert the Gospel of Christ.
    Sanctify Thy Son in our hearts, and enable us
    To give an answer for the hope in us
    With meekness and fear, and a good conversation.
    Make us hold fast Thy faithful Word as we have been taught
    And enable us by sound doctrine
    both to exhort and convince all gainsayers.

    Fill us with the Holy Ghost and faith;
    Give us a mouth and a wisdom
    Which all our adversaries shall not be able to gainsay or resist:
    Make us gentle unto all men, apt to teach, patient,
    In meekness instructing those who oppose us:
    And grant to them repentance to the acknowledging of the truth.
    Keep us in Thy love
    As we build ourselves up in Thy most holy faith,
    Praying in the Holy Ghost
    And looking for the mercy of our Lord Jesus Christ to eternal life.

    And now to Him that is of power to establish us
    According to this Gospel
    And the preaching of Jesus Christ
    According to the revelation of the mystery
    Which was kept secret since the world began,
    But is now made manifest, and by the Scriptures of the prophets
    According to the commandment of the everlasting God
    Made known to all nations
    For the obedience of faith:
    To God only wise
    Be glory through Jesus Christ forever.
    Amen.

18. What boldness have we, brethren, now to pray

1 What boldness have we, brethren now to pray
And enter into heaven's holiest place,
Since Jesus made that new and living way
Through His rent flesh unto the throne of grace!

2 Our great Priest standing o'er the house of God
Now saves His people to the uttermost:
There, where He entered in by His own Blood,
He lives and reigns o'er earth and heaven's host.

3 In faith then, let us to our God draw near;
In hope, let us hold our confession fast:
In love, let us still hold each other dear
Till that great Day when Christ returns at last!

10.10.10.10.

Preparatory Reading: Old Testament: Genesis 29;
  New Testament: Matthew 18 Psalm: 18

1 Timothy 2:1–2

1I exhort therefore, that, first of all, supplications, prayers, intercessions, *and* giving of thanks, be made for all men; 2For kings, and *for* all that are in authority; that we may lead a quiet and peaceable life in all godliness and honesty.

What to do? How to remedy the terrible bane of "any other doctrine," of "vain jangling" plaguing the Churches? How can I keep myself and my people on course from "making shipwreck of faith and a good conscience?" Paul does not warrant out a theological commission. Nor does he institute an inquisition. He prescribes no curriculum of books and seminars. The Apostle's antidote to the power of error begins in the hearts of pastor and people, at Church, in worship, in God's felt presence: *I exhort therefore . . . first of all . . . prayers.* Paul puts his arm round Timothy's shoulder; with fatherly care for "son Timothy" he embodies the mercy of the Holy Ghost as Comforter to saints in his counsel (John 14:26): *I exhort therefore—as if to say,* "Son, the answer is prayer!" The saint is always safe on his knees; the congregation is secure at prayer; the pastor and elders of Ephesus are best commended to God and the Word of his grace, when Paul kneels down and prays with them all (Acts 20:28,32,36; Eph 3:14–21).

First of all . . . prayers: This is more than ensuring an elegant, appropriate invocation leads off the service. Paul is bidding us give priority, significant time, and preparation for *prayers* at Church. Without this, there is no unction of the Holy Ghost for the preacher, and there is no illumination, or conviction of the Holy Ghost for sinners or saints. If God Himself is indeed our Refuge and Strength, if our help is in His Name, then without Him all is vain—so *first of all . . . prayers. I exhort . . . supplications, prayers, intercessions, giving of thanks:* The Apostle urges us to walk with God Triune through all life, and engage Him in reverent, yet intimate conversation. To seek His presence and counsel in *prayer;* to present our most pointed petitions at His throne for ourselves in *supplications* and for others in *intercessions;* and always to stir up our love for Him, praise to Him, and trust in Him by *giving of thanks.* This is spending "family time" in the household of faith; this is our common adoption as children of God by faith in Jesus Christ; this is our common prerogative as members of His royal priesthood (Eph 1:3–7, 2:13–20,3:8–12, 5:1–2; 1 Pet. 2:1–5,9–10). Paul calls us in our *prayers* to speak *for all men.* Abraham pleads even for Sodom because of Lot (Gen 18); Jeremiah calls the remnant to remember Babylon for its own peace (Jer 29); the Lord shortens days of tribulation for His elect (Mark 13)—so we too pray *for all men.* No class, color, condition is past prayer. Prayer informs us of, involves us with, and endears us to *all men,* as children of God (Matt 5:44).

19. Come, Holy Ghost, the Comforter

I.

1 Come, Holy Ghost, the Comforter
Which our Lord Jesus gives
To God's elect who by Thy power
Repent, believe and live!

2 Blest Holy Ghost, eternal God
The Father and the Son
Have sent Thee to impart the life
The Risen Christ has won.

3 Convince, convict of every sin,
Ill done, or good undone;
Reprove the world of righteousness
Of judgment yet to come!

4 Spirit of supplicating grace,
On every soul twice-born,
Pour out repentance, at the cross
To look on Christ, and mourn.

5 No man but by the Holy Ghost
Can call Christ Jesus Lord:
The gift of faith God gives by Him
Through preaching of the Word.

C.M.

Preparatory Reading: Old Testament: Genesis 30;
New Testament: Matthew 19 Psalm: 19

1 Timothy 2:1–2

1I exhort therefore, that, first of all, supplications, prayers, intercessions, *and* giving of thanks, be made for all men; 2For kings, and *for* all that are in authority; that we may lead a quiet and peaceable life in all godliness and honesty.

Timothy well knew Paul's "manner of life," he well knew how Paul himself prayed. The Apostle practiced what he preached; he prayed for believers just as he asked believers to pray for him. So he himself prayed for the Church just what he ordained us to pray for in Church.

Pray for kings? Paul dared to pray for Agrippa (Acts 26:25–29). Dare I not pray for Gospel grace when I say, "God save the Queen"?

Pray for all in authority? Paul astonished Sergius Paulus of Paphos and led him to faith (Acts 13:6–12); he made Felix and Drusilla tremble as he reasoned of the faith of Christ (Acts 24:24–25). He baptized his jailer at Philippi (Acts 16:23–34). His bonds for Christ were known in Nero's palace, and he found saints in Caesar's household (Phil. 1:12–13; 4:22). Do not the men and women in Parliament, in the police, in the courts, in civil service have souls, and families with souls?

Pray for all men? Paul makes himself servant to all to gain the more; he seeks the profit of the many, that they may be saved (1 Cor 9:22,10:32–33). Will he not pray for all? Will I not?

Lord Jesus, teach me to pray! Thou didst take a penny, and finding the image and superscription of Caesar on it, teach us to render to Caesar what is Caesar's (Luke 20). Teach me how *to pray for kings.*

Thou didst pay the Temple tax, though the Son by nature, exempt from the tribute due from Thy Father's servants. Thou didst put a coin in the mouth of the fish which Peter caught, to pay both for him, and for Thee (Matt 17:24–27). Teach me how *to pray for all that are in authority.*

Thou didst go about doing good, healing all that were oppressed of the devil, for God was with Thee (Acts 10:36). Thou, the chosen, beloved Servant of Jehovah, Thou didst not strive nor cry, neither did any man hear Thy voice in the streets (Matt 12:15–21). Let me not ask "Who is my neighbor?" Let me ask "To whom can I be neighbor?" (Luke 10:25–27). Teach me how to *pray that we may lead a quiet and peaceable life.*

From a Child didst Thou grow, waxing strong in spirit, filled with wisdom, and the grace of God was upon Thee; Thou didst increase in wisdom and stature and in favor with God and man; of Thy fullness have all received, and grace for grace (Luke 2:40, 52; John 1:16). Teach me how to *pray that we may lead . . . life in all godliness and honesty.*

Lord Jesus Christ, of the seed of David raised from the dead (2 Tim.2:8), who hast now all authority in heaven and earth (Matt 28:18), so overrule the conditions of our land, our nation, our society that Thy people may flourish and adorn the Gospel by leading *a quiet and peaceable life in all godliness and honesty.*

20. Come, Holy Ghost, the Comforter

II.
6 Spirit of witness, in our hearts
Shed forth the love of God,
Which gave His Son to die for us
And shed His precious Blood!

7 O Spirit of adoption, sent
Into our hearts to cry
To God, "Our Father!" now begin
In us to testify.

8 Spirit of promise, Earnest blest,
Thou hast believers sealed
Unto redemption's glorious day
When Christ shall be revealed.

9 O Holy Spirit of God, let not
Our sins Thy presence grieve:
The living temple of our hearts
Forsake not—never leave!

10 Our souls and bodies now possess,
Our minds and hearts renew:
Within us Thy good pleasure work
To think, to will, to do.

C.M.

The House of God

Preparatory Reading: Old Testament: Genesis 31;
New Testament: Matthew 20 Psalm: 20

1 Timothy 2:3–4

3For this *is* good and acceptable in the sight of God our Saviour;
4Who will have all men to be saved, and to come unto the knowledge of the truth.

O God, Thou art *our Savior!* "Behold, God is my salvation; I will trust, and not be afraid: for the Lord Jehovah is my strength and my song: He also is become my salvation" (Isa 12:2; 2 Sam 22:2–4). "God hath chosen you to salvation through sanctification of the Spirit and belief of the truth; whereunto He called you by our Gospel to the obtaining of the glory of our Lord Jesus Christ" (2 Thess. 2:13–14). "Now unto Him that is able to keep you from falling, and to present you faultless before the presence of His glory with exceeding joy, to the only wise God our Savior be glory and majesty, dominion and power, both now and ever. Amen" (Jude 24–25).

All that advances Thy good pleasure and purpose as *God our Savior* is *good and acceptable in* Thy *sight*. "So He was their Saviour. In all their affliction He was afflicted, and the Angel of His Presence saved them; in His love and in His pity He redeemed tem, and carried them all the days of old" (Isa 63:8–9). "I, even I am the Lord, and beside Me there is no Saviour" (Isa 43:11). "There is no God else beside Me; a just God, and a Saviour; there is none beside Me. Look unto Me, and be ye saved, all the ends of the earth, for I am God, and there is none else!" (Isa 45:21–22). "All flesh shall know that I the Lord am Thy Saviour, and thy Redeemer, the Mighty One of Jacob" (Isa 49:26). "Who is this . . .? I that speak in righteousness, Mighty to save" (Isa 63:1).

Paul who is "an apostle by the commandment of God our Saviour" (1:1), will surely enforce what is *good and acceptable in the sight of God our Savior*. What is that? Prayer—"first of all . . . prayers" (2:1). Prayer for all men puts us in the will of *God our Savior*, seeks His glory and reflects His likeness *who will have all men to be saved and to come into the knowledge of the truth*. Such prayer He finds *good and acceptable*: He will heed, honor, hear and answer it. This too is "the fervent effectual prayer of a righteous man" which "availeth much" (Jas. 5:16).

God our Savior . . . will have all men to be saved, and to come unto the knowledge of the truth: the election of His grace embraces every class, color, condition and clime of humanity—no sort of sinner is excepted. "A great multitude, whom no man could number" shall cry "Salvation to our God, which sitteth upon the throne and unto the Lamb" "Thou art worthy . . . for Thou wast slain and hast redeemed us to God by Thy Blood out of every kindred and tongue and people and nation" (Rev. 5:9–10; 7:9–17). So let me lay out my fullest powers of desire and expression to "magnify the Lord" and "rejoice in God my Saviour" in the service of "prayer . . . for all men", even the worst (1 Cor 6:9–11) body and soul, everywhere, always.

21. Come, Holy Ghost, the Comforter

III.
11 Spirit of truth, into all truth
Now written in Thy Word
Lead all the saints, by love to grow
In likeness to their Lord.

12 Come, Unction from the Holy One,
Anoint us all to learn
The faith delivered to the saints,
All error to discern.

13 No eye hath seen, no ear hath heard
Nor into any heart
Hath entered all the depths which God
The Spirit shall impart.

14 Yet built upon our holy faith,
We in the Spirit pray
To keep ourselves in God's own love
Till our Lord Jesu's Day.

15 Then shall the Spirit of Christ from death
To life immortal raise
The saints made perfect like the Son
To God's eternal praise.

Doxology
16 O Father, by thy Spirit lead
Our souls to Christ Thy Son,
And in Him grant us access free—
Praise God the Three in One!

C.M.

The House of God

Preparatory Reading: Old Testament: Genesis 32;
New Testament: Matthew 21 Psalm: 21

1 Timothy 2:5-6

⁵For *there is* one God, and one mediator between God and men, the man Christ Jesus; ⁶Who gave himself a ransom for all, to be testified in due time.

There is one God: to none other is my soul's devotion, my body's obedience, my heart's affection, my mind's delight, my will's submission due. I must love Him therefore with all. None, nothing less, else is worthy (Deut 6:4–5; Rev. 4:11). *There is one God:* hence it is "good and acceptable in the sight of God our Saviour" that "all men . . . be saved, and . . . come to the knowledge of the truth" (2:3–4). *There is one God:* apart, above all the din and duncery of "gods many and lords many," of the "gods of the heathen" which are "but idols"—like whom all who trust in them become—to the living and true God Triune I must live and die in time, appear and give account in eternity (1 Cor 8:6; Ps 115:4-8; Ps 97:7; Isa 40:18–25; Rom 14:7–8.12). Hence as *there is one God*, it is meet and right that there be but *one Mediator between God and men, the man Christ Jesus*. God He is, for His Name is "Jehovah saves"—Jesus; His Name is called Emmanuel, "God with us." Man He is, *the man Christ Jesus*. He can redeem for He our near Kinsman; we are members of His body, of His flesh and of His bones. "Forasmuch as the children are partakers of flesh and blood, He also Himself likewise took part of the same, that He might by death destroy him that had the power of death, that is, the devil, and deliver them who through fear of death were all their lifetime subject to bondage" (Ruth 2:20, 4:3; Eph 5:30; Heb.2:14–15). He is "mighty to save" as "God our Saviour," Jesus—"for it pleased the Father that in Him all fullness dwell"— "in Him dwelleth the fullness of the Godhead bodily," "God was in Christ" (Isa 63:1; Col.1:19–20,2:9; 2 Cor 5:19). What more could I need or want? Here is a Daysman to lay hold of God and man, heaven and earth, and bring us nigh—*one mediator between God and man* (Job 9:33; Eph 2:13–18).

This *one mediator, the man Christ Jesus . . . gave himself a ransom for all.* And what more could He give? "He loved me and gave Himself for me" "The Son of man came . . . to give his life a ransom for many." "He gave Himself for our sins." "He gave Himself for us, that He might redeem us from all iniquity, and purify unto Himself a peculiar people." "Christ loved the Church, and gave Himself for it." He said, "I lay down my life for the sheep;" "My flesh . . . I give for the life of the world;" "I gave my back to the smiters" "And He bowed His head, and gave up the ghost" (Gal 2:20; Mark 10:45; Gal 1:4; Tit. 2:14; Eph 5:25; John 10:15,6:51; Mark 15:37). What has He not given in that gift? "To them gave He power" "My peace I give unto you" "A Prince and a Saviour, to give repentance . . . and remission of sins" "I give them eternal life, and they shall never perish" (John 1:12, 14:27, Acts 5:30–31; John 10:28). Unspeakable gift! (2 Cor 9:15).

22. In the Spirit on the Lord's Day

1 "In the Spirit on the Lord's Day,"
Let us trace the steps once trod
By the aged, beloved disciple
Exiled for the Word of God,
Till the Lamb enthroned we worship,
Who hath bought us with His Blood!

2 See an open Door in Heaven:
Hear the Voice with trumpet sound
Beckon us to share the vision
Of the Throne, with all around,
Gathered in sublime submission
To our Savior, glory crowned.

3 Now attend unnumbered voices,
Surging like the boundless sea,
Of the saints in whom His choice is,
Loved, and washed, from sin set free:
How each ransomed heart rejoices
In His final victory!

4 "Thou art worthy!" hear them singing,
Praise outpouring like a flood,
"From all nations sinners bringing,
"Thou redeemed'st us by Thy Blood!
"Honour, riches, glory, blessing
"Is Thy due, O Lamb of God!"

5 "O come quickly—come, Lord Jesus!"
Every Sabbath let us pray!
May we thus in worship hasten
On until the Judgment Day.
When shall come new earth and heavens,
Which shall never pass away!

6 Father, Son, and Holy Spirit,
One, true, living God alone—
Grant us, on that Day assembling,
Grace to gather round Thy throne:
Make Thy Church Thy foursquare Temple,
Built on Christ the Cornerstone!

8.7.8.7.4.7.

The House of God

Preparatory Reading: Old Testament: Genesis 33;
New Testament: Matthew 22 Psalm: 22

1 Timothy 2:5–6

5 For *there is* one God, and one mediator between God and men, the man Christ Jesus; 6 Who gave himself a ransom for all, to be testified in due time.

One Mediator—who could possibly share the rights, the Name, the glory of *Christ Jesus* as that *one mediator between God and man?* None. "He saw that there was no man, and wondered that there was no intercessor: therefore His arm brought salvation unto Him, and His righteousness, it sustained Him" "Neither is there salvation in any other, for there is none other name under heaven given among men whereby we must be saved." He said it Himself: "No man cometh unto the Father but by Me" (Isa 59:16; Acts 4:12; John 14:6).

One Mediator . . . who gave Himself a ransom for all. All the diversity and depravity of the innumerable host of God's elect are fully compensated by the *one mediator . . . who gave himself*. For all my sin, in all my need, for all my days "Christ is all in all," "a ransom for all."

A ransom . . . to be testified in due time: In the fullness of time, God sent forth His Son, made of a woman, made under the Law, to redeem them that were under the Law (Gal 4:4). The times of ignorance God winked at, but now commands all men everywhere to repent (Acts 17:30). Now the revelation of the mystery in the preaching of Jesus Christ is made manifest, and by the Scriptures of the prophets according to the commandment of the everlasting God made known to all nations for the obedience of faith (Rom 16:25–26). And so Paul does not count his life dear to himself, but to finish his course with joy and the ministry he received of the Lord Jesus, to testify the Gospel of the grace of God (Acts 20:24). Paul, Peter, James, John, Jude, all the apostles and all the prophets bear witness that whosoever believes on Christ Jesus shall receive remission of sins (Acts 10:43; 1 John 1:1–4, 4:14–15). From them we have seen and do testify that the Father sent the Son to be the Savior of the world. Now then is the accepted time; today is the day of salvation (2 Cor 6:2).

O Father of mercies, so fill me with the Holy Spirit that I may *testify in due time* to my *one mediator . . . Christ Jesus,* that saving *ransom for all.* Exalt Thy Son, our Prince and Savior, to give repentance and remission of sins and constrain me to speak of what I have known, to obey God rather than men (Acts 4:19–20; 5:29). In this *due time* and day of salvation, open the doors of utterance and grant me boldness to speak plainly as I ought (Eph 6:19–20; Col. 4:3–4). Open Thou my lips, O Lord, and my tongue shall shew forth Thy praise; my tongue shall sing aloud of Thy righteousness, that I may teach sinners Thy ways, and they be converted unto Thee! (Ps 51:12–15). Let me *testify* the Gospel of Thy grace!

23. Come, Comforter and Holy Ghost

1 Come, Comforter and Holy Ghost,
O fill me in this hour,
To preach my Savior to the lost
With wisdom, love and power!
A pastor after God's own heart,
Make me, as Scripture saith,
With doctrine sound to build the saints
In their most holy faith.

2 O Holy Spirit of God, reveal
The things of Christ to me:
The mysteries of Thy Word unseal—
Let me His glory see!
Blest Unction of the Holy One,
Anoint mine eyes to know
The Father's witness to the Son
Which all the Scriptures show.

3 Now let all men be plainly taught
The counsel of our God,
Now feed the flock Christ Jesus bought
With His own precious Blood.
Thy power and demonstration give
That I should now proclaim
Christ crucified, in all I live
And preach in His great Name!

4 Thy people, wilt Thou not revive,
That they may yet rejoice
In our Good Shepherd, as they live
And follow at His voice?
A form of godliness alone
Forbid that we should have:
Come, Wind of Heaven, on these dead bones,
And show Thy power to save!

5 Father of mercies, show the face
Of Jesus Christ our Lord
In fullness of His truth and grace
By Thine own Spirit and Word!
O Triune God of holiness,

The House of God

Wisdom and might display
The foolishness of preaching bless
To save the lost today!

                                                                D.C.M.

Preparatory Reading: Old Testament: Genesis 34;
  New Testament: Matthew 23 Psalm: 23

1 Timothy 2:5-7

5 The man Christ Jesus; 6 Who gave himself a ransom for all, to be testified in due time. 7 Whereunto I am ordained a preacher, and an apostle, (I speak the truth in Christ, *and* lie not;) a teacher of the Gentiles in faith and verity.

Paul's ministry is to "testify the Gospel" of the *ransom for all* which *Christ Jesus* has paid. He commits "the testimony of our Lord" to Timothy (2 Tim.1:8; 2:2), and Timothy who holds the witness of the apostles and prophets in the Holy Scriptures passes *the truth in Christ . . . in faith and verity* on to us; to this I am called (2 Tim.3:15–4:2).

Not as an eyewitness of the sufferings of Christ (1 Pet. 5:1), not *an apostle,* as was Paul; no, Paul all his life contended for "his apostleship" from his earliest, even to the last of his Epistles (Gal:1:1; 2 Tim. 2:8–10). Even here he must say *I speak the truth in Christ, and lie not.* I have not seen the Lord Jesus physically, as Paul did, to qualify as an apostle (1 Cor 9:1; 15:8–11).We are rather blessed as those who have not seen, yet believe; we love Christ, and joy in Him seeing Him not (John 20:29; 1 Pet. 1:8–9).

But I am like Paul, with Paul and Timothy *ordained a preacher . . . a teacher of the Gentiles in faith and verity.* Now, can I have any part in the name *apostle?* Not directly, but derivatively, for I bear witness and declare what they have seen in fellowship with those who saw (Luke 1:1–4; 1 John 1:1–4). My ministry is "apostolic" as I continue steadfastly in the apostles' doctrine and bear the Biblical truth confessed by all the one, holy, catholic and apostolic church (Acts 2:41–42). Bearing their Word, and believing their Word, the Savior may say, "He that heareth you, heareth me" (Luke 10:16; 1 John 4:6). Even I can stand alongside Paul and Timothy, and say in concert with them, "We are ambassadors for Christ, as though God did beseech you by us; we pray you in Christ's stead, be ye reconciled to God." "We are not as many which corrupt the Word of God: but as of sincerity, as of God, in the sight of God speak we in Christ." "As we were allowed of God to be put in trust with the Gospel, even so we speak; not as pleasing men, but God, which trieth our hearts" (2 Cor 5:20;, 2:17; 1 Thess. 2:4). This is the *faith and verity* which makes the *preacher* and *teacher* apostolic. Total personal and public confidence in the Scripture; diligence and fidelity to confess and contend for "the faith once delivered to the saints" and "the common salvation" (Jude 3)—this is *the truth in Christ . . . in faith and verity.*

After this manner, Christ Jesus, my Lord and King, God and Savior, make me a minister; count me faithful to put me into the ministry (Eph 3:7; 1 Tim. 1:12–15).

24. Boats and Nets

1 Boats and nets they knew, in making
Trade as fishers by the sea:
All the night they toiled, yet taking
Nothing from Lake Galilee—
When they heard the Master calling
"All forsake, and follow Me!"

2 Boats and nets they ventured, taking
Jesus simply at His Word,
Then the catch their nets was breaking,
And they knew it was the Lord
Maker of all earth and heaven,
Who such bounty could afford.

3 Boats and nets and fish, forsaking
All they left to follow Him,
Who would teach and train them, making
Fishers of the souls of men:
To His service hence devoted,
All their days and hours to spend.

4 Fishers of the souls of sinners
Make us—in the path they trod,
Master, we in turn surrender
Lives redeemed by Thine own Blood:
Still to us Thy Word remember,
Jesus, Saviour, Lord and God!

8.7.8.4.7.

The House of God

Preparatory Reading: Old Testament: Genesis 35;
   New Testament: Matthew 24 Psalm: 24

1 Timothy 2:5–7

5 The man Christ Jesus; 6 Who gave himself a ransom for all, to be testified in due time. 7 Whereunto I am ordained a preacher, and an apostle, (I speak the truth in Christ, *and* lie not;) a teacher of the Gentiles in faith and verity.

Lord, speak; for Thy servant hears. Speak, O Lord, through me.

Enable me so to live, pray, deny myself, visit, and study that men may hear Thy voice, not mine; see Thee, not me; know what Thou wouldst impart, and not what little I know.

Make me *a preacher:* graciously grant me the unction, utterance, demonstration and power of the Spirit to "preach Christ and Him crucified," to "preach the unsearchable riches of Christ," to "preach upon the housetops" what I have heard with the ear from Thee (1 Cor 1:23; 2:2; Eph 3:7; Matt 10:26–27). Send me, like the prophets of old, to stand in Thy presence, to hear Thy words at Thy mouth, to find and feed upon Thy words, and then to warn the people from Thee, and turn them from their wicked ways, whether they hear or forbear (Jer 15:16, 23:22; Ezek 3:1–4,10,17). Make me a fisher of men, as I follow Thee; a servant to all, that I may gain the more; not pleasing myself, but seeking the profit of many, that they might be saved; doing the work of an evangelist to make full proof of my ministry (Mark 1:17, 1 Cor 9:19,10:33; 2 Tim.4:5). Make me, like Noah, a "preacher of righteousness;" let me never cease "teaching and preaching Jesus Christ" (Acts 5:42; 2 Pet.2:6).

Make me *a teacher of the Gentiles in faith and verity:* grant me the wisdom to give milk to babes and meat to men; to bring out of the treasures of the Bible "things old and new;" to provide each member of Thy house their portion in due season (1 Cor 3:1–2; Heb.5:13–14; Matt 13:52, 24:45–46). Train me to study that I may be a workman unashamed, rightly dividing the Word of truth; empower me to do and teach all that Thou hast commanded (2 Tim.2:15, Matt 5:19,28:20). Let me do all I do with charity, for without it I can do nothing; let me do all I do in Thee, for without Thee I can do nothing (1 Cor 13:1–4; John 15:5). Let me cherish an affectionate desire to impart to my people not the Gospel of God only, but even my own soul; make my heart's desire and prayer for them, that they should be saved (1 Thess. 2:7–8; Rom 10:1).

Keep before me Thy great commission to "go into all the world and preach the Gospel" as *a preacher . . . and teacher of the Gentiles* (Mark 16:15–16). Lift up mine eyes to look on the fields white to harvest (Matt 9:37–38, John 4:35–38); let me never forget that I myself was a bondman to sin (Deut 16:12, John 8:31–36, Rom 6:16–18, 22), and remain a debtor to Greek and barbarian (Rom 1:14). Make me willing to become all things to all men, that some might be saved (1 Cor 9:22).

I have received this ministry, even as I received mercy; I did not choose Thee, Savior, but Thou me; and to this I have been *ordained* (2 Cor 4:1–5; John 15:16. Let me take heed to what I have received and fulfill it.

25. When the Morning Light is Dawning

1 When the morning light is dawning,
As the shadows flee away
I can hear the Master calling
To the secret place to pray.
As I enter in the stillness
And behind me shut the door
My Lord Jesus from the fullness
Of His grace gives more and more.

2 When my burdened heart is bearing
Sorrow, bitterness and pain
Or the tempter comes ensnaring
Me to fall in sin again
I find refuge, pardon, mercy
As I call on Jesu's Name
He'll not fail me nor forsake me—
He'll not put my soul to shame.

3 In the day's long, weary hours
Filled with toil and anxious care
I receive the Spirit's power
As I raise my heart in prayer
For my great High Priest is pleading
There amid shining host
For the help my soul is needing,
Saving to the uttermost.

4 When the sun has set at evening
And my work at last is done
Once again I kneel, believing
On the Name of God's dear Son
And I pray our heav'nly Father
For His sake will safely keep
All who in my household slumber
Through the hours of darkness deep.

5 Every morning, every evening,
Through the hours of every day,
Savior, keep me ever heeding
Thine own Word, to watch and pray:
Till at last I stand before Thee

The House of God

Faultless at the throne of grace
And behold Thee in Thy glory
Safe in heaven—face to face!

                                              8.7.8.7.D
                       Tune: By the Riven Rock I'm Resting

The House of God

> Preparatory Reading: Old Testament: Exodus 1;
> New Testament: Matthew 25 Psalm: 25

1 Timothy 2:8

⁸I will therefore that men pray every where, lifting up holy hands, without wrath and doubting.

All that is "good and acceptable in the sight of God our Savior, who will have all men to be saved, and to come unto the knowledge of the truth;" all the Gospel's testimony to the "one Mediator . . . the man Christ Jesus, who gave Himself a ransom for many;" all must be effected by the ordained means of prayer (2:1,3–6). *Therefore* under God's good hand to effect salvation among mankind, Paul says, *I will . . . that men pray.* This is more than affectionate exhortation (2:1); it is his inspired "counsel," reflecting "all the counsel of God" revealed, and "the determinate counsel and foreknowledge of God" decreed (Acts 2:21; 20:27). It is a necessary part of the plan given the apostle "in all the churches" (1 Cor 3:10–11, 4:16–17). It is integral to what he has taught the elders and saints at Ephesus as "a preacher, an apostle . . . a teacher of the Gentiles in faith and verity" (Acts 20:36; Eph 6:18). No prayer, no Christian; no prayer, no church; no prayer, no Gospel ministry; no prayer, no missions. *I will therefore that men pray:* The fullness of the stature of the manhood of Christ is manifest in prayer. Real men are men of God; real men know God by prayer. Jacob became as a prince of power with God as he wrestled and wept all night in prayer, till he cried at daybreak, "I will not let Thee go, except Thou bless me" (Gen 32:24–31; Hos 12:3–4). The Church's hope for "a quiet and peaceable life in all godliness and honesty" rests on prayer; and such prayer is a man's job. Prayer requires all a man can be and bring to it: sanctifying his resolve, tenacity, courage, forethought, energy, initiative and responsibility for Christ's people and their households. *I will therefore that men pray:* what a man truly is, he is on his knees. King Solomon was never so regal as when he knelt down and spread forth his hands to dedicate the first Temple; almost all that followed that golden moment was his decline and fall (2 Ch.6:1–9:12). *I will therefore that men pray everywhere:* Wherever the congregation assembles, *men* must *pray everywhere.* Under any conditions, on all occasions, whatever else be lacking from the Church's worship *men* are to *pray.* The preacher may be absent, and the sermon with him; bread and wine may fail from the Lord's Table; perhaps no Bible is at hand to read—but in this the Church may still worship, and without this the Church does not worship—the *men pray.* So the Lord Christ ordains: "If two of you shall agree on earth as touching anything that they shall ask, it shall be done for them of My Father which is in heaven. For where two or three are gathered together in My Name, there am I in the midst" (Matt 18:19–20). Such worshippers the Father seeks (John 4:23–24).

26. Teach Us, Lord to Pray

1 As we wait upon Thee,
Jesus, day by day,
By Thy Word and Spirit,
"Teach us, Lord, to pray."
For us interceding
At the Throne on high,
Savior, hear us pleading:
"Teach us" to draw nigh.

2 After Thine own manner,
"Teach us Lord, to pray:"
In Thy chosen pattern,
From our hearts to say:
"O our heavenly Father,
Hallowed be Thy Name,
All Thy kingdom gather,
All Thy will make plain."

3 "For this day supply us
Daily bread and care;
All our sins forgive us,
As we others spare.
Keep us and deliver,
In temptation's hour:
Thine the kingdom ever,
Glory Thine, and power!"

4 Thou hast shown our Father
Is no unjust judge;
He his needy children
Never will begrudge.
"Ask: it shall be given,
Seek and ye shall find;
Knock—the door shall open"
Is Thy promise kind.

5 Jesus, let Thy Spirit
Lead us in Thy way,
Promised by the Father,
"Teach us, Lord to pray"!
Boldness with the Father,

The House of God

Access through the Son,
Unction in the Spirit,
Grant us, Three in One!

6.5.6.5.D

Preparatory Reading: Old Testament: Exodus 2;
   New Testament: Matthew 26; Psalm: 26

1 Timothy 2:8

⁸I will therefore that men pray every where, lifting up holy hands,
without wrath and doubting.

We employ all our faculties to pray: physical, vocal, emotional, social, not just mental and spiritual. "When ye pray," says the Master, "Say . . ." not "think." Jeremiah declares, "Arise, cry out in the night, pour out thy heart like water before the face of the Lord: lift up thy hands toward Him." David says, "O come, let us worship and bow down, let us kneel before the Lord our maker" (Luke 11:2; Lam 2:19; Ps 95:6). But the body without the soul is a corpse, as much as the soul without the body is a ghost. Any rite offered without righteousness is empty and vain. "When ye spread forth your hands, I will hide mine eyes from you: yea, when ye make many prayers, I will not hear: your hands are full of blood. Wash you, and make you clean . . ." (Isa 1:15).

So Paul outlines both physical posture and spiritual preparation—*I will therefore that men pray everywhere, lifting up holy hands.* "Who shall ascend into the hill of the Lord? Or who shall stand in His holy place? He that hath clean hands and a pure heart" (Ps 24:3–4).

What have my hands touched? "Touch not the unclean thing, and I will receive you" (2 Cor 6:17–18). What have my hands done? "These things doth the Lord hate . . . are abomination unto Him . . . hands that shed innocent blood" (Prov 6:17). What have my hands sought? "Let him that stole steal no more, but rather let him labour, working with his hands the thing which is good" (Eph 4:29). What have my hands held? "He that walketh righteously, and speaketh uprightly; he that despiseth the gain of oppressions, that shaketh his hands from holding of bribes . . . he shall dwell on high . . . thine eyes shall see the King in His beauty" (Isa 33:15–16).

How terrible for God to find our prayers offensive because our lives are sinful: "So is this people, and so is this nation before Me, saith the Lord, and so is every work of their hands; and that which they offer there is unclean" (Hag 2:14). How terrible when our laws issue licenses for iniquity: "that they may do evil with both hands earnestly" (Mic 7:3; *cf.* Lam 1:17–18). How terrible when God will not listen to us, because we are not listening to Him: "He that turneth away his ear from hearing the Law, even his prayer shall be abomination" (Prov 28:9).

How often has the Father of lights, from whom comes every good and perfect gift, with whom is neither variableness nor shadow of turning, who is of purer eyes than to behold iniquity, because of my stained hands, turned aside His eye and ear from my vain show of long prayers? Did I notice in all my much speaking? Did I care? Or have I like the Pharisee in the temple only really prayed with myself? (Jas. 1:17; Hab 1:13; Mark 12:40; Luke 18:11; Matt 6:1; Luke 18:11). *Pray every where, lifting up holy hands!*

The House of God

27. Lord Jesus, teach me how to pray

1 Lord Jesus, teach me how to pray,
And to my prayer give heed—
I know not what to ask or say
In all my sin and need!

2 My High Priest, who for me didst die,
Hear from Thy throne of grace!
Put in my *heart* to lift my cry
And boldly seek Thy face!

3 By precious Blood my *conscience* free,
That I may *walk* in white,
And lift up holy *hands* to Thee,
Accepted in Thy sight!

4 Lift up mine *eyes* to Thee above
From whence my help must come:
Loved with an everlasting love,
Be Thou my Shield and Sun!

5 Open my *lips* and let my *tongue*
Shew forth Thy glorious praise!
Be my salvation, strength and song,
My light through all my days!

6 O God that answerest prayer, to Thee
All praise and thanks be given,
Thou ever-blessed Trinity
Ruling in earth and heaven!

C.M.

Preparatory Reading: Old Testament: Exodus 3;
  New Testament: Matthew 27; Psalm: 27

1 Timothy 2:8

8 I will therefore that men pray every where, lifting up holy hands, without wrath and doubting.

Can an angry man pray? "Be ye angry, and sin not" Paul has told these very Ephesians among whom Timothy now labors (Eph 4:26). There are imprecations against God's enemies that are true prayer—and yet hard to utter rightly (Ps 137; 139:21-24). But to vent our own spleen into the ears of the Almighty cannot be prayer; to use the same tongue to bless God and curse men ought not to be (Jas 3:8-12). If we are to be slow to speak, slow to wrath because man's wrath works not God's righteousness, how much more ought we hesitate to pray out of anger? (Jas. 1:17-20). "Be not rash with thy mouth to utter anything before God; for God is in heaven, and thou upon earth: therefore let thy words be few . . . fear thou God" (Eccl 5:2, 7).

To pray, we must be still and know that the Lord is God; we must keep silence before Him when the Lord is in His holy temple. Our motive must be right: *pray . . . without wrath.*

And the object must be right, too: *pray . . . without doubting.* When our Savior gave us His pattern for our prayers, He taught us to seek God's kingdom and righteousness first, before anything might be added to us: "Thy Name . . . Thy kingdom . . . Thy will" precedes and puts in perspective "our daily bread . . . our debts . . . our debtors . . . temptation . . . evil." When we offer our supplications and intercessions "that the Father may be glorified in the Son;" when we can plead the "exceeding great and precious promises" our covenant God gives us for "all things pertaining to life and godliness" which are "yea and amen" in Jesus Christ; when our delight in the Lord governs the desires of our hearts; and when we may trust our dearest desires to His perfect wisdom and love with the words, "nevertheless, not my will, but Thine be done"—why then, we surely may pray *without doubting* (Matt 6:9-13, 33; John 14:13-14; 2 Pet. 1:3-4; 2 Cor 1:19-20; Ps 37:4-5; Luke 22:42).

To believers who pray "after this manner" come the promises: "What things soever ye desire, when ye pray, believe that ye receive them, and ye shall have them" "Let him ask in faith, nothing wavering" "Whatsoever we ask, we receive of Him, because we keep His commandments, and do those things that are pleasing in His sight. And this is His commandment, that we should believe on the Name of His Son Jesus Christ, and love one another, as He gave us commandment. And he that keepeth His commandments dwelleth in Him, and he in Him. And hereby we know that He abideth in us, by the Spirit which He hath given us." "This is the confidence that we have in Him, that if we ask any thing according to His will, He heareth us: and if we know that He hear us, whatsoever we ask, we know that we have the petitions that we desired of Him" (Mark 11:24; Jas.1:6-8; 1 John 3:22-24, 5:14-15). "Cease from anger, and forsake wrath . . . trust also in Him."

28. Faithful Savior Jesus, hear me!

1 Faithful Savior Jesus, hear me!
Thee I seek, poor and weak,
Naked, blind and needy:
Not my own, but Thine who bought me
Unto God by Thy Blood.
For Thy praise and glory!

2 May Thy grace suffice my weakness,
Sun and Shield, let me yield
To Thy Word in meekness
Humbly I would wait upon Thee:
Strength renew, will and do
All Thy pleasure through me!

3 Let Thy gracious Holy Spirit,
Dwell within, purging sin,
By Thy Blood and merit:
To our Father's praise redounding
Make me blest; righteousness
Joy and peace abounding!

4 Thus conformed to Thee in suffering,
Pain and loss, trial and cross,
Make my life an offering
Outpoured in Thy service wholly
To Thy praise, all my days,
Blameless, spotless, holy!

8.6.6. D.

The House of God

Preparatory Reading: Old Testament: Exodus 4;
   New Testament: Matthew 28 Psalm: 28

1 Timothy 2:8-10

⁸I will therefore that men pray every where, lifting up holy hands, without wrath and doubting. ⁹In like manner also, that women adorn themselves in modest apparel, with shamefacedness and sobriety; not with braided hair, or gold, or pearls, or costly array; ¹⁰But (which becometh women professing godliness) with good works.

I will . . . that men pray . . . in like manner also that women: The women pray too! For in Christ Jesus there is neither male nor female—we are all the children of God by faith in Jesus Christ; all one in Christ Jesus (Gal 3:26–28). The New Testament Church, like the Old Testament Church, must have men, women, and children all gathered before God to hear the Book of God, to worship, and to pray (Deut 31:9–18; Neh 8). The Twelve preached our Master, and the women followed to minister to Him (Luke 8:1–3). The Lord Jesus visited Bethany; there Martha served, and Mary sat at His feet to hear His word (Luke 10:39–42). Men and women added to the Church, baptized into Christ alike, continue in the apostles' doctrine, fellowship, breaking of bread and prayers—sharing the common priesthood of believers (Acts 2:41–42; 8:12; 1 Pet. 2:1–10). Brethren and sisters alike share the same tribulations for the testimony of Christ (Acts 8:3–4; Rev. 1:9). The household of faith embraces all members of the family who believe, so the Apostle has distinct instructions for husbands, wives, parents, children, young men, virgins and widows (Eph 5–6; 1 Cor 7; 1 Tim. 5; Tit. 2). *In like manner . . . women* are numbered with the redeemed of the Lord according to the election of grace. *In like manner also:* that is, as these women share in the prayers of the Church. Whether they may participate vocally or simply share the men's prayers in silence, these women do pray, and will pray alongside the men of the congregation (Acts 1:13–14). They share in the primary obligation of public worship to offer "first of all . . . prayers" (2:1). *In like manner* to the men as well, these sisters must prepare their hearts for prayer, and their hearts will be revealed and expressed in the dress and demeanor of the whole person. *Women* in Christ, like all women *adorn themselves* and here the tree is known by its fruit. Sinful, fallen, worldly woman values the superficial, the sensual, the self-centered beauty she attains by what she gets: *braided hair, gold, pearls, costly array.* Saved, redeemed *women professing godliness* value the "hidden beauty of the heart" revealed by what they give in *good works.* They can express their freedom and dignity in *modest apparel, shamefacedness and sobriety.* Abundant life in Christ needs not the abundance of possessions (Luke 12:15; John 10:9–10). The "beautiful people" God knows are not in the salons, but in Church.

29. Thou Art All Fair, My Love!

1 "Thou art all fair, my Love!"
His Spouse, the Bridegroom greets;
Their union, once-espoused,
Communion now completes:
"Thou art all fair, my Love!"
Th'eternal Prince of peace
Enfolds His chosen Bride,
Despite her sin-scarred face.

2 "Thou art all fair, my Love!"
The scorching sun revealed
Her shame, but in His eyes,
She stands in mercy veiled.
"Thou art all fair, my Love!"
His banner o'er her spread,
Within His banquet-house,
They share the wine and bread.

3 "Thou art all fair, my Love—
There is no spot in thee!"
God's well-beloved Son,
Christ Jesus, speaks of me!
"Thou art all fair, my Love!"
He loved me, and He gave
Himself to taste of death
My worthless soul to save.

4 "Thou art all fair, my Love!"
His nail-pierced hands embrace
And draw me to His heart
With cords of deathless grace
"Thou art all fair, my Love!"
On Jesu's riven breast,
My weary soul would lean,
And find in Him my rest.

5 "Thou art all fair, my Love!"
Mine eye in wonder scans
His visage, crowned with thorns,
More marred than any man's:
"Thou art all fair, my Love!"

The words impart a kiss
In raptured faith received—
A taste of endless bliss!

6 "Thou art all fair, my Love!"
We all with open face
As through a darkling glass
Upon King Jesus gaze:
"Thou art all fair, my Love!"
Transfigured by His Word,
The Spirit fits the Bride
In likeness to her Lord.

7 "Thou art all fair, my Love!"
When Christ shall come again,
Upon His glorious Bride
No spot shall then remain.
"This is my Spouse Beloved,
My Father, and my Guide!"
With God the Three in One
We ever shall abide.

6.6.6.6.D

The House of God

> Preparatory Reading: Old Testament: Exodus 5;
> New Testament: Romans 1; Psalm: 29

1 Timothy 2:11–15

¹¹Let the woman learn in silence with all subjection. ¹²But I suffer not a woman to teach, nor to usurp authority over the man, but to be in silence. ¹³For Adam was first formed, then Eve. ¹⁴And Adam was not deceived, but the woman being deceived was in the transgression. ¹⁵Notwithstanding she shall be saved in childbearing, if they continue in faith and charity and holiness with sobriety.

Let the woman learn: Modern minds can scarcely realize what a word the Holy Spirit has moved Paul to pen here. The Christian woman is commanded to *learn*—not merely permitted—but mandated as a full disciple of Christ, baptized into the Name of God Triune, to be taught to observe the Lord Jesus' commandments, secured in the better part of sitting at Jesu's feet to hear His Word (Matt 28:18–20; John 8:31–32; Luke 10:38, 42; Acts 8:12). Her intellect and conscience are recognized and devoted to read, reason, reflect and respond to Truth incarnate.

But more: this word falls from the Apostle Paul. As Saul of Tarsus he sat at the feet of Gamaliel (Acts 22:3); after the strictest, straitest sect of his religion he lived a Pharisee, exceeding zealous of tradition (Acts 23:6; 26:4–5; Gal 1:14). The traditions of the rabbis forbad women to learn the Law; but Paul, in whom God has revealed His Son to preach Him among the Gentiles, says, *Let the woman learn* (Gal 1:15–16; 1 Tim.2:7). The Savior who saved and sent Paul has given womankind a Word that sets us free. The Bible confirms the created order of man and woman: equal in God's image; distinctive in glory; consecrated to reflect the unity and diversity of the Triune Godhead (1 Cor 11:1–4; (Gen 1:28).

This word has divine guidelines: *let the woman learn in silence, with all subjection.* Her subjection, as under the Law, is betokened by her silence (1 Cor 14:33–36). She enters the same silent subjection of faith which moved the blessed virgin Mary to say, "Behold the handmaid of the Lord; be it unto me according to Thy Word" (Luke 11:38) and then to ponder all things in her heart (Luke 2:19, 51). Her faith made her blessed (Luke 1:45; 11:27–28).

When Paul says, *Let the woman learn in silence with all subjection,* he calls her into subjection not to man in himself, but to man under the Lord, and so at last to the Lord Himself (1 Cor 11:3,11–12). She expresses in her own unique way the silent subjection of all the Church to Christ, of the Bride to the Lamb. "Be still, and know that I am God" "In quietness and confidence shall be your strength" "It is good that a man should hope and quietly wait for the salvation of the Lord" "But the Lord is in His holy temple: let all the earth keep silence before Him." (Ps 46:10; Isa 30:15; Lam 3:25–28; Zech 2:13; Hab 2:20).

30. For Me to live is Christ

1 For me to live is Christ,
To die is but my gain:
To live and die to Him
His love my heart constrains.

2 For me to live is Christ,
Who gave Himself for me
In love, that I might live
In Him from sin set free.

3 For me to live is Christ,
Who shed His precious Blood,
And died for the unjust,
To bring me back to God.

4 For me to live is Christ,
Who ever lives to plead
Before the Throne of grace
In every time of need.

5 For me to live is Christ:
My heart with longing burns
To see Him face to face:
Lord Jesus, soon return!

6 My life is hid with God
In Christ, who reigns above:
His Spirit in my heart
Sheds forth the Father's love.

7 O Father, by Thy Son,
Thy Holy Spirit give,
That to the Triune God
I hence may ever live.

6.6.6.6.

The House of God

Preparatory Reading: Old Testament: Exodus 6;
New Testament: Romans 2 Psalm: 30

1 Timothy 2:11-15

¹¹Let the woman learn in silence with all subjection. ¹²But I suffer not a woman to teach, nor to usurp authority over the man, but to be in silence. ¹³For Adam was first formed, then Eve. ¹⁴And Adam was not deceived, but the woman being deceived was in the transgression. ¹⁵Notwithstanding she shall be saved in childbearing, if they continue in faith and charity and holiness with sobriety.

Learn . . . but . . . not . . . teach: Paul commands the Christian woman *to learn*, as he forbids her *to teach*. If she cannot abide *subjection with all silence*, she will *usurp authority over the man*. She cannot teach in the Church; it is a shame, Paul says, for her even to speak in the Church (1 Cor 14:34–35). But in Church she must *learn—let the woman learn*, that she may teach elsewhere. She is to teach younger women (Tit. 2:3–4). She is to teach children in the Holy Scriptures which are able to make them wise to salvation through faith in Christ Jesus (2 Tim. 3:14–15) so that faith by grace may dwell in grandmother, mother and child even as it did from Lois to Eunice to Timothy himself (2 Tim. 1:5). She may with all believers "exhort one another daily" against the deceits of sin (Heb. 3:12–13; and she may "speak the Word everywhere" to the lost (Acts 8:3–4). To an unconverted husband, this silent subjection to Christ makes for a witness "without word" (1 Pet. 3:1–2, 5–6). Silence has a potent force which we too freely squander in a welter of words. Our Lord Jesus could say much with silence (Matt 27:12–14). No woman in Christ need desire to usurp authority over the man, if men in Christ will live up to their calling to minister to women—when pastors and elders treat them as mothers and sisters (5:1–3), when husbands attend them with the self-sacrificial love Christ shows His bride (Eph 5:22–33). Woman in Christ is no chattel—she is an intelligent, devout disciple in her own right: *let the woman learn*. She exercises her life and service in Christ as the divine order of creation designed *in subjection* to God and to man under God. *To be in silence* is her privilege and her liberty from the burdens which *authority over the man* and the exertions to *teach* in the Church would bring. The roots of this commandment (2:11) are in creation (2:13), and of this sanction (2:12) in sin (2:14). Adam stands prior and principal in the human family; Eve, the helpmeet, stands second and subordinate. Woman is of man, for man; man is by woman, never without woman (1 Cor 11:3, 8–9, 11). Eve once taught and usurped authority over Adam; of this came all conflict of man and woman (Gen 3:6, 17–20). Adam chose Eve over God; he transgressed with open eyes in heeding her over Him. Yet Eve began, and led Adam, and all in Adam to our lost estate. In Christ creation is restored from the chaos of sin; woman is restored to her true glory—*saved in childbearing . . . in faith, charity and holiness with sobriety.*

31. O Triune God! Assembled Now Before Thee

1 O Triune God! Assembled now before Thee,
Gathered in reverence at the throne of grace,
We heed Thy call for hearts who worship truly,
We seek Thee, who hast said, "Seek ye My face!"

2 No temple made with human hands contains Thee:
Earth is Thy footstool, heaven of heavens Thy throne;
Yet to the contrite heart, at Thy Word trembling,
Hast Thou respect, and dost Thou look alone.

3 No graven image dare we make or offer;
Thou art a Spirit—only by Thy Word,
As it is written , we draw nigh to serve Thee,
Our Shield, and our exceeding great Reward.

4 Praise right and meet, we bring in adoration,
Raising in psalms, in hymns and spiritual songs,
Honor and blessing, for Thy great salvation:
Worthy Thou art—all praise to Thee belongs!

5 Prayer do we offer, fervent and effectual,
Led by Thy Spirit, in the Savior's Name:
Pleading Thy promise, holy hands extending,
That we should live before Thee without blame.

6 We hear Thy living voice—the Holy Scriptures;
These make us wise to trust Thee and obey:
Strengthen and bless our Pastors, Elders, Teachers,
That we may know by them what Thou dost say!

7 Keeping Thine ordinance, as the Savior told us,
Baptised in water, have we made our vows;
And as disciples, let Thy grace uphold us,
To do and teach whate'er the Scripture shows.

8 Gathered around the Table we remember,
How Jesus died, to bring us back to God:
Here do we meet, of Bread and Cup partaking,
In pledge and sign, the Savior's flesh and Blood.

The House of God

9 Thee would we fear, and keep the Sabbath holy,
Meeting upon the first day of the week;
Resting from all our works, and in Thee solely
Finding our hearts' delight, Thy ways to seek.

10 And every day, in labor and in leisure,
Our sweet communion with Thee would we keep:
Grant that Thy Word, and prayer may be our pleasure,
Alone, in family, when we wake and sleep.

11 Eternal Father, who in love hast sought us,
Eternal Son, who bought us with Thy Blood:
Eternal Spirit, who in mercy taught us
Worship in truth and spirit , Thou art God!

11.10.11.10.

The House of God

Preparatory Reading: Old Testament: Exodus 7
New Testament: Romans 3 Psalm: 31

1 Timothy: Reading over Chapter 2

The chapter I have completed has aimed to preserve the purity of worship, both in letter and spirit, both in form and fervor. Let me review and reflect on this chapter, calling on God to embody its precepts and principles in me and my hearers as that true circumcision who worship God in the Spirit and rejoice in Christ Jesus and have no confidence in the flesh.

Prayer before Worship in the Congregation

The LORD is in His holy temple:
Let all the earth keep silence before Him!
Heaven is Thy throne, O LORD, and earth is Thy footstool:
Where is the house man shall build to Thee? Where is Thy rest?
To this man dost Thou look
Even to him that is poor and of a contrite spirit,
Who trembles at Thy Word.
But wilt Thou indeed dwell on the earth?
Behold, the heavens and heaven of heavens cannot contain Thee:
There is no God like Thee
In heaven above or on earth beneath
Who keepest covenant and mercy with Thy servants
Who walk before Thee with all their heart:
Thou dwellest not in temples made with hands
Neither art Thou worshipped with men's hands
As though Thou needest anything.

But the hour is come, and now is
When Thou, O Father, seekest true worshippers
And they that worship Thee must worship Thee
in spirit and in truth
Now Thou hast brought us nigh who once were afar off
Without God and without hope in the world,
Nigh by the Blood of Christ
For by Him we have access to Thee in one Spirit
We are the circumcision which worship God in the Spirit
And rejoice in Christ Jesus
And have no confidence in the flesh.
Now we are fitly framed together an holy temple,
An habitation of God by the Spirit
Built upon the foundation of the apostles and prophets
Jesus Christ Himself the chief cornerstone.

The House of God

   Now hast Thou called us out of darkness into Thy marvelous light
   Us which had not mercy, but now have obtained mercy
   Which were not a people, but are now the people of God.
   Now are we Thy chosen generation
   A spiritual house, a royal priesthood and holy nation
   To offer up spiritual sacrifice acceptable to Thee
   By Jesus Christ.
   Worthy is the Lamb that was slain
   Who hast redeemed us to God by His Blood
   Out of every kindred, nation, tongue and people,
   Who loved us and loosed us from our sins,
   And has made us kings and priests unto Thee
   O God our Father!

   Open our lips, O Lord
   And our tongues shall shew forth Thy praise!
   Draw nigh to us as we draw nigh to Thee
   Grant us grace, whereby we may serve Thee
   Acceptably and with godly fear
   For Thou art a consuming fire
   Thy Name is Jealous:
   Cleanse our hands, purify our hearts
   To ascend and dwell in Thy holy place

   Grant us boldness to enter the holiest of all
   By the Blood of Jesus
   Through that new and living way
   Consecrated through the veil of His flesh.
   Let us draw near with true hearts, in full assurance of faith
   Sprinkled from an evil conscience
   our bodies washed in pure water
   Let us hold fast the profession of our hope
   As we assemble to exhort one another
   Provoking one another to love and good works
   Let us come boldly unto Thy throne of grace
   For mercy and help

   By Thy mercies, make our bodies a living sacrifice
   Holy, acceptable to Thy reasonable service
   Renew our minds to prove Thy good, acceptable and perfect will
   Set forth our prayers as incense
   And lift up our hands as sacrifice
   That we may pray lifting up holy hands without wrath or doubt
   By Jesus, who sanctified His people with His own Blood

The House of God

And suffered without the gate
Let us offer Thee the sacrifice of praise
The fruit of our lips giving thanks to Thy Name.
Fill us with the Holy Ghost
And let the Word of Christ dwell richly in our hearts
with all wisdom
In psalms, hymns and spiritual songs
Singing to Thee with grace in our hearts
That we may praise Thy Name in song
And magnify Thee with thanksgiving.

Fill us with joy and peace in believing:
Fill us with all goodness and knowledge to admonish one another
In reading, exhortation and doctrine
May we have hope
By patience and comfort of the Scriptures
And abound in hope
By the power of the Holy Ghost.
Convince us, judge us, manifest the secrets of our hearts
Till we fall down on our face and worship Thee
Knowing God is in our midst of a truth.

Add to Thy Church now and daily, O Lord
As many as should be saved
As they gladly receive Thy Word, are baptized
And continue steadfastly in doctrine, fellowship, prayer
and the breaking of bread.
Stand and knock, Lord Jesus, at our door
That we may hear Thy voice:
Enter in, that we may sup with Thee, and Thou with us:
Make Thyself known in the breaking of bread
That the bread we break be
the communion of the body of Christ
That the cup of blessing we bless be
the communion of the Blood of Christ.

O God, make Thy praise glorious!
Let Thy beauty be upon us
And be had in reverence in the assembly of Thy saints.
Dwell in every assembly of Thy Zion
By the Spirit of burning
As a cloud by day, a fire by night in all Thy glory
For Jesus Christ's sake alone.
Amen.

The House of God

32. Lord Jesus, let Thy Beauty Rest on All for Thee We Do

1 Lord Jesus, let Thy beauty rest
On all for Thee we do:
Let every *work of faith* be blest
From willing hearts and true!

2 On all *love's labors* which we show
To those who bear Thy Name,
Thine own reward, O God, bestow :
Thy faithfulness we claim !

3 Spirit of grace, help us to pray !
With *patient hope* we yearn
For our redemption, till that Day
Our Savior shall return.

4 Our words and works forever guide
With faith and hope and love
Which never fail, but shall abide
Before Thy throne above.

5 O Triune God, as we endure,
We pray that we might *make*
Our calling and election sure
For our Lord Jesu's sake!

C.M.

Preparatory Reading: Old Testament: Exodus 8;
   New Testament: Romans 4 Psalm: 32

1 Timothy 3:1

¹This *is* a true saying, If a man desire the office of a bishop, he desireth a good work.

A true saying is "a faithful saying" (1:15). The Gospel itself can be wholly relied upon: it can equally be relied upon that the service and ministry of the Gospel, the oversight of the Churches is *work,* fine, beautiful, noble, *good work*. To *desire the office*, to *desire* this *good work* is to "set our longings upon" it, to "be ambitious" for it. To set our heart upon spiritual good and stretch forth our hand to achieve it is a *desire* truly "good and acceptable in the sight of God our Saviour." To such even as to David the Lord says, "Thou didst well that it was in thine heart" (1 Kgs 8:18). But Paul refers not to *the office of a bishop* as a title, but as a task. The term is also translated "bishopric" (Acts 1:20). It is less the name "overseer", more the work of "overseeing" on which we are to set our hearts.

This true saying tests my heart and hand at once: what am I really after in seeking *the office of a bishop?* The letters of degrees? The show of pulpit, gown, collar and tabs? The prestige of a black suit and a big black Bible? A respectable income? A quiet job? The monikers "Pastor," "Reverend?" Paul demands that I lay my heart and hand on the plough of unsparing, Gospel *work* without looking back—that I seek the care, feeding, tending and guiding of "the flock of God" with resolve, humility and contentment (1 Peter 5:1–4). Would I take up this ministry unpaid? unappreciated? unsure of the future? Paul did (1 Cor 4:10–13; 2 Cor 6:4–10; Acts 20:17–35). Does Christ's love constrain me to take responsibility for the souls of saints and sinners; to watch over them prepared to give account for them? To nourish the lamb, tend the sheep, seek the stray, nurse the sick—this is to follow the good Shepherd; this is to love Him by loving them (John 21:15–18).

Lord Jesus, Thou knowest all things; Thou knowest that I love Thee! Take my heart and hands to shepherd Thy people, to work hard, unmindful of money or men's praise, to love them in Thy love for them, and so loving them, prove my love for Thee.

Make this one thing my longing desire and life's ambition. Keep me from losing my calling in a career; my principles for a pay-cheque; my desire to please Thee in the desire to please men; my love for others in my love of ease. Let me not bury my talent because it is small, or despise the day of small things; let me remember much is required of those to whom much is given, and that many masters shall receive a greater condemnation. Forbid that I should come before Thee in that great day, saying "Lord, Lord have we not in Thy Name done many wonderful works?" only to hear Thee say, "I never knew you: depart from me, ye that work iniquity." Put in my heart all my life long to *desire the office of a bishop, and desire this good work*.

33. Watchman, Wake—in Zion Stand

I.
1 Watchman, wake—in Zion stand,
Sound the trumpet through the land:
Take to heart the Word of God
Tell its living truths abroad—
Whether men forbear or hear,
Yield to none dismay or fear:
Warn the wicked, "Turn to God!"
And be clear of all their blood!   (Ezek 3, 33)

2 Watchman, early rise and wait
At the posts of wisdom's gate: (Prov 3:34)
To the doctrine taking heed,   (1 Tim. 4)
Daily on the Scriptures feed,   (Ezek 3)
Nourished in the words of life,
Take no part in jangling strife:
To thyself take heed and look,   (1Tim.4)
Meditate upon this Book!   (Josh 1)

3 Watchman, give the LORD no rest,
Pray that Zion may be blest,
Hold no peace by day or night
Till her righteousness shine bright
Till Jerusalem be raised
Through the earth and God be praised:
Till old paths again be found,
Till all fruits of grace abound.   (Jer 6; Isa 62)

4 Watchman, keep the flock of God,
Purchased by the Saviour's Blood:
House to house, go in and out,
Watch for souls, to give account:
Humbly serve the Lord with tears,
Warning each throughout the years;
All the counsel of our God,
Preach; be pure of all men's blood!   (Acts 20)

7.7.7.7D

Preparatory Reading: Old Testament: Exodus 9
   New Testament: Romans 5 Psalm: 33

1 Timothy 3:1–2

²A bishop then must be blameless, the husband of one wife, vigilant, sober, of good behaviour, given to hospitality, apt to teach; ³Not given to wine, no striker, not greedy of filthy lucre; but patient, not a brawler, not covetous

When Paul sketches before Timothy, the Church, and me in the Spirit-breathed words of Holy Scripture what *a bishop must be* he lays down the minimal essentials for his personal character (2–3), domestic habits (4–5), church standing (6), and general reputation in the world (7). These *a bishop then must be*; and without any one of them, he fails to be and cannot be *a bishop*. Lord Jesus, Author and Finisher of my faith, set down at God's right hand, I look to Thee: give me the patient endurance to run this race!

Why the Holy Ghost sets down these essentials becomes plain if I but ponder what would befall a man in this office without them. The intrusion of vice or defect of virtues spelled out here renders a man incompetent to "the office of a bishop"—he may "desire" this good work, but he cannot perform it.

Blameless: how can people trust a man of stained reputed, under a cloud of accusation? *Husband of one wife:* Who will put their wife or daughter under a leering eye or lecherous hand? *Vigilant:* Who will stay long under a sleep-walking, negligent, lazy oversight? *Sober:* Who can respect the self-indulgent carnality of a drunkard, glutton or dandy? *Of good behavior:* Who will tolerate a swine? *Given to hospitality:* Who can confide in a religious jack-in-the-box, whose home is off-limits? *Apt to teach:* Who will endure ignorant prating or vain jangling? *Not given to wine:* How can a man filled with wine pretend to be filled with the Holy Spirit of God? *No striker, no brawler:* Who will suffer violence, intimidation or abuse? *Not greedy of filthy lucre, not covetous:* How far can the sheep be sheared before they bleed? *Patient:* what flock will move when a drover harries them to market, instead of a shepherd leading them to pasture?

Paul could humbly, yet honestly appeal to his own character in writing to his converts: "Ye know what manner of men we were among you . . . ye remember, brethren, our labour . . . ye are witnesses . . . how holily and justly and unblameably behaved ourselves . . . as ye know how we comforted and exhorted and charged every one of you . . . " (1 Thess. 1:5; 2:9–11). Can I? I cannot be an elder, a pastor, a preacher, a *bishop* unless these I as *a bishop must then be*. My gifts are worthless without grace; my capacities vain without character; my potential nil without piety; my service sin without salvation. God's call is to believe and live in Christ; live and do for Christ; do and teach of Christ.

34. Watchman, Wake—in Zion Stand

II.

5 Watchman, sing, lift up thy voice!
With good tidings now rejoice!
All the ends of earth shall see
God's salvation full and free: (Isa 52)
Faith, repentance still proclaim,   (Acts 20)
Only in the Savior's Name: (Acts 4)
Work as God's evangelist,   (2 Tim. 4)
Preaching, teaching Jesus Christ!   (Acts 5)

6 Watchman, for the Savior's Name
Suffering comes: be not ashamed
Testifying to the Lord,   (2 Tim. 1)
In all seasons—preach the Word!   (2 Tim. 4)
Hunger, thirst, want, cold, or pain,
Tumults, stripes, or bonds are gain
When endured for Christ the Lord   (Matt 5)
Heaven brings thee great reward!   (2 Cor 6, 11)

7 Take heed, watchman—watch and pray,
Knowing not the hour or day
Evening, morning, midnight, dawn,
When the Master may return: (Mark 13)
Suddenly shall the Bridegroom come,
And His people gather home—   (Luke 12, Matt 25)
Finish then with joy thy race:
Tell the Gospel of God's grace!   (Acts 20)

8 Watchman, we shall all appear
At Christ's Judgment seat in fear;
All our deeds on earth confess,
Good or bad, as cursed or blest   (2 Cor 5)
Then thy righteous crown is won;   (2 Tim 4)
Jesus Christ shall say, "Well done!
Good and faithful! My reward—
Enter joy before thy Lord!"   (Matt 25)

9 Watchman, nothing know beside
Jesus Christ, Him crucified:
Foolish though thy preaching seem,
Christ alone can souls redeem,   (Rom. 1, 1 Col. 1)

Ever glory in the Cross,
Never count it shame or loss;   (Gal 6)
Praise Jehovah, Lord of hosts—   (Isa 6)
Father, Son and Holy Ghost!   (1 John 5)

7.7.7.7D

Preparatory Reading: Old Testament: Exodus 10;
    New Testament: Romans 6 Psalm: 34

1 Timothy 3:2-3

²A bishop then must be blameless, the husband of one wife, vigilant, sober, of good behaviour, given to hospitality, apt to teach; ³Not given to wine, no striker, not greedy of filthy lucre; but patient, not a brawler, not covetous

A bishop then must be blameless: Lord Jesus, I am not sinless. I cannot say I have no sin; One cannot say I have not sinned. There is no sin in Thee: Thou didst no sin; Thou knewest no sin. None convinced Thee of sin. Thou barest my sin in Thy Body on the Tree; Thou wast made sin for me. (1 John 1:8–10, 3:6; 1 Pet. 2:22, 24; 2 Cor 5:21; John 8:46).

Keep my life from sin, all sin; grant me so to live that none may lay upon me blame or shame, accusation or allegation. Keep from open sin, and cleanse me from secret sin. Make me *blameless* before Thee and among men (Ps 19:121–4).

A bishop . . . must be . . . the husband of one wife: Faithful Savior, Jesus, Bridegroom of Thy Church! Thou hast given Thyself in love for us, to sanctify and cleanse us by Thy Word; Thou wilt present us to Thyself a glorious Church without wrinkle, or spot, or any such thing. Thou hast appointed me a "friend of the Bridegroom" to watch over Thy people and present Thy Church a chaste virgin to Thee; and in all this Thou hast charged me to love, cherish, nourish and cleave to my own wife (Eph 5:25–33). My home must show what my pulpit tells; my wife should foreshadow the Church at her best—the most cared for, godly, and happy woman of the congregation must be the woman at my side.

By the power of an endless life, faithful, merciful High Priest, dost Thou ever live to make intercession for us. Do I pray for my wife, as Christ prays for His bride? How long dost Thou, Friend of sinners, bear with us—how touched art Thou with the feeling of our infirmities! Yet how little I can bear with my wife's frailties. What hast Thou not denied Thyself, my Savior, who became poor that we through Thy poverty might be rich toward God! Yet do I tend and provide for my spouse, even as much as I do for myself?

Thou, my Savior, cannot fail nor forsake us, nor deny Thyself. By Thy cross and Blood we are made of Thy bones and flesh. Yet I, O Lord, I am vile—fashioned in iniquity and conceived in sin. Every imagination of the thought of my heart is by nature only evil continually. Like a fool my eyes are in all the earth, and my heart walks after my eyes (Heb. 13:5; 2 Tim. 2:13; Ps 51:5; Gen 6:5; Prov 17:24; Job 31:7).

O wash me thoroughly from my iniquity, and cleanse me from my sin. Create in me a clean heart, O God, and renew a right spirit within me. Cast me not away from Thy presence, and take not Thy Holy Spirit from me. Make me, Lord Jesus, like Thee; make me to my wife as Thou art to me, and to all Thy Church—*the husband of one wife*—pure, true, clean, wholly of one heart with her. (Ps 51:2, 10–11).

35. Watch and Pray

1 From the Mount of Olives' seat,
Where again shall stand Thy feet
Jesus, Lord, we hear Thee say:
"Watch ye therefore, always pray!" (Luke 21)

2 In the night He was betrayed,
How our Savior watched, and prayed,
"Father, let Thy will be done!"
God's beloved, obedient Son! (Mark 14; Heb. 5)

3 In Gethsemane He wept,
E'en as His disciples slept:
See Him rouse them! Hear Him say:
"In temptation, watch and pray!" (Matt 26)

4 We, His household, watch and pray,
Waiting yet His glorious day,
Servant, steward, porter, all
Must attend the Master's call. (Mark 13)

5 Giving thanks, we watch in prayer,
For all saints, we persevere;
Supplicating for the lost,
Praying in the Holy Ghost. (Eph 6, Jude)

6 Sober, would we watch to prayer,
Fervent charity to share,
God's own oracles to speak,
Or in grace to serve the weak. (1 Pe 4:7–11)

7 With the end of all at hand,
Let us heed the Lord's command;
Knowing not His hour or day, (Mark 13)
Brethren, sisters: "Watch and pray!" (1 Pet. 4)

8 Thus His people glory brings
To Jehovah in all things:
To the Father, Spirit, Son,
Praise, dominion, e'er is won! (1 Pet. 4)

7.7.7.7.

The House of God

Preparatory Reading: Old Testament: Exodus 11;
New Testament: Romans 7 Psalm: 35

1 Timothy 3:2-3

²A bishop then must be blameless, the husband of one wife, vigilant, sober, of good behaviour, given to hospitality, apt to teach; ³Not given to wine, no striker, not greedy of filthy lucre; but patient, not a brawler, not covetous.

A bishop . . . must be . . . vigilant: "Could ye not watch with Me one hour?" My Master, how that question startled and searched Peter, and others who slept in Gethsemane. It rebukes me, for I too must be *vigilant*—awake, alert. Thou, Lord Jesus, Thou didst watch and pray many a night, all night, before that night. Early in the morning, a great while before day, didst Thou go to a desert place and pray. Morning by morning Thine ear was opened to hear the Father's voice. Thou dost yet keep Thine Israel, and wilt neither slumber nor sleep (Luke 6:12; Mark 1:35; Isa 50:4; Ps 121:3-4). Thou hast made me a porter in the household of faith. Thou hast set me as a watchman in Zion, to mention Thy Name and give Thee no rest. The trumpet is in my hand to sound the alarm and warn the wicked; if I fail, the blood of men is on my head (Mark 13:34; Isa 62:1,6-7; Ezek 33:6).

Savior, by Thine exceeding abundant grace enable me to make full proof of my ministry, and to watch in all things. Set a watch upon my lips, and let me take heed to myself. Let me watch and pray. Teach me to watch for my people's souls as Thy servant that I may give account with joy and not with grief (1:12; 2 Tim.4:5; Ps 141:3-4; 1 Tim.4:15; Col.4:2-4; Heb.13:17). Thy grace is sufficient for me; of that sufficiency make me able to take heed of myself and of all the flock, watching and warning the church of God, purchased by Thy Blood. Lord Jesus, make me, keep me *vigilant* (2 Cor 12,3:5-6; Acts 20:28-31).

A bishop . . . must be . . . sober: Eternal, only-begotten Son of God, Lord Jesus, Thou art the Word, who art God by whom all things were made. Thou art before all things, and by Thee all things consist, visible and invisible. In Thee dwelleth the fullness of the Godhead bodily; in Thee are hid all the treasures of wisdom and knowledge (John 1:1-5; Col. 1:16-17; 2:3, 9). Thou art the Rod of the stem of Jesse; on Thee rests without measure the Spirit of wisdom and understanding, of counsel and might, of knowledge and fear of the Lord (Is. 11:1-2). Even as a Child was the grace of God upon Thee; Thou didst grow in wisdom and stature, in favor with God and man. The gracious words of Thy mouth amazed men, and they cried out, "Whence hath this Man this wisdom?" (Luke 2:40, 52, 4:22; Matt 13:54). To me, Thou hast given not the spirit of fear, but the Spirit of love, power and a sound mind. The Holy Scriptures are able to make me wise; Thy Word is my wisdom. Let me not be wise in my own eyes, but fear Thee; give me subtlety, knowledge and discretion that I may speak the truth in love, in words of truth and soberness. O Lord, make me, keep me wise, and *sober*.

36. My Songs are Thine, Lord Jesus!

1 My songs are Thine, Lord Jesus—
Thy free, rich, sovereign grace
Awakes, and never ceases
To stir my lips to praise!
My glad heart's meditation
Of Thee is ever sweet—
Who can so great salvation
Extol in measures meet?

2 My songs are Thine, Lord Jesus:
What higher theme of praise
Is there that charms or pleases,
A sinner's heart might raise?
So altogether lovely,
Eternal Son of God,
Thou, sinless, in our nature,
Redeemed'st me by Thy Blood!

3 My songs are Thine, Lord Jesus!
None other name compares
With Thine, my heart who eases,
And all my burden bears:
O Alpha and Omega,
Emmanuel, the Word,
My Shepherd, Bridegroom, Kinsman,
Thou art my God, my Lord!

4 All songs be Thine, Lord Jesus!
Thy praise the world shall tell—
Thy kingdom yet increases
And storms the gates of hell,
Releasing untold numbers,
With Gospel liberty
To celebrate the wonders
Of Thy captivity.

3 Jehovah, my Salvation,
Is all my Strength and Song—
All praise and adoration
To Him alone belong:
To Father Son and Spirit

The House of God

Most Blessed Trinity,
Be honor, might and merit
To all eternity!

7.6.7.6.D

Preparatory Reading: Old Testament: Exodus 12
   New Testament: Romans 8 Psalm: 36

1 Timothy 3:2-3

²A bishop then must be blameless, the husband of one wife, vigilant, sober, of good behaviour, given to hospitality, apt to teach; ³Not given to wine, no striker, not greedy of filthy lucre; but patient, not a brawler, not covetous

A bishop . . . must be . . . of good behavior: Savior, Thy churches look to Thee as the Author and Finisher of our faith, the author, not of confusion, but of peace. On earth, Thou didst not strive, nor cry; no man heard Thy voice in the streets. Thou art meek and lowly of heart, and givest rest unto our souls. Thy love constrains us; that love does not behave itself unseemly (Heb. 12:2; 1 Cor 14:33; Matt 12:19, 11:29; 2 Cor 5:14-15; 1 Cor 13:5).

Thou hast called me to be a *bishop;* and *a bishop . . . must be . . . of good behavior.* I am to walk worthy of my vocation as a Christian minister. Let me be an example to others as an "elder" "in word, in conversation, in charity, in spirit, in faith, in purity." Lord Christ, let me walk after Thee in love, as Thou hast loved us. Let me walk after Thee, the Light of the world, in the light of life as a child of light. Let me walk in wisdom, circumspectly, not as a fool, but redeeming the time in these evil days (Eph 4:1-6; 1 Tim. 4:12, 5:17; Eph 5:1-6; John 8:12). Only one is good, who is God. Thou art my Lord and my God; Thou art well called "Good Master". Grant me to walk to please Thee in *good behavior* (Mark 10:17-18; John 20:28; Col. 1:10; Eph 5:9).

A bishop . . . must be . . . given to hospitality: Lord Jesus, my Master, how blessed were all who received Thee to their homes! How many thus received Thee to their hearts? Matthew, the publican; Zaccheus, the chief publican never had a like Guest before, and never had a like home after (Matt 9:9-13; Luke 19:1-10). And wast Thou not Thyself *given to hospitality?* Was this not how Thy first disciples came to faith in Thee? "Rabbi, where dwellest Thou? Come and see . . . They came . . . saw . . . and abode with Him that day" (John 1:35-41). Was this not Thy reproach, and glory? "This Man receiveth sinners, and eateth with them" (Luke 15:2). Thou didst host but two at Emmaus, and thousands on the fields of Bethsaida (Luke 24:28-35, 9:10-17). How blest shall we be when we shall break bread, and drink anew with Thee in Thy kingdom! (Matt 8:10-12; Luke 14:12-24; Isa 25:6-9; Mark 14:25; Rev. 19:5-10). Was not Thy *hospitality* the door of hope for Peter to be rebuked and restored to Thy service? "Come and dine" (John 21:9-19). Savior, teach me to open my heart, and my home to people. "He that hath friends must shew himself friendly"—here too often I fail. "And there is a friend that sticketh closer than a brother"—and here Thou hast never failed or forsaken me, Friend of sinners! (Prov 18:24). Use me to make Thy people "use hospitality without grudging" and "entertain angels unawares" (Heb. 13:2; 1 Pet. 4:9). King of glory, help me receive Thee in receiving others, that in the last day I and my house may hear Thee say, "Come, ye blessed of My Father, enter . . . for I was a stranger, and ye took me in (Matt 10:40-41; 25:31-35).

37. O hear my plea, most gracious Lord

1 O hear my plea, most gracious Lord
As I prepare to preach:
Give me to understand Thy Word,
With skill its truth to teach:
Awake, arouse, alert my mind
With insight deep and clear
Into the Scriptures, there to find
What Thou wouldst have us hear.

2 Engage, enlarge and warm my heart
To speak Thy truth in love;
Sound doctrine let me now impart
With unction from above:
Its bread and honey, milk and meat
Help me Thy saints to feed
To young and old, to strong and weak
According to their need.

3 My soul, subdued and captive, lead
And guide my footsteps still,
To show and tell by word and deed
Thy good and perfect will
Till found among Thy Blood-bought host,
I and my hearers praise
The Father, Son and Holy Ghost—
The Triune God of grace!

D.C.M.

Preparatory Reading: Old Testament: Exodus 13
   New Testament: Romans 9 Psalm:37

1 Timothy 3:2-3

2A bishop then must be blameless, the husband of one wife, vigilant, sober, of good behaviour, given to hospitality, apt to teach; 3Not given to wine, no striker, not greedy of filthy lucre; but patient, not a brawler, not covetous

A bishop . . . must be . . . apt to teach: Lord Jesus, Thou art my Master, my Teacher. Thou alone: "Be not ye called Rabbi: for one is your Master, even Christ; and all ye are brethren" (Matt 23:8). "Rabbi" the disciples called out after Thee, as they heard John Baptist, and followed Thee. "Rabboni," cried Magdalene through her tears as she heard Thy voice in the garden (John 1:38; 20:16). Even Thine enemies could not but acknowledge Thee as Teacher. Nicodemus says, "We know Thou art a teacher come from God." Simon the Pharisee must hear Thee out: "Master, say on." Herodian and Pharisee say more than they would admit in their flattery: "Master, we know that Thou art true, and carest for no man; for Thou regardest no the person of man, but teachest the way of God in truth" (John 3:2; Luke 7:39-40; Mark 12:14). For this work didst Thou come, to preach and teach the kingdom of God (Matt 9:35; Luke 13:22); for this wast Thou accused and crucified (Luke 23:5).

All that Thou didst begin to do and teach, Thou hast continued as the risen Lord and Head of the Church in and through us Thy people. Thou hast sent forth from the Father the Holy Ghost, the Comforter to teach us, to reveal the things of God to us, to furnish us with the anointing of the Holy One to discern truth and error (Matt 28:18-20; Acts 1:1-8; John 14:26; 1 Cor 2:12-13; 1 John 2:21, 4:6). To us as Messiah Thou showest all things; Thou alone dost teach us to profit (John 4:25-26; Isa 48:17).

Lord and Master, teach us by Thine example to love and serve one another John 13:12-15). Lord, teach us to pray (Luke 11:1-13). By Thy parables teach us the mysteries of Thy kingdom (Matt 13:10-17; Mark 4:33-34). Teach us by Thy grace to deny ungodliness and worldly lusts, and to live righteous, sober, godly lives, looking for the blessed hope of Thine appearing (Titus 2:11-15).

Lord Jesus, the common people heard Thee gladly (Mark 12:37); make me *apt to teach*. Make my words easy to be understood. Enable me to teach the people knowledge, to give good heed, to seek to find out words of delight, Thou one true Shepherd and Master of assemblies (1 Cor 14:9; Eccl 12:9-11). Open my ear to speak a word in season to the weary (Isa 50:4-5); let me never cease to preach and teach Jesus Christ (Acts 5:42). Risen Lord, lead my soul captive to Thee; grant me the gifts and give me to Thy people as a pastor and teacher, seen by them, a man wise in meekness and bridled in tongue, a brother to my brethren, keeping Thy law and teaching as Thy messenger (Eph 4:11; Isa 30:20; James 3; Matt 23:8-12; Mal 2:17). Teacher, Master, Rabbi, Christ—make me *apt to teach*.

38. Bought With A Price, and Not My Own

1 *Bought With A Price, and Not My Own*
Body and spirit His alone,
O let me glorify my God,
Redeemed by Jesu's precious Blood.

2 No more to this vain world conformed,
I would present, with *mind* transformed
To Him this living sacrifice:
My body, bought at such a price.

3 My opened *ears* would daily hear
The Shepherd's voice with love and fear;
O turn mine *eyes* from vanity
The wonders of Thy Law to see!

4 Lord Jesus, touch with holy flame
And purge my *lips* to speak Thy Name:
Let my whole body in my *tongue*
Be bridled, and Thy praise be sung.

5 From my full *heart*, let my *mouth* speak
To cheer the faint, and help the weak,
The law of kindness in me place,
To speak with words and lips of grace!

6 Lift up my *hands*; my feeble *knees*
Confirm, and, that my ways may please
My God in all things, let my *feet*
Run, Thy commandments to complete.

7 Clean *hands*, pure *heart*, a ready *mind*,
Vessels in honor sanctified
Members of righteousness alive
In Christ, and dead to sin are mine.

8 To my Lord Jesus let me give
My ev'ry pow'r, and for Him live,
Whate'er I do, or speak or think:
Yea, to His glory eat and drink.

9 No more my own, bought with a price,
My life and lips make sacrifice
Of praise to God, and make my boast
In Father, Son and Holy Ghost!

                    L.M.

The House of God

Preparatory Reading: Old Testament: Exodus 14
New Testament: Romans 10 Psalm:38

1 Timothy 3:2-3

²A bishop then must be blameless, the husband of one wife, vigilant, sober, of good behaviour, given to hospitality, apt to teach; ³Not given to wine, no striker, not greedy of filthy lucre; but patient, not a brawler, not covetous

A bishop ... must be ... not given to wine: Much, O Savior, has Thy Word instructed me *a bishop ... must be.* Much else, though, I must not be. Prevent and deliver me, O Savior, from defect and vice, even as Thou wouldst make and keep gift and grace in me.

May I be *not given to wine:* "Behold a Man gluttonous, and a winebibber, a Friend of publicans and sinners!" Lord Christ, what reproaches didst Thou bear as the Son of man simply for "eating and drinking" normally among men. This reproach hast Thou borne for me, for Thou hast received and befriended me, even as Thou didst the chief of sinners Paul (Matt 11:19; Luke 15:2; Rom 15:3; 1 Tim. 1:15).

How little have I regarded the dangers of indulgence and warning upon warning in Thy Word! "Wine is a mocker, and strong drink raging, and whosoever is deceived thereby is not wise" "When thou sittest to eat ... put a knife to thy throat, if thou be a man given to appetite" "Be not among winebibbers; among riotous eaters of flesh: for the drunkard and the glutton shall come to poverty; and drowsiness shall clothe a man with rags" "Who hath woe? Who hath sorrow? They that tarry long at the wine" "Behold, this was the iniquity of thy sister Sodom, pride, fullness of bread and abundance of idleness" (Prov 20:1, 23:1-2, 23:20-21, 23:29-35; Ezek 16:49).

How little have I heeded, my Savior, Thine own most solemn warnings that sealed Thy discourse of "things to come" on mount Olivet! "Take heed to yourselves, let at any time your hearts be overcharged with surfeiting and drunkenness and cares of this life, and so that day come upon you unawares ... watch ye therefore, and pray always" "That evil servant shall say in his heart, My Lord delayeth His coming; and shall begin to smite his fellow servants and to eat and drink with the drunken" (Luke 21:34-36; Matt 24:48-49).

How far from these slanders, Lord Jesus, didst Thou stand. Thy meat was to do the will of the Father which sent Thee, and to finish His work. The Paschal cup Thou didst put by, till Thy kingdom fully come. Thou didst refuse the vinegar, that Thou mightest taste death for every man, and drain the cup of God's just wrath for my soul (John 4:31-34; Matt 26:29; Matt 27:34; Heb.2:9; John 18:11; Mark 12:36; Ps 75:7-8).

Shalt Thou, my Redeemer, fast and pray to purchase Thy flock, and shall I but feed myself, and not the flock? Shall my life resemble the Good Shepherd, who gave His life for the sheep, or the hireling who cared nothing for the sheep? (Ezek 34:2; Matt 24:45-46; Luke 12:42-43; John 10:11-13). Let my affections and desires be given, my Savior, to Thee, to Thine, to Thy Word, to Thy work—but *not given to wine.*

39. King Jesus, teach me to forgive

1 King Jesus, teach me to forgive
As Thou hast me forgiven:
Then by Thy mercy I shall live
Before Thy Fath'r in heaven.

2 To endless torment once condemned,
How could I e'er repay
The riches which my sins did spend?
I wasted all away!

3 How can my thankfulness I show
Or how can I forget
The boundless mercy wherewith Thou
Forgav'st me all that debt?

4 Thy patience to forbear impart,
Thy wisdom not to judge
Those who might wound me, from my heart
To bear no bitter grudge.

5 King Jesus, who endured the cross,
From that right hand of God,
O strengthen me to suffer loss,
To strive with sin to blood!

6 By mercy lead me so to live
Before our Fath'r in heaven.
That I may freely all forgive
As I have been forgiven.

7 Within my heart, now shed abroad
The love of Father, Son,
And Holy Ghost, the living God.
Thou blessed Three in One!

C.M.

The House of God

Preparatory Reading: Old Testament: Exodus 15
New Testament: Romans 11 Psalm:39

1 Timothy 3:2-3

²A bishop then must be blameless, the husband of one wife, vigilant, sober, of good behaviour, given to hospitality, apt to teach; ³Not given to wine, no striker, not greedy of filthy lucre; but patient, not a brawler, not covetous

A bishop . . . must be . . . no striker: "What hast thou done? The voice of thy brother's blood crieth unto Me from the ground" (Gen 4:10). So didst Thou, O Lord, indict the murderer Cain, who was of that evil one, who hated his brother. Cursed was his hand that struck, and as cursed was his heart to say, "Am I my brother's keeper?" (Gen 4:8).

The blood of Abel cried out for vengeance, for justice; Thy Blood, Lord Jesus, speaks better things for me. Thou wast bruised for our iniquities, wounded for our transgressions; the chastisement of our peace was upon Thee, and with Thy stripes we are healed (Isa 53:5). The chief priest dealt the first blow, when he judged expedient for Thee to die for the people (John 11:50; 18:22). The guards of the Sanhedrin bloodied Thee. Over and over they buffeted Thee blindfolded: "Who smote Thee?" (Mark 14:65). Pilate laid Thee waste and scourged Thee. Thou didst yield Thy back to the smiters, and how were the plowed furrows laid into it! (John 19:1; Ps 129:3; Isa 50:6). And so the wicked, slothful servants cast Thee out and killed Thee, even as they had beaten and slain Thy servants the prophets before Thee (Luke 20:9-18; 1 Thess. 2:14-16). Yet Thou didst bid Peter put up the sword; Thou didst disclaim all force before Pilate (Matt 26:50-56; John 18:36). Doing no violence, Thou wast cut off for the transgression of Thy people; yet we did esteem Thee stricken of God (Isa 53:4, 9).

Lord Jesus, Master of the house, we Thy servants may expect no better; Thou hast warned us (Matt 23:34-35; Luke 11:49-51; Matt 10:16-26). The apostles approved themselves ministers of God by suffering; and we in turn are called to suffer for Thy Name. This marks our pedigree from the prophets and apostles alike (2 Cor 6:3-5; Acts 5:41-42; 2 Tim. 1:8-11; Matt 5:11-12).

Now what shall we say to these things, when Thou hast called us Thy ministers each to be *no striker?* Can the stricken dare strike? Shall we smite when the Master gave His cheeks to them that plucked off the hair, and bade us turn the other cheek? (Isa 50:6; Matt 5:38-39). Shall we join with wolves, thieves, robbers and hirelings to ravage, savage and scatter Christ's flock? None but an evil servant lays hand to Christ's house (Ezek 34:4-5; Jer 23:1-6; John 10:7-15; Matt 24:49).

Wretched man that I am! I must loathe, abhor myself, my ways and my doings for every evil impulse, every selfish motive to avenge myself, when my Christ died and left an example that I should follow in His steps (1 Pet. 2:21-25; Ezek 36:26-29, 31; Job 42:6). Vengeance is Thine, righteous Lord; Thou shalt repay. Let me give place to Thy wrath; let me overcome evil with good (Rom 12:19-21). Would that all men might say of me, even in sinful contempt, that I am *no striker.*

40. Silver and Gold have I None

1 Silver and gold have I none,
Neither my soul could redeem:
Only the Blood of God's Son
Jesus Christ can make me clean!
Though of all sinners the worst,
Grace to my soul did abound—
Seeking and loving me first,
Jesus my Ransom has found.

2 Silver and gold, Lord, is Thine!
Flocks, herds on all of the hills,
Treasures from depths of the mine
Thy hand provides as it wills:
Simple contentment I ask,
In this I find my great gain—
If for the Lord is my task,
I'll never labor in vain.

3 Silver and gold have I none,
Sinful, lost , perishing soul!
Hear now the Word of God's Son:
'Jesus Christ maketh thee whole!'
Silver and gold have I none,
Yet what I have would I give—
'Jesus the victory hath won!'
Hear, and your soul too shall live!

7.7.7.7.D

The House of God

Preparatory Reading: Old Testament: Exodus 16
  New Testament: Romans 12 Psalm:40

1 Timothy 3:2–3

²A bishop then must be blameless, the husband of one wife, vigilant, sober, of good behaviour, given to hospitality, apt to teach; ³Not given to wine, no striker, not greedy of filthy lucre; but patient, not a brawler, not covetous

A bishop . . . must be . . . not greedy of filthy lucre: "Woe unto you, scribes and Pharisees, hypocrites! For ye devour widows' houses, and for a pretence make long prayer; therefore ye shall receive the greater damnation." Lord Jesus, this spakest Thou openly to Thy disciples and the multitude, that none might miss Thy standard, nor presume to escape its censure or shame (Matt 23:1, 14). This single word speaks of "gain of shame." It is the evil itch to weasel wealth which robs parents to serve 'Corban' (Mark 7:9–13). How far wast Thou, our righteous Judge, from this: Thou didst take no gift, Thou wouldst be divider for none (Luke 12:13–21; Deut 16:19).

But one there was, my Savior, one of the Twelve was indeed *greedy of filthy lucre.* Elisha had Gehazi; Peter had Simon the sorcerer (2 Kgs 5; Acts 8). Thou hadst one of Thy companions, who dipped his hand with Thee in the dish; his feet Thine own dear hands washed, rinsed, toweled and relieved; he took from Thee the choice morsel of the feast, the sop. He left the Upper Room well fed, well shod of Thee, out into the night to sell Thee as a slave—just as he had pilfered the bag. This was Judas Iscariot, who betrayed with a kiss, with the honeyed words, "Hail, Master!" (Matt 26:21–25, 27:8–10, 47–50; John 13:1–5, 21–30; Mark 3:19; Luke 22:3, 47–48). This chosen devil and son of perdition had but one passion to move his heart, mouth, hands and feet after Thee, our Savior; his powers to preach, heal, cast out demons and do many mighty works left him graceless still (John 6:70–71; 17:12; Matt 7:22–23). He was *greedy of filthy lucre.* For this he went to his own place; even as I ponder this, he lifts up his eyes in hell, being in torments. What profit was it to have gained so little, and to have lost his own soul? (Acts 1: 25; Luke 16:23; Mark 8:36).

Peter read out his sentence from the Psalter: "He was numbered with us, and obtained part of this ministry . . . Let his habitation be desolate, and his bishopric let another take" (Acts 1:17,20,25; Ps 69:25). Judas left his chair empty and hell full.

Now I am called to "the office of a bishop;" Peter turns to me and says, "Feed the flock of God which is among you, taking the oversight thereof ; not by constraint but willingly, not for filthy lucre, but of a ready mind" (1 Pe.5:2). "No man can serve two masters . . . ye cannot serve God and mammon" (Matt 6:24). Will I be as many, that corrupt the word of God by peddling it, hawking it, speaking smooth things to please men; or will I speak in Christ, in sincerity before God? (2 Cor 2:17; Gal 1:10; Isa 30:8–13).

Lord, give me neither poverty nor riches; feed me with food convenient to me! (Prov 30:7–9). Cleanse me, keep me, let me *be not greedy of filthy lucre!*

41. Shepherd and Bishop of My Soul

1 Shepherd and Bishop of my soul.
Lord Jesus, hear a pastor's prayer:
Lead me, that I may lead Thy fold,
And guard them with Thy tender care:
Grant me to watch, to work, to weep,
And keep Thy charge to feed Thy sheep

2 Thy sheep so stray and turn aside—
Scattered among the woods and hills!
Teach me to be their faithful guide
To train and curb their stubborn wills
Thy rod and staff, give me to wield—
Thy Word till at Thy voice they yield.

3 Conflict within Thy flock is rife:
At stream and pasture, strong and sleek
With horn and shoulder, vexed with strife
Trample and push away the weak—
Grant me to lead them by Thy grace
In paths of righteousness and peace.

4 Before, about me, and behind
To steal, to kill and to destroy
Thieves, robbers, hirelings, wolves I find
Lay wait to spoil them of their joy:
Like Thee, O let me lay life down,
That all Thy people gain the crown.

5 The waters still, the pastures green,
The table spread before their foes
The oil which soothes and spreads its sheen,
The cup which with refreshment flows
Lead me to find, to tend and feed
Thy sheep in all their want and need.

6 Goodness and mercy show to me
Savior, through all my earthly days
In Thine abundance, full and free
Till all my people, to Thy praise
Are found as Thine, safe home above—
Lord Jesus, hear me, in Thy love!

8.8.8.8.8.8.

The House of God

Preparatory Reading: Old Testament: Exodus 17
  New Testament: Romans 13 Psalm:41

1 Timothy 3:2-3

²A bishop then must be blameless, the husband of one wife, vigilant, sober, of good behaviour, given to hospitality, apt to teach; ³Not given to wine, no striker, not greedy of filthy lucre; but patient, not a brawler, not covetous

A bishop ... must be ... patient: Of Thee, Lord Jesus, did Isaiah speak when He saw Thy glory John 12:41; Acts 8:34-35). Of Thee he wrote this—"Behold My Servant, whom I uphold; Mine Elect, in whom My soul delighteth. I have put My Spirit upon Him: He shall bring forth judgment to the Gentiles. He shall not cry, nor lift up, nor cause His voice to be heard in the street. A bruised reed shall He not break, and the smoking flax shall He not quench: He shall bring forth judgment unto truth. He shall not fail nor be discouraged till He have set judgment in the earth: and the isles shall wait for His law" (Isa 42:1-4; Matt 12:15-21). Of Thee, Savior, the Apostle writes—"Let us run with patience the race that is set before us, looking unto Jesus the Author and Finisher of our faith; Who for the joy that was set before Him endured the cross, despising the shame, and is set down at the right hand of the throne of God. For consider Him that endured such contradiction of sinners against Himself, lest ye be wearied and faint in your minds" (Heb. 12:1-3). Thou dost call us, saying, "Learn of Me, for I am meek and lowly of heart, and ye shall find rest unto your souls" (Matt 11:29).

How rarely, and rightly, didst Thou complain of our stupidity: "How long shall I suffer you?" "How is it that ye do not understand?" "O fools and slow of heart to believe ..." (Matt 17:17, 16:11; Luke 24:25-26). Yet never didst Thou simply berate or abuse; ever, having reproved didst Thou correct us.

Such is Thy kind patience, Lord Christ, to Thine unworthy servants, Thine unprofitable servants—"the meekness and gentleness of Christ" by which Paul sought to edify and not destroy his congregations, not seeking his own, but Thine (2 Cor 10:1, 8, 17-18). Such is the patience every saint must show: "Let your moderation be know unto all men. The Lord is at hand" (Phil 4:5). Such is the patience of a true pastor: "The wisdom that is from above is first pure, then peaceable, gentle and easy to be entreated, full of mercy and good fruit, without partiality and without hypocrisy" (Jas. 3:17).

Grant me, Savior Jesus, this patience to bear with others as Thou dost bear with me. Grant me more than endurance of circumstance, precious as that is (Col. 1:10-14; 2 Thess. 3:5). Grant me Thy large-hearted patience with people, more precious than all power or force among men (Prov 16:32; 2 Tim. 2:24-26). "Behold, the husbandman waiteth for the precious fruit of the earth, and hath long patience for it"—"blade ... ear ... full corn". So teach me to sow, weep, water—and wait (Jas. 5:7; Mark 4:28; Ps 126:5-6).

42. Now as the new-born Day Begins

1 Now, as the new-born day begins,
Lord Jesus, save me from my sins:
Unto Thy glory let me live
By all the grace that Thou dost give.

2 Thy Blood, once shed at Calvary,
From condemnation sets me free:
Yet daily cleanse my way, O Lord,
As I take heed unto Thy Word.

3 True wisdom grant, to know Thy will,
May Thy good, Holy Spirit fill
My heart to make entirely mine
Christ's Word of grace and truth divine.

4 O let me die to sin this day,
In all I think, and do and say:
With mind and soul in Christ renewed,
To live and walk in life anew.

5 Help me deny myself each day,
Take up Thy cross, and in Thy way,
A true disciple, follow Thee,
In service of humility.

6 At home, abroad, at work, at rest
In doing, let my faith be blest
And proven true by works of love
To praise our Father God above.

7 O Savior, let me clearer see
Thy glory; to me dearer be,
Walk with me nearer in Thy way,
That I may love Thee day by day.

L.M.

The House of God

Preparatory Reading: Old Testament: Exodus 18;
　New Testament: Romans 14 Psalm:42

1 Timothy 3:2-3

²A bishop then must be blameless, the husband of one wife, vigilant, sober, of good behaviour, given to hospitality, apt to teach; ³Not given to wine, no striker, not greedy of filthy lucre; but patient, not a brawler, not covetous

A bishop then must be . . . not a brawler: Lord Jesus, Prince of Peace, Wonderful, Counselor, neither hand nor voice didst Thou raise among us. Men fell into contentions and division all around Thee, but Thou didst speak the truth (John 6:41, 52, 60, 66; 7:40-53; 8:31-59). Thine enemies assailed Thee with guile, flattery, contempt and arrogance—Thou didst speak with the tongue of the learned, a soft tongue that could break bone (Isa 50:4; Prov 25:15). Thy foes arraigned Thee, tried Thee, heaping up slander and abuse—yet wast Thou led as lamb to the slaughter, and as a sheep before her shearers is dumb, so opened Thou not Thy mouth (Luke 20; Mark 14:55-62; Isa 53:7).

Even so, Lord, Thy servant must not strive. Where I see strife and railing, let me mark men of corrupt minds, destitute of the truth; and from all such strife, let me withdraw. The wisdom of Thy Word teaches me to avoid such (2 Tim. 2:22-26; 1 Tim. 6:3-5; Prov 22:24-25, 29:22). Set Thy balm of Gilead upon my wounded soul, that I may live at peace with all men as much as in me lies. Teach me to love pureness of heart, and have that grace of lips which marks me as the King's friend (Prov 22:11).

"The Lord is my light and my salvation: whom shall I fear? The Lord is the strength of my life: of whom shall I be afraid? . . . One thing have I desired of the LORD, that will I seek after; that I may dwelling the house of the LORD all the days of my life, to behold the beauty of the LORD, and to inquire in His temple. For in time of trouble He shall hide me in His pavilion: in the secret of His tabernacle shall He hide me: He shall set me up upon a rock" (Ps 27:1, 4-5).

"In Thee, O Lord, do I put my trust; let me never be ashamed: deliver me in Thy righteousness . . . Make Thy face to shine upon Thy servant: save me for Thy mercies' sake . . . O how great is Thy goodness which Thou hast laid up for them that fear Thee; which Thou hast wrought for them that trust in Thee before the sons of men! Thou shalt hide them in the secret of Thy presence from the pride of man: Thou shalt keep them secretly in a pavilion from the strife of tongues . . . O love the Lord, all ye His saints: for the Lord preserveth the faithful, and plentifully rewardeth the proud doer. Be of good courage, and He shall strengthen your heart, all ye that hope in the Lord" (Ps 31:1, 16, 19-20, 23-24).

43. Grant Me through the Night to Rest

1 Father, Son and Spirit blest,
Grant me through the night to rest
Trusting in Thy gracious care:
Triune God, O hear my prayer!

2 Father God, forgive my sin,
Holy Ghost, dwell me within
Never leave me nor forsake
For my dear Lord Jesu's sake!

3 Bless my kindred, friends and foes
Help the suffering in their woes
Save the lost, sustain the poor,
Let Thy Church in grace endure!

4 Turn all nations back to Thee
From all dangers set us free,
Bless the preaching of Thy Word
For the sake of Christ the Lord

5 Thru the hours of darkness deep,
Lord God, grant me peace to sleep
Till I wake, kept in Thy way,
With the new, returning day.

6 Let me serve Thee day and night,
Till at last I walk in white
With Thy people blest in heaven,
For Christ Jesu's sake, Amen!

7.7.7.7.

The House of God

Preparatory Reading: Old Testament: Exodus 19;
New Testament: Romans 15 Psalm:43

1 Timothy 3:2–3

²A bishop then must be blameless, the husband of one wife, vigilant, sober, of good behavior, given to hospitality, apt to teach; ³Not given to wine, no striker, not greedy of filthy lucre; but patient, not a brawler, not covetous

A bishop then must be . . . not covetous: We know Thy grace, Lord Jesus, that though Thou wast rich, yet didst Thou for our sakes become poor, that we through Thy poverty might be rich. Satan might set before all the kingdoms of this world, but Thou didst seek to serve Thy Father, the Lord our God. Thou wast born and swaddled a stranger in Bethlehem, hidden as an exile in Egypt; raised a carpenter in Nazareth; crucified in weakness at Calvary. "They parted His raiment among them, and cast lots. And the people stood beholding" (2 Cor 8:9; Matt 4:8–10; Matt 1–2; Mark 6:1–6; Luke 23:34–35). Thou didst bring nothing into the world but Thy love; Thou didst take nothing out of the world but our sins.

Thy Word we know, which declares: "Take heed and beware of covetousness: for man's life consisteth not in the abundance of the things which he possesseth" "No man can serve two masters: for either he will hate the one and love the other; or else he will hold to the one and despise the other. Ye cannot serve God and mammon" "Seek not ye what ye shall eat, or what ye shall drink, neither be ye of doubtful mind . . . But rather seek ye the kingdom of God: and all these things shall be added unto you. Fear not, little flock: for it is your Father's good pleasure to give you the kingdom" (Luke 12:15; 16:13; 12:29, 31–32).

Thou wast not covetous, but Thy foes were. "The Pharisees also, who were covetous, heard all these things: and they derided Him" (Luke 16:14). Their lives were driven, their worship, words and works all directed, not only by "filthy lucre" of unlawful gain, but by "love of money"—trust in uncertain riches rather than in God who gives us all things richly to enjoy (1 Tim.3:3; 6:17). They measured sanctity by profitability: "Woe unto you, ye blind guides," says Christ our Master, "which say, Whosoever shall swear by the temple, it is nothing; but whosoever shall swear by the gold of the temple, he is a debtor!" (Matt 23:16). They put a price on the head of Christ Himself: "Judas . . . went unto the chief priests to betray Him unto them. And when they heard it, they were glad and promised to give him money" (Mark 14:10–11, Matt 27:9–10). They sought to buy proof to deny His resurrection: "They gave large money unto the soldiers . . . so they took the money, and did as they were taught" (Matt 28:11–15).

A covetous heart is a root of all evil in the Church: heresy, simony, adultery, apostasy (1 Tim. 6:6–10, 17–19; Acts 8:19–23; 2 Pet. 2:12–16). Savior, let me not ask, "What shall we have?" (Matt 19:27–30). Neither leave me nor forsake me, and my life shall be without covetousness (Heb. 13:5–6).

44. Lord Jesus, in Our Home Abide

1 Lord Jesus, in our home abide
Our Strength and Stay, whate'er betide:
As at Emmaus, reign as Head,
And at our tables, bless our bread.

2 Savior, Thy Name is our High Tower,
Our Refuge in each trying hour;
Safe in Thy love, to Thee we flee,
O make our home Thy Bethany!

3 Hallow our marriage; let this house
Thrive in the love of man and spouse;
May wife and husband daily trace
The paths of Christ and Church in grace.

4 May son and daughter daily show
Thy likeness as in grace they grow;
To father, mother, honor give
That long before Thee they may live.

5 In kindness and forbearance long,
Let mercy overcome all wrong.
In rest and work, in joy and care,
Let all attend Thy Word and prayer.

6 Abide with us throughout the years,
In all our laughter and our tears,
Lord, save and bless our family,
In time and to eternity.

7 All that the Holy Scripture saith,
May we obey in Gospel faith,
Let grace on grace to us be given
To make our household part of heaven.

8 O Seed of Abraham, our Rest,
In Thee earth's families shall be blest:
Till all adore the Father, Son
And Holy Ghost—the Three in One!

L.M.

The House of God

Preparatory Reading: Old Testament: Exodus 20;
New Testament: Romans 16 Psalm:44

1 Timothy 3:2, 4–7

²A bishop then must be ... ⁴One that ruleth well his own house, having his children in subjection with all gravity; 5 (For if a man know not how to rule his own house, how shall he take care of the church of God?) ⁶Not a novice, lest being lifted up with pride he fall into the condemnation of the devil. ⁷Moreover he must have a good report of them which are without; lest he fall into reproach and the snare of the devil.

"The office of a bishop" is a "good work" for which grace is pre-requisite to gift, and gift manifested by grace. Character and conduct reveal a man's real capacity for this service much more than talent or talk. I can only fulfill the office as far as I have this character proven by my conduct—personal (2–3), domestic (4–5), relational (6) and social (7). Am I fit to serve in the ministry of the Gospel? All these aspects of my life will prove the reality of my call.

One that ruleth his own house: The church is gathered out of homes, and indeed the church may gather in homes. Nothing is hid from those closest to me; my family presents my first seminary and field work. Piety begins at home (Acts 16, 18, Col. 4; 1 Tim 5:8).

My Savior, Thou art a Son over Thine own house—Thy Church (Heb. 3:6). Among us Thou didst care for Thy house as the "carpenter's son" (Mark 6:3–4). Thou didst provide for Thy blessed mother (John 19:25–27). Thou didst love the home of Mary, Martha and Lazarus (John 11:5; Matt 21:17). Children loved Thee, and sought Thee out, as Thou didst watch them at play (Matt 11:16–17, 18:2). All I should need be as husband, father, or head of a home, Thou hast been for me in Thy justifying obedience; Thou canst work in me by Thy sanctifying grace.

Teach me to manage my substance without waste, as Thou didst (John 6:12–13). Teach me a loving firmness to train and discipline children (Eph 6:1–4). Enlarge my heart to serve and shepherd others (Matt 18:1–14). Make me skilled to feed my people at their capacities, to their needs (Matt 24:45–46; 1 Cor 3:1–2, John 21:15–17). Give me the wisdom of the Proverbs in all my household tasks. (Prov 3:33–35; 6:611; 11:24–25, 29; 12:11; 13:1,23–25; 15:15–17; 16:8, 20; 19:15, 18; 21:5, 17, 20; 22:6–7, 9; 23:20–21; 24:3–4, 27, 30–34; 27:23–29; 28:18–20.)

Master me, as a master *who ruleth well in his own house, having his children in subjection with all gravity* that I may know how to *take care of the church of God.* Give me then, Lord Jesus, a fatherly care, a mother love for my people—watchful, tender, diligent, loving, firm. Open my heart to them and strengthen me to hear and bear whatever heartache or heartbreak may come (Prov 4:1–13; 1 Thess. 2:7–8, 10–12, 20). So let me walk uprightly before Thee in my own house, and Thine.

45. Desiring I Desire

1 "Desiring, I desire
This Paschal feast to keep,
And here in My Last Supper,
With My disciples meet."
This said our Savior Jesus
The night He was betrayed,
Before He died to save us,
Before our debt He paid.

2 Desiring, He desired
His final hours to spend
With poor unworthy sinners
He loved unto the end.
For was not strife among them,
"Who shall be greatest soon?"
Did not their proud contention
Divide the Upper Room?

3 Yet He desired, desiring,
To show His love complete;
His own example giving,
He stooped to wash their feet.
"Among you as a Servant,
I came; in love for you,
I give this new commandment:
Love one another too."

4 Desiring, He desired
Yet greater love to show,
Than any man could ever
On any friend bestow:
For, from the throne of Heaven
Th'eternal Son of God
Stooped down to pay our ransom:
His sinless flesh and blood.

5 Desiring, He desired,
To do His Father's will
All that the Law required
He faithfully fulfilled;
To take away transgression,
As God's Passover Lamb,

The House of God

He entered in His passion
Redeeming sinful man.

6 Desiring, He desires,
With sinners still to eat;
For us He spreads this Supper,
And calls us here to meet:
Proclaiming Christ has suffered,
And risen from the dead,
We stedfastly continue
In "breaking of the bread".

7.6.7.6D

The House of God

Preparatory Reading: Old Testament: Exodus 24;
   New Testament: James 1 Psalm:45

1 Timothy 3:2, 6–7

²*A bishop then must be* … ⁶Not a novice, lest being lifted up with pride he fall into the condemnation of the devil. ⁷Moreover he must have a good report of them which are without; lest he fall into reproach and the snare of the devil.

A bishop . . . must be . . . not a novice: The Scripture makes plain that my Savior was no *novice* in entering His ministry. He was full of the Spirit and of wisdom as a mere Boy; He astonished the doctrines with His understanding and answers to their questions—but at twelve He learned, He did not teach. He was about His Father's business when He was subject to His legal parents (Luke 2:40, 47, 49, 51). He patiently waited, increasing in wisdom, stature, favour with God and man; at fully thirty years of age He emerged to be baptized and consecrated to His public work (Luke 2:52, 3:23). Nor even then did He hasten; He endured fasting and temptation in the wilderness before preaching in the synagogues (Luke 4:1, 14). So He at length appeared as a Man approved among the people by word and deed, as well as signs and wonders (Luke 24:19; Acts 2:22). Christ Jesus held no letters from the schools (John 7:15), but He was *not a novice*.

A bishop in the very nature of his work simply cannot be *a novice*. The graces of self-restraint and self-giving; the discipline of temper and appetite; the settled life of marriage, children, household—all these take too much time, experience and testing by the fellowship of saints for *a bishop* to be *a novice*. *A novice* cannot possess these in the usual run of life as they ought to be. A young man just out of the schools, newly-wed and fresh-faced may look well enough; but his enduring worth is as yet unproven. In time all may be clear; till then, *not a novice*.

To call an immature and unproven convert to this good work too soon is only to endanger him *lest being lifted up with pride he fall into the condemnation of the devil*. Satan fell from his high place as Lucifer *being lifted up with pride* (Isa 19:12–17). Satan tempted our mother Eve to fall by appealing to "the pride of life" (Gen 3:6; 1 John 2:16). Pride always goes before destruction, and a haughty spirit before a fall (Prov 16:18, 18:12).

And what is the *condemnation of the devil* into which the proud fall? "God resisteth the proud" "God knoweth the proud afar off" "The LORD plentifully rewardeth the proud doer" "Everyone that is proud in heart is an abomination to the LORD" "God is able to humble them that walk in pride" "and bring down high looks" (Prov 3:34, 1 Pet. 5:5; Ps 138:6; Ps 31:23; Prov 16:5; Dan 4:27; Ps 18:27).

Can anything be less like Christ than the self-preening pride of *a novice*? (2 Pet. 2:4; Jude 6). God of all grace, humble me under Thy mighty hand, and lift me up in due season when I may walk worthy of this most holy vocation as a proven man of God—*not a novice*.

46. Thou Art The Man !

1 In David's royal courts he stood,
Nathan the prophet, man of God:
With holy guile he pled his cause
To vindicate Jehovah's laws.

2 "O king! A poor man lived beside,
A man of wealth, who in his pride
And greed, to feed a passing guest,
The pauper's lamb he killed and dressed."

3 In indignation blazed the King,
And said, "The man who did this thing,
Must fourfold to the poor man give—
No pity show, he must not live!"

4 With David's sentence once pronounced,
The man of God the truth announced:
"With conscience stained and guilty hand,
Thyself hast sinned—*thou art the man!*"

5 "Thus saith the LORD—thy sin I see,
By murder and adultery,
Thou hast despised My law; My Name
The heathen hearing shall blaspheme!"

6 "*Thou art the man!*" O sinner, hear
How God shall find thee out, and fear:
He is not mocked, what thou dost sow
Shall soon be reaped in weal or woe!

7 "*Thou art the man!*" Thy heart's deceit
Thy conscience blinds in vain conceit:
Condemning others, thou, condemned
For like transgressions, dost offend!

8 "*Thou art the man!*" Thy soul's trespass
The Law reflects as in a glass;
"The soul that sinneth, it shall die!"
Hell at the Judgment draweth nigh!

9 *"Thou art the man!"* Who teacheth thee
From coming wrath of God to flee?
Deliverance find in Jesus Christ,
Who bids thee, "Come to Me and rest!"

10 "Behold the Man!" who on the Cross,
With His own Blood repaid our loss;
For many He the ransom gave:
Look unto Christ , and be ye saved!

L.M.

The House of God

Preparatory Reading: Old Testament: Exodus 32;
New Testament: James 2 Psalm:46

1 Timothy 3:7

7Moreover he must have a good report of them which are without; lest he fall into reproach and the snare of the devil.

Reproach . . . the snare of the devil: The "novice" falls as the devil fell; the scandal-ridden falls as the devil plans.

Even now Satan goes about as a roaring lion, seeking whom he may devour; his wrath is great and his time is short 1 Pet. 5:8, Rev. 12:12). At his will he takes captive in his snare those who oppose the Lord's servants and the Lord's truth (2 Tim. 2:24–26). This must be so, for such "are of the world" and "the whole world lieth in wickedness" (1 John 4:1, 5; 5:19). But the adversary's only foothold upon us can come with sin. "The accuser of our brethren" must find nothing against us, except our faith (Dan 6:4–5; 1 Pet. 2:11–12, 3:14–17, 4:14–16).

The tempter found nothing in my Lord Jesus (John 14:30). My Savior endured the contradiction of sinners against Himself (Heb. 12:3). He was reviled, pilloried as "a Samaritan," "a devil," "born of fornication," "mad," (1 Pet. 2:23; John 8:41, 48, 7:20, 10:20) yet He could publicly challenge His foes, "Which of you convinceth Me of sin?" and get no reply (John 8:46). When He called for even one among them "without sin," they slipped from His presence one by one in shame (John 8:7–9). In Him was no sin; He knew no sin; He did no sin (1 John 3:3; 2 Cor 5:21; 1 Pet. 2:22). Our reproaches fell upon Him; and reproach broke His heart (Rom 15:3; Ps 69:7, 9, 19–21). Over and over He bore the scorn of the passers-by, the soldiers, the scribes, the idle spectators, the thieves beside Him: "If thou be the Son of God, come down from the cross! . . . Save thyself . . . come down from the cross . . . let God deliver him, if He will have him! He saved others; himself he cannot save! . . . If thou be Christ, save thyself, and us!" (Matt 27:39–44 ; Mark 15:29–32; Luke 23:35–39). Thank God, He would not come down! Thank God, He saved not Himself, but us!

God be merciful to me, the sinner! God work in me that godly sorrow to repentance not to be repented of! (Luke 18:13; 2 Cor 7:10). Make not my name a byword among the heathen; suffer me not to cause the Lord's enemies to blaspheme (Deut 28:37; Ps 44:14; Rom 2:23–24; 2 Sam 12:14). Let me give offence to none; let me provide for honest things both in the sight of the Lord and of men; let me exercise myself to have always a conscience void of offence toward God and toward men (1 Cor 10: 32; 2 Cor 8:21; Acts 24:16). Let me pray daily: "Who can understand his errors? Cleanse Thou me from secret faults; keep back Thy servant also from presumptuous sins: let them not have dominion over me. Then shall I be upright, and I shall be innocent from the great transgression: Let the words of my mouth, and the meditation of my heart be acceptable in Thy sight, O Lord, my strength, and my redeemer," even Jesus Christ, Amen. (Ps 19:12–14).

47. We Serve the Tables, Deacons True

1 We serve the tables, Deacons true,
Of Christ our Servant-King;
We serve God's people and the poor;
In all our minist'ring
We free our Elders' hands for prayer
And preaching of the Word:
We serve, in all the Churches' care,
The business of the Lord.

2 The Lord Christ has appointed us
To each his several place;
The Holy Ghost anointed us
With wisdom, power and grace;
To every one of us is given,
By his ability,
The business of the house of God,
In works of charity.

3 With bread and wine we humbly serve
The Table of the Lord;
Our Pastor's table we would spread,
Who labors in the Word.
The table of the poor we help
To furnish in their need,
With this world's good, and show the love
Of Christ in truth and deed.

4 Not slothful in our business, we
In fervent spirit live
To serve the Lord, and cheerfully
Our alms of mercy give.
Our brother's keepers we would prove,
And even to the least
Of all His brethren, we our love
Would show as unto Christ.

5 *The King's own business now requires*
Our earnest zeal and haste:
We would not bear the traitor's bag,
And perish in his place.
As good and faithful servants, still

The House of God

We hold the mystery
Of Gospel truth, with conscience clear
And lives of purity.

6 To do His Father's business, once
Our Savior went about
In doing good, and in His steps
We follow, in and out:
As stewards in His household's care
We hold our brethren's trust:
Each others' burdens would we bear
And seek God's kingdom first.

7 In all the business of the Lord,
And service of the King,
His recompense of great reward
We seek in everything.
We do with all our might His work
In whatsoever thing,
In business, men of diligence
To stand before the King.

8 Savior, and Servant of the LORD,
We humbly pray that we
May well the Deacon's office use,
And gain Thy good degree;
In boldest faith to join the host
Of all the saints, to praise
The Father, Son and Holy Ghost—
The Triune God of grace!

D.C.M.

Preparatory Reading: Old Testament: Exodus 33
   New Testament: James 3 Psalm:47

1 Timothy 3:8–10

⁸Likewise *must* the deacons *be* grave, not doubletongued, not given to much wine, not greedy of filthy lucre; ⁹Holding the mystery of the faith in a pure conscience. ¹⁰And let these also first be proved; then let them use the office of a deacon, being *found* blameless.

Likewise, says Paul—for the character, tone, standards and spirit of the elders and Pastor as "bishops" must, will pervade the whole brotherhood of the Church, and shape the best of men from whom *the deacons* are to be chosen.

The congregation should seek *deacons* who are *likewise*—of the stature and spirit of their "bishop", for the men who wait on the Church's tables are to be as "filled with the Holy Ghost and wisdom" as the men who give themselves "to prayer and the ministry of the Word." The *deacons* must be fully in sympathetic spiritual support of the "bishop" if they are to render their needed help and manage matters which otherwise must fall to the elders (Acts 6:3–4, 11:29–30).

The deacons then, must have a character and grace akin to their Pastor and elders; their abilities and tasks are different, but in heart, mind and life they are to be as one.

Like the "bishop," *the deacons* are to be *not given to much wine, not greedy of filthy lucre*: personal pleasures and appetites, private profit and avarice have no place in the heart or life. These personal traits must be uniform in all the congregation's oversight.

Other traits are kindred one to other, but nuanced to the tasks of the different offices. Where the pastor and elder is to be *sober, vigilant, of good behavior*, the deacon is to be *grave*. Where the elder must not be *a brawler* in ruling the Church, the deacon must not be *double-tongue* in serving the Church. The pastor must be *apt to teach* in propagating the faith; the deacon must be *holding the mystery of the faith in a pure conscience* in protecting the faith in interests of the Church.

King Jesus, Prince and Savior, by Thy Word and Spirit, perfect that which concerns me and mine in the congregation—make me the best I can be as a Pastor; make the men under my care the best they can be, and of our best men give us elders and deacons after Thine own heart.

Sanctify to Thy Name and Thy service at the Lord's Table, the pastor's table and the table of the poor, all who bear the office of Deacon in their character, conduct and confession of the faith. Make them each one Thy good and faithful servants—*grave, not double-tongue, not given to much wine, not greedy of filthy lucre, holding the mystery of the faith in a pure conscience.*

48. Our Faithful, merciful High Priest

1 Our faithful, merciful High Priest,
Lord Jesus, from Thy glorious throne
Look down in pity on the least
Of all Thy brethren sad and lone.

2 Thy righteous saints, the poor and meek,
Bowed down with misery and grief
Are hungered, thirsty, cold and sick—
Be pleased by us to give relief.

3 To bring a cup of water cold,
To give a loaf the poor to feed
The naked in a cloak to fold:
Thus would we love in truth and deed.

4 The dying, sick, imprisoned, vile,
Widows and orphans in their need,
Religion pure and undefiled
Will visit, both in word and deed.

5 O Son of man, when Thou shalt come
In glory with Thine angels bright
Grant we may hear Thee say, "Well done,
Enter My kingdom—walk in white!"

6 "As ye have done it unto these
The least of all My brethren dear,
Ye have My Word fulfilled, Me pleased:
Ye have bestowed on Me your care!"

7 O King of glory, who prepared
Our place before the world began,
Grant us, with all for whom we cared,
On Thy right hand in life to stand.

L.M.

Preparatory Reading: Old Testament: Exodus 34
   New Testament: James 4 Psalm:48

1 Timothy 3:8-10

⁸Likewise *must* the deacons *be* grave, not doubletongued, not given to much wine, not greedy of filthy lucre; ⁹Holding the mystery of the faith in a pure conscience. ¹⁰And let these also first be proved; then let them use the office of a deacon, being *found* blameless.

First . . . proved: To our King we owe our best; we must serve when at our best. When the seven first deacons were sought, the apostles as elders asked for the best—"Look ye out among you seven men of honest report, full of the Holy Ghost and wisdom, whom we may appoint over this business" (Acts 6:3). And such as the first deacons were, so must our deacons be now. In being "grave", "not doubletongued" they are "of honest report"; "not given to much wine", "not greedy of filthy lucre" they prove to be "full of the Holy Ghost"; "holding the mystery of the faith in a pure conscience" they are "full of wisdom" (8–9).

The offices of the Church lead and model the vocation of all believers in our common priesthood before God and the Lamb. Each according to "the manifold grace of God" may "speak" or "serve." So just as the gifts of an elder and pastor are *proved* as all brethren admonish each other, so the gifts of a deacon are *proved* as members of the body of Christ serve one another in love (1 Pet. 4:10–11; Rom 12:3–8, 15:14).

So *proved*, and *found blameless*, they are admitted to *use the office of a deacon* (13). Well may our Deacons be *proved*, and *found blameless* before they *use the office of a deacon*, for on them rests the peace of the Church, the security of its treasury, the continuity of its orthodoxy, and the stability of its ministry "of prayer and of the Word". No elder may be "a novice;" every deacon must be *first proved*.

First . . . proved: By this apostolic ordinance the Lord Jesus promises there will be time enough to test a man for service. No need or emergency compels the Church to rash steps. It is written "Lay hands on no man suddenly" (5:22) and this maxim applies to deacons as much as to elders. The Apostle himself set apart elders about one year after planting the first churches in Galatia (Acts 14:21–23).

Proven . . . blameless . . . then . . . the office: Let me keep this before me without ceasing: no office without character, no gift without grace, no character without experience, no gift without exercise, no grace without evidence.

How much more confident our Deacons will be; how much more supportive the members will be; how much more cordial and co-operative all the oversight will be with one another as they are *proven . . . found blameless, then . . . use the office of a deacon*.

49. Young, Little, Infant Children

1 As our Lord Jesus journeyed,
It fell upon a day
They brought *young children* to Him,
That He His hands might lay
Upon them, and that, praying
He might them bless and touch:
For He has said His kingdom
Of grace belongs to such.

2 They brought Christ *little children*
For He His Word has given,
That of such helpless sinners,
The Kingdom is of heaven:
We cannot be forgiven
Or see Him face to face,
Except we be converted,
And humbly trust His grace.

3 They brought Him also *infants:*
We must be born again,
Cleansed by His Blood and Spirit
To share His gracious reign.
Young, little, infant children
They brought to Jesus Christ
For He alone can save them,
Our Prophet, King and Priest.

4 Rebuked by His disciples,
They turned to go away,
But Christ was sore displeased,
And to them all did say:
"Suffer these little children
To come; forbid them not!"
Receiving them, He blessed them,
The eternal Son of God.

5 Then on He took His journey
Which led Him to the Cross
Upon the hill of Calv'ry,
Where, to restore our loss,

He once for all would suffer
In death for us and bleed,
Bruised as the Seed of Woman
To meet our sin and need.

6 These are the seed of Abraham,
By faith in Jesus Christ,
Whom grace, by God's election
Hath purchased with that price
Our Saviour paid in dying—
His own most precious Blood!
The Spirit of adoption
Has made them sons of God.

7 Lord Jesus, Prince and Savior,
Thy promise now we plead:
To us and to our children
In all our sin and need,
Reveal Thy great redemption
Bought with Thy precious Blood—
Let all our households trust Thee,
As children born of God.

8 O hear us Holy Father,
Adopt us as Thine own:
O hear us Jesus, Savior,
High Priest upon the throne:
O hear us, Holy Spirit,
And witness with the Blood:
In Triune grace receive us,
As twice-born sons of God!

7.6.7.6.D

The House of God

Preparatory Reading: Old Testament: Deuteronomy 1;
New Testament: James 5 Psalm: 49

1 Timothy 3:11–12

¹¹Even so *must their* wives be grave, not slanderers, sober, faithful in all things.
¹²Let the deacons be the husbands of one wife, ruling their children and their own houses well.

Even so: The qualities of the true deacon must "likewise" reflect the pastor and elder. And the deacon's wife must *even so* reflect her husband. He must be "grave;" she must be *grave* (8, 11). He must not be "doubletongued;" she must be *not a slanderer* (6, 11). He must be "not given to much wine;" she must be *sober* (8, 11). He must be "not greedy of filthy lucre;" she must be *faithful in all things* (8, 11). In the service of a Deacon's office, his wife must mirror him as his helpmeet, like him in character, speech, self-discipline and fidelity.

Now Paul does not sketch such a profile for an elder's wife, though surely she too must cleave to her husband in his labors, as one flesh with him, and as joined in one Spirit by the Gospel. But the deacon's wife must needs work alongside her husband in all his care for widows and the distressed; so Paul well stresses her suitability.

Lord Jesus, Thou didst come not to be ministered unto, but to minister and to give Thy life a ransom for many. Thou didst take the form of a servant when humbled to save us; Thou camest among us as one that serves (Mark 10:45; Phil. 2:5–8; Luke 22:22–27). By Thy Spirit fill our Deacons and their wives to serve Thee with zeal as did Aquila and Priscilla; keep them from the works of Ananias and Sapphira, that they may be *faithful in all things.*

Let the deacons be the husbands of one wife, ruling their children and the own houses well: A deacon's marriage and home life must fully match any elder's or pastor's (2, 3, 12). Our Pastors, Elders and Deacons are none of them any better than their marriages, families and children reveal them to be.

The Church is "the house of God," and "the household of faith;" its peace, purity, and progress all require the steady, sure hands of proven family men, supported by their households to guide it, even as David once tended God's flock with hand and heart (Ps 78:70–72).

Risen Lord of glory, Christ our King, faithful Savior Jesus, lead captive in the captivity of Thy grace Thy chosen for the loving service of the Gospel. Fashion them according to Thy will in heart and life; make them Thy men above, before giving them Thy ministry. Make all Thy Deacons even as the first seven were—"men of honest report, full of the Holy Ghost and wisdom" to serve Thy tables and free Thy pastors and elders for "prayer and the ministry of the Word" (Acts 6:2–4).

50. "Give Ye Them to Eat!"

1 Among the multitudes in need
We see Thee stand, O Son of God,
In every gracious word and deed
Thy heart's compassion shines abroad:
To teach, to preach, to heal, to feed
We follow now where Thou hast trod.

2 We weary in our doing well:
We fain would send the crowds away,
Whose cries for mercy ever swell,
And bid them come another day:
Yet even as our plight we tell,
"They need not go," we hear Thee say.

3 Astonished, Savior, do we hear
Thee bid us, "Give ye them to eat!"
Our paltry store we count in fear—
"Whence shall we find all these their meat?
A few small fish and loaves are here.."
"Bring them to Me!" Thou dost entreat.

4 All that we bring, Thy hand will take,
Will to Thy Father lift and bless,
Will firmly, fully, freely break
And give to all, among the grass,
Set row on row, till all partake,
And thousands, filled, Thy reign confess,
And ever seek Thee King to make.

5 Yet Thou our debtor ne'er canst be:
Of all the gathered fragments found,
Our baskets full we all shall see—
All grace Thou wilt to us abound
Till eater's bread and sower's seed
Richly supply our every need.

6 O Father, no good gift deny
Thy children: give the Holy Ghost
To make us with our Savior's eye
Have deep compassion on the lost
For whom He wept, and bled and died,
And lives to save to uttermost!

8.8.8.8.8.8.

Preparatory Reading: Old Testament: Deuteronomy 2;
 New Testament: Luke 1 Psalm: 50

1 Timothy 3:13

13For they that have used the office of a deacon well purchase to themselves a good degree, and great boldness in the faith which is in Christ Jesus.

To *use the office of a deacon well* is to serve "nobly" or "beautifully." True service is an art which adorns the Gospel without garish show. The hypocrite's alms are given "to be seen of men" (Matt 6:1–4). The faithful deacon quietly serves and leaves in his wake the blessing, help and "the beauty of holiness" which his work effects.

This service is as much hard work as is the "good work" of a bishop. But it is the price a faithful man pays, an investment a good steward of God's manifold grace makes, which will at last *purchase* or acquire at a cost *a good degree*—a noble rank or standing within the Church. The "good work" brings *a good degree*. The harder the effort, the higher the esteem of the Lord who honors those who honor Him (1 Pet. 4:11; 1 Sam 2:30). What could be more noble than to serve the Servant of the Lord? The queen of the south once said to King Solomon, "Happy are thy men, happy are these thy servants, which stand continually before thee, and that hear thy wisdom" (1 Kgs 10:8). "Behold, a greater than Solomon is here" (Matt 12:42).

Along with that *good degree* is granted *great boldness in the faith which is in Christ Jesus*. Faithful service, which has *used the office of a deacon well* should mature and strengthen the soul's growth in grace, and enlarge our capacity to bless and be blessed. In receiving the Word, "whosoever hath, to him shall be given;" so too in service (Luke 8:18, 19:26; Matt 25:23). And are not the first seven deacons evidence of this?

Stephen becomes the first of the martyrs (Acts 6:5–7:60). Philip becomes the first of the evangelists; he is given to bring the Gospel first to Samaritans and a Gentile (Acts 8). Both these deacons anticipate the apostle and elder Peter both in doing and dying for Christ. In what affectionate esteem ought I to hold every deacon who follows in Christ's steps of humility, self-denial and sacrificial service?

Savior, and Lord, who didst come among us to serve, who washed our feet that we might learn how to love one another—Thou hast blessed the cup of cold water and received those who receive little children in Thy Name. Be pleased to raise up, sustain, bless and make fruitful those men gifted and called by Thy grace to serve Thy people, that they may *use the office of a deacon well,* and *purchase to themselves a good degree and great boldness in the faith* that is in Thee (Luke 22:23; John 13:12–13, 34; Matt 10:42, 18:4–5). Amen.

51. Lord Jesus Christ Our Risen King

1 Lord Jesus Christ, our risen King,
We meet in worship, wondering;
At Thine appointment gathered here
Our hearts are filled with joy and fear.

2 "All hail!" Thy voice doth gladly greet
Our souls, all trembling at Thy feet;
O still our doubts and strengthen faith
Fast holding all Thy Word now saith!

3 To Thee, our Prince of life, is giv'n
All power on earth ,all power in heaven;
We willing go at Thy command,
Thy peace to preach in every land.

4 We preach to all the world abroad,
Jesus, Thy righteousness and Blood:
We bid the lost repent, believe,
And to Thy Word forever cleave.

5 As Thy disciples thus we claim
All true believers in Thy Name:
In waters deep they sink and rise
Into the Triune God baptized.

6 To us, Thy Church redeemed by Blood,
Grant the whole counsel of our God:
Into all truth may we be led,
To do and teach what Thou hast said!

7 World without end, and all the days,
Redeemer, be with us always
To bring Thy scattered sheep and lost
To Father, Son and Holy Ghost!!

L.M.

The House of God

Preparatory Reading: Old Testament: Deuteronomy 3
New Testament: Luke 2 Psalm:51

1 Timothy 3:14-15

14These things write I unto thee, hoping to come unto thee shortly: 15But if I tarry long, that thou mayest know how thou oughtest to behave thyself in the house of God, which is the church of the living God, the pillar and ground of the truth.

These things—the focus on sound doctrine leading to godliness (1:3-7) on rightly using Law and Gospel (1:8-20); the zealous care for prayer and public worship (2); the high standards set for elders and deacons (3:1-13)—*these things* take such priority with Paul he must *write* of them even before he can visit Timothy in Ephesus. *These things write I unto thee, hoping to come unto thee shortly:* Paul does not rest the Churches' future on the uncertainties of his personal presence, nor on his availability to Timothy when needed, nor on Timothy himself as a supposed "successor to the apostles." No, the Holy Spirit inspires this Epistle and places it in Holy Scripture so that, long after Paul and Timothy have entered their rest, *these things* will endure to instruct and direct *the church of the living God*.

These things I write: In the only true "apostolic succession" required, I follow Paul, following Christ, with the other apostles and the prophets "believing all things that are written" (Acts 24:14-15, 26:22-23).

Here is my certainty in service: "the Holy Scriptures . . . are able to make thee wise unto salvation through faith which is in Christ Jesus" "given by inspiration of God, and profitable for doctrine, for reproof, for correction, for instruction in righteousness, that the man of God may be perfect, thoroughly furnished unto all good works" (2 Tim. 3:15-17).

Here is my certainty of knowledge: "It seemed good unto me also . . . *to* write unto thee in order . . . that thou mightest know the certainty of these things" (Luke 1:14). Here is assurance for my soul: "These things have I written unto you that believe on the name of the Son of God, that ye may know that ye have eternal life, and that ye may believe on the name of the Son of God" (1 John 5:13). Here is my sanctification: "My little children, these things write I unto you, that ye sin not" (1 John 2:1). Here is my joy: "And these things write we unto you, that your joy might be full" (1 John 1:4). Here is my soul's safety: "To write the same things to you . . . for you is safe" (Phil. 3:1). Here is comfort and hope: "What things were written aforetime, were written for our learning, that we through patience and comfort of the Scriptures might have hope" (Rom 15:4). Here is my readiness for Christ's return: "Blessed is he that readeth, and they that hear the words of this prophecy and keep those things that are written therein: for the time is at hand" Rev. 1:3; 22:10-20. And here is the pledge of all blessedness I may know for time and eternity: "As it is written, Eye hath not seen, nor ear heard, neither have entered into the heart of man the things which God hath prepared . . ." (1 Cor 2:9-14).

52. One Lord, One Faith, One Baptism

1 "One Lord, one Faith, one Baptism!"
Our joyful lips confess
Christ Jesus as our Savior,
"The LORD our Righteousness:"
Our Wisdom, our Redeemer,
Who sanctifies alone—
We praise, we bless and honor
The Lamb upon the throne!

2 "Once" has He come from heaven,
"Appeared in this world's end"
To put away transgressions,
His flesh and blood to rend:
"One offering" made and finished,
He has Himself, "sat down"
At God's right hand exalted,
With honor, glory crowned!

3 "One God, one Mediator
Between both man and God,
The Man Christ Jesus" only
Has given in that Blood
Which freely flowed at Calv'ry,
A ransom "once for all"
To sinners lost and needy
Who shall upon Him call.

4 "One Lord, one Faith, one Baptism!"
To all the world around
We now proclaim the Gospel,
Who know its joyful sound:
One God and Father blessing,
One Christ, as God the Son,
One Holy Ghost, confessing,
We praise the Three in One!

7.6.7.6.D

The House of God

Preparatory Reading: Old Testament: Deuteronomy 4
   New Testament: Luke 3 Psalm:52

1 Timothy 3:14-15

14These things write I unto thee, hoping to come unto thee shortly: 15But if I tarry long, that thou mayest know how thou oughtest to behave thyself in the house of God, which is the church of the living God, the pillar and ground of the truth.

These things write I . . . hoping to come unto thee shortly: Paul's remedy for his absence is to *write*. By his pen, his fingers touch, his hand comforts and his arm embraces his "own son in the faith," "son Timothy" (1:2, 18).

The Apostle John is led by the Spirit to say, "I would not write, but . . . speak face to face" (2 John 12). Paul, so much more uncertain of his future freedom says *These things write I . . . hoping to come.* In many ways, Paul came to Ephesus as well and better by pen than in person. Writing puts before Timothy Paul's mind, heart and voice directly, permanently, with definitive finality. Writing invests Timothy with Paul's authority and warrant for every step he must take.

Timothy passed all this on to faithful men, able to teach others also—and so now to me (2 Tim. 2:2). Wherever I go, the Bible goes; where the Bible goes, the Apostles and Prophets continue to herald our Lord Jesus Christ. And as they go with me, the Savior is with them and me always in the person of the Holy Ghost, the Comforter whom the Father has sent in Christ's name, the Spirit who joins the Bride calling all to "Come!" (Matt 28:18-20; John 14:26; Rev. 22:17). He who hears them through my preaching and teaching the Bible, hears Christ Himself. "Truly our fellowship is with the Father and with His Son Jesus Christ. And these things write we unto you, that your joy may be full" (1 John 1:3-4). "These are written, that ye might believe that Jesus is the Christ, the Son of God; and that, believing, ye might have life in His name" (John 20:31).

Paul writes *hoping to come:* thinking cannot add a cubit to Paul's stature, and he cannot boast of tomorrow. If the Lord will, he may live and do this or that; so Paul prepares for all events. It were well that we go and do likewise; we must redeem the time and so live "if the Lord will." In sowing the Word of the kingdom, or sowing to the Spirit, let us sow beside all waters; sow without heed to wind or sky; and sow bountifully (Matt 6:27; Prov 27:1; Jas. 4:15; Eph 5:16; Mark 4:14; Gal 6:7-8; Isa 32:20; Eccl 11:6; 2 Cor 8:6-9.)

But if I tarry long: Did Paul ever come? No; never again did he see Ephesus, just as he had said (Acts 20:25, 36-38). Long he tarried in other parts, and in prison; long now he tarries in death, dust to dust, ashes to ashes, his soul departed to be with Christ. But "he being dead yet speaketh." And while I tarry here, while it is day, let me put my hand to the plough and sow in hope; sow with tears, to reap with joy.

53. The Church of God

1 The Church of God! The Church of God,
Which Thou hast purchased with Thy Blood,
Lord Jesus, by Thy Spirit lead
The flocks Thy servants tend and feed.

2 The Church of God! We gladly give
Our hearts and service; hence we live
To watch, to work, to wait, to weep
To guard, to guide our Master's sheep.

3 The Church of God! Whose souls are led
Before the Table Christ has spread:
Upon Thy saints, O Savior, shine
Who break Thy bread and drink Thy wine.

4 The Church of God! O Father keep
Thy chosen, called and Blood-bought sheep
Which Thou hast given to Thy Son
In love and truth forever one.

5 The Church of God! The Bride, whose Spouse
Prepares on high a heavenly house:
Spirit of grace, our souls adorn
To see Him on that blessed morn!

6 The Church of God, in which is found
A pillar to the truth and ground
Lord, on her walls uphold and bless
The mystery great of godliness

7 The Church of God! In earth and heaven
All glory, praise and thanks be given
To Him who dwells in midst of thee
The ever-blessed Trinity!

L.M.

The House of God

> Preparatory Reading: Old Testament: Deuteronomy 5;
> New Testament: Luke 4 Psalm:53

1 Timothy 3:14–15

¹⁴These things write I unto thee, hoping to come unto thee shortly: ¹⁵But if I tarry long, that thou mayest know how thou oughtest to behave thyself in the house of God, which is the church of the living God, the pillar and ground of the truth.

Greatly I need *these things* which Paul writes, for hardly do I consider where I am working and barely comprehend how I am to work. Do I think much, or long, or hard on the fact I serve in *the house of God which is the church of the living God, the pillar and ground of the truth?* To look at them, any carnal eye can see very ordinary, sin-plagued, struggling believers—"babes," "the foolish, the weak, the base things" "no people in this world"—"publicans and sinners" whose leaders are "unlearned and ignorant men." But Christ sees in these "offscourings of the world" the makings of His bride. "Such were some of you: but ye are washed, but ye are sanctified, but ye are justified in the Name of the Lord Jesus, and by the Spirit of our God" (Matt 11:25, 1 Cor 1:27–28; 1 Pet. 2:10; Matt 11:19; Acts 4:13; 1 Cor 4:13, 6:11).

To *the living God,* here is His *church*. God who raises the dead, and speaks of things that are not as though they were—God with whom all things are possible and nothing is impossible—God has raised us from the dead, quickening us in "the great love wherewith He loved us" and raised us to sit with Christ Jesus in heavenly places, to show forth to all ages the exceeding riches of His grace and kindness to us (Rom 4:17; Luke 1:37; Matt 19:26; Eph 2:4–7). He has begotten us again to a lively hope by the resurrection of Jesus Christ from the dead; He has built us as lively stones onto the Lord Jesus as the living Stone (1 Pet.1:3; 2:4–5). This is whom I serve, and who I am. This Church is also *the house of God.* Every believer, yes, even myself, His Word declares the "temple of God . . . the temple of the Holy Ghost" (1 Cor 3:16–17, 6:19–20). The local assembly in its worship and fellowship is a holy temple to the Lord, "an habitation of God through the Spirit" (Eph 2:19–22); the entire communion of saints is a "household" a "family in heaven and earth" bearing the Name of the Father, indwelt by Christ in the strength of the Spirit and filled with the fullness of God (Eph 3:15–19). As every saint bears the life of God Triune in his soul, so the local congregation and the whole number of the elect is *the house of God:* how dreadful is this place, this *house of God!* The Lord is here, and so often I knew it not! (Gen 28:16–17). Does my knowledge puff up, or does my charity edify? Might I wound "a weak brother for whom Christ died" and so "sin against Christ" Himself? (Rom 14:15; 1 Cor 8:11–12). The life and sanctity of Christ's people is at stake, perhaps at jeopardy, in how I *behave* myself. Let me pause, pray, and purpose *to behave* myself *in the house of God, which is the church of the living God.*

54. O that the Lord's Salvation

1 "O that the LORD's salvation
From Zion soon should come,
When Israel's captive nation
Returns rejoicing, home!"
So sang the saints with longing
To see the distant day
Upon all peoples dawning
Of great Messiah's sway.

2 Salvation came from Zion
At dearest, direst cost,
When by His crucifixion
Christ died to save the lost:
When sore in His soul's travail
He shed His precious Blood
T' atone for sin's great evil
And bring us back to God.

3 Salvation comes from Zion
Whene'er the saints proclaim
The grace of God's election,
The power of Jesu's Name:
For all who, sin forsaking,
On Christ alone believe
Shall in His death partaking
Eternal life receive.

4 Lord Christ, send Thy salvation
From Zion in this hour:
In grace and supplication
Shed forth Thy Spirit's power—
Where'er Thy Bride is giving
To sinful souls and lost,
The call to waters living—
Send out the Holy Ghost!

5 From holy, heavenly Zion
Soon every eye shall see
Our Captain of Salvation
Return in victory:
Each day that Day is nearing;

The House of God

We pray, "Lord Jesus, come!
We long for Thine appearing—
O bring Thy captives home!"

6 All praise and exaltation
To God the Lord, Most High
The God of our salvation
Who brought His people nigh:
To Father, Son and Spirit,
Jehovah—Three in One,
Be giv'n all might and merit,
Be endless honors done.

7.6.7.6.D

Preparatory Reading: Old Testament: Deuteronomy 6;
   New Testament: Luke 5 Psalm:54

1 Timothy 3:14-15

14These things write I unto thee, hoping to come unto thee shortly: 15But if I tarry long, that thou mayest know how thou oughtest to behave thyself in the house of God, which is the church of the living God, the pillar and ground of the truth.

How I ought *to behave* myself greatly affects the purpose and mission of *the Church of the living God*. *The house of God* on earth, this Church is called in the world to be *the pillar and ground of the truth*. As a *pillar*, the Church must display *the truth*; as a *ground*, the Church must uphold *the truth*. How Timothy, pastors, elders, deacons and their families *behave* can vitally help or hurt the Church in its task, and so help or hurt *the truth*.

The Apostle insists absolutely upon wholesome orthodoxy, sound doctrine leading to godliness (ch. 1); urges a comprehensive, intense life of corporate prayer, with every man and woman engaged (ch. 2); demands a qualified leadership at church and home of elders and deacons (ch. 3)—all to hallow God's presence in His *house*, to enable the *church of the living God* to function as *the pillar and ground of the truth*.

Without the truth, without "a good confession" of "the glorious Gospel of the blessed God," of "sound doctrine," of "the truth" by whose knowledge "God our Savior . . . will have all men to be saved"—there is no *church of the living God*; God has as surely forsaken such a *house* as He forsook the temple of the Old Testament for its idolatries and apostasy. The Lord Jesus pronounced this sentence upon Herod's splendid temple: "Behold, your house is left unto you desolate . . . There shall not be left here one stone upon another" (Matt 23:38–24:2). In His glory as the Son of man, He yet warns the churches against losing their first love; against bearing a name to live when they are dead; against being lukewarm (Rev. 2:4–5, 3:1–2, 15–16). Shall God honor a house of prayer that has become a den of thieves? Shall His Son acknowledge a people who reject His written Word in unbelief and disobedience? (Jer 6:16–19; 7:1–28; 8:8–9; Hos 8:12–14; John 2; Mark 11:15–18).

Lord Jesus, keep my Bible clasped in my hand, open to my eyes, laid up in my heart, that I may *know how* I ought *to behave* myself *in the Church of the living God* as a Christian man and Pastor. Keep Thy fear before me in Thy *house, the church of the living God*. Make Thy church a glory and praise in the earth. Set her as a city upon a hill, which cannot be hid, that she may reflect the beauty and glory of her Lord and King. Teach me to teach her; prompt me to pray for her; enable me to exhort her; at all times let me live and minister to make her *the pillar and ground of the truth*.

55. The Faith We Now Confess

1 The Faith we now confess,
We preach in every place:
The Savior's only righteousness—
The Gospel of God's grace.

2 The Faith the saints receive,
On Holy Scripture rests:
All who in Christ alone believe
Shall be forgiven and blest.

3 By precious Faith we hold
Our Prophet, King and Priest,
We claim to God an access bold,
Alone in Jesus Christ.

4 The Faith of God's dear Son
To helpless sinners lost
Comes not by works which we have done
But by the Holy Ghost.

5 This Faith, the gift of grace,
Now works in us by love,
Till perfected, we see Christ's face
And reign with Him above.

6 Our God, the Three in One,
Who saves us, we confess:
The Father, Spirit, and the Son
We worship, praise and bless!

S.M.

Preparatory Reading: Old Testament: Deuteronomy 7;
   New Testament: Luke 6 Psalm:55

1 Timothy 3:16

16And without controversy great is the mystery of godliness: God was manifest in the flesh, justified in the Spirit, seen of angels, preached unto the Gentiles, believed on in the world, received up into glory.

As a diamond is clasped at the curve of a gold ring; as the yolk is cradled within the white and shell of an egg; and as a mother's heart beats and pulses with life within her—so lie amid the words of this Epistle these words which are the motive for all Paul writes. This is "the truth" of which "the Church of the living God" is "the ground and pillar;" this is "the truth" which "God our Saviour" wills that all men know; this is "sound doctrine" "according to the glorious Gospel of the blessed God." Here are the "words of faith and good doctrine" "the Word and doctrine," "the doctrine" as dear to God as His own "Name," "the doctrine according to godliness" committed to our "trust" (3:15, 2:4, 1:10–11; 4:6, 5:17, 6:1, 3, 5, 20, 21).

At the root of all vital, wholesome piety lies this *mystery of godliness*—the counsel of God's redemption in Christ, hidden from eternity, foretold in Old Testament Scripture, displayed at the coming of the Savior and disclosed by the Holy Spirit in the preached Gospel to the souls of saints (Rom 16:15–21; Col. 1:21–29; 1 Cor 2:7–13, 15:51–58; 2 Cor 4; Eph 3:1–13).

Without controversy great is the mystery says Paul. Its greatness defines the calling of the church and summonses all her servants to walk worthy of that calling (3:14–15). Its greatness encompasses *God, angels, the Gentiles, the world, and glory*—no less than the universe of "all things visible and invisible" through time and eternity (3:16). Here is reality in a nutshell, human existence in essence, all history in a sentence. How can it be otherwise that *without controversy great is the mystery of godliness?*

This *mystery* stands in Scripture with the poetry of a prophetic oracle—but it is no mere poetry. It may have been sung among the earliest "hymns and spiritual songs" that the New Testament churches joined to "psalms" in their worship, "singing with grace in their hearts unto the Lord" as the "word of Christ" dwelt richly in them and they were "filled with the Spirit" (Eph 5:18–19; Col. 3:16). But it is no mere canticle. *Great is the mystery of godliness* because it stands among other inspired declarations of "things most surely believed among us" as part of the biblical creed of "the faith once delivered unto the saints" (Deut 6:4–9, 26; Luke 1:1, 24:45–48; Rom 10:8–13; 1 Cor 15:3–4; Heb. 6:1–3; Jude 3).

Let me lay these words up in my heart and confess them with my mouth; let me ponder, wonder, and worship.

56. God in Flesh made Manifest

1 God in flesh made manifest—   (1 *Tim.* 3:16)
God who over all is blessed! —   (Rom 9:5)
Comes to save us from our sin: (Matt 1:21)
Let all angels worship Him!   (*Heb.* 1:6)
Hearken! Heaven's host all cry,
"Glory be to God on high!"
Sound the searing seraphim,
"Peace on earth! Good will to men!"   (Luke 2)

2 Now proclaim the glorious word
From the angel of the Lord,
Saying to us, "Do not fear!
All earth's peoples soon shall hear
These glad tidings of great joy:
Unto you a Baby Boy,
Christ the Savior now is born,
David's Son, this blessed morn!"   (Luke 2)

3 With the shepherds' humble mind
Let us seek until we find
In the manger mean and bare,
Swaddled by His mother's care,   (Luke 2)
That same holy Child who came,   (*Acts* 4)
With an angel-given Name,   (Matt 1, Luke 2)
To redeem us by His Blood: (*Heb.* 9:11–12)
Jesus Christ, the Son of God.   (Matt 1, Acts 8:37)

7.7.7.7.D

Preparatory Reading: Old Testament: Deuteronomy 8;
   New Testament: Luke 7 Psalm:56

1 Timothy 3:16

¹⁶And without controversy great is the mystery of godliness: God was manifest in the flesh, justified in the Spirit, seen of angels, preached unto the Gentiles, believed on in the world, received up into glory.

God was manifest in the flesh: here begins *the mystery of godliness,* and *without controversy great* it is. *Great* in the CONDESCENSION of our God to enter creation; *great* in the HUMILIATION of God to join humanity; *great* in the SUBMISSION of God to take His own most righteous curse upon a fallen world. See there, in a poor woman's womb, in her arms, amid the straw of a stable, the Eternal enters time, the Infinite takes up the space of a span, the Almighty lies helpless, the only wise God is dumb—the Creator appears as creature—CONDESCENSION! *Great is the mystery of godliness: God was manifest in the flesh.* God the Son was manifest before. Of old He appeared, the Messenger of the Covenant, the Angel of the LORD—to Abraham at his tent door; to Isaac upon the altar at Moriah; to Jacob, wrestling alone at Peniel; to Moses in the burning bush at Sinai; to Joshua, as the Captain of the hosts of heaven, to David on the threshing floor of the Jebusite (Gen 18, 22, 32; Exod 3; Josh 5; 2 Sam 24). Yea, "He said, Surely they are my people, children that will not lie; so He was their Savior. In all their affliction He was afflicted, and the Angel of His Presence saved them; in His love and in His pity He redeemed them, and carried them all the days of old" (Isa 63:8–9). But not now! "Christ Jesus . . . being in the form of God, thought it not robbery to be equal with God, but made Himself of no reputation and took upon Him the form of a servant . . . found in fashion as a man, He humbled Himself" (Phil. 2:5–8). Now He appears the virgin-born Emmanuel, the Man that is Jehovah's Fellow, David's Seed, the King's Son, the Seed of the Woman, the Seed of Abraham, the Son of man, the stem of Jesse's rod—"the Man Christ Jesus" (Isa 7:14; Zech 13:7; 2 Sam 7:12–15; Ps 72; Gen 3:16; Gen 22; Dan 7:13; Isa 11;1 Tim. 2:5). "Forasmuch then as the children are partakers of flesh and blood, He also Himself likewise took part of the same . . ." "The Word was God . . . the Word was made flesh and dwelt among us . . . the only-begotten of the Father, full of grace and truth" (John 1:1, 14; Hab 2:14, 16) HUMILIATION! *The mystery of godliness: God . . . manifest in the flesh:* "For when the fullness of the time was come, God sent forth His Son, made of a woman, made under the Law, to redeem . . ." (Gal 4:4–5). "Christ hath redeemed us from the curse . . . on a Tree" (Gal 3:13). He enters the world saying, "Lo, I come to do Thy will, O my God." He departs praying, "Thy will be done" (Heb 10:8; Matt 26:42). The Babe, the young child, the Boy, Carpenter, the Man of Sorrows, full of heaviness, not hid from shame and spitting, His hands and His feet pierced, stricken, smitten of God, afflicted, forsaken: *God . . . in flesh.* SUBMISSION!

57. Eye Hath Not Seen, Nor Ear Hath Heard

1 Eye hath not seen, nor ear hath heard,
Nor entered in the heart of man,
From the foundation of the world,
The things which God in love did plan.

2 But now, taught of the Holy Ghost,
We all may know the mystery—
The Lord of glory, Jesus Christ—
Which this world's princes could not see!

3 His grace to us has God revealed—
The glory once for us ordained
Before all ages, long concealed
Is now within His Word contained.

4 Deep things which God the Spirit shows:
The natural man will not receive;
He foolish counts, and cannot know
The saving truth which we believe.

5 We of the Spirit all possessed,
May freely learn what He imparts:
We now may have the mind of Christ,
His Word dwells richly in our hearts.

6 God's mercy chose us each by name,
Beloved in Christ ere time begun,
Predestined by His grace to shine,
In likeness of His only Son.

7 "The hope of glory—Christ in you":
Riches unsearchable, of grace!
The Gospel mystery brings in view
The Church, to angels' wond'ring praise.

8 Our God can do by Jesus Christ
Exceeding, and abundantly
Above all that we think or ask,
In us His glory to display.

9 So great salvation of our God,
Unknown to sinless angel-hosts,
Let all the Church proclaim abroad—
"Praise Father, Son and Holy Ghost!"

L.M.

The House of God

Preparatory Reading: Old Testament: Deuteronomy 30;
New Testament: Luke 8 Psalm:57

1 Timothy 3:16

¹⁶And without controversy great is the mystery of godliness: God was manifest in the flesh, justified in the Spirit, seen of angels, preached unto the Gentiles, believed on in the world, received up into glory.

God was manifest in the flesh, justified in the Spirit: the Lord of glory, Jesus Christ, reveals the wisdom and power of God in a mystery. *God manifest in the flesh*, was also *justified in the Spirit.* The Spirit of the Lord was upon Him, and empowered all of His incarnate life, ministry and atoning work. The Holy Ghost vindicated all His claims as Messiah, King, Lord and God (Isa 42:1–4, 11–12).

He is born the holy Son of God as the Holy Ghost overshadows His blessed virgin mother; Simeon, led of the Spirit, acclaims Him the Lord's Christ (Luke 1:35, 2:25–32). He grows, filled with the Spirit and wisdom; at His baptism, the Father anoints Him with the Holy Ghost and power for His public work (Luke 2:40; Matt 3:16–17, Acts 10:38). The Spirit drives Him into the desert, and fills Him with power to preach in the synagogues (Luke 4:1, 14). Gracious words proceed from His mouth because the Spirit is upon Him (Luke 4:18–22; Isa 61:1–2). He heals and casts out demons by the Spirit of God (Matt 12:15–21; Mark 3:33–40). At Calvary, the Lord Jesus offers His Blood without spot to God by the Eternal Spirit (Heb 9:14); He is declared the Son of God by the Spirit of holiness in His resurrection from the dead (Rom 1:4). Thus was He empowered "in the days of His flesh."

And now, exalted to the right hand of the Father, He has received the promise of the Father, to shed forth the Holy Ghost (Acts 1:4–8, 2:32–33).

The Holy Spirit of God comes as the Spirit of Christ to vindicate the Son. For Jesus has now prayed the Father; together Father and Son have sent the Comforter, with us, in us as the Spirit of truth, to supply the water of life freely, the washing of regeneration and renewing of the Holy Ghost, to lead us into all truth, and glorify Christ; convincing the world of sin, righteousness and judgment to come (John 14:16–17, 4:14, 7:37–39; Rev. 21:17; Titus 3:5–7; John 14:26, 16:7–14).

This so great salvation, spoken by the Lord Jesus Himself, confirmed to us by them that heard Him, God also bearing witness by signs and wonders and gifts of the Holy Ghost—this is the word of the Gospel now preached to us with the Holy Ghost sent down from heaven (Heb. 2:1–4; 1 Pet. 1:12). And now we who believe "are washed, are sanctified, are justified by the Name of the Lord Jesus, and by the Spirit of our God." "For no man can say that Jesus is the Lord, but by the Holy Ghost" (1 Cor 6:11, 12:3).

"This is He that came by water and by blood, even Jesus Christ . . . And it is the Spirit that beareth witness, because the Spirit is truth" (1 John 5:6). *Without controversy, great is the mystery of godliness: God was manifest I the flesh, justified in the Spirit!*

58. Now to the Cross draw nigh !

1 Now to the Cross draw nigh—
Jesus our Lord we see,
Condemned for all our sins to die
Upon the cursed Tree.

2 Here at the Cross we stand:
Him whom we pierced we mourn
Nailed to the cross, His feet and hands
His head now crowned with thorns.

3 See from His riven heart
Water and Blood now flow
Cleansing our souls in every part
Whiter than any snow!

4 Behold the Lamb of God,
Our Paschal Sacrifice!
Death passes o'er the sprinkled Blood
Which will for sin suffice.

5 Here would we look and live:
Once, once for all He died,
His finished work our peace shall give,
He shall be satisfied.

S.M.

The House of God

> Preparatory Reading: Old Testament: Deuteronomy 31;
> New Testament: Luke 9 Psalm:58

1 Timothy 3:16

¹⁶And without controversy great is the mystery of godliness: God was manifest in the flesh, justified in the Spirit, seen of angels, preached unto the Gentiles, believed on in the world, received up into glory.

"We see Jesus, who was made a little lower than the angels for the suffering of death, crowned with glory and honour" (Heb. 2:9). The wonder of God the Son's condescension, humiliation and submission when *manifest in the flesh* includes that He was *seen of angels*. Never had angels beheld the eternal, only-begotten Son who is in the bosom of the Father (John 1:18). So the prophet Isaiah tells us, "I also saw the Lord sitting upon a throne . . . above it stood the seraphim. Each one had six wings; with twain he covered his face . . . and one cried unto another, and said, Holy, holy, holy is the Lord of hosts" Isa 6:1–3). And the apostle John explains, "These things said Esaias, when he saw His glory, and spake of Him" (John 12:41). But now, in great moments of His obedience, sorrows, passion and triumph, the Son, before unseen, is *seen of angels: Angels* announce His birth—the archangel, Gabriel comes to His guardian Joseph, and His blessed virgin mother Mary (Matt 1:18–2:23; Luke 1:26–38). *Angels* see Him born, and summon the shepherds to witness it. They acclaim His royal degree and glory, for God, "when He bringeth in the Firstbegotten into the world, He saith, And let all the angels of God worship Him" (Luke 2:9–14; Heb.1:6). *Angels* see Him spent in the wilderness, tempted in all points like as we are, yet without sin, tempted of Satan amid the wild beasts—and minister to Him in victory (Mark 1:12–13). *Angels* at the close of His public work again view His secret agony in the garden of Gethsemane and strengthen Him in His submission (Luke 22:41–46). But these *angels*, twelve legion and more, must stand aside as they view His arrest, His manhandling, His willing substitution as the Good Shepherd releasing His sheep, and laying down His life for them (Matt 26:47–56; John 18:8–12). The Savior tells Peter just as much: "Thinkest thou that I cannot now pray to My Father, and He shall presently give me more than twelve legions of angels?" (Matt 26:53). Did they see Calvary—those angel hosts on high? Or did the deep darkness that hid the sun through those hours, also veil them from their burning gaze? Who can tell? Yet in resurrection *angels* once more appear—to silence in terror the keepers, and open the empty tomb to the world; to inform the mourning women, one after other, "He is not here: He is risen!" (Matt 28:1–8; Luke 24:1–9; John 20:11–16). The Lord's forty days of "many infallible proofs" closes as He ascends to heaven and once more *angels* confirm the promise of His return (Acts 1:11). Still they wonder at redemption (1 Pet. 1:12; Col. 1:25–27; Ep. 3:8–12. Still they minister to the heirs of salvation Heb. 1:14 cf. Acts 5:19–21, 8:4–11, 8:20, 12:23, 27:23–29). Still they go on Jacob's Ladder at Christ's behest (Gen 28:12–15; John 1:1). *God was manifest in the flesh, seen of angels—great is the mystery of godliness.*

59. Christ is Risen!

1 "Christ is risen!" Let the cry
Fill the earth, the sea, the sky:
Death is dead! Christ brings in might
Immortality to light!

2 "Christ is risen!" The empty tomb
Now dispels our fear and gloom:
Jesus, mighty now to save,
Brings us victory o'er the grave!

3 "Christ is risen!" Dead to sin,
We are raised to reign with Him:
Satan to the earth is hurled—
Christ now overcomes the world.

4 "Christ is ris'n!" In Him we died:
Fleshly lusts are crucified
Newness of eternal life
More than conquers in the strife.

5 "Christ is risen!" So shall we
Rise to immortality
At the dread last trumpet call:
God shall then be all in all.

6 "Christ is risen!"
Let us laud Him
who bought us with His Blood:
Prince and Savior, Paschal Lamb,
Jesus, Lord—the Great I Am!

7 Let us praise with angel hosts
Father, Son and Holy Ghost—
Praise, O praise, earth, sky and sea,
God the Blessed Trinity!

7.7.7.7.

The House of God

Preparatory Reading: Old Testament: Deuteronomy 32;
  New Testament: Luke 10 Psalm:59

1 Timothy 3:16

¹⁶And without controversy great is the mystery of godliness: God was manifest in the flesh, justified in the Spirit, seen of angels, preached unto the Gentiles, believed on in the world, received up into glory.

God . . . manifest in the flesh . . . preached unto the Gentiles: The Apostle's wonder ascends as he asserts *the mystery of godliness.* The first great truth involves the lowest stoop which God the Son took to save us—*God manifest in the flesh.* The last truth reflects the highest prize of which He is worthy—*received up into glory.* Between these each is a step upward in the Son's return to the Father's bosom and blessing (John 16:28; John 1:14, 18). *Justified in the Spirit,* the everlasting kindness of Christ Jesus to His church is displayed and *seen of angels.* So it is higher in the Apostle's mind than this that *God . . . manifest in the flesh* is *preached unto the Gentiles.* "For verily, He took not on Him the nature of angels; He took on Him the seed of Abraham" Heb. 2:16. To Paul, "less than least of all saints" and "chief of sinners," who magnifies his office not least to provoke his kinsmen to jealousy (Eph 3:8; 1 Tim. 1:15; Rom 11:13–14), is the grace given so to preach Christ as "a teacher of the Gentiles" that "principalities and powers" may admire the grace of the Gospel (1 Tim. 2:7; Eph 3:8–10). "Great is the Lord, and greatly to be praised; and His greatness is unsearchable" (Ps 145:3).

That Christ is preached gives Paul joy, even when silenced in prison, even when those who preach act in shameless, hypocritical malice toward him (Phil. 1:15–18). What comfort then must he have realizing the Gospel is preached in all the known world? (Col. 1:5–6).

If such is the servant's joy, is it not more the Master's—Jesus Christ, "Lord of all"? (Matt 10:16–20, 24–25; Acts 10:36). He comes as the Seed of the woman to deliver fallen mankind; He is that blessed Seed in whom all nations must be blessed (Gen 3:15, 22:15–18). He is the glory of Israel and the light of the Gentiles; He is Shiloh to whom the people will gather (Luke 2:28–32; Gen 49:10). The greatest Messianic sign He gives to the Baptist is this: "the poor have the gospel preached" (Matt 11:5). Just as angels in astonished adoration view His coming, so the brightness of His rising brings the nations to Him. Great light springs up in the regions and shadow of death before the Dayspring, the Sun of righteousness (Isa 60:1–3; Mal 4:2; Luke 1:78–79; Isa 9:1–2; Matt 4:15–16). So all through His obedience the Gentiles are there: the Magi, the multitudes beyond, the demoniac from Decapolis, the Italian centurion, the Syrophoenician, the Samaritans, the Greeks at the last Passover (Matt 2:1–12, 4:23–25; Mark 5:19–20; Luke 8:39; Matt 8:5–13; Mark 7:24–30; John 4:1–30, Luke 17:12–19; John 12:20–37). As the Good Shepherd He thinks of His "other sheep," claims and prays for all the elect (John 10:16, 12:32, 17:1–3). The cross proclaims Him to all (John 19:19–22; Luke 23:47; Mark 15:39. *Preached unto the Gentiles,* "All nations shall call Him blessed" (Ps 72:17).

60. Ascended Up On High

1 Ascended up on high,
Jesus our Lord is ris'n—
Exalted over every name
And power in earth and heaven!   (Eph 1, 4)

2 Into the heavens passed,
Jesus, our great High Priest,
Now ever lives to intercede
Before the Throne of Grace!   (Heb. 4, 7)

3 Glory and honor crown
The humbled Son of man
He who for us has tasted death
Now sits at God's right hand!   (Heb. 1, 2)

4 His Name shall all confess,
And every knee shall bow
Ye everlasting gates, receive
The King of glory now!   (Phil.2; Ps 24)

5 Sing praises to our King,
Praise, all the lands throughout!
To Father, Son and Spirit sing—
God, gone up with a shout!   (Ps 47)

S.M.

The House of God

Preparatory Reading: Old Testament: Deuteronomy 33;
New Testament: Luke 11 Psalm: 60

1 Timothy 3:16

16 And without controversy great is the mystery of godliness: God was manifest in the flesh, justified in the Spirit, seen of angels, preached unto the Gentiles, believed on in the world, received up into glory.

God . . . manifest in the flesh . . . preached unto the Gentiles: The amazing spread of the Gospel among *the Gentiles* marks the Pentecostal gift of the Holy Ghost, and hails the enthronement of our Lord Jesus over all. "This Jesus hath God raised up . . . Therefore being by the right hand of God exalted, and having received of the Father the promise of the Holy Ghost, He hath shed forth this which ye now see and hear" (Acts 2:32–33). God pours out His Spirit upon all flesh; the Comforter comes to convince the world (Acts 2:16–21; John 16:7–22). The Christ at God's right hand must command a willing people (Ps 110:1–3).

How soon then is *the mystery of godliness preached unto the Gentiles!* At Pentecost itself devout men from every nation, including proselytes, hear the wonderful works of God, of Jesus as Lord and Christ (Acts 2:7–11, 32–36). The worst persecutions only impel the saints to go everywhere preaching the Word—Philip to Samaria, and to the Ethiopian eunuch; Peter to Cornelius; believers from Cyprus and Cyrene to Antioch, where the disciples are first called "Christians" (Acts 8:4–5, 26–40, 10, 11:19–30. Before long, Paul and Barnabas set forth, the Word of the Lord has free course, increases and prevails (Acts 12:24, 13:1–5, 19:20; 2 Thess. 3:1–2). Truly, "they went forth and preached every where, the Lord working with them and confirming the Word with signs following" (Mark 16:20).

And what people are called by this Gospel! The rustic pagans of Lystra and Derbe (Acts 14); the Roman governor Sergius Paulus (Acts 13); the intellectuals of Athens (Acts 17); the riff-raff of Corinth (Acts 18, 1 Cor 6); the urban occultists of Ephesus (Acts 19); the first Europeans at Philippi—Lydia, the soothsayer, the jailer (Acts 16). Even kings and governors must hear the Savior's chosen vessel Paul: Felix, Drusilla, Festus, Agrippa, Bernice—yes, and Caesar too (Acts 24–26). Male and female, bond and free, Greek and barbarian—all in one first generation! (Rom 1:14; Gal 3:28). Those afar are brought nigh by the Blood of Christ; those once "no people" are now God's people (Eph 2:13, 1 Pet. 2:20).

"And this gospel of the kingdom shall be preached . . . unto all nations: and then shall the end come" (Matt 24:14). Soon, when the Son of man appears in His glory, the nations of the saved will gather into the Father's kingdom; from the north, east, west and south shall they sit down with Abraham, Isaac and Jacob; and they shall bring their glory into the holy city, the new Jerusalem (Matt 8:10–12, 25:32–34; Rev. 21:24). *Great is the mystery of godliness: God was manifest in the flesh . . . preached unto the Gentiles!*

61. Jesus Christ the Lord of Glory

(Based on Mark 16)

1 Jesus Christ the Lord of glory
Now is risen from the dead:
Over all enthroned, exalted,
As His Church's King and Head—
See, He sheds the Spirit's grace
On His Word in every place!

2 "Preach the Gospel" 's great glad tidings
"Jesus hath His people saved
From their sins" by living, dying,
Raised the third day from the grave:
He who came to seek the lost,
Saves us to the uttermost!

3 "Make disciples of all nations—
Into all the world" we go
Shewing forth so great salvation
Till all tribes and tongues shall know
Christ hath reconciled to God
Sinners by His precious Blood!

4 All who are baptized, believing,
Shall be saved because they call
On the Savior's Name, receiving
Jesus Christ as Lord of all:
All rejecting His command
For their unbelief are damned!

5 Thus we heed the Great Commission
Spoken to us by the Lord
Who repentance and remission,
Gives, still working with the Word
As His people yet go forth
To the ends of all the earth!

8.7.8.7.7.7.

The House of God

Preparatory Reading: Old Testament: Deuteronomy 34;
New Testament: Luke 12 Psalm:61

1 Timothy 3:16

¹⁶And without controversy great is the mystery of godliness: God was manifest in the flesh, justified in the Spirit, seen of angels, preached unto the Gentiles, believed on in the world, received up into glory.

God was manifest in the flesh . . . believed on in the world: "The Word was made flesh and dwelt among us . . . His glory as of the only-begotten of the Father, full of grace and truth . . . the true Light . . . He was in the world, and the world was made by Him, and the world knew Him not. He came unto His own and His own received Him not. But to as many as received Him, to them gave He power to become the sons of God, even to them that believe on His Name: which were born . . . of God" (John 1:14, 9–13). The faith of God's elect is itself part of *the mystery of godliness:* "the preaching of Jesus Christ . . . now is made manifest . . . made known to all nations for the obedience of faith" (Rom 16:25–30). For it is a gift of grace to believe on Christ Jesus: "It is given unto you to believe" "For by grace are ye saved through faith, and that not of yourselves: it is the gift of God" (Phil. 1:29; Eph 2:8).

What a wonder to *believe*! The world says of the Lord Jesus, "He hath no form nor comeliness . . . there is no beauty that we should desire Him: He was despised, and we esteemed Him not" Yet believers see far otherwise, and of Christ say, "Whom having not seen, ye love: in whom, though ye now see Him not, yet believing, ye rejoice with joy unspeakable and full of glory, receiving the end of your faith, the salvation of your souls" (1 Pet. 1:8–9).

What a wonder to believe on Him *in the world!* "If our Gospel be hid, it is hid to them that are lost: in whom the god of this world hath blinded the minds of them which believe not, lest the light of the glorious Gospel of Christ who is the image of God should shine unto them" (2 Cor 4:3–4). "Christ crucified, to the Jews a stumblingblock, to the Greeks foolishness . . . but to us who are called . . . Christ the power of God and the wisdom of God" (1 Cor 1:22–24).

To us who believe, Christ is our chief cornerstone, elect and precious; we believe on Him, and are not confounded. To those who stumble at His Word, being disobedient, He is a stone of stumbling, a rock of offence; and to this they were appointed (1 Pet. 2:6–8).

Nothing can extinguish that faith, "for the Lord knoweth them that are His." Nothing can render that faith unfruitful, for "let every one that nameth the Name of Christ depart from iniquity" (2 Tim. 2:15–19). Christ's flock, His church, can never die, nor His cause ever fail. "My sheep hear My voice, and I know them, and I given unto them eternal life; and they shall never perish" (John 10:27–28). And the Gospel shall never lack a hearing, nor a harvest. "Be it known therefore unto you, that the salvation of God is sent unto the Gentiles, and that they will hear it" (Acts 28:28). *God . . . in the flesh . . . believed on in the world.*

The House of God

62. Jesus, the Lamb upon the throne

1 To Thee, in worship would we gather
O Savior, on Thy Name to call,
Upon the right hand of Thy Father
Now raised, exalted Lord of all!

Refrain:
With lowly hearts we fall before Thee!
We bow the knee to Thee alone!
Thy Name we bless, as all confess
Jesus—the Lamb upon the Throne!

2 Thy love, for us and our salvation
Embraced us as Thy Bride, by name
And stood before the world's foundation
To be the Lamb for sinners slain!

3 We echo "Holy, holy, holy!"
The song of angel hosts on high:
While they their faces veil before Thee,
We as dear children now draw nigh!

4 We raise a glad new song in victory,
For Thou art worthy, Lamb of God—
Once slain upon the Cross of Calv'ry,
Thou hast redeemed us by Thy Blood!

5 When raised to endless life and glory,
When for us Thou shalt come again,
We'll cry, "O grave, where is thy vict'ry?"
With Thee as kings and priests we'll reign!

9.8.9.8.9.8.8.8.
Tune: Welsh Song "MYFANNWY" or "ARABELLA"
(Sir Joseph Parry)

The House of God

Preparatory Reading: Old Testament: Joshua 1;
    New Testament: Luke 13 Psalm:61

1 Timothy 3:16

¹⁶And without controversy great is the mystery of godliness: God was manifest in the flesh, justified in the Spirit, seen of angels, preached unto the Gentiles, believed on in the world, received up into glory.

God . . . manifest in the flesh . . . received up into glory: What can astonish and dazzle us more—the first, or the last wonder of this *great mystery of godliness?* The Son in His Deity revealed to the eyes of angels and men *in the flesh*—the Son glorified and exalted in His humanity, returned to the right hand of the majesty on high—Jesus the Son of God passed into the heavens? (Heb. 1:1–4; 4:14–15). The Son of man stands before the Ancient of Days to receive the kingdom of the saints; the King of glory, the Lord mighty in battle enters the uplifted gates and everlasting doors; ascended on high to take captivity captive and give gifts to men, He sits at the Lord's right hand till all His enemies be made His footstool, a High Priest forever after the order of Melchizedek (Dan 7:13–14; Ps 24:7–10; Ps 68:17–2; Eph. 4:8; Ps 110:1–4, 1 Cor 15:25; Mark 12:35–37; Heb. 5:5–6, 7:15–28). Taken up in a cloud before His eyewitness apostles, He is exalted to the Father's right hand as our Prince and Savior, Lord and Christ, given a Name above every name that is named, far above all principality and power; set over all for His Church (Luke 24:50–51; Acts 1:9; Acts 2:35–36, 5:30–32; Phil. 2:1–11; Eph 1:20–23). Now lifted up whence He came, He draws all men to Himself; He prepares a place for His own; He has sent the Comforter, glorified of the Father, to glorify the Father, till at length His people may see His eternal glory with the Father—His Father and ours, His God and ours (John 3:11–13, 6:62; 8:14, 21, 29; 12:32; John 14:3, 16–18; 16:5–7; 17:1, 25, 20:18). How much more astonishing to consider Him *received into glory* in light of His lowly life on earth! (Isa 52:13–15). Only in the holy mount did the first three glimpse at that glory (Luke 9:23–36, 51; 2 Pet. 1:16–18; Matt 17:1–9). How dumbfounding to our unbelief to hear the Savior "in the days of His flesh" calmly, confidently speak of it, even at trial, even on the cross: "The Son of man cometh in His glory" "I shall not taste of this fruit of the vine till I drink it new with you" "Many shall say to Me in that day" "When the Son of man cometh in His glory . . . on a great white throne" "Hereafter shall ye see the Son of man seated at the right hand of power, and coming in the clouds of heaven" "Verily I say unto thee, Today thou shalt be with Me in paradise" (Mark 8:38, 14:29; Matt 7:21–23, 25:31, 26:64; Luke 23:43). But so it is now—now Christ Jesus is *received up into glory* whence we look for Him, whence He shall be revealed to avenge His enemies and be glorified in His saints; where He shall receive us to Himself and present us as children of God (Phil. 3:20–21; 2 Thess. 1:7–10; Heb. 2:10–13, 5:8–20). Here may I draw aside, dare to look, and pray, "Shew me Thy glory!" (Exod 3:1–6; 2 Cor 3:18; Exod 33:18).

63. Hearken, the trumpet sounds!

1 Hearken, the trumpet sounds!
See how the angels fill the skies!
All of the saints are gathering round
To gaze with longing eyes!
Jesus the Lord appears,
Clothed in His Father's glory now!
Gone are our sins and gone are our fears
As we before Him bow!

2 Let every tongue confess!
Let every creature bend the knee:
Jesus is Lord, yes, Jesus is Lord
O'er Heaven and earth and sea!
All shall adore His Name
And to His Father's glory praise
Jesus who bore our sin and our shame
Jesus our King of grace!

3 God shall be all in all!
Suffering and sin shall be no more!
Ended the curse which came in the fall!
O worship, and adore!
Praise to the living God
Father and Son and Holy Ghost
Praise to the Lamb who bought with His Blood
His chosen, ransomed host!

6.8.9.6.D
Tune: Musical Theme of Film "GETTYSBURG"

The House of God

Preparatory Reading: Old Testament: Joshua 2;
   New Testament: Luke 14 Psalm: 63

1 Timothy: Reading over Chapter 3

The chapter I have tarried over has called me to consider thoroughly what manner of man I must be as a Pastor, and what manner of men I must call my brethren to be as Elders and Deacons. It has also made me look intently upon my Savior in all the facets of His person and work. Let me review and reflect on this chapter, seeking "the exceeding abundant grace of Christ Jesus with faith and love" to "enable" my brethren and me to do our duty as unworthy, unprofitable servants of our glorious Master.

Prayer for Elders and Deacons of the Church

Blessed be the LORD who daily loadeth us with benefits
Even the God of our salvation!
Thou hast ascended up on high, Thou hast led captivity captive
Thou hast received gifts for men, yea for the rebellious also
That the LORD God might dwell among them:
The LORD gave the Word:
great was the company of those that published it.
A Father of the fatherless, and a Judge of the widows
Is God in His holy habitation.
Bless ye God in the congregations,
Even the LORD from the fountain of Israel.
Thy God hath commanded thy strength;
Strengthen, O God, that which Thou hast wrought for us.

Father of lights, from whom cometh every good and perfect gift
With whom is neither variableness nor shadow of turning,
We give Thee thanks for Thine unspeakable gift
The gift of eternal life through Jesus Christ our Lord:

Thou hast not spared Thine only Son
but given Him freely for us all
and with Him
Thou hast given us all things that pertain to life and godliness:
Thou hast sent forth Thy Son to redeem us,
And Thou hast sent forth the Spirit of Thy Son into our hearts:
Thou hast given to everyone of us grace
according to the measure of the gift of Christ:
Thou hast made us stewards of Thy manifold grace,
To speak the oracles of God,

The House of God

to serve as of the strength Thou suppliest
That Thou mayest be glorified in all things by Jesus Christ.
God and Father, above all, through all, in all,
Who hast by the gift of Christ Thy Son, ascended on high,
Given to us in Him
Pastors and teachers, bishops, elders and deacons,
Grant to these Thy servants
the manifestation of Thy Spirit to profit withal:
Give us pastors after Thine own heart,
To feed Thy people wisdom, understanding and sound doctrine;
By the grace of the Lord Jesus,
our Good Shepherd, our Chief Shepherd
Enable them to feed the flock of God and take oversight
Not by constraint, but willingly
Not for filthy lucre, but of a ready mind
Neither as lords over God's heritage,
but being ensamples to the flock.
Give them to strengthen the diseased, heal the sick,
bind up the broken, bring again those driven away
and seek what is lost
that they may feed them by the integrity of their hearts
and guide them by the skillfulness of their hands.

God our Savior, by that one Mediator Christ Jesus
Who gave Himself a ransom for all to be testified in due time
Make Thy servants who are deacons
Servants of all, even as the Son of man came
Not to be ministered unto, but to minister
And to give His life a ransom for many.
Fill them with the Holy Ghost and wisdom over their business
That like their Master they may go about doing good
To the least of His brethren, as unto Him.

O Lord our strength, save Thy people
Bless Thine inheritance;
Feed them also, and lift them up forever.

Make us to watch and pray;
Keep and deliver us
from grievous wolves which enter into Thy flock,
From perverse disciples
False brethren, false teachers, false apostles, false prophets
From thieves, robbers and hirelings

The House of God

    From wicked and slothful servants
    From heretics subverted of themselves
    And from all who think Thy gifts may be purchased with money
    Whose heart is not right with Thee.

    O God of peace,
    Which brought again from the dead the Lord Jesus,
    That great Shepherd of the sheep
    By the blood of the everlasting covenant
    Make them perfect in every good work to do Thy will;
    Work in them what is well-pleasing in Thy sight
    Through Jesus Christ
    To whom be glory forever and ever. Amen.

64. "Come, Lord Jesus!" This We Pray

"Come, Lord Jesus!": this we pray,
Haste the glorious, dreadful Day,
When with angels Thou shalt come
And Thy people gather home.
"Come, Lord Jesus!" In the air,
For Thy saints shalt Thou appear,
While the final trumpet's sound,
Echoes all the world around.

2 "Come, Lord Jesus!" every tomb
Open, bid the dead to come
Stand before Thy great white throne,
Give account for all deeds done.
"Come, Lord Jesus!" On Thy right
Set the children of the light;
Set the sons of sin, bereft
Of Thy mercy, to the left!

3 "Come, Lord Jesus!" Shepherd good,
Separate the flock of God
For Thine own eternal fold,
In the City paved with gold.
"Come, Lord Jesus!" Thy decree
Now proclaim, "Depart from Me,
All ye sinners doing ill—
Enter now the flames of Hell!"

4 "Come, Lord Jesus!" On that Day
Heaven and earth shall pass away,
Then new heavens and earth shall come
Filled with righteousness alone.
"Come, Lord Jesus!" Wipe away
Every tear from every eye,
Let the former things be o'er,
Death, and pain, and sorrow sore.

5 "Come, Lord Jesus!" Shining bright,
Let Thy Church now stand in light,
Sinless, spotless in Thy sight
As Thy Bride arrayed in white.
"Come, Lord Jesus!" Make us meet

The House of God

Our great Bridegroom soon to greet;
O prepare us now to taste
Of th'eternal wedding feast.

6 "Come, Lord Jesus!" This we pray
With each new, returning day;
Still we watch, and work and wait,
Trim our lamps before the gate:
"Come Lord Jesus!" Every knee
At Thy Name shall bow to Thee:
Every tongue shall Thee confess,
And Thy Father's glory bless.

7 At the Father's own right hand,
Stands the once-slain, risen Lamb,
With the seven-fold Spirit true,
Reigning, making all things new.
To the Father, with the Son
And the Spirit, Three in One,
Hallelujahs loud we raise:
Riches, honor, blessing, praise!

7.7.7.7D

The House of God

Preparatory Reading: Old Testament: Joshua 3;
   New Testament: Luke 15 Psalm: 64

1 Timothy 4:1-3

¹Now the Spirit speaketh expressly, that in the latter times some shall depart from the faith, giving heed to seducing spirits, and doctrines of devils; ²Speaking lies in hypocrisy; having their conscience seared with a hot iron; ³Forbidding to marry, *and commanding* to abstain from meats, which God hath created to be received with thanksgiving of them which believe and know the truth.

Paul has been setting the highest standards for Timothy, for all elders and Pastors, and for me: fidelity of doctrine, purity of worship, integrity of character. Nothing less can befit "the mystery of godliness" I must teach; "the church of the living God" I must serve; and *the latter times* I must face. How we need "men that have understanding of the times . . . to know . . . what to do" (2 Chr 12:32). These *latter times* are "the last days" (2 Tim. 3:1). "The end is not yet" though we live "in these last days" (Matt 24:6; Heb. 1:2). The Apostle sees the whole New Testament era as "the end of the world" (Heb. 9:26); he can envision time to come, and warn us not to be gullible that "the day of Christ is at hand" (2 Thess. 2:2). Throughout the Churches' long pilgrimage and warfare "perilous times will come." O God our Father, for Christ Jesu's sake, grant even to me an "understanding of the times" and teach me what to do. Now is my salvation nearer than when I believed; it is high time to awake out of sleep, to put on the Lord Jesus Christ, to make no provision for the flesh to fulfill its lusts (Rom 13:14). Of these *latter times—our times—the Spirit speaketh expressly,* for the Scripture of truth is the voice of the Holy Spirit who moved holy men of old to prophesy (2 Pet. 1:21). Whether the Lord Christ speaks as the Fountainhead, or the prophets and apostles as rivers and streams—the Spirit moves through all as the water of life (John 3:33-34; 1 Cor 7:40). By Christ Jesus, by Paul, by Peter *the Spirit speaketh expressly that in the latter times some shall depart from the faith* (Matt 24:23; 2 Thess. 2:3, 9; 2 Pet.3:1-5). *Some*, but not all; "many" but not all—for the foundation of God stands sure and sealed (2 Pet. 2:2; 2 Tim. 2:19). This dismaying apostasy neither lessens the truth of the Gospel, nor should it shake the faith of believers (Matt 24:11-13). Just as the Lord Jesus foretold the sufferings of the elect, so He predicted betrayals and desertions from His cause lest we be offended and stumble (John 16:1-4). Such departure proves reprobation (1 John 2:19). So intent is Satan to sow tares among wheat; so varied are the soils of the souls on which the good seed of the Word falls (Matt 13:18-22), the wonder is not that some wither away, or that others are choked and unfruitful, but that He has prepared, ploughed and given us to be "good ground . . . with good and honest heart" to take root downward and bear fruit upward (Luke 8:15; Isa 37:31). If *some shall depart from the faith*, might not I?

65. Lord Jesus, Friend of Sinners

1 Lord Jesus, Friend of sinners,
To Thee I now draw nigh:
I long to hear Thy Gospel—
How Thou didst come to die
In shame and Blood at Calv'ry
To save me from my sin:
Lord Jesus, Friend of sinners,
Be pleased to take me in!

2 Lord Jesus, Friend of sinners,
How wholly am I lost!
A wandering sheep in peril—
A coin of squandered cost—
A child whose life is wasted
In riot and enslaved:
Lord Jesus, Friend of sinners,
Seek me, till I am saved!

3 Lord Jesus, Friend of sinners,
I have no right to heaven—
Unclean, unjust, unworthy,
My soul must be forgiven:
O let Thy Name and Spirit
Both justify me now,
And wash, then sanctify me
Till at Thy throne I bow.

4 Lord Jesus, Friend of sinners,
Receive me, with me meet!
Though from beneath Thy table
But crumbs I fain would eat,
Grant me to share Thy kingdom,
And by Thy sovereign grace,
Among Thy chosen people
To find the lowest place!

5 Lord Jesus, Friend of sinners—
Thou dost my soul receive!
Thou dost forgive and cleanse me!
I on Thy Name believe,
And all my sins forsaking,

With those Thy Blood hath bought,
I now embrace Thy promise:
Thou wilt not cast me out!

6 Lord Jesus, Friend of sinners,
No greater love could be
Than this, which laid Thy life down
For us at Calvary:
Thou knowest that I love Thee!
O bid me follow still,
Thy most unworthy servant,
To do Thy perfect will.

7 O Lord our God, where is there
A God like unto Thee?
Thou pardonest transgression,
And castest in the sea
The depths of our trespasses
Till all is gone and lost:
We praise Thy mercies, Father,
And Son, and Holy Ghost!

7.6.7.6.d

The House of God

Preparatory Reading: Old Testament: Joshua 4;
New Testament: Luke 16 Psalm: 65

1 Timothy 4:1–3

¹Now the Spirit speaketh expressly, that in the latter times some shall depart from the faith, giving heed to seducing spirits, and doctrines of devils; ²Speaking lies in hypocrisy; having their conscience seared with a hot iron; ³Forbidding to marry, *and commanding* to abstain from meats, which God hath created to be received with thanksgiving of them which believe and know the truth.

Giving heed . . . speaking . . . forbidding . . . commanding: Paul earmarks the lethal symptoms of heinous apostasy; he tells us whence error arises; how it possesses men; where it expresses its influence; and what blights it brings on believers' lives. *Seducing spirits and doctrines of devils* supply those who *depart from the faith*. Just as an infected well supplies disease, disability and death through the pumps, pipes and taps of a town, so error may turn a man from a channel of blessing to a ditch of defilement. Am I a vessel of honor, purged of evil, fit for Jesus my Master's use? Does secret sin taint my life and bring decay to my zeal—does malignant contention sour my service—does a self-willed, unteachable spirit leave me vulnerable to become a messenger of Satan through subtle error? To what am I listening? What dominates my talk? What do I oppose? What do I promote? Do these put me in the way of Christ or antichrist in *giving heed . . . speaking . . . forbidding . . . commanding*?

Seducing spirits . . . doctrines of devils . . . lies in hypocrisy represent the danger of "another spirit . . . another Jesus . . . another gospel" which beguiles and corrupts the Bride from "the simplicity of Christ" (2 Cor 11:2–4). How may I discern these? When have I shifted from solid rock to shifting sand? I must "try the spirits" by the good confession of the Word (1 John 4:1–6). I must hold fast the Word I have received (2 Thess. 2:1–3, 13–17; Titus 1:9–11). I must study the Word as a thorough workman and shun all "vain babblings" that eat away as a cancer in the soul (2 Tim. 2:15–17). Whatever cannot "pass muster" in the plain testimony of the Bible and the doctrines which the Churches have drawn from them, cannot and must not claim my time or thought; has no authority to bind my conscience, or my people's. Let me ask nothing of God's children they cannot safely gather from their Bibles and "the form of sound words" which are the heritage of their fathers.

> Otherwise I may be falling into the devil's snare (2 Tim. 2:22–24).
> "They draw nigh that follow after mischief:
> they are far from Thy Law.
> Thou art near, O LORD;
> and all Thy commandments are truth" (Ps 119:150–151).

66. Lord of the Sabbath, Jesus Christ

1 Lord of the Sabbath, Jesus Christ,
In Thee we now would find our rest:
Upon the first day of the week
Thy face in worship would we seek.

2 Thou glorious Sun of righteousness,
Shine forth, and all the nations bless:
Arise with healing in Thy wing
Till all the earth Thy praise shall sing.

3 Raised to Thy Father's own right hand,
Shed forth on this and every land
The fullness of the Holy Ghost
To quicken, call and save the lost.

4 Our blind eyes open, now to view
The wonders of Thy Law anew:
And as the Gospel's grace abounds,
Grant us to hear its joyful sounds.

5 Show us Thy glory and Thy power
In every place and every hour
Where holy hands are raised in prayer
To cast upon Thee all our care.

6 O Father, Son and Spirit bless
Thy people as we now confess
Thee God Triune alone, and praise
Thy Name on this and all our days!

L.M.

The House of God

Preparatory Reading: Old Testament: Joshua 5;
New Testament: Luke 17 Psalm: 66

1 Timothy 4:1–3

4:1Now the Spirit speaketh expressly, that in the latter times some shall depart from the faith, giving heed to seducing spirits, and doctrines of devils; 2Speaking lies in hypocrisy; having their conscience seared with a hot iron; 3Forbidding to marry, *and commanding* to abstain from meats, which God hath created to be received with thanksgiving of them which believe and know the truth.

Speaking lies in hypocrisy, having . . . conscience seared with a hot iron: Exposing myself to these baneful influences will leave me with a *conscience seared*. The effect of the truth is quite opposite: "the end of the commandment is . . . a good conscience" "war a good warfare, holding faith and a good conscience" "holding the mystery of the faith in a pure conscience." A man's flesh *seared with a hot iron* loses all sensation and can no longer ward off infection. Is this not the very tell-tale symptom of heresy? The conviction of sin is cauterized; the fear of God is dulled; the assurance of truth disappears. There is no feeling of heart for the Gospel nor sense of its need first personally, then publicly. There is no more "trembling at the Word of the Lord", and no scruples at double-minded, double-tongued dealing with creed or confession. Sincerity gives way to sophistry. Such men not only *speak lies* and advance deviant teaching, but they *speak lies in hypocrisy*, in brazen pretence of conforming to the faith. Do I mean what I say, and say what I mean? Christ Jesus our Lord Himself will cast out all "salt without savour" (Luke 14:34–35). Out of the fullness of the heart the mouth speaks; with the heart man believes and with the mouth confesses. *Seducing spirits* by *doctrines of devils* will *sear the conscience with a hot iron* till men *depart from the faith, speaking lies in hypocrisy*. What does this apostasy lead to, that we may see, hear, and touch? The Savior bids us look for the fruits of a tree, good or corrupt in words (Matt 12:33–37) and in deeds (Matt 7:16–20). We do as we teach at best; we say and do not at worst (Matt 5:19, 23:3). The wisdom of our words is shown in the way of our works (Jas. 3:1, 13–18). So Paul warns us to watch for these evil fruits—*forbidding to marry, and commanding to abstain from meats*. The *seducing spirits, doctrines of devils, lies in hypocrisy* lead us at last to all that is external, ritual, ascetic and even superstitious. *Forbidding to marry . . . abstain from meats*—how many "world religions" are trade-marked by rulings like these? But Christ demands "the weightier matters of the law, judgment, mercy, faith"; His kingdom is "not meat and drink, but righteousness, peace and joy in the Holy Ghost" "Be not carried about with divers and strange doctrines. For it is a good thing, that the heart be established with grace, not with meats" (Matt 23:23–24; Rom 14:17; Heb. 13:4, 8–9).

67. Turn Ye, Turn! Why will ye die?

1 Turn ye, turn! Why will ye die?
All who pass my Savior by,
God's salvation comes today!
Will ye also go away?

2 Passing on in evil's path,
Now ye treasure up the wrath
Which the Righteous Judge shall send
On the wicked at the end!

3 Plainly doth the Scripture tell,
"All the nations go to Hell
Which forget the God of heaven,"
Who His only Son hath given!

4 In this world Christ Jesus came,
Sinners lost to seek and claim,
Hanging on the cursed Tree,
By His Blood to set us free.

5 Dare ye trample on that Blood
Of the gracious Son of God—
Put Him to an open shame,
And despise His holy Name?

6 Sinner, vile, condemned and vain,
Doomed to Hell's unending pain,
Do not pass my Savior by,
Turn ye, turn! Why will ye die?

7 From the broad way now relent
Turn to God, of sin repent!
In th'accepted time, receive
Jesus Christ the Lord, and live!

7.7.7.7.

The House of God

Preparatory Reading: Old Testament: Joshua 6
　　New Testament: Luke 18 Psalm: 67

1 Timothy 4:1–3

¹Now the Spirit speaketh expressly, that in the latter times some shall depart from the faith, giving heed to seducing spirits, and doctrines of devils; ²Speaking lies in hypocrisy; having their conscience seared with a hot iron; ³Forbidding to marry, *and commanding* to abstain from meats, which God hath created to be received with thanksgiving of them which believe and know the truth.

Forbidding to marry, and commanding to abstain from meats: What attracts *seducing spirits* to such matters in framing the *doctrines of devils* and *speaking lies in hypocrisy?* This is well-worked ground. Here is where the old serpent subverted our first parents with "the lust of the eyes, the lust of the flesh and the pride of life" (Gen 3:1–6; 1 John 2:16). Here the devil can fix men's minds on "meat and drink" so as to miss "the kingdom of God" (Rom 14:17). Here Satan reduces holiness to "the beggarly elements of this world", crying, "Touch not, taste not, handle not" (Col. 2:20–22). Here the accuser can tempt sinful man's vainglory beyond what his fallen nature can bear—to burn rather than to marry (Matt 19:10–12; 1 Cor 7:1–9). In short, heresy confuses and directs us away from God's Word to man's, from the spirit to the flesh, calling evil good and good evil, putting darkness for light and light for darkness. This marks the hand of the Antichrist, and of many antichrists (1 John 2:18, 4:3); false prophets (1 John 4:1) and the spirit of error (1 John 4:6). Such teaching directly undermines the wholesome example and sound doctrine of an apostolic ministry of the Word, whose pastors and elders honor marriage and use meats in hospitality (1 Tim. 3:2, 11–12).

The work of *seducing spirits* is always injurious to men in soul and body. So *to receive and give thanks* for marriage and meats is a tangible fruit of faith in *them which believe and know the truth.* As I *believe and know the truth* from Scripture, the "knowledge of the truth" whereby "God will have all men saved" I will safeguard its central truths: "There is one God, and one mediator between God and man, the Man Christ Jesus, who gave Himself a ransom for all to be testified in due time" (2:4–6). When marriage and meats are *received with thanksgiving of them which believe and know the truth,* access to the Gospel's saving truth to all people is kept open. How often do matters of "meats" divert men's minds from Christ? What evils have the unnatural exactions of false celibacy created in promoting secret vice, demeaning family life, and turning men from the Savior as *some depart from the faith . . . forbidding to marry?* Let me remember to keep first things first; let me "put the brethren in remembrance of these things" as "a good minister of Jesus Christ" (4:6).

68. Afar from Thee I Stand

1 Afar from Thee I stand;
I dare not lift mine eyes:
Upon my breast I strike my hand
With tears, and broken cries.   (Lk 18)

2 I blush and am ashamed
To look up unto Thee: (Ezra 9)
More than my hairs can all be named
Is mine iniquity.   (Ps 40)

3 I humbly bring this plea,
This only prayer I make:
"O God, be merciful to me
A sinner!" for Christ's sake!   (Lk 18)

4 Thy faithful Word I have,
Worthy of all belief,
"Christ Jesus came from sin to save
Poor sinners—e'en the chief!"   (1 Tim 1)

5 O God, regard Thy Son
Who suffered, bled and died: (Rom 8)
And to my house I shall go down
In mercy justified.   (Lk 18)

6 Thou dost resist the proud,
But Thou hast giv'n Thy grace   (1 Pet 5, Prov 3)
Unto the lowly, and avowed
The shining of Thy face.   (Num 6)

S.M./ D.S.M

The House of God

> Preparatory Reading: Old Testament: Joshua 7;
>   New Testament: Luke 19 Psalm: 68

1 Timothy 4:1–3

4:1Now the Spirit speaketh expressly, that in the latter times some shall depart from the faith, giving heed to seducing spirits, and doctrines of devils; 2Speaking lies in hypocrisy; having their conscience seared with a hot iron; 3Forbidding to marry, *and commanding* to abstain from meats, which God hath created to be received with thanksgiving of them which believe and know the truth.

To marry . . . and . . . meats . . . God hath created: This world, and man's bodily life in it, sustained by *meats*, satisfied and propagated by *marriage*, is God's workmanship; God said in making it, "It is good." And despite man's fall, despite his abuse, it is still good. *God hath created* these *to be received with thanksgiving of them which believe and know the truth.* Disciples of the Christ Jesus "know the truth" and that truth makes us free (John 8:31–32). As saints restored to the adoption of sons, we may receive our Father's primal gifts to His children, and use them rightly, cleanly, joyfully. *Marriage* in the hands of fallen sinners is so easily blighted with false expectations, infidelity, strife and self-interest. *Marriage* is too often a farce to the godless (Prov 21:9, 25:24). *Meats* in the mouths of the wicked can be a false god, an occasion to gluttony and excess (Prov 23:20–21, Phil.3:19). But with God's children, who *believe and know the truth*, whose faith has brought sight and insight, *meats* and *marriage* bring *thanksgiving*.

Marriage and meats could well sum up all the course of common life. The calling to lawful work, trade, commerce, the social and legal relations that bring *meats* to the table *which God hath created to be received* are sanctified to *them which believe and know the truth.* All the blessings of family, social, and civil life whose foundation is in God-ordained *marriage* fulfill His first mandate for mankind to "have dominion . . . fill. . . replenish the earth." *Marriage and meats* alike are the fruits of that *which God hath created to be received with thanksgiving of them that believe and know the truth* (Gen 1:23–29; 2:15–18). Under the rule of Scripture, then, let me *receive with thanksgiving* every good and perfect gift from the Father of lights, who gives good gifts to His children, because He spared not His own Son but delivered Him up for us all (Jas. 1:17, Matt 7:11, Rom 8:32).

> "O LORD, how manifold are Thy works!
> In wisdom hast Thou made them all; the earth is full of Thy riches . . .
> I will sing unto the LORD as long as I live
> I will sing praise to my God while I have any being.
> My meditation of Him shall be sweet: I will be glad in the LORD."
> (Ps 104:24, 31, 33, 34).

69. O God Most Holy, God Most High

1 The azure skies all glow with light;
The blazing sun shines forth in might:
O God most holy, God most high—
Our Sun and Shield, to us draw nigh!

2 The laden dew has left its sheen
Upon the fields of emerald green:
O God most holy, God most high—
Our Fount of life, to us draw nigh!

3 The chorus of the waking birds
Voices its praises without words:
O God most holy, God most high,
Our Strength and Song, to us draw nigh!

4 The mountain peak and forest flower
Reveal Thy wisdom and Thy pow'r—
O God most holy, God most high—
Creator blest, to us draw nigh!

5 The purple nightshades show afar
The sparkling of the evening star—
O God most holy, God most high—
In all Thy greatness, now draw nigh!

6 Through summer, winter, spring and fall
Thy throne endureth over all:
O God most holy, God most high,
Eternal King, to us draw nigh!

7 We praise the Father's love which gave
His Son beloved our souls to save
And sent His Spirit in our hearts
With every gift that grace imparts!

8 Almighty Father, gracious Son
And Holy Spirit—Three in One!
Our God, most holy and most high—
In sovereign grace to us draw nigh!

L.M.

The House of God

> Preparatory Reading: Old Testament: Joshua 8;
> New Testament: Luke 20 Psalm: 69

1 Timothy 4:4-5

4For every creature of God *is* good, and nothing to be refused, if it be received with thanksgiving: 5For it is sanctified by the word of God and prayer.

All of life in this world, whose sum is "marriage and meats," Paul says, "God hath created . . . to be received with thanksgiving of them that believe and know the truth" (4:3). Only by faith, as I "believe" the truth, do I "know the truth." I believe in order to see; without faith, I know and see nothing as it is. If I am ruled by "philosophy and vain deceit, the traditions men, after the rudiments of the world, and not after Christ," my mind and conscience will become "subject to ordinances (Touch not, taste not, handle not) . . . after the doctrines and commandments of men" (Col. 2:8, 20–22). In eating and drinking, I may profess to know God, but in works deny Him, and with defiled mind and conscience find nothing pure (Titus 1:15–16). But, since I "believe and know" "the truth as it is in Jesus," I have in these present verses the reality of life. Whatsoever I do, whether I eat or drink, I do all to the glory of God (1 Cor 10:31). Whatever I do in word or deed, all I must do in the Name of the Lord Jesus, giving thanks to God the Father by Him (Col. 3:17). So, very tangibly, my plate preaches, my table testifies, my kitchen honors or dishonors the Lord and Savior who bought me (Zech 14:20–21; 2 Pet. 2:1, 12–13). *Every creature of God is good, and nothing to be refused:* While all meats are lawful, not all eating is expedient or profitable (1 Cor 10:23–24; Prov 20:1, 21:17, 23:20–21, 29–35). The food God gives may be *good*, but not the abuse of gluttony (1 Cor 6:12–13). *Nothing is to be refused;* even meat from a pagan altar carries no jot of moral taint once it is "sold in the shambles" (1 Cor 8:8, 10:25). Only the danger of offense to the weak, or the danger of temptation to myself can bar its use (1 Cor 8:7, 9–13; 10:27–29; Rom 14:14–21). Within bounds of liberty, safety, and charity, *every creature of God is good, and nothing to be refused.* One sole pre-requisite stands: *if it be received with thanksgiving for it is sanctified by the Word of God and prayer. Thanksgiving* sanctifies our daily portion of good on earth *by the Word of God and prayer.* The act is a gesture of *prayer* which complies with and confesses God's *Word* and truth, that He has created what we receive, that it is good, that He has graciously given it to us. We recognize our dependence upon Him, and our responsibility to Him for the use and enjoyment of this life; we acknowledge our sinful tendencies to waste His gifts and despise His goodness. And what we begin at the table at meal-times, we continue throughout each day, *sanctified by the Word of God and prayer.* This is the priestly privilege of every believer; how much more of the pastor and elder, called to give himself "to prayer and the ministry of the Word?" (Acts 6:4).

70. See, Pray, Go, Serve

1 Lord Jesus, who of old didst go
To cities, villages and towns,
And teaching, preaching, healing show
Thy power and mercy all around:
Before us go, in every place
In fullness of Thy saving grace!

2 Good Shepherd, who of old didst see
The multitudes as scattered sheep,
And gathered, in compassion free,
Thy flock into Thy fold to keep:
Grant us like Thee the world to view—
"The harvest, plenteous—labourers, few!"

3 O Lord of harvest, who of old
Didst bid Thine own disciples pray
For labourers, till with hearts made bold,
Themselves Thou send'st in their own day:
Teach us to pray, till we shall see
Our call, and answer, "Send Thou me!"

4 Into the harvest white, now sent
Grant us to labour willingly—
Spending, and in Thy service spent,
Till all flesh Thy salvation see:
Uplifted Saviour, hear our plea:
Now let all men be drawn to Thee!

8.8.8.8.8.8.

The House of God

Preparatory Reading: Old Testament: Joshua 23;
New Testament: Luke 21 Psalm: 70

1 Timothy 4:6

⁶If thou put the brethren in remembrance of these things, thou shalt be a good minister of Jesus Christ, nourished up in the words of faith and of good doctrine, whereunto thou hast attained.

A good minister of Jesus Christ: Here is the sum of all my proper ambitions, the crown of my labors, an epitaph for my tomb. Not how many I cared for, but how well; not how I pleased men, but Him. "We labour, that, whether present or absent, we may be accepted of Him" (2 Cor 5:9). This citation I seek, and can only receive with the crown of life, righteousness, and unfading glory when the Lord, the righteous Judge, shall appear as Chief Shepherd of the flock: "His Lord said unto him, 'Well done, thou good and faithful servant; thou hast been faithful over a few things, I will make thee ruler over many things: enter thou into the joy of thy Lord'" (Jas. 1:12; 2 Tim. 4:6–8;1 Pet. 5:4; Matt 25:21–23).

The word *minister* here translates a word usually given for "deacon;" it emphasizes the task of service, the function. "Servant" as in the parable of the talents stresses our standing as the Master's property. As Joseph was both a bondman and a butler to Potiphar; as Paul himself both a servant of Christ and an apostle, so is Timothy, so am I, the willing captive and liveried herald of King Jesus. As such, Peter charges me to feed God's flock "not by constraint but willingly; not for filthy lucre, but of a ready mind, not as lords . . . but as ensamples" (1:1, 4:6; Gen 39:1, 4; Rom 1:1; 1 Pet. 5:2).

What luster lights the smallest service to the Lord of glory! As Paul did, so do all pastors declare to men and angels the unsearchable riches of the mystery of Christ in His saints, the hope of glory (Eph 3:6–12; Col. 1:25–27). What blessing God deigns to bring through our meanest ministry! John Baptist rejoiced, as the Bridegroom's friend, to hear His voice and present the bride, saying, "He must increase, but I must decrease." The least in the kingdom of God is greater than he (John 3:29–30; Matt 11:11). As Paul writes, "We preach not ourselves, but Christ Jesus the Lord, and ourselves your servants for Jesus' sake" (2 Cor 4:5). We note a constable's uniform before his face or features; so ought we see Christ revealed in His servants—"Follow me as I follow Christ." We are to be a "sweet savour of Christ" among men (1 Cor 11:1; 2 Cor 2:14–17).

A good minister of Jesus Christ, Paul says, prepares well for his work, and performs well in his work. Nourished up in the words of faith and good doctrine I am to put the brethren in remembrance of these things. These two balance the promise of approval; so the whole course of my race must be taken in hand most earnestly from start to finish. Let me study hard; let me labor hard. Let me preach my best—for my latest sermon might be my last. Let me then be in every good word and work a good minister of Jesus Christ.

71. Go, Stand and Speak these Words of Life!

1 "Go, stand and speak these words of life!"
Among the temple's eager throngs:
To hear the Name of Jesus Christ
A chosen people waits and longs.

2 "Go, stand and speak these words of life!"
Along the quiet riverside
Though few may gather, yet a heart
The Lord has opened to abide.

3 "Go, stand and speak these words of life!"
As, wondering, heathen minds and hearts
Turn from their idols vain to God,
Freed by the truth which Christ imparts.

4 "Go, stand and speak these words of life!"
Against the worldly-wise and blind
Who turn to fables from the truth
The Spirit gives, in pride of mind.

5 "Go, stand and speak these words of life!"
Although the proud self-righteous toss
And wag their heads in mockery,
Preach Christ, and glory in His cross!

6 "Go, stand and speak these words of life!"
Arraigned, to governor, king and prince
With boldness plead the Savior's cause:
The Holy Ghost will some convince.

7 "Go, stand and speak these words of life!"
And, by the preaching of the Word
Shall all, Jew, Gentile, bond or free
Believe in Jesus Christ our Lord!

L.M.

The House of God

Preparatory Reading: Old Testament: Joshua 24;
New Testament: Luke 22 Psalm: 71

1 Timothy 4:6

⁶If thou put the brethren in remembrance of these things, thou shalt be a good minister of Jesus Christ, nourished up in the words of faith and of good doctrine, whereunto thou hast attained.

Nourished up in the words of faith and of good doctrine, whereunto thou hast attained: O Lord Christ, Thou hast twice declared "Man shall not live by bread alone, but by every word that proceedeth out of the mouth of God" (Deut 8:3; Matt 4:4). Clearly hast Thou taught us, "The words that I speak unto you, they are spirit and they are life." So, "to whom shall we go? Thou hast the words of eternal life, and we believe and are sure that Thou art that Christ, the Son of the living God" "Lord, evermore give us this bread" (John 6:34, 63, 68–69).

These are *the words of faith and of good doctrine* by which my soul must live—*nourish* me in these. Daily let me pray for soul as well as body, "Give us this day our daily bread" (Matt 6:11). By Thy Spirit, work in me to will and do Thy good pleasure, that I may sing with David, "How sweet are Thy words unto my taste! Yea, sweeter than honey to my mouth!" and say with Jeremiah, "Thy words were found, and I did eat them; and Thy Word was unto me the joy and rejoicing of mine heart: for I am called by Thy Name, O Lord God of hosts" (Ps 119:103; Jer 15:16). Let me desire the sincere milk of Thy Word, that I may grow thereby, for I have tasted that Thou art gracious (1 Pet. 2:2–3). Let me sing from a full heart, "O taste and see that the Lord is good: blessed is the man that trusteth in Him. O fear the Lord, ye His saints, for there is no want to them that fear Him" (Ps 34:8–9).

To these words let me *attain* and follow closely. Grant my soul and intellect, heart and affections keep pace and measure with Thy truth, so that I may grow from milk to strong meat, no longer a babe unskillful in the Word of righteousness, but of full age, my senses by use exercised to discern both good and evil (Heb. 5:13–14). Make my hope and desire that of David who sings, "I will run the way of Thy commandments when Thou shalt enlarge my heart" (Ps 119:32). May these *words of faith and of good doctrine* impart to me their own life and power; imprint on me the graces they reveal. "Let my heart be sound in Thy statutes" that I may be "a good man, full of faith and of the Holy Ghost" (Ps 119:80; Acts 6:5, 11:24). So may I hold fast "sound doctrine according to the glorious Gospel of the blessed God, which was committed to my trust" (1:10–11).

As an athlete hones his skill by the buffeting exercise of his own body, so must I prepare for the Gospel ministry by "taking heed to" myself as much as "to the doctrine" (4:16; 1 Cor 9:25–27). The great task of my office is to take myself in hand, and learn to rule myself before, in order to rule others. Let me begin at once, *nourished up in the words of faith and of sound doctrine whereunto* I have *attained*.

72. Come Apart and Rest Awhile

1 Come apart and rest awhile
From your heavy toil and care:
Malice lay aside, and guile,
Enter in the House of Prayer,
And among His people sit
At our Savior Jesu's feet!

2 Hear the Word of life and peace
Which the Holy Scriptures tell;
From your sins and self now cease—
Jesus hath done all things well:
Now behold the Lamb of God,
Trust in His atoning Blood !

3 Through the quiet hours of rest,
Enter in the secret place:
Seek the Father, and be blessed
With His Spirit's strength and grace,
As you plead Christ's Name in prayer,
Casting on Him all your care.

4 Fathers, mothers, girls and boys,
In God's favor break your bread
At your tables, and rejoice
That His providence has led,
Sheltered, helped you all your days:
Show your thanks and keep His ways.

5 Thus let Christian Sabbaths prove
Festive, restful days of bliss:
Filled with faith, and hope and love,
And all fruits of righteousness,
Till our Triune God we see,
Blessed to all eternity.

7.7.7.7.7.7.

The House of God

Preparatory Reading: Old Testament: Ruth 1;
  New Testament: Luke 23 Psalm: 72

1 Timothy 4:6

⁶If thou put the brethren in remembrance of these things, thou shalt be a good minister of Jesus Christ, nourished up in the words of faith and of good doctrine, whereunto thou hast attained.

If thou put the brethren in remembrance of these things, thou shalt be a good minister of Jesus Christ: The kind of Christian a pastor can best disciple is the kind of Christian he is himself, and he secures in his wife and family (3:2, 4-6; Titus 2:7). It is a work for which the weak in faith and the novice need not apply.

And in large measure, this ministry involves *putting in remembrance*—literally, "placing under" the eyes, noses and faces of others the fundamentals of faith and principles of practice which are *the words of faith and of good doctrine,* the "great mystery of godliness," "godly edifying in faith" (1:4, 3:16). I must constantly, consistently steer my people on this course lest under the influence of "seducing spirits" and "doctrines of devils" they "depart from the faith" (4:1-2). My ministry must have a practical turn; it must be systematic, catechetical; and it must flow from my own personal progress being *nourished up in the words of faith and of sound doctrine.*

In all my preaching and visiting, I must cherish sympathy, affection and humility toward my people as *the brethren*—my fellow saints (Eph 2:19), the children of God (1 John 3:10-11), fellow-heirs with Christ Jesus (Rom 8:16-17), members of the household of faith (Eph 3:6), new creatures begotten by the Word of truth (Jas 1:18) and born of the Spirit (John 3:3), to whom I owe the love I owe to God Himself (1 John 3:14, 4:14-21). Their souls' good is my own; they are my crown and rejoicing (Phil 4:1; 1 Thess. 2:8, 19-20). They are men called to "pray with holy hands" (2:8) and "women professing godliness" (2:10), "the believers" (4:12) whom I must entreat as "fathers ... brethren ... mothers ... sisters" (5:1-2).

Put the brethren in remembrance: We are often called in the Bible to remember (Deut 8:2, 16:12; Luke 17:32, 22:19-20, John 16:4; 2 Pe.3:1-2; Acts 20:35). For so often it is not that we do not know, but that we do not do. Paul wrote to the troubled Church of Corinth as an assembly "enriched in all utterance and in all knowledge." He could appeal to them as "wise men," and say "We know that we all have knowledge" (1 Cor 1:5, 8:1, 10:15). Yet they failed to understand the implications and obligations of that knowledge: "Know ye not?" Paul asks them (3:16; 6:2, 9, 24). So the Lord Jesus says, "If ye know these things, blessed are ye if ye do them" (John 13:17). James says, "Whoso looketh into the perfect law of liberty, and continueth therein, he being not a forgetful hearer, but a doer of the work, this man shall be blessed in his deed" (Jas. 1:25). Let me *put the brethren in remembrance* as *a good minister of Jesus Christ.*

73. What Gift or Offering Can I Bring?

1 What gift or offering can I bring
To lay before His throne,
In tribute of my Savior King
Who saves by grace alone?

2 All honor, riches, blessing, strength
And glory is His worth,
Whose love exceeds depth, breadth and length
And heights of heaven and earth!

3 But what can fully show the grace
Of Christ, our Lord and God,
Who suffering, took poor sinners' place
And dying, shed His Blood?

4 No gold, like wise men's, could I bear
No frankincense, nor myrrh:
Nor have I Mary's ointment rare
To lavish out, like her.

5 My heart alone may I bestow,
All contrite, broken, poor:
From day to day O let me show
Thy great salvation sure!

6 A thousand songs my voice would raise
But all shall have one theme:
To tell of my Lord Jesu's praise—
My song shall be of Him!

7 To Father, Son, and Holy Ghost
One true and living God
Be glory given through heaven's hosts
And all the earth abroad!

C.M.

The House of God

Preparatory Reading: Old Testament: Ruth 2;
  New Testament: Luke 24 Psalm: 73

1 Timothy 4:7-8

7But refuse profane and old wives' fables, and exercise thyself *rather* unto godliness. 8For bodily exercise profiteth little: but godliness is profitable unto all things, having promise of the life that now is, and of that which is to come.

Body and soul alike thrive through diet and exercise. If I eat poorly, or too much, I desecrate my body as a temple of the Holy Ghost. I cannot neglect my regimen and improve.

Paul is advising Timothy, instructing, commanding him to keep on course with the diet and exercise of his own soul. "The words of faith and of good doctrine" to which I "have attained" will not "nourish" me as they ought if I am distracted by heeding *profane and old wives' fables*—I must *refuse* such. I must push these aside and get busy elsewhere—*exercise thyself rather unto godliness*.

Whatever I cannot trace to Holy Scripture as "good doctrine" must be rejected as no better than *profane and old wives' fables*—*profane* in character, alien and demeaning to the faith; *old wives'* in origin, having contemptible and incredulous sources. The Bible does not consign its readers to *fables*; it keeps me from *fables* (1:4; 2 Tim. 4:4; 2 Pet. 1:16).

Exercise thyself unto godliness, says Paul. Constantly give yourself to the discipline, diet and dog-work of an athlete in intense commitment to godliness. What every believer should do, I must do; these are the rules:

1. "Run to win" (1 Cor 9:24-27)

2. "Compete by the rules" (1 Tim. 2:5)

3. "Travel light" (Heb. 12:1-2)

4. "Focus on the goal" (Heb. 12:1-2)

5. "Never look back" (Phil. 3:13-14)

6. "Watch your step" (Gal 5:9)

7. "Pull no punches" (1 Cor 9:26)

8. "Always in control" (1 Cor 9:25)

9. "Use it or lose it" (1 Cor 9:27).

Godliness is my goal. I must keep my heart with all keeping, for out my heart flow the issues of life (Prov 4:23). "Godly edifying in faith" will result in "charity out of a pure heart, and of a good conscience, and of faith unfeigned" (1:4-5). I must model to my people what I call them to be. I pray that they "may live in all godliness and honesty" (2:2); I tutor them to live as those "professing godliness" (2:10); I preach the Gospel as "the mystery of godliness," "the doctrine according to godliness" (3:16, 6:3). Only as I "follow after godliness" am I truly a "man of God" (6:11). The success of my life is the "great gain" of "godliness with contentment" (6:6). *Exercise thyself rather unto godliness.*

74. No Cross, No Crown

1 "No cross, no crown", this saying true,
Ye saints, this watchword keep with you
And arm yourselves to suffer pain
That ye with Jesus Christ may reign!

2 "No cross, no crown!" Our Shepherd good
Has in His people's place once stood,
Condemned to suffer, bleed and die
To gain His Father's throne on high.

3 "No cross, no crown!" Our risen Lord
Now bids you trust and keep His Word:
In His own steps ye now must tread
To serve your glorious King and Head.

4 In sorrow, toil, reproach and loss
Ye feel the weight of Christ's own cross:
To death be faithful mid the strife,
And ye shall win the crown of life!

5 "No cross, no crown! No cross, no crown!"
A cloud of witnesses around—
Saints, martyrs and apostles—cry
To urge you on to victory.

6 Soon shall we join that countless throng
To raise our voices high in song:
"We triumphed through the Lamb's shed Blood—
Praise to the living, Triune God!"

L.M.

The House of God

Preparatory Reading: Old Testament: Ruth 3;
New Testament: Ephesians 1 Psalm: 74

1 Timothy 4:7-8

7But refuse profane and old wives' fables, and exercise thyself *rather* unto godliness. 8For bodily exercise profiteth little: but godliness is profitable unto all things, having promise of the life that now is, and of that which is to come.

Godliness is profitable unto all things having promise of the life that now is, and of that which is to come: The Lord Jesus came "that they might have life, and have it more abundantly" (John 10:10). His kingdom is within, with righteousness and peace and joy in the Holy Ghost (Luke 17:21, Rom 14:17). Seeking His righteousness and kingdom first, His disciples may live without the gnawing care, "What shall we eat, what shall we drink, wherewithal shall we be clothed?" (Matt 6:31, 33). Whatever we forsake for Christ, He will recompense us a hundredfold "now in this time" (Mark 10:28-31). "He that heareth My Word, and believeth on Him that sent Me, hath everlasting life, and shall not come into condemnation ,but is passed from death unto life" (John 5:24). Here is the *promise of the life that now is, and of that which is to come.* Now I shall never hunger, never thirst; then, I shall never perish (John 6:35, 3:16).

In the same vein Peter writes to assure us that Jesus our Lord "in His divine power hath given unto us all things that pertain unto life and godliness, through the knowledge of Him that hath called us to glory and virtue" (2 Pet. 1:3). Virtue now; glory then. Now, we "add to" our faith "godliness" to be "fruitful in the knowledge of the Lord Jesus Christ; then we look to have "an abundant entrance into" His "everlasting kingdom". If these things abound in me, my calling and election is sure (2 Pet. 1:5-8, 10-11).

Compared to this *bodily exercise profiteth little*. The runner, the wrestler, the boxer each "striveth . . . to obtain a corruptible crown; but we, an incorruptible" (1 Cor 9:25). Ours is a crown of life, of glory, of righteousness (James 1:12; 1 Pet. 3.5:4; 2 Tim. 4:9). With it, the Savior shall say, "Well done . . . enter into the joy of thy Lord" (Matt 25:23-24)."The LORD taketh pleasure in them that fear Him, in those that hope in His mercy. Praise the LORD, O Jerusalem; praise my God, O Zion" (Ps 147:11-12).

O faithful Savior Jesus! Exercise me to godliness. "Turn away mine eyes from beholding vanity, and grant me Thy law graciously" (Ps 119:18). Let me study to show myself an approved workman to Thee, rightly dividing the Word of truth . . . let me shun profane and vain babbling whose words eat like a canker, and which only increase unto more ungodliness (2 Tim. 2:14-16,17; Psalm 32:6-7).

75. How My Heart Exults in Gladness

1 How my heart exults in gladness
At the sound of Jesu's Name—
Gone is all my care and sadness,
Banished is my guilt and shame!
Of Ten Thousand He is Fairest—
Now and to eternity,
As the Rose of Sharon rarest
Only Jesus would I see!

Refrain:
Sing of Jesus—my Lord Jesus,
Who for our salvation came:
How my heart exults in gladness
At the sound of Jesu's Name!

2 All my boasting, all my glory
Is in Christ the Crucified:
O my soul, now tell the story
How for me He bled and died!
How the Father in compassion
His own Son to us did send,
Laying down His life a ransom,
Loving us unto the end!

3 Oh to see Him in His beauty!
When mine eyes behold my King,
All His grace and all His glory,
Shall my soul forever sing!
Hence away, all doubt and sorrow,
All my anxious, fretful fear—
All that comes upon the morrow
Heralds my redemption near!

8.7.8.7. D (Refrain).
Tune: Choral Fantasia in C (Ludwig von Beethoven)

The House of God

Preparatory Reading: Old Testament: Ruth 4;
New Testament: Ephesians 2 Psalm: 75

1 Timothy 4:8–10

⁸For bodily exercise profiteth little: but godliness is profitable unto all things, having promise of the life that now is, and of that which is to come. ⁹This *is* a faithful saying and worthy of all acceptation. ¹⁰For therefore we both labour and suffer reproach, because we trust in the living God, who is the Saviour of all men, specially of those that believe.

As I take up the Bible and read, I sit at Christ Jesu's feet to hear Him. Do I act in faith, and listen for His voice as I read?

Godliness is profitable unto all things . . . This is a faithful saying for the saint, just as the previous *faithful saying* speaks to the sinner (1:15). Gladly I embrace the promise of the Gospel; do I as eagerly desire the promise of godliness? This *faithful saying* is *worthy of all acceptation.* Its obligation falls on all the redeemed; its hope heartens every true believer. Let me entirely, honestly put my weight upon this promise; let me consider Him faithful who promised it, and claim it as *worthy of all acceptation.*

The pursuit of godliness must bring 'toil and trouble' in its nature, and should for its value—*for therefore we both labor and suffer reproach. We labor* as we "exercise ourselves to godliness," as we give heed to "godly edifying in faith" and "war a good warfare, holding faith and a good conscience", as we "behave . . . in the house of God" (4:7; 1:4, 18–19; 3:15). *We suffer reproach* from the "vain jangling" "blasphemy," "usurping authority" "departing from the faith" "lies in hypocrisy" and "profane and old wives' fables" which all who in pride "teach otherwise" thrust in our faces out of scorn and contempt for "the glorious Gospel of the blessed God," the "great mystery of godliness" (1:6, 20; 2:12; 4:1, 7; 6:3–5, 20–21; 1:11, 3:16).

Our pursuit of godliness fully acknowledges God's mercy as a Creator and grace as a Savior: *we trust in the living God who is the Savior of all men, specially of those who believe.* As a faithful Creator, "the LORD is good to all; and His tender mercies are over all His works." As the King of saints, "the LORD is nigh unto all them that call upon Him, to all that call upon Him in truth. He will fulfill the desire of them that fear Him: He also will hear their cry and save them" (Ps 145:9, 18–19). So we "exercise" ourselves "unto godliness" as we receive all created good, "sanctified by the Word of God and prayer" (4:4–5, 7).

Lord Jesus, teach me to trust Thy Father's care, submit to His will, live upon His provision, and seek first His kingdom. Let me labor and suffer reproach but that I may be godly. Grant me this in the fullness of the Holy Spirit for Thy Name's sake. Amen.

76. In Breaking Bread

1 In breaking bread I seek Thee,
Lord Jesus; how I need
Thine out-poured Blood to pardon,
Thy flesh my soul to feed!
In breaking bread, I hear Thee:
Thy written Word is true—
"In sign of loaf and chalice,
I give Myself for you!"

2 In breaking bread I view Thee:
The stripes, the prints, the wounds—
In David's house that Fountain,
Where grace o'er sin abounds;
In breaking bread I taste Thee,
The tender Lamb so sweet—
O come, indwell and fill me,
My soul's true Drink and Meat!

3 In breaking bread I know Thee:
In faith my soul discerns
Thy presence through the symbols,
My heart within me burns,
Rememb'ring all the Scriptures
Revealing all Thy love,
Who suffering bore our sorrows,
And risen reigns above.

4 In breaking bread, I trust Thee:
On Thee my sins are laid—
Thy voice cries, "It is finished!"—
My every debt is paid:
In breaking bread, I love Thee,
For Thou hast first loved me—
O Savior, take me wholly,
To live and die for Thee

5 In breaking bread, I pray Thee,
"Lord Jesus, quickly come!"
The night must soon be over;
When Thou shalt bring the dawn!
The former things shall vanish,
The shadows flee away;

The House of God

In Zion's courts with singing,
I'll greet Thee on that day!

6 How blest within God's kingdom,
Who on that day break bread!
With Abr'ham, Isaac, Jacob,
From all the nations led,
Thy Church to Thee shall gather,
A countless, ransomed host—
One God to praise: The Father,
The Son and Holy Ghost!

7.6.7.6D

Preparatory Reading: Old Testament: 1 Kings 17;
   New Testament: Ephesians 3 Psalm: 76

1 Timothy 4:11–12

¹¹These things command and teach. ¹²Let no man despise thy youth; but be thou an example of the believers, in word, in conversation, in charity, in spirit, in faith, in purity.

These things are in sum all Paul has charged, exhorted and committed to Timothy, and to me (1:3, 28; 2:1, 8; 3:15; 4:6). The whole counsel of God in doctrine; all the ordinances the Lord Jesus delivered for worship; all the truth into which the Holy Ghost leads—*these things* I hold in trust as "a good minister of Jesus Christ" (Acts 20:27; 1 Cor 11:2; John 14:26, 16:13; cf. 1:18, 4:6, 6:13-14, 20-21). *These things command and teach:* The work of the ministry is to apply *these things* to Christ's people with authority as Christ's servants—as "ministers of the Word" (Luke 1:2). This authority is neither inherent in us as personalities, nor tied to the mere possession of office. It is delegated through the commission of Christ Himself "to preach the gospel to every creature." The King of glory declares, "All authority is given unto *Me* . . . therefore go *ye* . . . make disciples . . . baptizing . . . teaching . . . and lo, *I am with you*" (Matt 28:18–20; Mark 16:15). If I abide by the doctrine of Christ; if I enjoin what the Bible teaches; if as a servant to all I care for the house of God; if as a steward I feed the whole household; if as a shepherd I take heed to all the flock, then with Christ's own authority I may *these things command and teach.* Our Prince and Savior gives His Spirit to all who obey Him—He must and will be obeyed. *These things command.* And to obey, believers must understand *these things* in every what, why, where, when and how. *These things teach.* O Father of mercies, how can I lift up my face to Thee, and not blush? I teach, but do not do; I teach, but do not command. In so many ways I offend. Make my life authentic; grant my ministry authority. Make me like Thy dear Son; enable me to speak for Thy dear Son. Forgive, hear, do, lest Thy people turn away empty and unfed, straying and unled, scattered and torn. Cleanse me in the Blood of Christ Jesus; fill me with the Holy Ghost, the fullness of Thy grace in light, love, life and labor. Thy Word commands "Be thou," I pray Thee, make me so to be for the sake of the Lord Jesus Christ, Amen.

Let no man despise thy youth, but be thou an example of the believers: The Greek word suggests "let no one think down;" as we might say, "look down his nose." This "down" attitude attaches to Timothy's *youth.* Our day attaches little value to age—we live in a "never-land" society that desires to "never grow up." But in Paul's day, age was expected to carry the weight of experience and maturity. Yet age and maturity are neither inseparable nor inevitable cause and effect. In God's kingdom the calculations of flesh do not count (1 Cor 1:27–29; Eccl 9:11). Timothy must live beyond his years, and temperament, not in the flesh but in the Spirit, following Christ. "The Lord looketh on the heart." (Rom 8:1–3; 2 Cor 3:5–6; 1 Cor 11:1; Phil. 3:13–17; 1 Sam 16:7).

77. Called to share the Holy Supper

Before Communion

1 Called to share the Holy Supper
At the Table of the Lord,
Let my heart with love remember
From the pages of His Word,
All my Savior's love to me
Now and to eternity.

2 Here in grief and true repentance
Let me now my sin recall—
All its bitterness and bondage
Darkness, sorrow, wormwood, gall,
From which Christ to set me free
Paid the price at Calvary!

3 Then with thankful tears o'erflowing
Let me come His bread to break,
All His pain and torment showing
As my part in Him I take,
Hearing Jesus say to me,
"This, My Body, is for thee!"

4 With what mingled joy and trembling
In my hands I hold the Cup,
Filled with mercy, grace and blessing
All because my Lord drank up
God's just wrath and judgment dread
As for me His Blood He shed!

After Communion

5 Who can show the matchless glory
Of His everlasting love?
Who can tell the wondrous story
How He left His throne above
Humbled, dying on the Cross
There to seek and save the lost?

6 Pardoned, cleansed, redeemed, forgiven
Let me spend my ransomed days

The House of God

In His service, till in heaven
I shall share the song of praise
"Worthy, worthy Lamb of God,
Thou hast bought us by Thy Blood!"

7 Thus with all the saints attending
Shall I rightly show His death
And at last there comprehending
Height and depth and length and breadth
Of the love of Christ to me,
Live to all eternity.

8 "Hallelujah! Hallelujah!"
Let all heaven and earth proclaim;
To our Lord and God Jehovah
Give the glory due His Name:
Father, Son and Holy Ghost,
Three in One, the Lord of hosts!

8.7.8.7.7.7.

The House of God

Preparatory Reading: Old Testament: 1 Kings 18;
  New Testament: Ephesians 4 Psalm:77

1 Timothy 4:11–12

[11] These things command and teach. [12] Let no man despise thy youth; but be thou an example of the believers, in word, in conversation, in charity, in spirit, in faith, in purity.

Be thou an example of the believers: The first charge of our Lord Jesus to every scribe in His kingdom is "do and teach" (Matt 5:19). Our King's commission is "teach . . . to observe" (Matt 28:20). So my calling is first "take heed unto thyself" and then "the doctrine" (4:16). "In all things shewing thyself a pattern of good works: in doctrine shewing incorruptness, gravity, sincerity, sound speech" (Titus 2:7–8). Titus is no different from Timothy—no preacher is exempt. "Who is a wise man, and endued with knowledge among you? Let him shew out of a good conversation his works with meekness of wisdom"—*an example* (James 3:13). *Be thou an example,* says Paul, in speech and conduct—*in word, in conversation;* in soul—*in charity, in spirit, in faith;* in body—*in purity.* All I am, all I do, all I say must be *an example.*

How far, far short I fall from this! How quickly I fret over the natural limitations of life which Providence has allotted me—once youth, and since, age; once alone, now married; once in need of books, now with books in surfeit. All this I fret over, but how slothful and slow to struggle, strive to be *an example of the believers.* How easily my private moments, my anonymous actions outside my public vocation can become anything but Christ-like, in speech, conduct, soul and body. "O wretched man that I am!" Should I not fear, "lest having preached to others, I myself should be a castaway?" (Rom 7:25; 1 Cor 9:27).

Lord Jesus, make me *an example of the believers in word:* Could I but bridle my tongue, I might master my whole body; I would be perfect and entire, wanting nothing, could I not offend in word (James 1:4; 3:1–2). For every idle word must I give account; "out of the fullness of the heart the mouth speaketh" (Matt 12:32–40). Lord Christ, teach me the truth as it is in Jesus. Let no corrupt communication proceed out of my mouth, but that which is good to the use of edifying, that it may minister grace to the hearers. Let me not grieve the Holy Spirit of God, whereby I am sealed unto the day of redemption. Put from me all bitterness, and wrath, and anger, and clamor, and evil speaking, with all malice. Make me kind, tenderhearted, forgiving even as God has forgiven me for Christ's sake (Eph 4:21, 29–32). Grant me sound speech that cannot be condemned; make me *an example of the believers in word* (Titus 2:8).

> "LORD, I cry unto Thee; make haste to hear me:
> Give ear unto my voice, when I cry unto Thee.
> Set a watch, O LORD, before my mouth: keep the door of my lips"
>   —Psalm 141:1,3.

78. Have Faith in God

O Savior God, Lord Jesus Christ,
Our faithful, merciful High Priest,
Who hast redeemed us by Thy Blood,
To us Thou say'st: "Have faith in God!"

2 A morning came, in Thy last week,
When from a fig tree Thou didst seek
But find no fruit; then didst Thou say,
"Of this tree none shall eat for aye!"

3 The day that followed, all could see,
Accursed, and dead, the barren tree:
All thy disciples hast Thou taught,
From this the truth: "Have faith in God!"

4 "Have faith in God!" He meets our need
Though faith be like a mustard seed;
Our little faith could mountains move,
If rested on His power and love.

5 "Have faith in God!" Dare to believe,
All that ye ask, ye shall receive;
Rely on what the Savior saith,
And, nothing wavering, ask in faith!

6 Ask in His Name, for in His will,
Ye shall receive, and joy shall fill
Your cup to overflow with praise
To glorify His sovereign grace!

7 Only-begotten Son of God,
Who as the Man of sorrows trod
Our path on earth, now hear and heed:
Grant grace, and help in time of need!

8 Our Mediator, in Thy Name
Alone we would Thy promise claim:
"Let not your hearts still troubled be,
Believe in God; also, in Me!

The House of God

9 By faith we come to God the Lord,
The promise stands within His Word:
"All who believe He is, and seek
His face with zeal, reward shall take!"

10 Lord God, may we Thy glory see,
In faith, and hope, and charity,
Saved unto all the uttermost
By Father, Son, and Holy Ghost!

L.M.

Preparatory Reading: Old Testament: 1 Kings 19;
   New Testament: Ephesians 5 Psalm: 78

1 Timothy 4:11–12

¹¹These things command and teach. ¹²Let no man despise thy youth; but be thou an example of the believers, in word, in conversation, in charity, in spirit, in faith, in purity.

Be thou an example . . . in conversation: "if any man be in Christ, he is a new creature: old things are passed away; behold, all things are become new" (2 Cor 5:17). How new am I? "Like as Christ was raised up from the dead by the glory of the Father, even so we also should walk in newness of life" (Rom 6:4). How new is my walk? "He that saith he abideth in Him, ought himself also so to walk, even as Himself also walked" (1 John 2:6).

My past conduct as a sinner is all too clear—vain (1 Pet. 1:18), filthy (2 Pet. 2:7), wasteful (Gal 1:13), led by the devil, the flesh and the world, under wrath (Eph 2:1–3). My present *conversation* as a saint is to be utterly different: holy (1 Pet. 1:15, 2 Pet. 3:11), chaste (1 Pet. 3:1), good (1 Pet. 3:16), godly, simple and sincere (2 Cor 1:12), free of the old, full of the new (Eph 4:22–24), becoming the Gospel (Phil.1:27), free of covetousness, full of contentment (Heb. 13:5–6), in Christ (1 Pet. 3:16). "To him that ordereth his conversation aright will I shew the salvation of God" (Ps 50:16–17, 22–23).

Be thou an example . . . in charity: Father of heaven, Thou didst so love the world that Thou gavest Thine only-begotten Son; Thou commendest Thy love toward us in that, while we were yet sinners, Christ died for us. Thou hast shed abroad Thy love in our hearts by the Holy Ghost given us (John 3:16; Rom 5:5, 8). Every one of Thy true children loves as begotten of God—"he that loveth not, knoweth not God" (1 John 4:8). Every believer is called to "follow after charity" (1 Cor 14:1).

But Thy Word here commands me to *be . . . an example . . . in charity*. My doctrine and preaching, in Law and Gospel, has this end: "charity out of a pure heart" (1:5). In taking heed to myself I must be *an example . . . in charity*. Who is to be the most loving saint in the assembly? I am. Who is to "do all things with charity"? (1 Cor 16:14). I am. Who is to prize charity above tongues prophecy, knowledge, generosity? 1 Cor 13:1–3). I am. Can I replace the word "charity" in 1 Cor 13:4–8 with my name and speak the truth? Does the love of Christ constrain my service, whatever the cost? (2 Cor 5:14–15). Do I affectionately desire my people's good, as would a father, even a nurse-maid? (1 Thess. 2:7–12). My Savior has one question for my ordination: "Lovest Thou me?" (John 21:15–17). Lord Jesus, let me love without dissimulation; teach me to abhor evil and cleave to good. I pray my love would abound more and more in knowledge and judgment. Make me kindly affectioned to others in brotherly love, in honor preferring others. Let me love not in word or tongue, but in deed and truth. Clothe me with charity as the bond of perfectness. Let me walk in love, as Thou hast loved us and given Thyself for us, Amen. (Rom 12:9–10; Phil. 1:9; 1 John 3:15; Col. 3:13, Eph 5:1–2).

The House of God

79. Lord, Our Faith Increase!

1 Wearied in well-doing, *Savior*,
Cumbered with our care—
We for strength would wait upon Thee:
Hear our prayer!

2 Hear and answer our petition:
"Lord, our faith increase*!"*
From ourselves, our sins, our struggles
Grant release!

3 *Jesus,* make Thy grace sufficient!
In our weakness prove
All Thy strength, and never part us
From Thy love!

4 *Christ,* who makest intercession
At the Throne of God,
From our sins give full remission
In Thy Blood!

5 We would cast on Thee our burden,
Cast on Thee our care:
All our griefs and all our sorrows
Thou dost bear.

6 Hear we now Thine invitation:
"Come to Me, and rest!"
In Thy Word we have salvation
And are blest!

7 From Thy Father's richest glory
All our needs supply:
For Thy Holy Spirit's fullness
Hear our cry!

8.5.8.3.

The House of God

Preparatory Reading: Old Testament: 1 Kings 20;
  New Testament: Ephesians 6 Psalm: 79

1 Timothy 4:11–12

¹¹These things command and teach. ¹²Let no man despise thy youth; but be thou an example of the believers, in word, in conversation, in charity, in spirit, in faith, in purity.

Be thou an example . . . in spirit: "The spirit of a man is the candle of the LORD, searching all the inward parts of the belly" "For what man knoweth the things of a man, save the spirit of man which is in him?" (Prov 20:27; 1 Cor 2:11).

"Soul" and "spirit" and not two separate elements of my humanity—they are two distinct aspects of my "inner man." The soul viewed in relation to self and this world is "soul" the soul viewed in relation to God and the other world is "spirit." The soul in life inhabits the body as "soul;" the soul in death departs the body as "spirit" (Matt 26:38; 27:30; Luke 23:46). As the "joints and marrow" are the outward and inward elements of a man's bones, so is "the dividing asunder of soul and spirit" (Heb. 4:12; cf. Gen 2:7, Eccl 12:7; Ps 97:10; Heb. 12:23). It is as the eternal, God-ward aspect of the soul that the 'spirit' of a man receives and interacts with the Spirit of the Lord and the Word of God Heb. 4:12, 1 Cor 2:10, 12). Thus our full salvation reaches the whole man, inner and outer, in time and eternity: "Now the very God of peace sanctify you wholly: and I pray God your whole spirit and soul and body be preserved blameless unto the coming of our Lord Jesus Christ. Faithful is He that calleth you, who also will do it." "Having therefore these promises, dearly beloved, let us cleanse ourselves from all filthiness of the flesh and spirit, perfecting holiness in the fear of God" (1 Thess. 5:22–24; 2 Cor 7:1).

As "spirit" the believer's soul bears the graces of the Gospel in its inner life and motive; there we are "renewed in the spirit of our mind" (Eph 4:20–24, Rom 12:2). Paul in communion with the saints can say he is "present in spirit" with Churches over which he labors, or that "his spirit is refreshed" by their good news (Col. 2:5; 1 Cor 16:18; 2 Cor 7:13). All saints must rule their spirits as much as their flesh by the Holy Ghost (Prov 16:32, 25:28, 1 Cor 14:32). To any Christian the call comes: "Ye are bought with a price: therefore glorify God in your body and in your spirit which are God's" (1 Cor 6:20). Every saint receives the promise: "The Lord Jesus Christ be with thy spirit" (2 Tim. 4:20).

Regeneration resurrects the inner man as a new creature in Christ Jesus. "That which is born of the flesh: and that which is born of the Spirit is spirit" (John 3:6). The regenerate soul receives the circumcision of heart which is of the Spirit (Phil. 3:3 cf. Rom 2:29). Baptized into , indwelt by, led by, filled with the Spirit of grace the soul endures the conflict of the flesh and the Spirit (1 Cor 12:13; Rom 8:9, 14; Eph 5:18; Gal 5:16–17, Jas. 4:5–6). And as a "good minister of Jesus Christ," walking in the example of the Apostle, I also am called to "serve God with my spirit in the Gospel of His Son" (Phil. 3:17; 2 Cor 12:17; Rom 1:9).

80. Assembled in the Upper Room

1 Assembled in the Upper Room
Beset by doubt and fear,
Through bolted doors they saw Him come,
And knew that He was near.

2 Amidst them standing, Christ our Lord
Revealed Himself anew,
And kept the promise of His Word—
"My peace I give to you!"

3 The Savior showed His wounded side,
His pierced hands and feet;
He ate before their wond'ring eyes,
And made their joy complete.

4 Upon them breathing, as a sign,
The Holy Ghost He gave
As witness to the grace divine
Which by their Word would save.

5 Lord Jesus, now to us draw near
As Thee by faith we seek
When we assemble to Thee here
Each first day of the week.

6 In all the Scriptures which we read
And preach, O let us learn
Of Thee, till Thou hast met our need,
And made our hearts to burn!

7 And may the gracious Comforter,
The Holy Ghost, reveal
To all our hearts, that Thou art near,
Thy promises to seal!

8 Instill our hope, inflame our love,
And, Lord, our faith increase:
Till, filled with power from above
We know Thou art our Peace!

C.M.

Preparatory Reading: Old Testament: 1 Kings 21;
   New Testament: 1 Peter 1 Psalm: 80

1 Timothy 4:11–12

¹¹These things command and teach. ¹²Let no man despise thy youth; but be thou an example of the believers, in word, in conversation, in charity, in spirit, in faith, in purity.

Be thou an example . . . in spirit: In what way would Paul have every "good minister of Jesus Christ" to be *an example . . . . In spirit?* By the graces and gifts of the Holy Ghost, "God hath not given us the spirit of fear; but of power, and of love, and of a sound mind" (2 Tim. 1:7). Of all believers, I as a pastor and elder must first and foremost pray for the Holy Ghost to work in me (Eph 1:15–23) that I may walk and work with the Spirit and the understanding (2 Cor 14:15–16) and discern the spirits of men as they claim to speak for God (1 John 4:1–6). Tragic it is when Christ's servants do not know "what manner of spirit" they are of (Luke 9:55). The Savior calls me in spirit to be fervent (Rom 12:11), contrite (Isa 57:15; Ps 51:17), broken (Isa 66:2; Ps 34:18), honest (Ps 32:2), faithful (Prov. 11:13), humble (Prov 16:18), believing (2 Cor 4:13), poor and meek (Matt 5:3, 5). This is to follow God wholly as did Caleb and Joshua of old (Num 14:24) with a spirit of "power, love and a sound mind" (2 Tim. 1:7). Blessed Comforter, Lord and Giver of life: Holy Spirit of God, Spirit of Christ, who searchest the deep things of God—dwell in me as the Spirit of revelation in the knowledge of God, the Father of glory, the God of our Lord Jesus Christ—enlighten my eyes to know the hope of my calling, the riches of the glory of His inheritance in the saints, and the exceeding greatness of His power to believers, the power that raised Christ from the dead, and set Him at His own right hand (Eph 1:21–23). Lord Jesus Christ, be with my spirit!

Be thou an example . . . in faith: As all the saints have charity, have the Holy Spirit and by Him a new heart and a new spirit, so all who are Christ's possess saving *faith*—"the faith of God's elect" (Tit. 1:1). "By grace are saved through faith, and that not of yourselves: it is the gift of God" (Eph 2:8) "Unto you it is given in the behalf of Christ . . . to believe on Him" (Phil. 1:29). This faith is more precious than tried gold, and receives the salvation of our souls (1 Pet. 1:7–9; Heb. 10:39). Yet Paul admonishes Timothy, all elders, and me, *Be thou an example of the believers . . . in faith.* He bids me to abound in "the grace of faith" (2 Cor 8:7). Lord Jesus, Author and Finisher of my faith, too often mine is "little faith" (Matt 6:30). Like Israel of old which "believed not in God and . . . limited the Holy One of Israel" (Ps 78:22, 41). I show "no faith" but fear (Mark 4:40). Grant me "full assurance of faith" (Heb. 10:19–25); leave me not "weak in faith" (Rom 14:1) but fulfill "the work of faith with power" that it may "grow exceedingly" (2 Thess. 1:3–11). Make me "strong in faith" to give Thee glory, fully persuaded that what Thou hast promised, Thou art able to perform (Rom 4:20–21). Give me to work and pray in faith (1 Th.1:3; Mark 11:24;

Jas. 5:13). Support me through every trial of my faith (Jas. 1:2–4; 1 Pe.1:7). Against the devil, the world, and death itself, grant me the victory of faith, enduring as seeing Thee, the Invisible (Eph. 6:16; 1 John 5:4–5; Heb. 10:39, 11:27).

81. O what a sweet Exchange is this!

1 O what *a sweet exchange* is this!
The King of glory took my place,
My sin, my hell, His righteousness,
His heaven to give to me in grace!

2 *For me*, Lord Jesus, didst Thou leave
The glory of Thy throne on high?
For Thee, blest Savior, shall I grieve
When earthly honors pass me by?

3 *For me* didst Thou, who knew no sin,
In our frail flesh partake of pain?
For Thee, who sought my soul to win,
Should I in suffering e'er complain?

4 *For me*, eternal Son of God,
Didst Thou embrace the cursed Cross?
For Thee, who bought my soul with Blood,
Shall I disdain reproach or loss?

5 *For me*, my Lord and God, hast Thou
A ransom free, Thy life laid down:
For Thee my life to spend, I vow
To bear Thy cross and win Thy crown!

L.M.

Preparatory Reading: Old Testament: 1 Kings 22;
New Testament: 1 Peter 2 Psalm: 81

1 Timothy 4:11–12

¹¹These things command and teach. ¹²Let no man despise thy youth; but be thou an example of the believers, in word, in conversation, in charity, in spirit, in faith, in purity.

Be thou an example . . . in purity: Lord Jesus, Thine eyes are as a flaming fire; Thou art of purer eyes than to behold evil, and canst not look on iniquity (Hab 1:13; Rev. 1:14). Thou hast declared, "Blessed are the pure in heart: for they shall see God" (Matt 5:8). Without holiness no man shall see Thee (Heb. 12:14) and Thou hast called us, not to uncleanness, but unto holiness (1 Thess. 7–8). Everywhere Thy servants are to pray as men "lifting up holy hands, without wrath and doubting" (1 Thess. 3:8; 1 Tim. 2:8). In this am I called to be *an example of the believers . . . in purity.*

By Thy Holy Spirit given to us, cause me to flee youthful lusts, and follow righteousness, faith, charity and peace with them that call on Thee from a pure heart (1 Thess .4:7–8; 2 Tim. 2:22). Let me so treat women in the Church "with all purity" even as their brother or son, that they may learn to be chaste, and I may prove myself a minister of God by pureness (1 Tim. 5:2; Tit. 2:5; 2 Cor 6:6).

Thou hast said, "He that loveth pureness of heart, for the grace of his lips the King shall be His friend" O may I cleanse my way as I take heed thereto according to Thy Word! (Prov 22:11; Ps 119:9).

Turn mine eyes away from beholding vanity, O Lord, and grant me Thy Law graciously (Ps 119:29–37). Make straight paths for my feet, hands and eyes that my heart may safely walk after my eyes and I may keep my heart with all diligence (Heb. 12:12–13; Prov 4:24–27; Job 37:1–2; Prov 4:23). And as I hope to see Thee as Thou art, let me purify myself even as Thou, Christ Jesus, art pure (1 John 3:2–3).

Father! God of peace, sanctify me wholly, that my whole body, soul and spirit be preserved blameless unto the coming of our Lord Jesus Christ! Thou art faithful who callest; also do it (1 Thess. 5:23–24). So shall my days pass fulfilling Thy call:

> I am the Almighty God: walk before Me, and be thou perfect"
> "Be ye holy, for I am holy"
> "Be ye clean, ye that bear the vessels of the LORD"
> "Be ye therefore perfect,
> even as your Father which is in heaven is perfect"
> —Gen 17:1; Lev 19:2; 1 Pet. 1:16; Isa 52:11; 2 Tim. 2:2:21; Matt 5:48.

82. Christ is the Power of God

1 Despised, derided and defamed,
Yet shall we never be ashamed
Of Christ's most precious Blood:
The Gospel brings God's righteousness
To Jew and Greek, and ever is
The saving power of God. (Rom 1:16–17)

2 We preach the Christ, who at the cross
Atoned for sin, and saved the lost
Who bore God's wrath and rod
To Jews who signs and wonders seek,
A scandal; folly to the Greek,
To us the power of God. (1 Cor 1:23–24)

3 The testimony of our Lord
We hold according to His Word
And where th'apostles trod,
We follow still, and yet partake
Of suffering for our Savior's sake
Held by the power of God. (2 Tim. 1:8)

4 Our last inheritance awaits
In undefiled and perfect state
A kingdom vast and broad,
In heaven above for us reserved
Who persevere and are preserved
Kept by the power of God. (1 Peter 1:3–5)

5 In God alone we make our boast:
To Father, Son and Holy Ghost
Whose wisdom and whose power
In our Lord Jesus is displayed
To men and angels' wond'ring gaze
Be glory evermore!

8.8.6.D

The House of God

> Preparatory Reading: Old Testament: 2 Kings 1;
> New Testament: 1 Peter 3 Psalm: 82

1 Timothy 4:13

13 Till I come, give attendance to reading, to exhortation, to doctrine.

"These things command and teach"—this is *what* my ministry is to enjoin and enforce, the sum and substance of this Epistle. *How* my ministry can achieve these goals effectively follows in 4:11–16. These instructions move steadily from "self" (4:12) to "doctrine" (4:16), first in particular detail (4:12–14), then in general summary (4:15–16). The order never varies—character (12), discipline (13), gifts (14) in priority; inner, then outer progress (15); perseverance first with self, then others (16). Whatever gifts I may possess, they are squandered without considerable attention to character, and then concerted action on the discipline of a pastor's duties: *reading, exhortation, doctrine*.

Give attendance, "hold close" to *reading . . . exhortation . . . doctrine* says Paul, because all manner of minor matters will otherwise fritter away your energy, capacities and opportunity. A pianist relentlessly practices his physical technique and constantly ponders the interpretation of his repertoire. Even so, a pastor practices holiness, ponders Holy Writ and pursues active service in the Gospel, the Word, the ordinances, the cure of souls and prayer. Early celebrity and its indulgences have spoiled many a promising musician; how much more dangerous when a minister is treated as an oratorical performer! (Ezek 33:30–33). "We will give ourselves to prayer, and to the ministry of the Word" (Acts 6:4). Paul makes no sharp distinction between private study and public ministry. I must taste the bread I bake; I must proclaim what I hear; what I learn I must teach. Nothing is to go without use (Matt 10:27; Eccl 12:9–11).

Give attendance to reading: The apostle supremely directs every "good minister of Jesus Christ" to the *reading* of Holy Scripture. What does this discipline entail? 1. Humbly to sit at Christ's feet (Luke 10:38–41). 2. Constantly to meditate in the Word (Ps 1). 3. Continually to read them (Josh 1:8; Deut 17:18–21). 4. Daily to search them Acts 17:11). 5. Publicly to read them in order, distinctly, giving the sense (Neh 8:8; 9:3). 6. Prayerfully to exercise the mind of Christ by the Spirit to know them well (1 Cor 2:9–13 cf. Luke 24:44–49). 7. Honestly to examine myself by them (Jas. 1:21–23). 8. Intently to behold Christ through them (2 Cor 3:17–18). 9. Watchfully to hide them in my heart against sin (Ps 119:11). 10. Trustingly to abide in the Lord Jesus through them (John 15:7). When the Savior asks, "How readest thou?" how will I answer? (Luke 10:26; Acts 8:30). He who is my wisdom in the fullness of the Godhead (Col. 2:1–3, 6–9; 1 Cor 1:30–31; Prov 8) beckons me to my Bible, saying, "Cease . . ." (Prov 19:27) "Bow down thine ear . . . " (Prov 22:17–21) "Turn you at my reproof" (Prov 1:23; 2:1–9; 8:34) "Give me thine heart!" (Prov 23:26). Master, help me *give attendance to reading* (Eccl 12:9–12).

83. Of all Thy Fullness

1 Of all Thy fullness, grace on grace,
Lord Jesus, let me now receive
Till I shall see Thee face to face
In whom, not seeing, I believe.

2 Fill me with faith to rest upon
The precious promise of Thy Word
Ever to pray and labor on
To gain at last Thy great reward.

3 Fill me with love, for Thee, for Thine,
For all who need Thy mercy free:
Shed forth that charity divine
Which brought Thee down to die for me!

4 Fill me with hope, assured and strong,
In quiet confidence to wait
For Thy return, for which I long:
The blessed hope of all Thy Saints!

5 O fill me with Thy Spirit's power
Savior, who bought me with Thy Blood,
Till I am filled each day and hour
With all the fullness of my God.

L.M.

The House of God

> Preparatory Reading: Old Testament: 2 Kings 2;
> New Testament: 1 Peter 4 Psalm: 83

1 Timothy 4:13

¹³Till I come, give attendance to reading, to exhortation, to doctrine

Give attendance to reading, and I will furnish myself with "these things" which are my trust as a "steward of the mysteries of God" (4:11; 1 Cor 4:2). *Give attendance to doctrine*, and I shall be skilled to "teach these things" (4:11). *Give attendance to exhortation*, and I shall be equipped to "command these things" (4:11). As faith works by love, and faith without works is dead, so the Gospel is proclaimed "for the obedience of faith" (Gal 5:6; Jas. 2:20; Rom 1:5; 16:25–27) and all who in unbelief reject and scorn my Savior "obey not the Gospel" (John 3:36; 1 Pet. 2:7–8, 4:17; 2 Thess. 1:8; Rom 10:3, 16). My God who has reconciled me to Himself through the death of His Son, has committed to me that ministry of reconciliation as an ambassador for Christ, to "pray," "beseech" and "persuade men" (Rom 5:10; 2 Cor 5:10–11, 20, 6:1). So I must wait on *exhortation* as well as teaching in the ministry of the Gospel (Rom 12:6–8).

All preaching, specially of the Gospel, reported in Scripture flows seamlessly from *doctrine* to *exhortation*. Paul's great Epistles and our Lord's own preaching blend *doctrine* and *exhortation* (Eph 1–3, 4–6; Romans 1–11, 12–16; Luke 24:45–49, Mark 1:14–15). In what areas must I *give attendance to exhortation*? 1. Are my motives and aims pure and sound as I exhort? (1 Thess. 2:3–8) 2. Does my life unmistakably model what I ask my hearers to do? (1 Thess. 2:10–14; Acts 27:22, 25; 1 Cor 11:1; Acts 11:23–24). 3. Am I providing practical, relevant application to the lives and conditions of my hearers as the Spirit of God grants wisdom? (Luke 3:1–18; 2 Thess. 3:4–15; Titus 2; Jude 3). 4. Because there is no deviating to right or left from the path of life, am I clear in reproving, rebuking, correcting as I exhort? (Rom 15:14, Col. 1:27–29; 2 Tim. 3:16–4:12; Acts 13:15, 38–41 cf. Deut 12:32; Jas. 1:7–9; 1 Thess. 2:11–12). 5. Do I abundantly illustrate and illumine my exhortation? (Luke 11:27–12:40, Mark 4:24–45). 6. Do I seek a holy skill to persuade, encourage and move my hearers? (Acts 3:19–4:2, 26:22–29, John 14:21, 15:9–13; Hab 12:5–17). 7. Do I use sung praise to enforce and assimilate my exhortation? Col.3:16). 8. Do I exhort with authority derived from confidence in Christ and His Word? (Tit. 2:15; 1 Thess. 4:1–2). 9. Do my exhortations express an affectionate devotion to my hearers in Christ? (2 Thess. 2:7, 8, 11, 3:8). 10. Do I exhort in dependence upon the Holy Ghost to make His Word effectual in our lives, with faith that God will indeed will and work in us to will and do His good pleasure? (Acts 11:23–24; 1 Thess. 2:13; Phil. 2:13).

Holy Father, who hast loved me, and in Thy blessed Son Jesus Christ given me everlasting consolation and good hope through grace, comfort me in every good word and work for Thy kingdom. Make me as Thy servant Barnabas "a good man, full of the Holy Ghost and of faith," that I may exhort Thy people with purpose of heart to cleave to the Lord Jesus, for whose sake I ask it, Amen. (2 Thess. 2:16–17; Acts 11:22–24, 4:36).

84. Great Grace upon us All

1 Lord, Thou art God alone!
All heaven and earth is Thine:
Behold us from Thy gracious throne
Thine ear to us incline.

2 In earnest, urgent prayer
We join to seek Thy face:
As we assemble, meet us there
In might, and shake the place!

3 Behold our threatening foes:
Restrain their wrathful ways
Till all who now Thy reign oppose
Be made to sing Thy praise!

4 Stretch forth Thy hand to seal
The preaching of Thy Word:
In Jesus Christ Thy Son, reveal
The glory of the Lord!

5 Grant all our longing hearts
To feel the Holy Ghost,
Till in the fullness He imparts
We boldly seek the lost.

6 O Father, in this hour,
In Jesu's Name we call:
Send in Thy Holy Spirit's power
Great grace upon us all!

S.M.

The House of God

> Preparatory Reading: Old Testament: 2 Kings 3
> New Testament: 1 Peter 5 Psalm: 84

1 Timothy 4:13

13 Till I come, give attendance to reading, to exhortation, to doctrine

Give attendance . . . to doctrine: From *reading* the Scriptures I am to furnish the *doctrine* which grounds and shapes my *exhortation*. From *doctrine* I am to "reprove, rebuke, and exhort with all longsuffering" (2 Tim. 4:2). Without "sound doctrine" which is "the truth," I would have nothing but "fables" or "the traditions of men" 2 Tim. 4:2–3; Mark 7:7). How precious, vital and liberating is the blessing of every true Christian to "abide in the doctrine of Christ!" So to abide by faith is to abide in the Lord Jesus Himself (2 John 9; 1 John 2:24, 27–28). How humbling and heavy then the charge laid upon me for my congregation and community both for this time and time to come, to "feed the flock of God, which He hath redeemed with His own Blood" (Acts 20:28); to work as "a faithful and wise steward . . . a ruler over the Lord's household, to give them their portion of meat in due season" (Luke 12:42), providing milk for babes and strong meat for men (1 Cor 3:1–2, Heb. 5:11–14). Has my God fulfilled in me to those I shepherd His promise: "I will give you pastors according to Mine heart, which shall feed you with knowledge and understanding?" (Jer 3:15). Or will I be to them His threat: "Woe be unto the pastors that destroy and scatter the sheep of my pasture! saith the LORD" "His watchmen are blind; they are all ignorant, they are all dumb dogs, they cannot bark . . . they are shepherds that cannot understand" "In vain do they worship Me, teaching for doctrines the commandments of men?" (Jer 23:1; Is. 45:10–11; Mark 7:7). Surely I must keep as close a watch on "the doctrine" as on my own soul, and "wait on teaching" (1 Tim. 4:16; Rom 12:7). Let me *give attendance . . . to doctrine:*

1. Does my teaching carry the authority of Christ from His Word, proven by my own experience of faith and obedience? (Matt 7:29, Mark 1:27, Luke 4:14–32, John 7:14–17. 2. Has my teaching simplicity common folk can grasp? (Mark 4:1, 33–34, 12:37–40). 3. Do I teach with confident faith that sound doctrine will effectually work in my hearers? (John 17:17; Acts 20:32; 1 Tim. 6:2–3) 4. Is my doctrine presented to advance the Gospel of Christ crucified? (Mark 8:31–38, 9:30–32; Luke 24:25–27, 44; Acts 8:35, Luke 9:1,6; Matt 28:18–20; Acts 19:11, 20:20–21). 5. Is my teaching rounded, comprehensive of the whole counsel of God in Scripture? (Acts 11:26, 20:25–27; Luke 1:1–4; Acts 26:22–23, 1 Cor 2:12–14:6). 6. Do I teach boldly, zealously, constantly, despising sham, pretence or complacency? (Mark 11:13–18; Acts 4:31, 18:24–28, 28:31, 5:42; Luke 20:21–26; Mark 12:38–40, John 18:19–23). 7. Do I teach with sincerity, untouched by mercenary or vain ambitions? (2 Cor 2:17, 4:1–6; Tit. 2:7–8). 8. Is my teaching sustained by prayer? Am I learning to pray through the doctrines I teach? (Luke 11:1–13; John 15:7). 9. Am I teaching wisely, fitting the doctrine to the needs of my hearers, applying the doctrine practically to their lives? (Mark 6:2; Luke 6:20–7). 10. Am I teaching sound doctrine with entire dependence on the Spirit of truth indwelling me and my hearers? (1 Cor 2:1–5, Luke 21:13–15; John 14: 23–26, 16:13–14, Acts 5:28–32, 18:4–5, 11).

85. Ye People, Great and Small

1 Ye people, great and small,
Of every clan and race—
Now hear the Savior call,
In words of truth and grace:
"The Son of Man His life did give
A ransom free, that ye might live!"

2 Ye straying sheep, and lost,
See our Good Shepherd come
To save at highest cost
And bring you safely home!
"His life did this Good Shepherd give—
O follow, hear His voice and live!"

3 In this world, without hope,
Ye strangers far from God,
From heaven Christ did stoop
To bring you nigh by Blood!
The Son of God Himself did give
In love for you, in Him to live!

4 Ye serpent-bitten souls,
Sickened and soon to die—
Upon a wooden pole
The Son is lifted high!
God loved the world, His Son to give—
Upon His Cross now look, and live!

5 In sin and trespass dead,
Ye dwellers in the grave,
Christ hath for sin once bled,
And died and ris'n to save!
Eternal life the Son shall give—
O hear His call, 'Come forth and live!'

6 Whoso receives the Son,
This record has within:
"The Blood of Jesus Christ
Doth cleanse us from all sin."
This is the record God doth give:
Believe on Christ, and thou shalt live!

The House of God

7 Three Witnesses in Heaven
On high—the Father, Son,
And Holy Ghost have given
This record—They are One:
Unspeakable the Gift God gives:
In Jesus Christ believers live

6.6.6.6.8.8.

The House of God

Preparatory Reading: Old Testament: 2 Kings 4;
  New Testament: 2 Peter 1 Psalm: 85

1 Timothy 4:14–15

14Neglect not the gift that is in thee, which was given thee by prophecy, with the laying on of the hands of the presbytery. 15Meditate upon these things; give thyself wholly to them; that thy profiting may appear to all.

As Paul unfolds to Timothy how to "command and teach these things" which are "the doctrine according to godliness" (4:11, 6:1–3) in this paragraph (4:11–16) he begins with our *example* (12). He continues with our practice and *education* through means (13). He then turns to our *endowments* from the Holy Spirit (14) and next to our consecrated *efforts* to advance in usefulness (15). At last he sums up his charge to the careful *examination* of our own life and ministry (16).

Nothing can replace saving, sanctifying grace in my soul as a minister of the Gospel. Though I speak or understand or give, "if I have not charity, I am nothing" (1 Cor 13:1–3). This charity is the love of God shed abroad in the heart by the Holy Ghost, commended to us in that while we were yet sinners, without strength, enemies, and ungodly, the Lord Christ Jesus died for us (Rom 5:5–11). From this springs all that I am as a pattern to others: "Be thou an example of the believers" (12). I can neither do nor teach without knowledge, so I must hear and do the royal law of liberty in the Word before I attempt to preach to others, lest I myself be found a castaway (Jas. 1:25, 3:13; 1 Cor 9:27). Hence, "give attendance to reading, to exhortation, to doctrine" (13).

Yet these cannot 'make' me a minister of the Word—even as a man may be trained in music but have no heart for it as a life-work. The gift and calling of God makes and marks a true minister of Christ and steward of His mysteries. Every pastor, teacher, elder should say no less than the Apostle, "I was made a minister according to the gift of the grace of God given unto me by the effectual working of His power. To me is this grace given, that I should preach . . . the unsearchable riches of Christ" (Eph 3:7–8). "As every man hath received the gift, even so minister . . ." (1 Pet. 4:10–11). So Paul points Timothy, once his conversion and character are assured, once his convictions are matured, to his own personal divine call to the ministry: *neglect not the gift that is in thee* (14). *The gift*: this is the skill, aptitude, and constraining compunction for which our "reading . . . exhortation . . . doctrine" are but tools. *The gift that is in thee*: this is a unique bestowal of the Holy Ghost by the Lord Jesus; it is not an attainment we achieve, not a talent we possess, but rooted in our souls as new creatures in Christ—*the gift* that fits and places us in the Body of Christ for our designed role (Eph 4:11–15, *the gift* which marks the proprietary rights of the ascended Christ over His captives (Ep. 4:4–10; Ps 68:18–19), *the gift* which shows the "manifestation of the Spirit" given to all for the care of all (1 Cor 12:4, 7, 25). By *gift* we wait on our ministering, teaching exhortation (Rom 12:6–8).

86. Jesus, Lord over All

1 Jesus, Lord over all,
To all Thou art the same ,
Thy mercy rich to such as call
Upon Thy saving Name!

2 How then, can men confess,
Except they first believe?
And how believe Thee and be blest,
Except Thy Word receive?

3 How can Thy truth be heard,
Without a preacher sent
With beauteous feet, to bring Thy Word,
Glad tidings to present?

4 Thus faith by hearing comes,
And hearing, by Thy Word:
To nations, kindreds, hearths and homes
O call and send us, Lord!

5 Now is that Word brought nigh,
The Word of faith we preach,
To heart and mouth; ye need not die,
But to the Gospel reach.

6 Now with thy mouth confess
Jesus the Lord of all,
Trust with thine heart His righteousness
And on His Name now call!

7 Believe with all thine heart,
God raised Him from the grave:
Christ shall to thee His grace impart—
Thou surely shalt be saved!

8 To all the world's wide ends
Proclaim this glorious Word—
His great salvation God now sends
Through Jesus Christ our Lord!

S.M.

The House of God

Preparatory Reading: Old Testament: 2 Kings 5;
   New Testament: 2 Peter 2 Psalm: 86

1 Timothy 4:14-15

¹⁴Neglect not the gift that is in thee, which was given thee by prophecy, with the laying on of the hands of the presbytery. ¹⁵Meditate upon these things; give thyself wholly to them; that thy profiting may appear to all.

Paul reminds Timothy *the gift . . . was given thee by prophecy*. Much more led Timothy to this holy work than the commendation of other believers among the churches—though that was given (Acts 16:2-3); more than Paul's assessment and enlistment—though he clearly loved him as a son (Acts 16:2-3). Timothy received this charge "according to the prophecies which went before on thee" (1:9). Paul says, *the gift that is in thee . . . was given thee by prophecy*. Now what does this mean? And how does it relate to other pastors, elders, teachers called to be bishops and stewards in God's household? Am I charged to the ministry, is mine a *gift given by prophecy*? There can be no doubt Paul himself was given his apostolic ministry *by prophecy*. The Lord Jesus Himself revealed to Ananias His choice and sovereign appointment of the persecutor and blasphemer Saul to this end (Acts 9:15-16). He later bade Paul leave Jerusalem for Tarsus with this charge (Acts 21:17-23). Then, at the appointed time, after his year or more of ministry alongside Barnabas at Antioch (Acts 11:25-26, 36; 12:24-25), the Spirit called him to go (Acts 13:1-5). Extraordinary revelation of the Word by the Spirit called Paul *by prophecy*, just as he knew his future trials *by prophecy* (Acts 20:22-23, 21:4, 8, 18). Perhaps in some such way the Word of the Lord *by prophecy* singled out young Timothy to his labors. Was this common in those early days of "signs and wonders . . . divers miracles and gifts of the Holy Ghost?" (Heb. 2:4). No such oracles are recorded of John Mark (Acts 12:24-25). And though Mark failed and faltered at the start of his service (Acts 13:5, 13; 15:28), through Barnabas' wise care he returned to ministry and at last proved himself profitable even to Paul (Acts 15:39; Col. 4:10; 2 Tim. 4:11). No word of any such things concerns Titus. Looking back through Scripture, the Word of the Lord was given in old time to appoint God's servants by name. So Moses was directed to Joshua (Num 27:15-23; Deut 31:7-8, 34:9). Elijah was sent to Elisha (1 Kgs 19:15-21; 2 Kgs 2). Samuel was pointed to "little David" (1 Sam 16:1-13. So what of today, of me? Certainly the congruence of a man's life and gifts with the standards of the office in the Bible verifies a *gift . . . given . . . by prophecy*. John the Apostle says, "Demetrius has good report of all men, and of the truth itself" (3 John 12). The preaching of the Word in the Spirit's unction which at ordination lays upon us the charge of ministry in a sense confirms a *gift . . . given . . . by prophecy* (1 Cor 2:4-5; Ps 68:11; 2 Tim. 4:1-5; 1 Tim. 1:18, 6:11-16, 10-11; Josh 1:2-9). And in every man's call the Spirit uses the Word in different ways to move us inwardly to offer our lives to the Lord in service, just as the Word works effectually in all saints by faith (1 Thess. 2:13). The Spirit confers His gifts through His Word, and so *by prophecy*.

87. Wilt Thou not Revive us, Lord?

1 "Wilt Thou not revive us, Lord?"
Hear our prayer with one accord:
Let us hear Thy quickening voice,
That Thy people may rejoice!

2 Father and Almighty God,
Underneath Thy chastening rod,
For Thy mercy now we plead,
And Thy grace in time of need!

3 Prince and Savior, Jesus, Lord!
Now refresh us by Thy Word:
O revive us in this hour
By thy risen, saving power!

4 Holy Spirit, Lord and God,
To our souls apply the Blood
Which our Savior on the Tree
Shed for sin to set us free!

5 Fill our souls with in ward might,
Holy boldness, life and light,
Till we show in prayer and praise
Thy salvation all our days!

6 Lord Jehovah—Father, Son,
Holy Ghost—the Three in One
In the midst of wrath, recall
Mercy, and revive us all!

7.7.7.7.

Preparatory Reading: Old Testament: 2 Kings 6;
   New Testament: 2 Peter 3 Psalm: 87

1 Timothy 4:14–15

¹⁴Neglect not the gift that is in thee, which was given thee by prophecy, with the laying on of the hands of the presbytery. ¹⁵Meditate upon these things; give thyself wholly to them; that thy profiting may appear to all.

Paul verifies Timothy's call and *gift . . . given . . . by prophecy* through an objective confirmation. Later he will recall, "the gift of God which is in thee by the putting on of my hands" (2 Tim. 1:6); here he says, *the gift . . . which was given thee . . . with the laying on of the hands of the presbytery*. Elders are ordained in every local church (Acts 14:23; they, like the members at large (Acts 16:2) have their part in discerning, declaring and endorsing the gift and calling of God. Letters of commendation cannot replace the gift (2 Cor 3:1–6, 10:17–18), but the gift will not lack commendation and letters as needed (Acts 18:24–28). In every letter of reference, in the certificate of ordination, in the accreditation which the local church and sister churches afford, formally or informally, the Lord Jesus as King and Head has confirmed *the gift that is in* me. A wider brotherhood of faithful men who in each congregation form *the presbytery* recognizes and reckons me accountable before God and men, for the stewardship of *the gift*.

The gift is mine, as it was Timothy's; no less valid because it is ordinary and not extraordinary; no less precious to my Master Christ because it is one talent and not five; no less solemn a task to feed a few lambs than to lead teeming flocks—for the King takes the least of His brethren as one with Himself, and appoints His angels before the Father as ministering spirits even to the little ones who believe on Him (Luke 19:20–26; John 21:15–16; Matt 25:40; Heb. 1:14; Matt 18:1–10).

So, says Paul, *neglect not the gift that is in thee*. *Neglect* is the careless use or omission of duties required of us or privileges granted us. Let me heed what Scripture sets down as my proper stewardship of *the gift*: "As every man hath received the gift, even so *minister* the same" "*Seek earnestly* the best gifts" "*Stir up* the gift that is in thee" "Having then differing gifts . . . let us *wait on* [them]" (1 Pet. 4:11, 1 Cor 12:31, 14:1; 2 Tim. 1:6, Rom 12:6–8). I *neglect the gift* when I do not humbly acknowledge it as Christ's treasure, talent and trust to me; when I do not use it in earnest faith; when I do not actively strive for its best, fullest use; when I do not seek its widest sphere to the good of saints or sinners; when I do not persevere in practicing or perfecting it to the profit of all; when I presume upon it without prayerful dependence on the Holy Spirit effectually to work by it; when I grieve the Holy Spirit of God by sin and serious decay of piety or morality.

Lord Jesus, let me not be ashamed at Thy coming to have my one pound tied in a napkin and buried in the earth! Grant me to *neglect not the gift that is in* me, *given . . . with laying on of hands!*

88. Break Forth, My Soul

1 Break forth, my soul, in freedom
Stand in that liberty
From sin to service given
Wherewith Christ made thee free:
The Blood He shed at Calv'ry
All enmity hath slain:
Now to thy God and neighbor
Be reconciled again.

2 Break forth, my soul, with longing
God's Law now to fulfill:
The Comforter shall teach thee
To do His holy will.
Continue in the Scriptures—
King Jesus set thee free
In love to keep His statutes
And His disciple be.

3 Break forth, my soul, and journey—
The pilgrim's path take home.
The Dayspring, Star of Morning,
The Light of life has come!
His righteousness before thee,
His glory round, thy Shield;
His voice shall say, "Behold Me!"
And to thy prayer shall yield

4 Break forth, my soul, rejoicing
The word of Christ goes forth
To prosper in its purpose
Of grace through all the earth.
Afflicted saints, take comfort—
That Word goes not in vain:
The Church shall see her children
Rebuild her wastes again.

5 Break forth, my soul, in singing—
With mountain, hill and plain,
With field and forest ringing
Praise to the Lamb once slain!
He hath redeemed His people!

To ends of earth abroad,
All nations see in wonder
Salvation from our God

7.6.7.6.D

The House of God

Preparatory Reading: Old Testament: 2 Kings 7;
New Testament: John 1 Psalm: 88

1 Timothy 4:14–15

¹⁴Neglect not the gift that is in thee, which was given thee by prophecy, with the laying on of the hands of the presbytery. ¹⁵Meditate upon these things; give thyself wholly to them; that thy profiting may appear to all.

Meditate upon these things: Every believer is to find delight in the Law of the Lord by meditating in it day and night (Ps 1, 119:97). Every family is to be exercised in the Word through the day's work and rest (Deut 6:6–7). What I am to command and teach, what I read in order to give exhortation and doctrine, what I am to be as an example among believers (4:11–13)—I must *meditate upon these things*; I must consider and study them (2 Tim. 2:7, 15). A careful eater slowly, deliberately chews, a mouthful at a time, and swallows to digest and grow. Even so am I to ruminate over the Word (Josh 1:6); let Christ's sayings "sink down into" my "ears" (Luke 9:44); eat the roll of the Book proffered in vision, tasting the sweet and taking the bitter (Ezek 2:9–3:3; Jer 15:16–17; Rev. 10:5–11). The more the Word sanctifies me, the more will the Master fit me for His use (John 17:17; 2 Tim. 2:21). To give my ministry a disciplined, deliberative, designed direction, I must *meditate upon these things*. *Give thyself wholly to them:* In meditation, the ministry of the Word pre-occupies my thoughts. "Think on these things" says Paul; do not work mechanically, tediously by rote but intelligently, prayerfully, increasing in the knowledge of God and His will, growing in the grace and knowledge of the Lord Jesus Christ (Phil. 4:8; 1 Cor 14:15–19; Col. 1:9–14; 2 Pet. 3:18). In such concentrated devotion and effort, the ministry must pre-occupy my time and action. "Why call ye Me Lord, Lord, and do not the things that I say?" (Luke 6:46). King Ahab "sold himself to do evil;" shall I not give myself to do good? (1 Kgs 16:33, 21:25; Rom 6:11–23). Archippus deserved and received public rebuke for his lackadaisical ministry—a blot that stains his name to all generations in Holy Scripture (Col. 4:17), as much as Demas who forsook Christ's cause for the world (2 Tim. 4:10) or Iscariot who betrayed Him (Mark 3:19). A common magistrate works diligently as an agent of providence; must I not be more diligent as a herald of redemption? (Rom 13:6). I am to watch for men's souls so as to give account—what account will I give of my stewardship? (Heb. 13:17; Luke 16:2). A farmer, an athlete, a merchant, a laborer draw full-time pay for full-time work (2 Tim. 2:4–5). Have I a workload that justifies full-time support, in my prayer, closet study of the Word, sermon preparation, visitation, Gospel outreach, administration of church business, and opportunities for wider ministry by preaching or writing? Paul declares, "Even so hath the Lord ordained that they which preach the Gospel should live of the Gospel" "The laborer is worthy of his reward" (1 Cor 9:14; 1 Tim. 5:17–18). *Give thyself wholly to them.*

89. Good Tidings of Great Joy

1 *Good tidings of great joy*
Angels to shepherds bring:
"A Savior, Christ to you is born,
Of David's line the King!"

2 To seek and save the lost
Has this Good Shepherd come:
Upon His shoulders He will bear
His sheep rejoicing home.

3 The joy before Him set
Endured the Cross of Blood,
Despising all its shame to gain
The right-hand Throne of God.

4 *His joy in us remains:*
Abiding in His love,
We taste the great exceeding joy
Which we shall share above.

5 O magnify the Lord
In song lift up thy voice:
"In God my Savior—Jesus Christ
My heart and soul rejoice!"

6 Unspeakable this joy!
We full of glory raise
To Father, Son and Holy Ghost,
Our God and Savior's praise!

S.M.

The House of God

Preparatory Reading: Old Testament: 2 Kings 8;
New Testament: John 2 Psalm: 89

1 Timothy 4:14-15

14Neglect not the gift that is in thee, which was given thee by prophecy, with the laying on of the hands of the presbytery. 15Meditate upon these things; give thyself wholly to them; that thy profiting may appear to all.

Meditate . . . give thyself . . . that thy profiting may appear to all: Love for my Savior should move my mind ever to stray home toward His Word and His work, as an ox to its crib, the bird to its nest; all I do, even in leisure, recreation or daily living should be honed to serve my fitness to ministry. All I do ought to work together to this goal as my master passion—*that thy profiting may appear to all*. Well would it serve me to review each year, or more often, what *profiting may appear to all* in my service. Am I more constant, fervent as "an example of the believers in word, in conversation, in charity, in spirit, in faith, in purity?" (12). Has my "reading" of the Holy Scriptures, of sound books, of general knowledge really deepened, broadened or ripened my understanding and discernment? How rounded, clear, simple, practical is the "doctrine" I expound? How much more wise, wooing, winsome or winning has the "exhortation" become? (13). Have I really grown up into the fullness of the stature of the manhood of Christ? Have I profited others, or are they simply hearing year by year the same tyro's prattle? Paul demands that Timothy make such progress *that thy profiting may appear to all*. So what *profiting* appears to the small children? the teens? The young couples? the seniors? the newcomers to our land? The support I receive is a sacred trust; I "live of the Gospel" from the tithes and offerings of God's people. Let me ask myself straight out: Is there value for money? Is there better value this year than last? *Give thyself wholly to them; that thy profiting may appear to all.*

Forgive me, merciful God and Father, for wasted years standing pat instead of growing; for routine instead of excellence; for closing up instead of opening up to all the needs and challenges of the present age; for ready contentment with small things, rather than longing to call upon Thee to shew "great and mighty things" which I know not; for the sake of Thy dear Son Jesus Christ, by His Blood and merits, forgive all that is past and restore the years which the locusts have eaten! Cast me not away from Thy presence, nor take Thy Holy Spirit from me. Restore unto me the joy of my salvation, and uphold my with a willing spirit. Open my lips to show forth Thy praise, that I may teach Thy ways, and sinners be converted unto Thee. These things I dare to ask in the Name of Thy Son, Thy Servant, meek and lowly of heart, who neither breaks the bruised reed nor quenches the smoking flax, even the Lord Jesus, Amen. (Eph 4:13; Jer 33:1-3; Joel 2:23-27; Ps 51, Matt 12:20-21).

90. My Soul in Exultation will magnify the Lord

1 My soul in exaltation
Will magnify the Lord
Who brought to me salvation
According to His Word!
His precious Blood and merit
Has rescued me from night
And caused me to inherit
With all the saints in light!
O bless His Name and bear it
All glory, riches, might!

3 In humble expectation
I waited for His Word
Till, tasting His salvation
I cried, "It is the Lord!
He heals all my diseases,
From bondage sets me free,
I'll praise Thy Name, Lord Jesus
To all eternity!"
O bless the Name of Jesus,
The Christ of Calvary!

4 "All praise and adoration,
All glory to our King,
Our Captain of salvation,"
To Jesus, let us sing!
Who reigns in endless power
O'er earth and heaven's host,
One with th'Almighty Father,
One with the Holy Ghost!
One Triune God forever,
In Him alone we boast!

7.6.7.6.D with refrain.
Tune: German Lieder "Die Forelle" (Franz Schubert)

The House of God

Preparatory Reading: Old Testament: 2 Kings 9;
New Testament: John 3 Psalm: 90

1 Timothy 4:16

¹⁶Take heed unto thyself, and unto the doctrine; continue in them: for in doing this thou shalt both save thyself, and them that hear thee.

Paul had placed Timothy in Ephesus, in its own way as tranquil as Crete was turbulent—as suited to Timothy as Crete was for Titus (1:3; Tit. 1:12). Paul had left Timothy in a Church placed on alert. This is how he left its elders on his farewell at Miletus: "Take heed therefore unto yourselves, and to all the flock over the which the Holy Ghost hath made you overseers, to feed the Church of God, which He hath purchased with His own Blood . . . Therefore, watch . . . " (Acts 20:28, 31). Paul put Timothy on alert, too, as their pastor: "Charge some . . . this charge I commit unto thee. . . . I exhort . . . I will therefore . . . these things write I . . . I charge thee that thou observe these things . . . these things teach and exhort . . . I give thee charge that thou keep this commandment . . . charge them . . . O Timothy keep that which is committed to thy trust" (1:3, 18; 2:1, 8; 3:14–15; 5:21; 6:2, 13–14, 20). But Paul's supreme charge to Timothy is this: *take heed unto thyself and unto the doctrine*. The man and his message, his life and labor, his soul and his service need as much vigilant watch-care, as much close surveillance as the threat of heresy, the emergence of disorder, the decay of fellowship or the temptation to besetting sin. As a mother or nurse keeps wary of any symptom of illness or signs of mischief in her child; as an athlete 'listens' to the body's stresses and pains—so a true pastor must *take heed to self and doctrine*. All Paul has encouraged Timothy to do as an example (12), to use in his endowments (14), to make of his exertions (15) show how I too must *take heed unto myself*. All that the Apostle demands in advancing Timothy's education (13) and effectiveness (15)—these show how I must *take heed unto the doctrine*. Sedulous, jealous self-watch and constant attention to the Word are my work. The porter minds the door; the steward minds the larder (Mark 13:34; Matt 24:45–46). *Continue in them:* In the truths of the Scriptures (John 8:31–32; 2 Tim. 3:14), in the fellowship and faith of the local assembly (Acts 2:42), by these we keep the Savior's commandments and continue in His love (John 15:9–10, Jude 20–21). Only those who hear and keep the word, bringing forth fruit with patience are at last blessed (Luke 8:15); "he that endureth to the end shall be saved" (Matt 10:22. Continuing in the "perfect law of liberty" not as a forgetful hearer, but "a doer of the work" am I blessed (Jas. 1:25). The people's perseverance lies in part with the pastor's, no less in affliction than in joy (2 Cor 11:1; 1 Thess. 1:6; 2:24–26, 19–20; 3:3–4, 8; 4:1–2; 5:12–13). *For in so doing this thou shalt both save thyself and them that hear thee:* Isaiah bound himself and his disciples to the Word of the Lord (Isa 8:16–18); the Lord Jesus will present Himself with God's children (Heb. 2:10–13); Paul's crown of joy will be his children in the faith (1 Thess. 2:19–20; Gal 4:19–20; 1 Cor 4:14–17). What of me and mine?

91. Lord, Here We Stand!

1 *Lord, here we stand!* Our consciences are captive
Unto Thy Word; forbid our hearts should faint:
Loose Thou our tongues, to tell in praises festive
The faith delivered once unto the saints!
Lord, here we stand! Keep Thou our hearts receptive
To hear and hold Thy Gospel without taint!

2 *Scripture alone!* Thy Word is truth unerring,
Breathed by the Holy Ghost through holy men;
To Christ's redemption witness fully bearing,
Sole rule of faith, life, worship now as then.
Scripture alone! Teach us, its truths comparing,
To hear Thy voice above the din of men.

3 *By grace alone!* Apart from human merit,
God shows His love to sinners lost, undone;
That He might freely grant us to inherit
Life everlasting, He sent forth His Son.
By grace alone! To all the world declare it—
In Jesus Christ, God has salvation won!

4 *By Christ alone!* To us has come salvation—
Through His obedience and atoning Blood!
Our only High Priest, and our sure Foundation;
King and sole Head to all the Church of God!
By Christ alone! Our Shepherd great is risen,
And leads His people by His staff and rod.

5 *By faith alone!* Our hearts are resting solely
On that one offering made at Calvary
Which our Lord Jesus finished, paying wholly
For our transgressions, and iniquity.
By faith alone! We've peace with God Most Holy,
Now justified, accepted and set free.

6 *Only in Scripture* is the truth that frees us
Only by grace in liberty we stand
Only in Christ accepted God now sees us:
Only by faith we live; for us is planned
A life of loving service that Him pleases:
Upon this Gospel true—*Lord, here we stand!*

The House of God

7 We praise Thee now, Thy saints, redeemed, forgiven,
Triune Jehovah, God our Shield and Sun!
All praises to the Holy Father in heaven,
Only begotten, and eternal Son,
Blest Holy Spirit, to His people given—
All glory give to God the Three in One!

11.10.11.10.11.10
Tune: Finlandia (Jean Sibelius)

Preparatory Reading: Old Testament: 2 Kings 10;
 New Testament: John 4 Psalm: 91

1 Timothy: Reading over Chapter 4

The Apostle has taken this chapter to set before me two paths of conduct, two courses for my future, two directions my life may be spent to influence the churches and the world. He faithfully reflects the challenge our Savior issues to everyone in every age: choose the goal, guides and grounds of your life for time and eternity (Matt 7:13–29). Which will I choose? The narrow or the broad? The way of life, or the way of destruction? An enduring bedrock, or a shifting surface? Let me once more read over this chapter, and choose, not my own, but the things of Jesus Christ.

Prayer for the Gospel Ministry

O Lord, I have heard Thy speech, and was afraid:
O Lord, revive Thy work in the midst of the years,
In wrath remember mercy.
Wilt Thou not revive us again,
That Thy people may rejoice in Thee?
Shew us Thy mercy, O Lord, and grant us Thy salvation.
I will hear what God the Lord will speak
For He will speak peace unto His people and to His saints
But let them not turn again to folly.

Speak, Lord, for Thy servant heareth.
O Lord, truly I am Thy servant:
I am Thy servant, and the son of Thy handmaid;
Thou hast loosed my bonds.
I am not worthy of the least of all the mercies and of all the truth
Which Thou hast shewed unto Thy servant
For I am an unprofitable servant,
Unworthy to loose Thy shoe's latchet.
Fain would I cry, Depart from me, O Lord, for I am a sinful man!

Yet all power is given Thee, Lord Jesus, in heaven and in earth:
Raised from the dead, set in heaven
Far above all principality and power, and might and dominion,
And every name that is named in this world or that which is to come.
Behold, Thou comest with clouds, and every eye shall see Thee
In the glory Thy Father with His angels,
And then shalt Thou reward every man according to his works.
By Thee shall God judge the secrets of men according to Thy Gospel

The House of God

Every knee shall bow
Of things in heaven, in earth and under the earth
And every tongue shall confess Thee
Jesus is Lord
To the glory of God the Father.
We must all appear before that judgment seat of Christ
That everyone may receive the things done in his body
According that he hath done, whether good or bad.

Hide not Thy face from me; put not Thy servant away in anger;
Leave me not, neither forsake me, O God of my salvation.
To each according to his ability
Hast Thou put us in trust of the Gospel:
Thou hast said, 'Occupy till I come'.

Thou art our Prince and Savior,
The blessed and only Potentate,
King of kings and Lord of lords;
We are ambassadors for Christ, reconciled and committed the Word of reconciliation.
Thou art the good Shepherd which gavest Thy life for the sheep
Brought again from the dead
By the Blood of the everlasting covenant
And Thou hast made us overseers to feed the flock of God
Which Thou hast purchased with Thine own Blood.

Thou art the Bridegroom
And we are Thy friends and servants,
Rejoicing to hear Thy voice:
Thou must increase,
We must decrease.

Thou art the Lord of the harvest:
And we are Thy laborers, sent forth into Thy harvest,
And Thou hast said,
'He that heareth you hearth Me,
And he that heareth Me, heareth Him that sent Me.'

Who shall stand before Thee in the day that Thou appearest?
Who is sufficient for these things?
Make us able ministers of the New Testament;
Not of the letter that killeth, but the Spirit that giveth life!
Let Thy love constrain us to live to Thee
Who for us hast died and risen again;

The House of God

Let me take heed to myself
Let me take heed to all the flock
Let me take heed to the doctrine:
Make me a workman approved and unashamed,
Rightly dividing the Word of truth,
Knowing the Holy Scriptures
Which are able to make us wise to salvation through faith in Thee
Christ Jesus.

Lord, Thou knowest that I love Thee:
Let me feed Thy sheep and feed Thy lambs:
Shew me now Thy way, that I may know Thee;
If Thy presence go not with me, carry me not up hence;
I beseech Thee, shew me Thy glory!

O God, reveal Thy Son in me
That I might preach Christ,
Warning, teaching every man in all wisdom
That I might present every man perfect in Christ Jesus;
Labouring, striving according to Thy working
which worketh in me mightily

Make us unto Thee a sweet savor of Christ
As of sincerity, as of God, in the sight of God
Speak we in Christ.

We ask it
That the Father be glorified in the Son by the Holy Ghost;
We ask it in the Name of Jesus.
Amen.

92. How great Thy love to me!

1 How great the love to me,
Savior which Thou hast given,
From all eternity
To leave the throne of heaven
Angels in wonder gaze
Down at the mystery
Of Thy humility
Glorious in all its grace.

2 How great to me that love,
Jesus, Thou Son of God,
Which brought Thee from above
To take our flesh and blood
Incarnate Holy Child,
Seeking to save the lost
Conceived of Holy Ghost
Born of the Virgin mild

3 How great the love to me
Which angel hosts declare
Which shepherds come to see
Laid in a manger bare
Heaven and earth now sings
How in His love He came
To bear our sin and shame,
Jesus, the King of kings.

4 How great that love and true
Jesus, Thou Servant meek
Did all thy steps pursue
Sinners to save and seek
All of our woe and pain,
And our afflictions sore
Thou in Thy Body bore
Our sinful souls to gain.

5 How great the love to me
Jesus, Emmanuel
Which led to Calvary
And to the depths of hell
There on the cursed cross

The House of God

To death Thou didst obey
My ransom price to pay
All to redeem my loss

6 How great Thy love and free
Jesus, whose Blood was shed
Which won the victory
Raising Thee from the dead
Exalted to the throne
Ever for me to plead
High Priest and King, my need
Thou shalt supply alone.

6.6.6.6.D
Tune: Quebecois Song
"Un Canadien Errant"

The House of God

Preparatory Reading: Old Testament: 2 Kings 11;
New Testament: John 5 Psalm: 92

1 Timothy 5:1-2

¹Rebuke not an elder, but intreat *him* as a father; *and* the younger men as brethren; ²The elder women as mothers; the younger as sisters, with all purity.

Elder . . . younger men . . . older women . . . younger women: "Ye are all the children of God through faith in Christ Jesus. For as many of you as have been baptized in Christ have put on Christ" (Gal 3:26–27). We are "predestinated unto the adoption of children by Jesus Christ unto Himself" (Eph 1:5). Our Lord Jesus says, "Whosoever shall do the will of My Father which is in heaven, the same is My brother and sister and mother" (Matt 12:50). "One is your Master, even Christ; and all ye are brethren" (Matt 23:8). All these testimonies show the blessing of adoption and the family bond it creates in the Churches as the "household of faith" (Eph 2:19; 3:14–16). That bond must be nourished and cherished at cost: "If there be any consolation in Christ, if any comfort of love, if any fellowship of the Spirit, if any . . . mercies . . . be likeminded, having the same love, being of one accord, of one mind" (Phil. 2:1–2). "Be ye all of one mind, having compassion one of another, love as brethren, be pitiful, be courteous" (1 Pet. 3:8).

Paul now instructs Timothy how to care for the relationships among the members of the congregation (chapter 5) as closely and practically as he has directed his ministry, life, doctrine and conduct toward heresy (chs.1–4). All my dealings with Christ's people, whether member, officer, adherent or seeker must be governed by the Savior's new commandment, enforced by Peter—"a new commandment I give unto you, that ye love one another; as I have loved you, that ye also love one another. By this shall all men know that ye are My disciples, if ye have love one to another." "Love the brotherhood" (John 13:34–35; 1 Pet. 2:17).

Once more, Timothy sets the tone and terms of all working relations in this brotherhood; he leads by example, as must I. As I deal with them, they will tend to deal with each other. "Be kindly affectioned one to another with brotherly love" "Let brotherly love continue" (Rom 12:10; Heb. 13:1). The *elder* now in view fits into the pattern of age and gender which God has ordained from the creation (Gen 1:27–28, and which the Moral Law at the heart of Holy Scripture sustains: "Honour thy father and thy mother" (Exod 20:12; Mark 7:10–13). These created distinctions still govern the relations in the Church of saints who before God are "all one in Christ Jesus" (Gal 3:28; 1 Cor 11:3, 8–9, 11; 1 Tim. 2:11–15). To undermine them is to destroy the family; to ignore them in the Church is to create confusion, not peace (1 Cor 14:33–35; Rom 1:26–30). What our catechisms tag "the duty and honor belonging to everyone in their several places and relations" is here outlined in divine order as *elder, younger men, elder women, younger women.*

93. Where shall I find the Holy Child?

1 Where shall I find the Holy Child,
Born of the Virgin blest,
Who comes to earth in mercy mild
To bring us heaven's rest?

2 Where may I see the infant King,
Whose long-awaited birth
Bids heaven's host all join to sing
"Praise God for peace on earth!"

3 The night reveals no beaming star
To guide my doubting feet:
No anxious Magi from afar
In search of Him I meet!

4 Through princes' palaces I look,
But cannot find Him there;
Proud scholars cite the sacred Book
But for Him do not care.

5 Yet may I find Him in the place
To which the Scriptures lead;
And from His fullness, grace on grace
Receive in all my need

6 I trace the path which once He trod
From manger to the Tree,
Where by His merits and His Blood
He bought redemption free.

7 Beyond the Tomb whence He arose
I seek the Throne of grace
Where He shall bring the saints He chose
And see them face to face.

8 O glorious Dayspring from on high,
O Sun of righteousness,
Shine in my heart, to me draw nigh,
With Thy salvation bless!

The House of God

9 According to His promised Word,
When days on earth shall cease,
I shall, still trusting Christ the Lord,
To heaven depart in peace!

C.M.

Preparatory Reading: Old Testament: 2 Kings 12;
  New Testament: John 6 Psalm: 93

1 Timothy 5:1–2

5:1 Rebuke not an elder, but intreat *him* as a father; *and* the younger men as brethren; 2 The elder women as mothers; the younger as sisters, with all purity.

Rebuke not an elder, but intreat him as a father, says Paul. Toward older men the abiding norm of my ministry is respect and deference. "Thou shalt rise up before the hoary head, and honour the face of the old man, and fear thy God: I am the Lord" (Lev 19:32). That respect is the higher as the elderly show the wisdom and integrity age should bring: "The hoary head is a crown of glory, if it be found in the way of righteousness" (Prov 16:31). But old men are not always wise, or right, even as saints in Christ, because of age. "Great men are not always wise, neither do the aged understand judgment" (Job 32:9). Then, even then, Paul checks the exasperation of younger men; he bridles the tongue from impertinence, he directs us to express humility and preserve goodwill in our response—*rebuke not . . . intreat him as a father.* Would the tact and even-tempered gentleness of this entreaty be any less than the servants of Naaman the Syrian showed when "he turned and went away in a rage?" It is written, "His servants came near and spake unto him saying, 'My father, if the prophet had bid thee do some great thing, wouldest thou not have done it? how much rather then, when he saith to thee, Wash and be clean?'" (2 Kgs 5:12–13). The defects or deficiencies of older men require the full measure of charity that humbly, meekly forbears and forgives to sustain the "bond of perfectness" (Col. 3:13–14). How much bitterness, contention, alienation and suspicion has festered in congregations, among elders, deacons and members because we have forgotten to humble ourselves before God? "Ye younger, submit yourselves unto the elders. Yea, all of you, be subject one to another and be clothed with humility; for God resisteth the proud, and giveth grace to the humble" (1 Pet. 5:5–7). Were our hearts wholly given to Christ and governed by His mind, would this not be our proper impulse? *Rebuke not an elder, but intreat him as a father.*

Father of mercies, pardon and forgive all my vehemence, rash zeal, brusque manner, all that has been so unlike the meekness and gentleness of Christ toward older men in the ministry, toward older brethren, toward my father and older relatives. Wash me thoroughly from mine iniquity, and cleanse me from my sin by the Blood of the Lamb, offered once for all at Calvary, who sits now at the right and hand of the majesty on high. Forbid me so to sin again. Teach me this: *rebuke not an elder, but intreat him as a father.* Hear me, fill me with the Holy Ghost and faith, so to do and teach, for Jesu's sake, Amen.

94. Sing Forth Salvation's Glad New Song

1 Sing forth salvation's glad new song,
As kings and priests redeemed to God
From every people, tribe and tongue
By Christ the Lamb's most precious Blood!

2 Called out of darkness into light
A people formed to tell His praise,
Declare in all the nations' sight
The glory of the God of grace!

3 To north and south, to east and west
Now let the Bride and Spirit call,
Bid all earth's families to be blest
Proclaiming Jesus Lord of all!

4 Throughout the earth, the seas, the sky,
From streaks of dawn to sunset glow,
Let all the saints of God most High
Each day Thy great salvation show!

5 O Father, Son and Holy Ghost,
Jehovah, glorious One in Three,
We make Thy Name alone our boast
Through time and to eternity!

L.M.

Preparatory Reading: Old Testament: 2 Kings 13;
   New Testament: John 7 Psalm: 94

1 Timothy 5:1–2

¹Rebuke not an elder, but intreat *him* as a father; *and* the younger men as brethren; ²The elder women as mothers; the younger as sisters, with all purity.

And the younger men as brethren: to these members, no less than to older men, Paul's injunctions apply: *rebuke not . . . intreat.*

How little brotherly love, brotherly kindness has marked the relations of believers, even within families? The story of God's elect Church is stained through the ages by strife: Cain and Abel, Isaac and Ishmael, Esau and Jacob, Joseph and his brethren, Adonijah and Solomon, in the Old Testament (Gen 4, 21, 26, 37; 1 Kgs 1–2); Zebedee's sons and the ten disciples, Diotrephes, the envious brethren at Rome who preached only to plague Paul, in the New (Mark 10; 3 John, Phil. 1).

How rare, and beautiful, to see that love of the brethren which marks the grace of the Gospel in regenerate souls—"Behold, how good and how pleasant it is for brethren to dwell together in unity! . . . For there the LORD commanded the blessing, even life forevermore." "We know that we have passed from death unto life, because we love the brethren. . . . And this is His commandment that we should believe on the Name of His Son Jesus Christ, and love one another, as He gave us commandment" (Ps 133:1, 3; 1 John 3:14, 23–24).

Paul's Epistles breathe with this humility while he teaches, exhorts, admonishes, warns and reproves his converts as "beloved brethren;" whether the faithful Philippians or contentious Corinthians, he never condescends, always appeals to this bond—"Brethren!" If Timothy's own youth need not be despised (13), neither should others. Says aging John, "I have written unto you, young men, because you are strong, and the Word of God abideth in you, and ye have overcome the wicked one" (1 John 2:14). *Do not rebuke . . . but intreat . . . younger men as brethren*: aim to retain their zeal while restraining their zeal without knowledge; keep their confidence and loyalty by affection rather than constrain it by bare authority.

The elder women as mothers: Womankind, ever the fount of human life, can bring to us either precious blessing or pernicious bane (Gen 3:20). Paul looks for great grace in younger and older women (2:9–10, 15; 5:9–10, 14; Titus 2:3–5), yet he also knows to what errors they are prey (1 Tim. 2:11–12, 4:7, 5:11–13; 2 Tim. 2:16, 3:6). Every believing woman of age should receive the affectionate respect, attention and patient entreaty due to our *mothers*. The God of all grace truly sets us in families, even as He raises us from paupers to princes (Ps 113:7–9). How happy would our older sisters be to have the pastors, elders, and members embrace and cherish them as *mothers*. No assembly of Christians can afford to neglect or discard their *elder women* as *mothers* to the Church, with their love, wisdom and devotion to Christ Jesus.

95. With All My Heart I Hearken

1 With all my heart I hearken
Unto Thy voice, O Lord,
And turn from my transgression
To keep Thy written Word: (Deut 30)
With all my heart I seek Thee
And find Thy truth and grace
Revealed with all Thy glory
In my Lord Jesu's face.   (Jer 29; 2 Cor 4)

2 O Lord my God, *to love Thee*
With all my heart and soul
And mind and strength within me
Thy Law hath e'er me told.   (Deut 8)
To walk in Thy commandments
With all my soul and heart,
I stand to keep the Covenant
Thy written Words impart.   (1 Kg 22)

3 With all my heart I praise Thee,
O Lord my God; Thy Name
I glorify, Thy mercy—
From age to age the same: (Ps 108)
With all my heart I trust Thee
And e'er in all my ways
Acknowledge Thee to guide me
Thy wisdom's path to trace.   (Prov 3)

4 With all my heart I love Thee,
And serve Thee, O Lord God—
That heart is circumcised,
And washed in Jesu's Blood: (Deut 30)
O Father, Son and Spirit,
To Thee my heart I raise
Most promptly and sincerely
In sacrifice of praise.   [Calvin's Motto]

7.6.7.6D

The House of God

Preparatory Reading: Old Testament: Nehemiah 1;
  New Testament: John 8 Psalm: 95

1 Timothy 5:1–2

¹Rebuke not an elder, but intreat *him* as a father; *and* the younger men as brethren; ²The elder women as mothers; the younger as sisters, with all purity.

The younger as sisters, with all purity: The women who heard and believed the Gospel in Ephesus, where Timothy was sent to labor, had been translated from darkness to light. In a city shadowed by the temple of Artemis, filled with shouts of "Great is Diana of the Ephesians!" no doubt some, possibly most, had passed the whole of girlhood and womanhood shaped by squalid heathen immorality in heart, mind, speech and act (Eph 4:17–19, 5:3–5). So many girls and women of today pass their lives into old age, soiled and stained, "laden with divers lusts" (2 Tim. 3:6). But these who as children of wrath, as fornicators, adulteresses, and harlots could not enter the kingdom of God, these were "washed, sanctified, justified in the Name of the Lord Jesus, and by the Spirit of our God" (1 Cor 6:9–10). They found compassion, mercy, forgiveness, cleansing from the Savior, a Friend to publicans and harlots, who receives sinners, calls them to repentance and eats with them (Matt 11:10; Luke 15:1–2; Mark 2:17). They became members of His mystical Body, joined to Him by one Spirit (1 Cor 6:15–20).

Can there be then anything more treacherous, or disgusting, than to witness or suspect that a minister of Christ stains his exhortation with "uncleanness or guile" (1 Thess. 2:3); to discern the lineaments of a false teacher in "an unstable, beguiling soul . . . having eyes full of adultery, that cannot cease from sin?" (2 Pet. 2:14). The Jezebel or Balaam in the Church who condones or encourages any trifling with impurity among believers—their damnation is just (Rev. 2:20–24; 2 Pet. 2:15).

The tempter respects no person, and no place. Not without reason Solomon warns us, "I was almost in all evil in the midst of the congregation and assembly" (Prov 5:14). A deceived heart can stray into sin from the very courts of the Lord (Prov 7:13–18).

Grace constrains, and holiness demands, that all my dealings with *younger women* show the humility, kinship, kindness, cleanness and empathy of a brother to *sisters with all purity. All purity*—of heart, thought, eye, tongue, and hand (Matt 5:27–30; Prov 4–7; Eph 5:1–6).

> Create in me a clean heart, O God;
> And renew a right spirit within me.
> The sacrifices of God are a broken spirit:
> A broken and a contrite heart, O God,
> Thou wilt not despise.
> —Psalm 51:10, 17.
> *The younger women as sisters, with all purity!*

The House of God

96. Lord Jesus, living King and Head

1 Lord Jesus, living King and Head,
We as Thy saints confess
One, holy, apostolic church
Most catholic and most blest!

2 The sweet communion of the saints
Through every age and place
Joins all our souls and minds and hearts
In deathless bonds of grace.

3 Good Shepherd, for that chosen flock
Thou cam'st to earth and died;
Now risen, reigning, Prince of life
Call forth and claim Thy bride!

4 Our faithful, merciful High Priest
And Advocate on high
Plead for us in our daily need
And for our help draw nigh!

C.M.

Preparatory Reading: Old Testament: Nehemiah 2;
  New Testament: John 9 Psalm: 96

1 Timothy 5:3-7

3Honour widows that are widows indeed. 4But if any widow have children or nephews, let them learn first to shew piety at home, and to requite their parents: for that is good and acceptable before God. 5Now she that is a widow indeed, and desolate, trusteth in God, and continueth in supplications and prayers night and day. 6But she that liveth in pleasure is dead while she liveth. 7And these things give in charge, that they may be blameless.

The apostles and prophets by whom the Holy Scriptures have come to us speak with one voice, divinely inspired, in all that they teach. Most forcefully so, when the Spirit of God moved them to deal with *widows:* "Ye shall not afflict *any widow*" (Exod 22:22–24); "Thou shalt rejoice in thy feast, thou . . . and *the widow*, that are within thy gates" (Deut 16:14); "a Father of the fatherless, and a Judge of the *widows*, is God in His holy habitation" (Ps 68:5); "Leave thy fatherless children, I will preserve them alive; and let thy *widows* trust in Me" (Jer 49:11); "Pure religion and undefiled before God and the Father is this, to visit the fatherless and *widows* in their affliction, and to keep himself unspotted from the world" (Jas. 1:27).

The poorest, weakest and least of all ordinary society (perhaps excepting the leper and outcast) *widows* figure largely in God's great works for our redemption. The prophet Elijah works miracles among widows (1 Kgs 18). The final Prophet of the Church, the Lord Jesus Himself, shows His divine power specially in their aid (Luke 7:11–17). The Saviour sees in their desperate cries the prayers of God's elect for vengeance (Luke 18:1–8); in their meager gifts the devotion of their whole living to God in faith (Mark 12:41–44). If all *elder women* have honor in the Church as mothers, then especially we must *honour widows that are widows indeed.*

Widows indeed: for not all *widows* meet the apostolic standard of *widows indeed.* Those with family, immediate or even extended, must and should be cared for by family, for believers must *shew piety at home.* Those with such wealth as might *live in pleasure,* have no claim on the Church's care; such are spiritually *dead* given not to Christ but to self and sin (6, cf. 11–13). Such decay, corruption and hypocrisy must be prevented and stopped among our families—for there is no "retirement age" or "off duty" condition to any believer, certainly not to "women professing godliness" (2:9–10). Hence, *these things put in charge that they may be blameless* (5:7).

97. Come, All Ye Sisters in the Lord

1 Come, all ye sisters in the Lord
Your voices join in Jesu's praise:
Sit at His feet, and hear His Word
The choicest portion of your days!

2 Walk worthy of His heavenly call,
As royal daughters of our God—
Freed from the curse of Adam's fall,
Bought by the Lamb's most precious Blood.

3 Now saved by sovereign grace alone,
By His own Spirit born and led,
Call on the Father, at whose throne
Your High Priest lives who for you bled.

4 With Sarah's and with Rahab's faith,
Still cleave to Christ with all your heart—
Believing all the Scripture saith,
Never from Him alone depart.

5 In all love's labors persevere
With hope as did our mother Ruth
Who served the LORD with godly fear
And found Him full of grace and truth.

6 Adorn the Gospel with good deeds,
As Dorcas' coats once clothed the poor,
Till without word, men shall you heed,
And ye make your election sure.

7 Old Deborah's courage, Hannah's zeal,
Martha's devotion, Mary's love,
The wisdom of an Abigail.
Our Father gives us from above.

8 Our God shall thus supply your needs
From all the riches of His grace
By Jesus Christ who intercedes
For you within the Holy Place.

L.M.

The House of God

Preparatory Reading: Old Testament: Nehemiah 3;
   New Testament: John 10 Psalm: 97

1 Timothy 5:3–7

3 Honour widows that are widows indeed. 4 But if any widow have children or nephews, let them learn first to shew piety at home, and to requite their parents: for that is good and acceptable before God. 5 Now she that is a widow indeed, and desolate, trusteth in God, and continueth in supplications and prayers night and day. 6 But she that liveth in pleasure is dead while she liveth. 7 And these things give in charge, that they may be blameless.

Widows indeed whom the Church must *honor* are *desolate* of human family and devoted to the faith of God's elect (5:5). Such a widow *trusteth in God*—God is her Redeemer, her Maker and her Husband (Isa 54:5). Like Anna, who received and blessed the Saviour along with Simeon, she *continueth in supplications and prayers day and night* (Luke 2:36–38).

Few indeed are such *widows indeed.* Are the girls and women growing, maturing, aging in our Churches such women of faith and prayer through all their years of youth, marriage and motherhood that when at last left on earth *desolate,* they too shall *trust in God and continue in supplications day and night?* Will my "doctrine and exhortation" (4:13), my "example of the believers" (4:12) and habit to "intreat . . . younger women as sisters with all purity" (5:2) be His tool to prepare them to such a life of devotion? Or will I fail to ready their families *to learn first to shew piety at home*—will my ministry leave them carnal, deceived, to *live in pleasure* as souls *dead while they live?* The Scriptures, even as they unfold and reveal the "glorious Gospel of the blessed God" in the covenant of grace, also hold up "the royal law," "the law of liberty" which the Lord Jesus has fulfilled for us on the Tree, and yet fulfills in us by the Spirit of life. It is to this end that the Holy Ghost has stocked the Bible's pages with the words and deeds, the lives and labors of mankind—saints and sinners alike. The sinfulness of sin, and the wages of sin are writ large in lives like Cain, Ahab, Joab, Saul, Diotrephes, Demetrius, Demas or Judas. Are they not also written for our learning when we meet Potiphar's wife or Pilate's, Athaliah, Orpah, or the Jezebels? Shall we mark Samuel and not Hannah? James and John, and not Martha and Mary? As believers we all need models to live by, not to dress by.

If as a preacher I am called to prepare sinners to enter eternity, am I not to ready them to die well? And if to die well, then am I not to prepare them to live well, and age well too? Paul includes such topics in declaring "These things command and teach" (4:11) as much as any other. Says Paul, *these things give in charge that they may be blameless—widow, children, nephews* and all who believe.

98. Thy will be done!

1 Father, I know not by what way
Thy hand would lead me on:
Only uphold me day by day
Through Thy beloved Son.

2 Savior, I cannot see ahead
Amid the darkening night:
By Thee alone I would be led
Who art the world's true Light.

3 Spirit of grace, by whom are led
The children of our God
For whom the Lamb His Blood has shed:
Lead me through paths untrod.

4 I know not whither I may go
Through this world's wilderness:
My God, I ask but this to know
Thou art with me to bless!

5 Almighty Father, just and true
Eternal, gracious Son,
Blest Spirit, making all things new—
My God, Thy will be done!

C.M.

The House of God

Preparatory Reading: Old Testament **Nehemiah 4;**
   New Testament: John 11 Psalm: 98

1 Timothy 5:8

⁸But if any provide not for his own, and specially for those of his own house, he hath denied the faith, and is worse than an infidel.

Ever since our first parents' fall into sin under the curse, our homes have been torn by selfish strife. We hardly know at times how to be families. How Boaz discovered this in Naomi's nearest kinsman, forever consigned to anonymity as "Such an one," when he said, "I cannot redeem it, lest I mar mine own inheritance; redeem thou my right to thyself" (Ruth 4:1, 6). Content to see a branch of his family die rather than sacrifice aught for himself, was he really less guilty than another, who dared to say in God's face, "I know not: am I my brother's keeper?" (Gen 4:9).

The God of all grace who gathers the outcasts, also sets the solitary in families (Ps 147:2–3, 68:6). He displays the glory of His risen Son in the Church as He fills believers with the Spirit to live as husbands and wives, children and parents (Eph 3:20–21, 5:18–6:4). And so Timothy must "command and teach" the family duties of the saints also— "these things give in charge that they may be blameless" (4:11, 5:7).

Every Christian has a debt of gratitude to discharge *for his own, and specially for those of his own house*—a duty as sacred and serious as prayer (2:8)—*to provide for his own and specially for those of his own house*. The Master bids me be neighbor to any stranger in distress who crosses my path (Luke 10:25–37); can I doubt I must be kinsman to all who share my lineage, my name, my blood—with whom I am bound n the bundle of life itself? (1 Sam 25:29). If I am to "do good unto all men, specially to those of the household of faith" (Gal 6:10), can I do less to "my own" whether or not they believe? Even if for Christ's sake "a man's foes shall be they of his own household" (Matt 10:36; Mic 7:6), shall I not "love my enemies" and "overcome evil with good?" (Matt 5:44; Rom 12:21).

If any man provide not for his own—no exceptions. The cause of Christ may require us to sacrifice ties to family Mark 10:28–31), to choose allegiance to Him over them (Luke 14:23–35), or to forego duties which others can fulfill (Luke 9:54–60; Matt (8:21–23), but never to neglect the responsibilities which are ours in the family. Our Savior Jesus Himself *provided for His own, specially for those of His own house,* when on the cross He committed His blessed mother to John the Apostle, both as His beloved disciple, and as her *nephew* (John 19:23–27 cf. 1 Tim. 5:4). Never did He sanction the willful neglect of family under a cloak of religious zeal (Matt 15:3–9). How can Pastors, elders or deacons claim to "rule their own houses well" and yet *provide not for their own, and specially for those of their own house?* (3:4, 12).

Do I *provide*—readily supply love, attention, advice, help, means—*for my own?* Do I give my wife her due as *of my own house?* Do my relatives near and far know and feel practically they are of *my own?*

99. Called out of darkness into light

1 Called out of darkness into light
To show forth all Thy praise,
God of all grace, my heart delights
To Thee my song to raise.

2 How shall I praise thee, Father God,
Whose love to me untold
Redeemed me by the Lamb's shed Blood
More precious far than gold?

3 My faithful Savior Jesus, where
Can I thy praise begin?
Thou on the Cross my guilt didst bear
To save me from my sin!

4 Lord God the Holy Ghost, what praise
Can celebrate Thy worth,
Who in the fullness of Thy grace
Hast wrought my soul's new birth?

5 "This people have I formed Myself—
They shall show forth My praise!"
Then let me sing Thy saving wealth,
O Triune God of grace!

C.M.

Preparatory Reading: Old Testament: Nehemiah 5;
   New Testament: John 12 Psalm: 99

1 Timothy 5:8

⁸But if any provide not for his own, and specially for those of his own house, he hath denied the faith, and is worse than an infidel.

If ... not ... he hath denied the faith, and is worse than an infidel: We deny the Lord who bought us in works no less than in words, in deeds no less than in doctrines (Tit. 1:16). Persecution may occasion it (Matt 10:33; 2 Tim. 3:5). Heresy amounts to it (2 Pet. 2:1; 1 John 2:22). But disobedience effects it. "Why call ye me 'Lord, Lord' and do not the things that I say?" the Master demands of us (Luke 6:46–49). Hearing without doing is self-deceit (Jas. 1:22); knowing and doing is alone blessed (John 13:17).

When Paul was Saul of Tarsus, he killed the saints; but he obtained mercy because he did it "ignorantly in unbelief" (1:12–16). What can we expect if we sin willfully against the knowledge of the truth? (Heb. 10:26–31). To neglect the least of Christ's people is to neglect Him (Matt 25:45). How much more is it sin to neglect our own flesh and blood who believe?

There can be no division or discrepancy between the public and domestic life of an elder in God's Church. An impressive preacher—but a negligent son? A diligent visitor—but an improvident husband? An ever-available counselor—but an absent kinsman? Such a man, like the "such an one" who abandoned Naomi and Ruth to Boaz out of self-interest, is a monstrosity. We trespass the whole Law when we violate any one part of it (Jas. 2:10–13). So the Lord God declares by the lawgiver Moses, "Ye shall fear every man his mother, and his father, and keep My Sabbaths: I am the LORD your God ... Thou shalt rise up before the hoary head, and honor the face of the old man, and fear thy God: I am the LORD" (Lev 19:3, 32). Our Savior roundly damns all who draw nigh to God with the lips while the heart is far from Him as "hypocrites." And the pious evasion of duty to parents is just such hypocrisy (Mark 7:6–13).

> Unto the wicked God saith,
> What hast thou to do to declare My statutes,
> Or that thou shouldest take My covenant in thy mouth?
> Seeing thou hatest instruction,
> And castest My words behind thee.
> Thou sittest and speakest against thy brother;
> Thou slanderest thine own mother's son.
> —Ps 50:16–17, 20

Merciful Savior, Holy Child Jesus, subject to Thy mother and earthly stepfather, faithful to care for Thine own kindred even while hanging on the Cross; first to claim the allegiance of Thy brethren who had not believed—pardon all my sins of omission; instruct, empower and enable me to be the son, brother, cousin, nephew, husband, uncle or father I should be to *provide for my own, and specially for those of my own house.* Amen.

The House of God

100. Our Father, bless this house

1 Our Father, bless this house today
Which we would enter in:
Safeguard us in its walls always
And keep our souls from sin.

2 Lord Jesus, build the home we make
Within this house henceforth
Grant us to live for Thy dear sake
To praise Thy Name and worth.

3 O Holy Ghost, bind now the hearts
In love which make this home;
With every grace Thou dost impart
Into our midst now come!

4 Lord God Triune, exalted King,
Reign over us, we pray,
Till all our hearts and homes shall sing
Within Thy house for aye.

C.M.

Preparatory Reading: Old Testament: Nehemiah 6;
 New Testament: John 13 Psalm: 100

1 Timothy 5:9-10

9Let not a widow be taken into the number under threescore years old, having been the wife of one man, 10Well reported of for good works; if she have brought up children, if she have lodged strangers, if she have washed the saints' feet, if she have relieved the afflicted, if she have diligently followed every good work.

"Honour widows that are widows indeed" (5:8); this "honour" must include the same practical, financial support which honors elders devoted to "the Word and doctrine" (5:17). The ordained, devoted pastor, teacher, elder is the congregation's "staff," biblically; no less are the "widows indeed." How wisely has our Lord Christ as Head of the Church combined family men who "give themselves to prayer and the ministry of the Word" (Acts 6:4) with "mothers" in the faith who "continue in supplications and prayers day and night" (5:2, 5) as "teachers of good things" to "younger women" (Tit. 2:3–5). We need no Jezebels to play prophetess in the congregation; we must needs "honour widows that are widows indeed" (5:3; Rev. 2:20).

Paul first sets down the spiritual, inward qualifications for such widows (5:3, 5); now he details their social, outward credentials (5:9–10). The woman whose life-long trust in God and continual prayer to God fits her when desolate to service, and the support of the assembly, has borne these fruits of life among others. Anna models the true widow (Luke 2:36–37), as Dorcas models the consecrated virgin (Acts 9:36; 2 Cor 7:32–34). These alone are to be *taken into the number* and may rightly expect "the daily ministration" of the Church (Acts 6:1).

The opening requirement touches age: *let not a widow be taken into the number under threescore years old*. This rule determines that she is truly alone, with no wish or prospect to re-marry (5:5, 11); that she has entered the final term of expected life-span at "threescore years and ten" or "fourscore" (Ps 90:10), and that she may rightly look to the Church for care in her neediest, most infirm years. The Word of God thus scorns the vain wisdom of this world which prizes the passing beauty and strength of youth (Isa 40:6–8). "Favour is deceitful, and beauty is vain: but a woman that feareth the LORD, she shall be praised" (Prov 31:30). The "inner man is renewed day by day" and her beauty is "the hidden man of the heart" (2 Cor 4:16; 1 Pet. 3:4). Blessed woman, whose last years are made the best, and crowned with glory that fades not away!

The second requirement touches her character—*having been the wife of one man.* This establishes a blameless reputation both for chaste fidelity in the married years, and settled singleness in widowhood. This also speaks to a practiced domestic life experience, from which she may instruct younger women. Every pastor would be wise to take counsel of such a "mother" to "rule his own house well."

101. May Children Come to Jesus?

1 May children come to Jesus?
The Bible tells us so:
None other can release us
Of all the guilt and woe
Which Adam's fall has brought us
In sinful hearts and hands:
The Savior came and sought us
To save us from all lands.

2 Christ called a young child to Him
And children watched at play;
His arms received and blessed them
His hands on them He lay:
He spoke of honoring parents
Of those who disobeyed
In all of their afflictions
He shared, and wept, and prayed.

3 He raised the ruler's daughter,
He raised the widow's son
He heard a Gentile mother
And a centurion,
Who, outside Israel's nation,
Great faith in Him revealed,
To such He brought salvation,
Their loved young folk He healed.

4 He took the loaves and fishes
A young lad gladly brought
Then, with His own disciples,
A miracle He wrought:
He fed the famished thousands
Out in the wilderness
With those few loaves and fishes
He deigned to break and bless.

5 Can any doubt Christ Jesus
Who came to save from sin
Who bled, and died and suffered
Eternal life to win?

The House of God

Will not such little children
As on His Name believe
Have all their sins forgiven,
And all His love receive?

6 We cannot see His kingdom
Till we are born again:
We all must be converted
And humbled, thus to gain
A place among His chosen
Whom He by grace shall call—
The Church His Blood has ransomed
And purchased once for all.

7 Forbid not little children,
But suffer them to come
To Christ, whose Blood a ransom
Was once paid to atone
For trespass and transgression,
For sin, and guilt and shame:
His Spirit gives repentance
And faith to plead His Name!

7.6.7.6.D

The House of God

> Preparatory Reading: Old Testament: Nehemiah 7;
> New Testament: John 14 Psalm: 101

1 Timothy 5:9–10

9Let not a widow be taken into the number under threescore years old, having been the wife of one man, 10Well reported of for good works; if she have brought up children, if she have lodged strangers, if she have washed the saints' feet, if she have relieved the afflicted, if she have diligently followed every good work.

Paul's third requirement to "honour widows that are widows indeed" (5:5) touches a widow's record and reputation of service to Christ in her sphere of life—*well reported of for good works . . . if she have diligently followed every good work*. The known reality of her life must fully match the reputation gained—hers is a lifetime of good works, not a select few, pursued by preference; not an occasional display for emergency use. *Every good work,* is *diligently followed:* major or menial, long-term or short, for every sort of need. At every opportunity, to all of her ability, with all humility, sincerity, and piety such a woman has daily lived and wrought *every good work* for her Lord Jesus. This sister's righteousness is wrought not "to be seen of men" but to the Father which "seeth in secret" and "shall reward . . . openly" (Matt 6:1, 4).

The Apostle illustrates those *good works* which are *well reported* in four cases. There is much to ponder here, not merely in the work assigned with honor to "women professing godliness" (2:10) but also in the nature of *good works.* Our Savior bade us care for those who would be unable to "reply in kind" (Luke 14:12–14). Here are those whose condition would make any recompense unlikely—*children, strangers, the saints, the afflicted.* So to serve the needs of others is very truly to "trust in God" (5:5) who is faithful to reward such labors of love (Heb. 6:10, 10:35).

All the good works which are here reported are domestic, physical and even menial acts of mercy and comfort, both to the outer and inner man. Who does not know the endless toil which befalls those who *have brought up children?* or the rush and press to take proper pains to *lodge strangers?* The anxious, patient care needed to *relieve the afflicted?* Or the humiliation of *washing . . . feet?* Such are the good works of the saints throughout the Bible. Amram and Jochebed labored over Moses (Exod 2) in *bringing up children.* Abraham and Sarah hurried to receive the Lord of angels (Gen 18; Heb. 13:2), as did Lot to his own danger (Gen 19) in *lodging strangers.* How good was the Samaritan to assist the traveler to Jericho (Luke 10:33–35) and so *relieve the afflicted.* And how gracious was our Master first and best to *wash the saints' feet* among the Twelve in the Upper Room, even beyond to Judas (John 13:3–5). The security, health, comfort of others takes hard work.

102. "Ye did it unto Me!"

1 When Christ, the King of glory,
As Son of Man shall come,
The nations shall be gathered
Before His great white throne:
Then, as He has decided,
Each shall be made to stand,
As sheep and goats divided,
On His left or right hand.

2 The King shall tell the righteous,
"Come, enter in, ye blest!
My Father's realms inherit
With everlasting rest:
Before the world's foundation,
This kingdom was prepared
For all who to salvation
Were named predestined heirs."

3 "The Holy Ghost has sealed you
With all of faith's effects,
With love whose works reveal you
To be of God's elect;
Each act of kind compassion
In want and misery
To e'en My lowliest brethren,
Ye did it unto Me!"

4 In love to one another
We surely show to all
We are Christ's true disciples
Who at His saving call,
Deny ourselves to follow
And count the world but loss
His holy Name to hallow
And bear our Savior's cross.

5 So let us now remember
How our Lord Jesus said,
That every saint as member
Is one with Him, the Head
Of that one mystic Body,

The House of God

The Church for whom He died,
And love all who embody
Our Savior crucified.

7.6.7.6D

The House of God

Preparatory Reading: Old Testament: Nehemiah 8;
   New Testament: John 15 Psalm: 102

1 Timothy 5:9-10

9Let not a widow be taken into the number under threescore years old, having been the wife of one man, 10Well reported of for good works; if she have brought up children, if she have lodged strangers, if she have washed the saints' feet, if she have relieved the afflicted, if she have diligently followed every good work.

If she have diligently followed every good work: Who can demean this labor of love, this work of faith, this patient hope as mere "woman's work" in the home or the Church? Without these unpleasant and unsung labors there would be no reality to the Church as "the ground and pillar of the truth" (3:15). Who can take seriously a religion whose love is all in word and tongue, and not in deed and in truth? (1 John 3:18). Who can credit a dead faith, which must be shown by its works to be alive? (Jas. 2:17–19). It should give me pause to consider what I think important to the effective witness of the Churches to the Gospel, when the Scriptures of the New Testament never mention music, masonry or marketing as means by which the Gospel swept the known world of the apostles' day. The Spirit of God was pleased to use Christ's people simply in speaking and serving; in the Word of the Gospel and good works; in holiness and righteousness. "Pure religion and undefiled before God and the Father is this, to visit the widow and the fatherless in their affliction, and to keep unspotted from the world" (Jas. 1:27). God the eternal Son, the King of glory, Jesus Christ Himself, has set His seal of Yea and Amen to such good works with these great and precious promises: "Whosoever shall give to drink unto one of these little ones a cup of cold water, only in the name of a disciple, verily I say unto you, he shall in no wise lose his reward" (Matt 10:42). "Whoso shall receive one such little child in My Name receive Me" (Matt 18:5). "Come, ye blessed of My Father, inherit the kingdom prepared for you from the foundation of the world: for I was an hungered, and ye gave Me meat; I was thirsty, and ye gave Me drink; I was a stranger, and ye took Me in; naked, and ye clothed Me; I was sick, and ye visited Me; I was in prison and ye came unto Me . . . Inasmuch as ye have done it unto one of the least of these My brethren, ye have done it unto Me" (Matt 25:34–36, 40). "Ye call Me Master and Lord: and ye say well; for so I am. If I then, your Lord and Master, have washed your feet, ye also ought to wash one another's feet. For I have given you an example, that ye should do as I have done to you. Verily, verily I say unto you, the servant is not above his lord; neither he that is sent greater than He that sent him. If ye know these things, happy are ye if ye do them" (John 13:13–17; 3 John 5–8).

103. No Fruit!

1 *No fruit!* How could it ever be,
A branch in Christ, the living Vine,
Could fail to grow and thrive to Thee,
Lord Jesus, as Thou didst design?

2 *Taken away!* No fruit was found
To show that His engrafted Word
Was truly to the soul e'er bound
Of those whose lips had named the Lord.

3 As from it there decay and die
The outward forms of godliness,
Cast forth, and withered, see it lie
All barren of true righteousness.

4 Full soon the day of judgment comes,
To dash all hypocrites' desire
Gathered before th'eternal throne,
They all are *cast into the fire.*

5 Thus is the Word of God fulfilled,
"The Lord His chosen knows and sees"
"Let all who name our Savior still,
Depart from their iniquities."

6 O Father, may I not profess
The faith of Christ in word alone;
Born of the Holy Ghost, possess
And graft my soul into Thy Son!

7 Abiding in the Savior, clean,
And purged, before our Father's eye
Let fruits of righteousness be seen
In me, His Name to glorify!

L.M.

The House of God

Preparatory Reading: Old Testament: Nehemiah 9;
   New Testament: John 16 Psalm: 103

1 Timothy 5:11–13

¹¹But the younger widows refuse: for when they have begun to wax wanton against Christ, they will marry; ¹²Having damnation, because they have cast off their first faith. ¹³And withal they learn *to be* idle, wandering about from house to house; and not only idle, but tattlers also and busybodies, speaking things which they ought not.

"Be not rash with thy mouth, and let not thine heart be hasty to utter anything before God: for God is in heaven, and thou upon earth; therefore let thy words be few . . . Better is it that thou shouldest not vow, than that thou shouldest vow, and not pay" (Eccl 5:1–7, esp. vv. 2, 5). So spoke Solomon, himself at once a wise child and an old foolish king (Eccl 4:13). And so to the purpose spoke our Lord Jesus, greater far than Solomon (Matt 12:42) when He taught His disciples "Swear not at all" (Matt 5:33–37; Jas. 5:12). Any vow or engagements we make to our Savior, Bridegroom and Lord are as serious as any marriage vows between man and wife—if we fail them, we break *faith*.

The apostolic command to *refuse younger widows* (5:11–12) seems to imply such an engagement by vow on the part of the Church's *widows* to devote themselves with special fidelity to the Savior and His service. Such have upon them *their first faith* which to *cast off* is to *wax wanton against Christ*. If such younger widows undertake this commitment, and then break it because *they will marry*, is this a lesser or other offense than an adulterous breach of marriage vows? Is *damnation*, as distinct from "condemnation" really too strong a consequence, in view of the decay of character Paul predicts of such offenders?

What infinite mischief can distempered "over-much" zeal wreak upon "unlearned and unstable souls!" (Eccl 7:16; 2 Pet. 3:16 cf. Rom 10:2). Haste is waste as much with *widows* as with elders (5:22, 24–25). What could be further from this apostolic caution in Scripture than the press of young girls into the impossible vows of a convent life? As if to prove the mischief of the one extreme by the other, Paul shrewdly foretells the reaction of these unsuitable women to their former pledge (5:13). Not only *they will marry*; but *they will marry* in a spiritual decay as *wanton against Christ*. In such a state of soul, how can they marry but badly, for the worst, not the best motives? The hardened heart of many young women from convent schools gives uncanny corroboration to this warning. A "widow indeed" will not fall this way, "having been the wife of one man" (5:8–9).

Ordination will place me as well under vows; I also shall have a *first faith* which I must keep and not *cast off*. Will I put my hand to the plough, and not look back? (Luke 9:62). Or will I in time *wax wanton against Christ*? (Cf. Jas. 4:1–10).

The House of God

104. The Wicked shall be turned to Hell

1 Hear! All who now God's Word despise,
"The wicked shall be turned to Hell"
Shalt *thou* in torment lift thine eyes—
In everlasting burnings dwell?

2 A lake of everlasting fire
And brimstone is prepared of old
For men or devils, who desire
Sin's wages, and themselves have sold.

3 Fearful, and unbelieving, liars,
Who work uncleanness, steal and kill,
Shall with their idols face the fires
The second death will bring them still.

4 Ye who fare sumptuously each day,
With no regard to God or man,
Sin's wages ye shall ever pay
A great gulf fixed, that none may span.

5 In outer darkness shalt thou wail,
Thy teeth shall gnash as in the flame
All torments shall thy soul assail
With guilt and everlasting shame.

6 Cut off and cast away thine eye.
Thine own right hand or foot, lest burn
Thy body and thy soul for aye,
Where never dies the smoke or worm.

7 Now, now is the accepted time!
Repent and flee the wrath to come!
Today shalt thou salvation find—
Trust in the Blood of Christ alone!

L.M.

The House of God

Preparatory Reading: Old Testament: Nehemiah 10;
New Testament: John 17 Psalm: 104

1 Timothy 5:11–13

¹¹But the younger widows refuse: for when they have begun to wax wanton against Christ, they will marry; ¹²Having damnation, because they have cast off their first faith. ¹³And withal they learn *to be* idle, wandering about from house to house; and not only idle, but tattlers also and busybodies, speaking things which they ought not.

When lust of pleasure and love of ease move a woman to marry, the pursuit of pleasure will take up the whole life. There is no heart in such to "follow diligently every good work"; the needs of "children . . . the afflicted . . . strangers . . . the saints" are not in view; no deep "trust in God" will move the soul "to continue in supplication and prayers day and night" (5:5, 10). Any life, of woman or man, so controlled by pleasure, must only spawn vanity and vice. "A virtuous woman is a crown to her husband: but she that maketh ashamed is rottenness in his bones" (Prov 12:4). Here are found the houses of "silly women, laden with sins, led away with divers lusts" that afflict the Church (2 Tim. 3:6).

Idleness is the fount both of emptiness and evil: *they learn to be idle . . . and not only idle . . .* God made us in His image, male and female, for labor and worship, not for leisure and wantonness. The godly woman makes her home a centre of industry and charity, as a "keeper at home" (Titus 2:5; Prov 31)—her home may be the hub to the widest circle of social, public and financial interest and enterprise. This sort, in contrast, *wandering about from house to house,* achieves nothing. The "widow indeed" gives voice to "prayer" and hand to "good works" (5:5, 10). This woman, "dead while she liveth", gives voice and hand to the life of a *tattler and busybody* (5:6, 13; 1 Pet. 4:15).

A woman truly "professing godliness," leaves the memory of "supplications and prayers day and night" (2:10, 5:5), whereas this sort is remembered for *speaking things which they ought not*—and this Paul catalogues in detail to the elders and saints at Ephesus: "lying," "corrupt communication" "bitterness, wrath, anger, clamour, evil speaking with all malice" "fornication, all uncleanness" "covetousness" "filthiness, foolish talking, jesting" "threatenings" (Eph 4:25, 29, 31; 5:8, 4; 6:9). If any religion leave these mouths, Paul foretells little good: "slander," "profane and old wives' fables" (3:11; 4:7 cf. Jas. 1:26). Can anyone doubt this is the tone and temper of too many older women who are "dead while they live" "in pleasure?" (5:6). Will my ministry and pastoral care simply serve as a chaplaincy to such women? (Mark 12:38–40; 2 Tim. 3:5–7) or a stimulus to nurture "widows indeed?" O Father and Judge of the widow, for our Lord Jesus Christ's sake, visit our sisters with great grace, to redeem the time of their life; grant them the beauty of holiness, and lead them in every good work. Amen.

105. Lord God, we make this Covenant

1 LORD God, we make this covenant,
And pledge before Thee now
Our love, life-long and constant
In this, our marriage vow:
All other, we, forsaking,
To one another cleave,
As wife and husband taking,
Ne'er to forsake or leave.

2 Forsaking father, mother,
In poverty and wealth,
And taking one another,
In sickness and in health,
We'll comfort, honor, cherish
Each other from the heart
With love which shall not perish
Till death us twain shall part.

3 By grace, this day we promise
To walk as spouse and bride,
As does our Savior Jesus,
Who for His Church once died
To sanctify and cleanse us
With washing by his Word—
Who shall present us faultless,
"Forever with the Lord."

4 And thus, with hands, and tokens,
We plight our solemn troth
Of faithfulness unbroken
Upon this vow and oath:
By Father, Son, and Spirit
Most Holy Trinity,
May we as one inherit
Life to eternity!

7.6.7.6.D

The House of God

Preparatory Reading: Old Testament: Nehemiah 11;
  New Testament: John 18 Psalm: 105

1 Timothy 5:14–16

14 I will therefore that the younger women marry, bear children, guide the house, give none occasion to the adversary to speak reproachfully. 15 For some are already turned aside after Satan. 16 If any man or woman that believeth have widows, let them relieve them, and let not the church be charged; that it may relieve them that are widows indeed.

I will therefore: As "a preacher, apostle . . . and teacher of the Gentiles in faith and verity" Paul thus hands down a ruling, a sum of duty in practice as in worship (2:7, 8). Inspired by the Holy Ghost, given the mind of Christ, proclaiming the Word of God, he commands what he teachers and gives orders (2 Cor 14:37; 1 Cor 2:12–13, 16; 16:1–2 cf. 7:10, 12, 25, 40). To Timothy and all elders following down to me, he passes them with the mandate: "Command and teach" (3:14–15; 4:11). This too is a divine ordinance given to "all the churches" (1 Cor 4:17, 11:16).

More than this, as a true "apostle of Jesus Christ by the commandment of God our Saviour" (1:1), Paul's *I will* carries the authority of the Savior's own "I say unto you" (Matt 5:22, 28, 32). Paul can say, "Follow me, as I follow Christ" (1 Cor 11:1) because Christ Jesus has said to His apostles, "He that receive you, receiveth Me" (Matt 10:40, and of all those He sends to preach, "He that heareth you, heareth Me" (Luke 10:1–2, 16). And so Paul says to Titus, "Let no man despise thee" Tit. 2:15, and for Timothy, "Let no man despise him" (1 Cor 16:10–11).

Paul has received the Gospel by the revelation of the Lord Jesus Himself (Gal 1:11–12), been recognized by the pillar Apostles (Gal 2:4), so, though he is called late, he is no less than the chief of apostles, though in himself he is nothing (2 Cor 12:11–12, 15:3–11). If these words do not come from the Savior's own mouth, they do come through His own mouthpiece; by apostolic revelation, if not by apostolic report. They are every whit "the word of Christ" and "the mind of Christ" for today, for us now. Jesus the Lord is saying through Paul, *I will therefore.*

What is the Master's will, His normative design for the course of life of *younger women?* Do not ask, "What would Jesus do?" Do not say, "I feel a peace about what I am praying for." Read, hear, trust and obey. If God has not given to a *younger woman* the gift of continence and singleness, here is His Word and will cf. (1 Cor 7). Our faithful Savior Jesus says through His apostle, *I will therefore.*

Just as every young man called to be a bishop, elder, pastor, teacher in the Church may prayerfully trust his heart's desires to the Lord Jesus to become "the husband of one wife" (3:2), and unless given single life as a gift, may expect a prudent wife from the Lord (Matt 19:10–12; Prov 19:14), so all *younger women* may expect to *marry, bear children, guide the house* as they "trust in God" (5:5). His way is perfect. (Psalm 18:30) SIXTY.

106. Christ Jesus, Now Thy Help We Seek

1 Christ Jesus, now Thy help we seek
In time of need we call on Thee:
"Lord, he whom Thou dost love is sick!"
Incline Thine heart to hear our plea!

2 Thy hand once cooled the fever'd brow,
And made the leper whole again:
Thy virtue staunched the issue's flow,
And set the cripple free of pain.

3 O Man of Sorrows, who hast borne
Our sins, and carried all our grief:
Lay on Thine hands, by nails once torn,
To grant Thy children now relief!

4 The healing balm, the bed of rest,
Many physicians' art and skill,
Do nought except Thy mercy blest
Should deign to work in them Thy will!

5 Thy way is perfect; if Thou wilt,
Thy power can make us fully whole,
Or grant us in our weakness still,
Grace all-sufficient to the soul.

6 Thou givest, and Thou tak'st away—
Forever we Thy Name must bless!
Thy chastening, painful in its day,
Shall work our good and holiness,

7 "Our light affliction" in its grief,
We "suffer" but "a little while":
"The Resurrection and the Life"
His grace and glory shall reveal.

8 Draw near to us, Lord Jesus Christ,
Thou feelest our infirmity:
Faithful, and merciful High Priest,
Keep us to all eternity!

9 No pain, no pang, disease nor death,
Can wrest us from Thy love's embrace:
We own Thee with our latest breath,
Till we shall see Thee face to face.

10 Till all the new creation sings:
" To Father, Son and Spirit, praise!
The end has come of former things,
Our God shall reign now and always!"

                                                                  L.M.

The House of God

Preparatory Reading: Old Testament: Nehemiah 12;
　New Testament: John 19 Psalm: 106

1 Timothy 5:14

14I will therefore that the younger women marry, bear children, guide the house, give none occasion to the adversary to speak reproachfully.

I will therefore that the younger women marry: Both men and women are normally given the desire and need for marriage; to some God grants the single state (Matt 19:11–12). Marriage is not a spree; it is a high privilege, an important duty, a created natural necessity for Christ's people. So the apostle commands us to *marry*—not cohabit, not fornicate, but marry. Paul ordains this for *younger women;* and while the ruling on widows suggests this covers all women under sixty years (5:4, 11, 14), the entire pattern here seems to view the godly woman's lifespan from adulthood and childbearing years: *marry, bear children, guide the house.* This implies marriage is not for girls, but *younger women* come of age physically, socially, spiritually and emotionally. Believers in their families need to take careful stock of their children's education and training for vocation with a view to preparing both men and *younger women* to *marry* within the natural years these sisters may *bear children.* This might mean Christian men must take a vocation requiring shorter years of training; or that the age difference between groom and bride be somewhat longer. Our sense of calling and work must reckon on the timely foundation of house and family by marriage. The Lord GOD gave Adam work, home then wife—and this would be well to keep (Gen 2:8, 15, 18, 24). So must *the younger women marry. I will therefore that the younger women marry, bear children:* while the Church, local and visible, is a gathered community of believers in the Lord Jesus by the Word and Spirit, a household of saints called by grace to faith, the families of believers are under the tutelage of the Church and claimed for the kingdom of heaven (Eph 2:13–22; Rom 11:18–23, 1:7; Matt 19:13–15, Isa 44:1–6, Acts 2:38–39). Where in the Old Testament church, mixed marriages were dissolved and children disinherited (Ezra 10:10–11, 44; Neh 13:29–29), in the New Testament church, marriages mixed after the conversion of one spouse are respected, "sanctified" so that the children are heirs of Gospel privilege (1 Cor 7:12–15). Timothy himself was precisely such a child, perhaps outcast to the synagogue, yet nurtured in the Scriptures by grandmother and mother (Acts 16:1–3; 2 Tim. 1:5, 3:15). And so we may believe that the Gospel as much as the Law seeks to realize "a godly seed" among the saints (Gen (1:27–28; Mal 2:15–16). This underlies the high honor of motherhood among Christian women (2:15, 5:2; Isa 56:1–8; Ps 113:9). While the barren suffer no stigma under the Gospel, *younger women* in Christ should hope prayerfully to *bear children.* Blessed is the woman, who with the support of a godly husband gives her time and talent to nurture, discipline, and train her children for Jesus! (Eph 6:4, 1 Sam 1–2).

107. The Night is Far Spent

1 The night is far spent:
At hand is the day
When heaven and earth
Shall soon pass away—
Our King is returning,
The Bridegroom will come,
Presenting His people
Their glorious home!

2 The night is far spent:
While others may sleep,
Or long may carouse
In drunkenness deep—
Now let us be sober
As children of day—
Give heed to our Savior,
Who said, "Watch and pray!"

3 The night is far spent:
'Tis high time to wake
From cares of this world,
And sin to forsake—
To lusts of the flesh
No provision we give:
We put on Christ Jesus
In Him hence to live!

4 The night is far spent:
We all must prepare
Our Savior and Prince
To meet in the air:
This blessed hope seeking,
We grow in His grace
Till we shall be like Him
When seen face to face.

5 The night is far spent:
And soon every eye
His glory shall see—
Redemption draws nigh!
The angels shall gather

The House of God

A numberless host
In praise to the Father,
Son and Holy Ghost!

10.10.11.11

Preparatory Reading: Old Testament: Nehemiah 13;
    New Testament: John 20 Psalm: 107

1 Timothy 5:14–16

14I will therefore that the younger women marry, bear children, guide the house, give none occasion to the adversary to speak reproachfully. 15For some are already turned aside after Satan. 16 If any man or woman that believeth have widows, let them relieve them, and let not the church be charged; that it may relieve them that are widows indeed.

I will. . . that the younger women . . . guide the house: Just as Christian men are to "rule their own houses well" (3:4, 12), Christian women are to *guide the house.* The husband holds ultimate responsibility and accountability for the direction of the family; he is to "provide for his own, specially them of his own house" (5:8). The wife holds immediate management and stewardship of the family's means; she is to *guide the house.* Abraham and Sarah so worked together (Gen 18; 21:9–13); Abigail so worked despite her husband's stupidity (1 Sam 25); the virtuous woman is praised for managing her family's interests adroitly (Prov 31). What better proof of a wise match than the complete trust of husband and wife in each other's integrity, competence and devotion in "ruling" and *guiding the house?* Such a family may sing Psalm 128 both as prayer and testimony.

In this quiet, holy vocation, sanctified by God's Word and prayer, sweetened by praise, *younger women* will *give none occasion to the adversary to speak reproachfully.* The devil finds many spokesmen—themselves far from any conformity to God's commandments, but ever ready and willing to lay blame upon the righteous and drag them down into their own ditches. In her own conduct, a godly woman must guard her heart to be "grave, not a slanderer, sober, faithful in all things," not "living in pleasure" and "waxing wanton against Christ" but to "adorn herself in modest apparel" and "good works," and "continue in faith and charity with holiness and sobriety" (3:11, 2:9, 15, 5:6, 9, 11). She must aim to raise her *children* to be "in subjection with all gravity" to father and mother, "faithful . . . not accused of riot or unruly" (3:4; Titus 1:6). Sincere piety and circumspect morality must govern her so to *guide the house* as to *give none occasion to the adversary to speak reproachfully.*

Not all who begin and seem to run well endure to the end, and win the prize. Some who "would be teachers" at last "make shipwreck concerning faith," and so are "delivered unto Satan" (1:7, 19–20). Even as an elder must avoid the "reproach and snare of the devil" (3:7) so must every sister in Christ *give none occasion for the adversary to speak reproachfully.* The warning is needed, *for some are already turned aside after Satan.* How terrible so to end! (2 Pet. 2:19–22).

The House of God

108. O Triune God, before Thy Throne

1 O Triune God, before Thy throne
By faith in Christ we now draw near:
Thou art our Sun and Shield alone—
To us and to our prayer give ear!

2 Almighty Father, now embrace
The child that we present to Thee,
In Thine electing love and grace
Predestined from eternity!

3 Eternal Son, regard our plea:
By Thine own Blood and righteousness,
Suffer this child to come to Thee
By faith, and with repentance bless.

4 Blest Holy Ghost, come and breathe forth
Thy quickening grace and freely give
Newness of life in that new birth
By which this child to God may live!

5 So may this child Our Father take
Our Savior Jesus hold and bless
Our Comforter, the Spirit make
Anew and fill with holiness!

6 Our children bless! We humbly plead,
Vouchsafe, Most Holy Trinity,
To be to us and to our seed
Our God, now and eternally!

L.M.

Preparatory Reading: Old Testament: Proverbs 1;
   New Testament: John 21 Psalm: 108

1 Timothy 5:14-16

14 I will therefore that the younger women marry, bear children, guide the house, give none occasion to the adversary to speak reproachfully. 15For some are already turned aside after Satan. 16If any man or woman that believeth have widows, let them relieve them, and let not the church be charged; that it may relieve them that are widows indeed.

Some have already turned aside after Satan: Had some of these women lapsed into the occult arts the Ephesian believers renounced, "taken captive by the devil at his will?" (Acts 19:18-20; 2 Tim. 2:26). Possibly; more probably they reverted to the vanity and vice of living "without God and without hope in the world" (5:6, 11-13; cf. Eph 2:12). Once more "the prince of the power of the air" had them walking "according to the course of this world" as those "dead in trespasses and sins" (Eph 2:1-3). All who habitually "do not righteousness" nor "love the brethren" are "manifest" as "children of the devil" (1 John 3:10). The tempter needs not show his hand to pull his snares. Heretics must be disciplined and "delivered unto Satan, that they may not learn to blaspheme" (1:20). Should any less drastic measure protect the Church from *some who are already turned aside after Satan?*

The safety and sanctity of these *younger women* will prepare some to be "widows indeed" whose precept, example and supplications will train generations to come, not unlike Timothy himself in preparing future elders (5:3; Titus 2:3-5; 2 Tim. 2:2).

Paul now argues to his specific point—*if any man or woman that believeth have widows, let them relieve them and let not the Church be charged. The Church* must not undermine but undergird the proper function of the home, specially of believers called to "shew piety at home" (5:4). Delinquency here is denial of the faith (5:8). *The Church* will serve the needs of those truly in need and no other.

Let not the Church be charged is a fair motto for believers, and for me as a pastor, to take in all the costs allied to the Lord's service. Sometimes I may need to "preach the Gospel without charge" (1 Cor 9:18). I must also avoid plying my people with every imaginable expense for which they could reimburse me cf. (Acts 20:33-35; 1 Thess. 2:5, 9).

Let not the Church be charged, that it may relieve them that are widows indeed: relieving those who have through life "relieved the afflicted" (5:10), we are to "honour widows that are widows indeed", upon the Lord's promise: "Them that honour me will I honour" (1 Sam 2:30). None who forsake or lack for Christ's sake the supports of the family are to miss them, but be more recompensed in the communion of saints (Matt 19:29-30; Mark 8:34-35, 10:29-31).

109. We Greet the Day of Light

1 We greet the Day of Light
When God our Maker stood
The Day dividing from the night
And saw that it was good.

2 We take the Day of Rest
Jehovah sanctified:
One of the seven, which He blessed,
For man did He provide.

3 We hail the Day of Grace:
The Gospel Jubilee,
When Christ proclaims in every place
The truth that sets us free.

4 We see the Day of Power
On which the Spirit gains
A willing people in the hour
Our risen Savior reigns.

5 We haste the Day of God
And seek the rest to come
For all the saints redeemed by Blood
In their eternal home.

6 Lord God, upon us shower
These blessings rich, we pray:
Grant us Thy light, rest, grace and power
On this, Thy holy Day!

7 In Thee alone we boast,
In Thee alone we rest:
The Father, Son and Holy Ghost,
One God, forever blest!

S.M.

Preparatory Reading: Old Testament: Proverbs 2;
   New Testament: Hebrews 1 Psalm: 109

1 Timothy 5:17-18

17Let the elders that rule well be counted worthy of double honour, especially they who labour in the word and doctrine. 18For the scripture saith, Thou shalt not muzzle the ox that treadeth out the corn. And, The labourer *is* worthy of his reward.

Paul calls on the household of faith to honor those most devoted to the Lord and His people with financial support—"widows indeed" (5:3) and *the elders that rule well*. The cause of the Gospel requires men and women of proven maturity, fidelity and integrity; the mothers of the Church are to be supported at the end of their life's course, the elders during their life's course. "Even so hath the Lord ordained that they which preach the Gospel should live of the Gospel" (cf. 1 Cor 9:14).

To become an elder demands much (3); to be *elders that rule well* demands much more. This might suggest that not all elders of the Church are supported, at least not before a period of proving. If deacons, whose labors are voluntary, must be "first proved" (3:10), should not *elders* likewise show that they *rule well* before they receive *honor*? Perhaps a basic support is needed for them to *rule* at all, and once proven that they *rule well* are they to receive *double honor*. What then is *double* in *double honor*? A figurative "much" or a factual "twice?" and if "twice," then twice what? The rate of satisfactory *elders*—or the rate of the *widows* whom we are to *honor*? Perhaps our widows should be somewhat better cared for rather than our elders somewhat less!

To *rule well* is to fulfill the tasks of ministry Paul has assigned in his charge to (Timothy 1:4-6; 2:1-6; 3:2, 4; 4:6-8, 11-16). While every elder must abhor "filthy lucre" (3:3), there is no sin in recognizing and rewarding the competence and conscientious service of *elders that rule well*; such are to be *counted worthy of double honor*. Disparities of income and amenities among pastors and elders will naturally reflect the financial condition of the congregations in varied settings, but also to some measure the gifts and abilities of elders' service. Paul highlights one area *especially—especially they that labor in the Word and doctrine*. To engage in "godly edifying in faith" and be "apt to teach," the truth of the Word effectually needs the priority of the Churches' care, as this is vital to defend, confirm and propagate the Gospel. Such men are to *labor in the Word and doctrine*—and all Paul demands in 4:11-16 is surely hard *labor*: "command . . . teach . . . be an example . . . give attendance . . . stir up . . . neglect not . . . meditate . . . give thyself . . . take heed . . . continue." This is no merely human, pragmatic measure (1 Cor 9:7)—it is warranted by *the Scripture* both in Old and New Testament; we have a moral principle of equitable recompense for service rendered, especially to God's cause.

110. My Joy is Full, whate'er betides!

1 Of Thee, Lord Jesus, would I sing,
My Savior, Prophet, Priest and King,
Thy Words do light and joy impart,
As Thou abidest in my heart:
Joy! Joy! Thy joy in me abides—
My joy is full whate'er betides!

2 Now justified in Thine own Blood,
By faith my heart has peace with God
Clothed in Thy righteousness alone,
With access to Thy gracious throne:
Joy! Joy! Thy joy in me abides—
My joy is full whate'er betides!

3 In tribulations here below,
I glory in Thy Name also,
Enduring patience thus to gain
With hope that never makes ashamed:
Joy! Joy! Thy joy in me abides—
My joy is full whate'er betides!

4 O let Thy Spirit from above
Now shed within my heart Thy love
That in believing, joy and peace
May overflow, and never cease:
Joy! Joy! Thy joy in me abides—
My joy is full whate'er betides!

5 We joy in God, whose only Son
For all our sins did once atone.
And through whose Holy Spirit's power
Our hope abounds in every hour:
Joy! Joy! Thy joy in us abides—
Our joy is full whate'er betides!

Based on Romans 5:1–11, 15:13.
8.8.8.8.8.8.
Tune: Sussex Carol

Preparatory Reading: Old Testament: Proverbs 3;
   New Testament: Hebrews 2 Psalm: 110

1 Timothy 5:17-18

17Let the elders that rule well be counted worthy of double honour, especially they who labour in the word and doctrine. 18For the scripture saith, Thou shalt not muzzle the ox that treadeth out the corn. And, The labourer *is* worthy of his reward.

The scripture saith: as he wrote to Corinth (1 Cor 9:9-10), Paul cites a precept of the Law, *Thou shalt not muzzle the ox that treadeth out the corn* cf. (Deut 25:4), arguing "from lesser to greater" that if an animal is to be fed by its labors, so much more the farmer (cf. 2 Tim. 2:6-7). He further quotes from the Gospels (Matt 10:10, Luke 10:7) perhaps Luke's account, compiled during Paul's imprisonment in Caesarea (Luke 1:1-4; Acts 23:11-26:32). He thus remembers the words of the Lord Jesus, how He said, *The laborer is worthy of his reward.*

An unpaid ministry is an exception and not the rule in *the scripture.* Aaron and the tribe of Levi received maintenance from the tithes, offerings and sacrifices of the altar Num 18. Isaiah and Jeremiah came from priestly families as did Ezekiel and Samuel (Isa 1:1, 6:1; Jer 1:1; Ezek 1:3; 1 Sam 3). On the other hand, Ahijah the Shilonite, Elijah the Tishbite, Amos of Tekoa, Elisha the son of Shaphat clearly come at God's call outside the house of Levi. Certainly Amos repudiated any mercenary motive in his calling (Amos 7:10-17; cf. 1 Kgs 11:29-40, 12:15, 17:1, 19:19-21).

Our Savior Himself was supported by the help of devout women and the hospitality of His disciples and others, after working as a carpenter (Mark 6:3; Luke 8:1-3; John 12:6). The twelve disciples, later apostles left working life to follow Him (Luke 5:1-11; Matt 9:9-13) and were instructed to accept the willing support of those who received the Gospel (Matt 10:5-13).

Paul deliberately waived his asserted and acknowledged claims for support, in order to model responsible discipleship (Acts 20:34-35), to preach the Gospel more creditably (1 Cor 9:19; 1 Thess. 2:1-9), and to claim the Lord's reward in glory (1 Cor 9:18; 2 Tim. 4:6-8). His personal renunciation, and lifelong labor as a tent-maker lends all the more weight to his insistence here that *the elders that rule well be given double honor, especially they that labor in the Word and doctrine* (Acts 18:1-4).

While a dispensation of the gospel is committed to my charge, I must needs preach the Gospel whenever and wherever the Savior opens the door of utterance. I cannot be right to quarrel or complain over the support I receive in doing so, as an hireling might. Yet I may put my trust in God to sustain me by the means He provides, whether in whole or part from the people's gifts or my own labor.

The trust, support and esteem of my people takes tangible form in my stipend. O that I might *rule well* not merely to be *worthy of double of honor,* but of my Master's "Well done, thou good and faithful servant! Enter thou into the joy of thy Lord!" (Matt 24:46-47, 25:21, 23).

111. Lord Jesus, Prince of Peace

1 Lord Jesus, Prince of peace—
Most Wonderful Thy Name!
Thy throne and kingdom still increase
O'er all the earth to reign:
Great Shepherd, good and meek,
True Prince of David's seed—
Thy scattered flock search out and seek
To gather, save and feed!

2 Lord Jesus, *Prince of life*—
Our true Messiah, Prince,
Cut off in troublous times of strife
To make an end of sins:
By promise, sent to bless,
And turn us from our sin,
An everlasting righteousness
Thy finished work brings in.

3 Lord Jesus, Thou dost live!
From God's right hand, draw nigh—
Repentance and remission give
Thou Prince and Savior high!
O Prince of princes, reign!
Those who against Thee stand
Shall at Thy footstool soon be slain,
All broken without hand.

4 Lord Jesus, quickly come !
Thou Prince of all earth's kings,
O'er sin and death Thy victory won
We wait and long to sing:
To Thee who hast us loved,
And washed us in Thy Blood,
Who mad'st us kings and priests above
Be glory—Lamb of God!

D.S.M.
Based on the Holy Scriptures at
Isa 9:6–7; Ezek 34; Acts 3:11–26; Dan 9:24–27;
John 19:30; Acts 5:29–32; Dan 8:25; Luke 19:27; Rev. 1:4–6, 5:9–10.

Preparatory Reading: Old Testament: Proverbs 4;
  New Testament: Hebrews 3 Psalm: 111

1 Timothy 5:19–21

19Against an elder receive not an accusation, but before two or three witnesses. 20Them that sin rebuke before all, that others also may fear. 21I charge *thee* before God, and the Lord Jesus Christ, and the elect angels, that thou observe these things without preferring one before another, doing nothing by partiality.

Against an elder . . . an accusation: No faithful pastor or elder can pass many years of service without an accusation, however much he is and "must be blameless" (3:2). Our Lord Jesus warned us plainly, "Ye shall be hated of all men for My Name's sake . . . if they have called the Master of the house 'Beelzebub,' how much shall they call them of His household?" (Matt 10:22, 25). He Himself "knew no sin," "did no sin," and "in Him is no sin;" yet He could be pilloried as "born of fornication," "having a devil," "mad." Can we expect at all times to "have a good report with them that are without?" Christ Jesus says, "I have chosen you out of the world, therefore the world hateth you . . . if the world hate you, ye know that it hated Me before it hated you" (2 Cor 5:21; 1 Pet. 2:22; 1 John 3:5; John 8:43, 10:20; 1 Tim. 3:7; John 15:18–19). With this ever present hazard, Paul moves us to the greatest caution. He has already warned us against any hard and ill-considered treatment: "Rebuke not an elder" (5:1). He teaches us to be cautious even in our self-defense: "Being reviled, we bless; being persecuted, we suffer it; being defamed, we intreat" (1 Cor 4:12–13), "in all things approving ourselves as the ministers of God . . . by honor and dishonor, by evil report and good report: as deceivers, yet true . . . " (2 Cor 6:4, 8). It is a mark of the false teacher to lash out against others with loose tongue: "not afraid to speak evil of dignities" (2 Pet. 2:10; Jude 8). Therefore he writes *against an elder receive not an accusation, but before two or three witnesses.* As there is to be no sparing of heresy (Titus 1:9, 13); so there is to be no shielding of sin—*them that sin rebuke before all.* An *accusation* must have *two or three witnesses*—definite proof and due process in accord with divine standards of evidence (Deut 19:15, 17:6; Num 35:30; Matt 18:16). Even in faithful, authentic churches, some elders may *sin* so grievously as to merit *rebuke before all.* The Master warned us it would be so; the apostle John dealt openly with the likes of Diotrephes—so upon proof, the pastor, elders, deacons and people must visit upon a serious offender a *rebuke before all* grave enough to underscore the public responsibility of the office. This *rebuke* seems to carry no implied restoration to office; the loss of character and reputation make an end of service. As all members are liable to excommunication *before all* (1 Cor 5) so are offending elders open to *rebuke before all.* This biblical deterrence remains: *that others also may fear* (5:24; cf. Deut 13:11, 17:13, 19:20).

The House of God

112. Lord Jesus Christ Good Shepherd

1 Lord Jesus Christ, *Good Shepherd*
Thy lost to seek and save,
Obedient to Thy Father,
Thy life a ransom gave;
Thy Blood was shed, more precious
Than silver far, or gold,
Thine other sheep to bring Him—
One Shepherd, and one fold.

2 Lord Jesus, Smitten Shepherd
That dark and cloudy day,
Thy stripes our souls were healing,
Our griefs to take away.
The Just for unjust dying,
Thou cam'st to Calvary.
In Thine own Body bearing
Our sins upon the Tree.

3 Lord Jesus, now arisen
Great Shepherd of the sheep,
The Covenant everlasting,
Thy Blood has sealed to keep.
The God of peace within us
Shall work with that same might
In every work Thy likeness,
Well pleasing in His sight.

4 Lord Jesus, Thee we worship:
Thy love each heart extols
Which led Thee as *the Shepherd*
And Bishop of our souls
To seek us out in searching,
From mountain, hill and glade
To bring us home rejoicing,
Upon Thy shoulders laid.

5 Lord Jesus, come—come quickly!
Chief Shepherd, soon appear
Upon the clouds in glory!
O grant that we may wear
The crown of life and glory

That fadeth not away,
As good and faithful servants,
Upon Thy glorious day!

6 Lord Jesus Christ, *my Shepherd*,
My thirsting soul now lead
To founts of living waters,
Me in Thy pastures feed,
Till with that countless number
Washed in Thy Blood alone
I worship Thee in wonder
The Lamb upon the Throne!

7 Make joyful noise, with singing
All lands that are the Lord's!
With praise and with thanksgiving,
Enter into His courts!
Ye pastured sheep, His people,
His truth and mercy bless!
Praise Father, Son, and Spirit,
One God of holiness!

                                                                         7.6.7.6.D

The House of God

Preparatory Reading: Old Testament: Proverbs 5;
New Testament: Hebrews 4 Psalm: 112

1 Timothy 5:19–21

19 Against an elder receive not an accusation, but before two or three witnesses. 20 Them that sin rebuke before all, that others also may fear. 21 I charge *thee* before God, and the Lord Jesus Christ, and the elect angels, that thou observe these things without preferring one before another, doing nothing by partiality.

The inspired Apostle has now laid before me in this solemn Epistle governing "the church of the living God" (3:15) the hardest, most trying challenge to her purity, peace and progress—sin among her elders. And he lays upon the pastor and elders, especially those "who labour in the Word and doctrine" (5:17) the full burden to follow through in meeting it. *I charge thee that thou observe these things. I charge thee:* not a committee, not the deacons, not pagan magistrates, but *thee*. As our good Shepherd laid down His life for the sheep in face of the wolf, thief and robber, so must I (John 10:4–14). *I charge thee.* This painful duty must be discharged as in the presence of heaven, with no regard to earthly connection or consequence—this is Paul's emphasis in closing this direction and *charge*. He puts Timothy under heaven's witness thrice: concerning the pastor's impartiality (5:19–20), probity (6:11–16), and fidelity (2 Tim. 4:1–2). *I charge thee before God and the Lord Jesus Christ and the elect angels. Before God:* how blind we are in the moment, in the weakness of the flesh, to the central reality of God in Whom we live , move and have our being! (Acts 17:28). How far do we stray in the delusion, "How doth God know?" (Ps 73:11). Of all who should look upon things unseen and eternal, rather than seen and temporal, should not we most, who have received the ministry by mercy—we who know the terrors of the Lord and proclaim, "We must all appear before the judgment seat of Christ"; "Every one of us must give account to God?" (2 Cor 4:1, 8, 5:4–11, Rom 14:10–12). We are commissioned to call all men everywhere to repent, seeing God has appointed a day in which to judge the world in righteousness—can we forget we too must stand there? (Acts 17:30–31). This reality should possess us and awaken us. Like Jacob of old, we should cry out, "How dreadful is this place! . . . surely the LORD was in this place, and I knew it not" (Gen 28:16–17). The first thought we must take to our homes, our studies, our pulpits is this; "Thou God seest me" (Gen 16:13). Before Him we confess, "O LORD, Thou hast searched me and known me;" to Him we pray, "Search me, O God, and know my heart" (Ps 139:1, 23). "The LORD looketh from heaven; He beholdeth all the sons of men" (Ps 33:13–18). So much more He regards those who take His words into their mouths. "Am I not a God at hand, saith the LORD, and not a God afar off? Can any man hide himself in secret places that I shall not seen him? Saith the LORD. Do not I fill heaven and earth? Saith the LORD" (Jer 23:16–29, esp. 23–24).

113. O God, before Thy Throne I Stand

O God, before Thy throne I stand
Now charged to preach Thy holy Word:
For all I do, at His command,
I give account to Christ the Lord
When He in clouds shall soon appear—
The righteous Judge shall I not fear?

2 Grant me all grace to preach the Word,
Instant, in season and without,
With patience to reprove, exhort
Rebuke, and doctrine sound give out
To watch, endure, and hold the truth
My ministry to make full proof.

3 When my departure is at hand
Let me have fought a goodly fight,
My course all finished, let me stand
Before Thee in eternal light:
The faith well kept, grant me the crown,
Lord Jesus, Thou shalt give Thine own.

Based on 2 Timothy 4:1–8
8.8.8.8.8.8.

The House of God

> Preparatory Reading: Old Testament: Proverbs 6;
> New Testament: Hebrews 5 Psalm: 113

1 Timothy 5:21

²¹I charge *thee* before God, and the Lord Jesus Christ, and the elect angels, that thou observe these things without preferring one before another, doing nothing by partiality.

I charge thee before God, and the Lord Jesus Christ: Paul protested "if I yet pleased men, I should not be the servant of Christ" (Gal 1:10). As surely as I am to *observe these things before God*, I must walk and work for the Lord Jesus, laboring to be accepted of Him, living to Him who for me died and rose again (2 Cor 5:9–15). He is the Chief Shepherd for whom I am to feed the flock, whose is the crown of glory to give me (1 Pet. 5:1–4). He is the Son of Man, the King on the throne of His glory, who "after a long time" comes to reckon with His servants—His is the joy I would enter (Matt 25:19–23). He is the Righteous Judge who will give the crown of righteousness to all who fought the fight, finished the course and kept the faith (2 Tim. 4:2, 8). He is the Bridegroom, who will return to honor and reward the watching, waiting servant (Luke 12:35–38). He is the Lord in the midst of His two or three, binding and answering prayer even in the throes of discipline (Matt 18:15–20). To this *Lord Jesus Christ* we must give account as we watch for our people's souls—will that be joy, or grief? (Heb. 13:17). Let me, whatever the cost on earth, *observe these things . . . before God, and the Lord Jesus Christ. Before . . . the elect angels:* "The angels which kept not their first estate, but left their own habitation" the Lord "hath reserved in everlasting chains under darkness unto the judgment of the great day" (Jude 6). "The Lord knoweth how to . . . reserve the unjust unto the day of judgment to be punished" (2 Pet. 2:4). And "the time is come that judgment must begin at the house of God" (1 Pet. 4:17). Shall He not then spare us any less than the devil and his angels? *The elect angels* ever attend upon the Church of God—in midst of our worship (1 Cor 11:10), in service to the saints' needs (Heb. 1:14), wondering at the triumphs of the Gospel (1 Pet. 1:12), expecting to adore our God Triune for His wisdom displayed in the Church to eternity (Eph 3:10–11) and behold the saints judge angels (1 Cor 5:2–3). They bear witness to my ministry; my daily prayer for bread holds them as models of fidelity, devotion and obedience—"Thy will be done on earth, as it is in heaven" (Matt 6:10). They stand guardian to the weakest of God's children, lest I offend one (Matt 18:1–14). Let me *before the elect angels,* sing: "Bless the Lord, ye His angels, hearkening unto the voice of His word . . . ye ministers of His, that do His pleasure!" (Ps 103:20–21). *Without preferring one before another, doing nothing by partiality:* blind to no one's sin, none made an offender for a word; no need ignored or neglected; no fault condoned to keep my place or purse; no tie of friend or family higher than duty. Before Thee, O God; before Thee, *Lord Jesus Christ;* before Thee, Holy Spirit, as all *the elect angels* bear witness, help me, in grace enable me to observe these things.

114. From Sea to Sea

1 From sea to sea, to earth's remotest bound,
Let our Dominion hear the joyful sound
Which to repentance and to faith will call:
"Our Savior, Jesus Christ, is Lord of all!"

2 Where springs, streams, rivers, lakes their waters pour
Out to the rugged coast and ocean shore;
Through mountains, forests, prairies, glaciers fields,
Shine forth in mercy, God our Sun and Shield!

3 O God our Father, bare Thine arm in might
To bring our land from darkness into light:
Crime and injustice, vice and hate repress,
Exalt our nation with true righteousness!

4 Lord Jesus, Sun of Righteousness, arise
And bring salvation marvelous to our eyes:
From east to west bear healing in Thy wings
Through grace the preaching of Thy Gospel brings.

5 Come, Holy Ghost, to Christ Thy witness bear—
Convict, convert and quicken those who hear:
All races, classes, tongues and kindred call
To crown our Savior Jesus, Lord of all!

6 Our people perish without hope or God:
Redeem them by the Lamb's most precious Blood!
Triune Jehovah, now do all things well,
To pluck our souls as burning brands from Hell!

7 Grant us Thy truth alone which makes men free:
Proclaim Thy kingdom here, from sea to sea,
Fulfill the promise of Thy written Word:
"Blest is the nation whose God is the Lord!"

10.10.10.10.

The House of God

Preparatory Reading: Old Testament: Proverbs 7;
New Testament: Hebrews 6 Psalm: 114

1 Timothy 5:22

22Lay hands suddenly on no man, neither be partaker of other men's sins: keep thyself pure.

Paul has set down very clear guidelines to "honour" or "rebuke" elders in the Church according to their fidelity or fault, service or sin (5:17, 19), just as he has established criteria to "honour" or "refuse" widows in the Church (5:3, 11). He now supplements these with three "footnotes" of practical importance to any pastor or elder or teacher in working with the men who bear office in a congregation: (i). We must be timely in invoking discipline (5:22) (ii). We must be temperate and healthy to render good judgment (5:23). (iii). We must test the character of men over time for good or ill, and not rely on single events (5:24–25).

If my own character and repute is indispensable to my ministry, I must not hazard it by unwise haste or delay in protecting it—I must heed the Apostle's demand, *keep thyself pure*. Not only must I seek to walk before God with integrity; I must *keep pure* of sinful influences or associations, to be "a vessel unto honor, sanctified and meet for the Master's use" cf. (2 Tim. 2:15–21; Ps 101). To this end Paul counsels me to avoid two opposite extremes: *lay hands suddenly on no man, neither be partaker of other men's sins.*

Is the Apostle referring to laying hands on men in ordination? That "laying on of the hands of the presbytery" which set Timothy apart? (4:14). While this is possible—and too hasty ordination has brought grief to the churches—the context around this admonition might also suggest a warning not to arrest or receive accusations against an offender too quickly. "Lay hands on" another is a phrase used of arrest (Mark 12:12; Matt 26:50; John 7:30, 44; Acts 4:3). We are not to apprehend a man either *suddenly* nor too late—and so *be partaker of other men's sins*. Such a caution would fit the counsel to test both sins and good works by a measure of time (5:24–25).

An unseasonable delay in facing matters of discipline can increase both the difficulty of remedy and the extent of mischief an offence causes. For that reason Paul roundly reprimanded the Church at Corinth for 'looking away' from the scandal of incest sheltered in the congregation (1 Cor 5). The Son of God Himself rebukes the churches in Pergamos and Thyatira for 'tolerating' error and evil among them (Rev. 2:14, 20–25).

In either case, time is on the side of the truth; haste does not help—neither does delay. Some pastors have relative "youth," but none can afford to be a "novice" (4:12; 3:6.

Lord Jesus, keep me pure, as Thou art pure—"holy, harmless, undefiled and separate from sinners" (1 John 3:3; Heb. 7:26; Ps 26).

115. One Loaf, One Cup, One Table

1 One loaf, one cup, one Table
Received from Christ the Lord,
We keep, and would be faithful
To follow His own Word:
As week by week we gather
In Christ's simplicity,
We prove ourselves, and heed Him:
"This Do—Remember Me!"

2 One loaf we break, confessing
Our sins on Jesus laid;
Our guilt and our transgressions
His stripes have fully paid.
One loaf each other giving,
We sharing, all partake
In Him, One Body living
And serving For His sake.

3 One cup, in sign and symbol,
His precious Blood shows forth;
One cup, the pledge and token
Of all His matchless worth:
This cup, the cup of blessing,
From His own hand we take,
And humbly drink, remembering
He suffered for our sake.

4 One Table stands before us;
One Table would we share—
One Household, we our burdens
For one another bear.
With all baptized believers
In faith's true unity,
Forgiving, and forbearing,
We live in charity.

5 One loaf, one cup, one Table
His love must oft proclaim;
We keep the feast, still faithful,
Until He come again:
His reign in power and glory

The House of God

Archangels shall declare,
The trumpet sound, and like Him,
We'll meet Him in the air.

7.6.7.6D

Preparatory Reading: Old Testament: Proverbs 8;
   New Testament: Hebrews 7 Psalm: 115

1 Timothy 5:23

23 Drink no longer water, but use a little wine for thy stomach's sake and thine often infirmities.

Paul's second counsel to Timothy also seems to assist the right use of discipline among the elders of the congregation—here in being personally temperate and fit in health to act wisely. Timothy is to *drink no longer water* alone but *a little wine for* his *stomach's sake and . . . often infirmities.*

Now why would Timothy have been otherwise, in common parlance, a "total abstainer?" For so he was. Timothy, considering his office and work hitherto and even hereafter kept clear of beverage alcohol. *Water* alone he drank—not always in ancient times a wholesome choice, as his *stomach and . . . often infirmities* might suggest.

The reason clearly lies in the standards of the Old Testament Church, whose teaching and praying priests serving at the altar were stipulated to abstain totally while on duty (Lev 10:8–11; Ezek 44:21; cf. 1 Cor 9:13–14). This sobriety was a royal virtue too (Prov 31:4-9), and the New Testament mandates sobriety in elders (3:3-8). "Not given to wine" applies to elders and deacons alike.

What is Paul's intent in this advice? It does not seem to encourage the beverage but medical use of alcohol for digestive and other ailments: *for thy stomach's sake and thine oft infirmities.*

A little wine is not contrary to the earlier command "not given to wine." Where real medical knowledge sanctions *a little wine* God's Word does not forbid it, no more than the sacramental use of wine at the Lord's Table violates the Biblical polemic against strong drink (Prov 23:24–33; Mark 14:23–26). If anything, Paul's advice commends total abstinence to a wise pastor, and as a model disciple, to a wise people.

Even more broadly, these inspired words recall that pastoral service brings stress and strain which must be recognized and treated by proper attention to health, personal well-being, and preventative measures. For many an elder will have need of concern for his *stomach's sake and . . . oft infirmities.*

Father of mercies, who hast paid the price of Thy dear Son's precious Blood to redeem me; who hast given the highest gift of Thy Holy Spirit to renovate, renew and fill my soul and body as Thy temple; who indwellest me through Thy Son by Thy Spirit; grant me to prosper and be in health both in body and in soul. Let me be temperate in all things, let me glorify Thee with my body and spirit which are Thine, through Jesus Christ, Amen.

116. "My Grace Sufficient is for thee"

1 The thorn will not from me recede,
Though oft I may beseech and plead;
Yet comes the Savior in my need
Jesus, the Lord my Strength and Song!

2 I hear His Word; He speaks to me,
"My grace sufficient is for thee,
My perfect strength in weakness be
Thy lot; thou dost to Me belong!"

3 In weakness and infirmity
Reproach, distress, necessity,
The power of Christ doth rest on me:
When I am weak, then I am strong!

4 Through time and to eternity
Is nothing that can sever me
From my Lord Jesu's love so free,
So high, so deep, so broad, so long!

5 To God our Father, with the Son
And Holy Spirit ever One,
Our praises, here on earth begun,
Shall know no end in heaven's throng!

L.M.

Preparatory Reading: Old Testament: Proverbs 9;
  New Testament: Hebrews 8 Psalm: 116

1 Timothy 5:24-25

24Some men's sins are open beforehand, going before to judgment; and some *men* they follow after. 25Likewise also the good works *of some* are manifest beforehand; and they that are otherwise cannot be hid.

Paul's final counsel to Timothy concerning the discipline of elders states one truth twice—"the truth will out." Sooner or later, subtly or suddenly, overt or covert, the tree is known by its fruits, and our sins will find us out (Num 32:23; Matt 12:33).

Let me think over this long and hard when I am tempted, when I imagine I am far, far removed from public view and duty. Let me remember this when my prayers, and labors and efforts seem so much wasted ointment, fragrant, but fleeting. Truth will out.

Some men's sins are open beforehand going before to judgment. Let me never forget that the decay of personal godliness, the cherishing of vain thoughts or secret sins, sours and stales my soul in public duty—sooner or later. The spiritually minded members of the Church will discern it—sooner or later. It will taint and tarnish my preaching, prayer, study, visits and witness—sooner or later. It will produce powerless formality if not real heresy—sooner or later cf. (Ps 32:3-4). Paul speaks from real and bitter experience as well as by inspiration of the Holy Ghost. He can remind Timothy pointedly of Hymenaeus, Philetus and Alexander (cf. 1:19-20; 2 Tim. 2:16-18). He has warned of grievous wolves and smooth schismatics with mercenary minds (Acts 20:28; Rom 16:17-18). Peter likewise warns us of the "unlearned and unstable;" John warns of the likes of Diotrephes (2 Pet. 3:16; 3 John 9-11). Yes, truth will out.

And some men they follow after: "He that covereth his sins shall not prosper" (Prov 28:13). Even if men can perceive nothing amiss, the evil heart of unbelief will bring forth its cursed fruits Heb. 3:12-13; 6:4-6; 12:14-17). "Judas Iscariot, which also betrayed Him" (Mark 3:19) surely proves the case; he stood numbered with the Twelve, and bore the bag, unnoticed and indistinguishable to the last moment—all the while Satan filled his heart (John 13:2, 21-30, 18:1-3; Luke 22:3). Paul has met them too in his travels—he has known the "perils of false brethren" (2 Cor 11:26). He expects them in Ephesus (Acts 20:30). He would in time report Demas' sad plight to Timothy (2 Tim. 4:10). Peter bids us watch and pray against any such fall; John and Jude note the apostasy of yet others (2 Pet. 3:17, 2 John 2:19; Jude 17-19). Truth will out (cf. 2 Cor 12:20-13:3).

Have I not myself witnessed men stronger, abler, more widely useful than ever I might be, yet fallen from ministry, yea, making shipwreck of faith? *Some men's sins are open beforehand going before unto judgment, and some men they follow after.* Sooner or later—truth will out.

117. As drew on the Evening Hours

1 As drew on the *evening hours*
Of a far-spent Sabbath day,
Two poor, weary, worn disciples
To Emmaus made their way:
As they passed, Another joined them—
Jesus, risen from the dead,
To them shown in all the Scriptures,
Then made known in breaking bread.

2 Jesus, as the Lord's Anointed
Spent *a night* in ceaseless prayer
Ere the Twelve He called, appointed
Sent, His Gospel to declare:
So His people, wise as serpents
Meek as doves, go forth as sheep
In the midst of wolves and violence
Trusting Him their souls to keep.

3 Through *the watch of deepest darkness*
On the Lake of Galilee
Toiled the Twelve, alone and helpless
Crossing o'er the storm-tossed sea;
Walking on the water, glorious
In His Godhead's majesty,
Came our Savior King victorious
From their fears to set them free.

4 As the shadows dark were fleeing
At the dawn of that First Day,
Asked the women, mourning, weeping,
"Who shall roll the stone away?"
Coming to anoint the Master
Filled with sorrow, pain and dread
Yet they found the tomb was empty
Christ had risen from the dead.

5 So, when *doubt* assails, assure us
Savior, of Thy truth and grace:
In our *duties,* go before us,
Where we serve in every place:
Making bare Thine arm, relieve us

From all *danger* yet in store,
And, *at death*, Lord Christ, receive us
To Thy kingdom evermore.

6 O Redeemer, heed and help us
As for refuge now we flee
To Thy throne of grace: behold us
Day and night, alike to Thee:
Shine upon us out of darkness,
Jesus, Lord, our one true Light
Save, preserve, protect and bless us
Through the hours of this night.

8.7.8.7.D

The House of God

Preparatory Reading: Old Testament: Proverbs 10;
New Testament: Hebrews 9 Psalm: 117

1 Timothy 5:24–25

24Some men's sins are open beforehand, going before to judgment; and some *men* they follow after. 25Likewise also the good works *of some* are manifest beforehand; and they that are otherwise cannot be hid.

If Paul's words of warning put me in fear, and well they should, then there is also great comfort to assure me my labor cannot be in vain in the Lord Jesus (1 Cor 15:58). *Likewise also the good works of some are manifest beforehand, and they that are otherwise cannot be hid.*

While we are not to do righteousness to be seen of men, we are so to let our light shine that men may see our good works and glorify the Father in heaven (Matt 5:16; 6:1). The conversion and testimony of believers may well draw the admiration of the world to God's glory; with such why should I not rejoice? (Rom 16:19; 1 Thess. 1:7–8, cf. Acts 2:46–47; 5:12–13). The impact of a notable pastor or teacher may be celebrated as God's gracious work (1 Cor 15:10; Gal 1:23–24). *The good works of some are manifest beforehand.*

But while this is true of *the good works of some,* it is not true of all. We cannot infallibly foresee the outcome of our labors, because we do not walk by sight but by faith. King Solomon wisely counsels us to take no risks in well-doing: "Cast thy bread upon the waters: for thou shalt find it after many days. Give a portion to seven, and also to eight: for thou knowest not what evil shall be upon the earth . . . In the morning sow thy seed, and in the evening withhold not thine hand: for thou knowest not whether shall prosper, either this or that, or whether they both shall be alike good" (Eccl 11:1–2, 6).

And they that are otherwise cannot be hid. If my own labors are not so known, they are by no means, unknown. The Father who sees in secret will not fail to reward me openly (Matt 6:3–4). The promise stands: *they that are otherwise cannot be hid.* As in time, so in eternity, truth will out. And the Apostle himself says much the same: "Be not deceived; God is not mocked: for whatsoever a man soweth that shall he also reap. For he that soweth to his flesh shall of the flesh reap corruption; but he that soweth to the Spirit shall of the Spirit reap life everlasting. And let us not be weary in well doing: for in due season we shall reap, if we faint not. As we have therefore opportunity, let us do good unto all men, especially unto the who are of the household of faith" (Gal 6:7–10).

Let me in fear, humility, charity and zeal be vigilant, watchful of myself, my brethren and of all the flock over which the Holy Ghost has made me an overseer. And let me take this caution from the Apostle:

"Judge nothing before the time, until the Lord come, who both will bring to light the hidden things of darkness, and will make manifest the counsels of the heart: and then shall every man have praise of God" (1 Cor 4:5).

118. Bless us, O God, as now we wait upon Thee

1 Bless us, O God, as now we wait upon Thee
Before we leave and from this place depart:
Make us to taste the grace the Gospel mystery
Brings through Thy Word and Spirit to our hearts.

2 God of all grace, who hast to glory called us
After a little while of suffering here,
Make us all perfect, strengthen, settle, 'stablish
Through Jesus Christ, our Lord and Savior dear.

3 Father of mercies, God of consolation,
Through Jesus Christ we cast on Thee our care:
All that befalls us, work for our salvation
In answer to Thy children's earnest prayer.

4 Thou God of peace, who our Lord Jesus rais'ed
Up from the dead again, by Covenant Blood,
By Jesus Christ, whose Name be ever prais'ed,
Perfect us all to do the will of God.

5 O God of hope, Thy joy and peace bestowing,
Make hope abounding by the Holy Ghost
That we, the grace of Jesus Christ still knowing,
May grow in grace, unto the uttermost.

6 Blest be our God, who from the heavenly places
Hath blessed our lives in Jesus Christ His Son
Sealed by His Spirit with all saving graces,
Praise we our God—the blessed Three in One!

11.10.11.10.

The House of God

Preparatory Reading: Old Testament: Proverbs 11;
  New Testament: Hebrews 10 Psalm: 118

1 Timothy: Reading over Chapter 5

The chapter I now review has impressed upon me the importance of honoring and protecting the Church as a "household of faith;" of treating its members as brethren, sisters, fathers and mothers in that "whole family in heaven and earth" bearing the Name of the Father of our Lord Jesus Christ; of supporting those the Savior has called and gifted to teach and encourage believers, whether as widows or elders; and of keeping each other accountable, responsible and faithful to our callings. Let me read once more this portion, praying that the Holy Spirit who inspired these words of spirit and life, will translate them into my love and labor for Christ Jesus and all the saints.

Prayer for the Brotherhood of the Church

Behold, how good and how pleasant it is
for brethren to dwell together in unity
For there the LORD commanded the blessing,
Even life forever.
No man hath seen God at any time:
If we love one another,
God dwelleth in us, and His love is perfected in us.
Hereby know we that we dwell in Him and He in us,
Because He hath given us of His Spirit.
Whosoever shall confess that Jesus is the Son of God,
God dwelleth in him, and he in God.

O Father of glory, God of all grace,
Thou hast blessed us with all spiritual blessings in Christ;
Thou hast predestinated us unto the adoption of children
By Jesus Christ unto Thyself:
Thou hast predestinated us
To be conformed to the image of Thy Son,
the Firstborn of many brethren.

Thou hast called us into the fellowship of Thy Son
In whom we have redemption through His Blood,
Even the forgiveness of sins
According to the riches of Thy grace.
Thou knowest what we have need of before we ask,
And yet Thou dost bid us ask, and knock and seek
For Thou givest Thy Holy Spirit and all good gifts to Thy children

The House of God

Even as Thou hast not spared Thine only Son
But delivered Him up for us all.
Lord, Thou pitiest us as Thy children
Thou chastenest us as sons
Thou numberest the hairs of our heads
Thou hast sent the Spirit of Thy Son,
The Spirit of adoption,
Into our hearts, and we cry to Thee, Abba, Father!

O Lord Jesus, Thou hast loved us and given Thyself for us
Thou hast loved us to the end
Thou art not ashamed to call us Thy brethren
Thou dost declare the Father's praise among Thy brethren
In the midst of the Church.

As the Father hath loved Thee, Thou hast loved us
And given us commandment to love one another.
Thy Father is our Father; Thy God is our God.
Thou art our faithful and merciful High Priest,
passed into the heavens
touched with the feeling of our infirmities
yet without sin
In all our afflictions Thou art afflicted;
Thou art able to succor the tempted,
as Thou Thyself hast been tempted.

Holy Ghost, Spirit of Christ, Spirit of adoption, Spirit of life,
Spirit of grace and supplications
Thou hast given us new birth, and newness of life in Christ
Thou hast baptized us into Christ
One Body with many members,
One Church of all nations, kindred and tongues of earth
A royal priesthood, an holy nation, a spiritual house

Once no people, now the people of God
Thou art our God, and we are Thy people.

Shed abroad Thy love in our hearts—
The love of Jesus, the love of the Spirit, the love of the Father
That we may love one another with a pure heart fervently
Forbearing and forgiving one another
As Thou hast forgiven us.

The House of God

Give us one heart and mind, soul and strength to love Thee
And keep Thy commandment
To abound in love to one another and to all men
To serve one another by love,
In honor preferring one another.

Make our older men fathers
Make our older women mothers
Make our young men brethren,
our young women sisters with all purity
Preserve among us the unity of the Spirit in the bond of peace
Bring us in the unity of the faith
To the fullness of the stature of manhood in Christ Jesus
That we may at last with all saints
Comprehend the length, breadth, depth and height
And know the love of Christ which passes knowledge.

This we ask for the sake of Jesus Christ:
And unto Him that loved us,
And washed us from our sins in His own Blood,
And hath made us kings and priests unto God and His Father:
To Him be glory and dominion for ever and ever!
Amen.

119. Humbly to walk with God

1 O God, now let me walk with Thee—
My Shield and great Reward:
Order my steps, that all may be
According to Thy Word.

2 Mercy to love, justly to do,
Humbly to walk with God
Thus hast Thou shown me what is good
The path which Christ hath trod.

3 Lord Jesus, as I follow Thee,
I stumble not in night:
Thy precious Blood still cleanseth me,
I walk with Thee in light.

4 As in the Holy Ghost I live,
So let me walk in Him:
Rich fruits of grace O let Him give
Striving against all sin.

5 Throughout the length of all my days
I'll walk my God before
Till I at last behold His face
When I am here no more.

C.M.

The House of God

Preparatory Reading: Old Testament: Proverbs 12;
New Testament: Hebrews 11 Psalm: 119:1–16

1 Timothy 6:1–2

6:1Let as many servants as are under the yoke count their own masters worthy of all honour, that the name of God and *his* doctrine be not blasphemed. 2And they that have believing masters, let them not despise *them*, because they are brethren; but rather do *them* service, because they are faithful and beloved, partakers of the benefit. These things teach and exhort.

Where chapter 5 of this Epistle focuses on the relationships of the pastor with others in official and moral leadership of the congregation—its elders and widows—chapter 6 directs the pastor in guiding the wider brotherhood of the Church, those who work in the world. The poorest and richest of the saints all represent *the Name of God and His doctrine* among men; their own souls' good and their witness to the world depends on the right use of work and money.

No greater anxiety undermines the devotion of believers to God's kingdom than the cares of this life (Matt 6:19–34, 13:22). We all need to echo the wisdom of Agur's prayer for "neither poverty nor riches" (Prov 30:7–9). So the Apostle addresses a solemn charge to Timothy, commanding him, and me to enforce "godliness with contentment" and "trust in the living God" as part of the "doctrine according to godliness"—*these things teach and exhort* (6:2–3, 6, 18).

The heaviest cross to be borne by disciples in *these things* lies upon *as many servants as are under the yoke*. They are bondmen, slaves, reduced to legal chattel, like oxen *under the yoke*. Yet they can, as Christ's freemen, as His people, safeguard and adorn and glorify *the Name of God and His doctrine* even in such degraded conditions. *The yoke* can be transcended even as it is borne by their own willing service for the Name of the Lord Jesus: *count their own masters worthy of all honor*. Do not be forced and constrained to comply; obey with a willing, free heart as a free man in Christ Jesus, for in Him "there is neither bond nor free" (Gal 3:28; 1 Pet. 2:18–25, Eph 6:5–8). To render eye service or to disobey or answer back, does not assert but subvert the believer's liberty from sin and prompts *the Name of God and His doctrine* to *be blasphemed*.

What fellowship with Christ's sufferings do so many saints share amid the hard work of life, and with what new hope may we then hear His well-loved words, "Come unto Me, all ye that labor and are heavy-laden, and I will give you rest. Take My yoke upon you, and learn of Me, for I am meek and lowly of heart, and ye shall find rest unto your souls" (Matt 11:28–29). Timothy must move his hearers with method and motive to live as the Lord's freemen even in bond-service, rendering their duties to Christ as His servants (1 Cor 7:21–22). *These things teach and exhort*.

120. Stretch forth, O God, Thy Hand in Power

1 Stretch forth, O God, Thy hand in power
In this, our nation's darksome hour,
And by the truth that makes men free,
Turn back our hearts to Thee!

2 For sake of Thy beloved Son,
Christ Jesus, Who for us hath won
Redemption through His Blood from sin—
Thy Kingdom now bring in!

3 Shed forth Thy Spirit, send Thy Word
Proclaiming peace through Christ the Lord,
Till all our troubled land across
Be gathered to the Cross!

4 So, truly reconciled to Thee
And to each other, O may we
Make this Dominion, sea to sea,
Thine own, both just and free!

5 To Father, Son and Holy Ghost,
The living, true Lord God of hosts,
Who reigns forever—One in Three—
Be praise eternally!

8.8.8.6.

The House of God

Preparatory Reading: Old Testament: Proverbs 13;
New Testament: Hebrews 12 Psalm: 119:17–32

1 Timothy 6:1-2

⁶:¹Let as many servants as are under the yoke count their own masters worthy of all honour, that the name of God and *his* doctrine be not blasphemed. ²And they that have believing masters, let them not despise *them,* because they are brethren; but rather do *them* service, because they are faithful and beloved, partakers of the benefit. These things teach and exhort.

If *our own masters* are unworthy of honor, our duty is not lessened—we must *count* them *worthy* and render obedience, respect, service as required—*worthy of all honor*. If I refuse my *yoke*, when it is Christ's yoke, *the Name of God and His doctrine* may well be *blasphemed*. Now as then we are to be living "epistles of Christ, known and read of all men" (2 Cor 3:2–3). Paul could count his bonds the chains of office for an ambassador of Christ (Eph 6:20)—we must take on *the yoke* of labor as His yoke.

Our duty is no lesser either, when we have *believing masters*: we dare not *despise them because they are brethren*. If anything, Paul says, the ties of love replace and increase the former obligations of outward constraint and law. Such *believing masters* are not merely *counted worthy of all honor*—they are to receive *service* as truly worthy, because they are *brethren, faithful, beloved* and *partakers of the benefit*.

A believing master is a *brother*, sharing the same predestinating grace (Rom 8:29, adoption of children (Eph 1:5) and regenerate life (1 Pet. 1:22–25) I have received in the Lord Jesus—is not his *honor* and interest mine? He is also *faithful*—holding the same form of sound doctrine, trusting the same Savior, making the same good confession: is not his *service* then a help to the cause of *the Name of God and His doctrine?* (Rom 6:17; 2 Pet. 1:1; 1 Tim. 6:12–13). Further, he is *beloved* of God, and shall I not love those begotten of God, if I love God Himself? How can I love God unseen, and yet not love a brother I have seen? (1 John 4:20, 5:1). Then too he is a *partaker of the benefit*—he is a joint heir with Christ of God and of all things (Rom 8:14–17; Gal 4:7), a servant who shall receive the Master's reward as well as I, and who must answer for his work, and care of me, in his turn. Every true Christian must seek so to *honor* those over him in work, that he will be seen as an asset to the workplace and an advertisement for the Gospel. This is the necessary duty of saints even in wage slavery. *These things teach and exhort.*

O Father of heaven, for the Lord Jesu's sake, grant all Thy people who labor daily in hard conditions that abundance of grace to take their "yoke" from the Savior, finding that yoke easy, their burden light, because He bears it beside them and gives rest. Amen.

121. Lord Jesus Christ, I Came to Thee

1 Lord Jesus Christ, I came to Thee,
And claimed Thy promise blest:
"All ye that labor, come to Me,
And I will give you rest."

2 With heavy-laden heart I spoke,
"Jesus, I trust in Thee!"
And Thou didst answer, "Take my yoke
Upon you—learn of Me."

3 That yoke upon me did impart
Release so unexprest;
Thou saidst, "My meek and lowly heart
Shall to your souls give rest."

4 Savior, the promise I have heard
Is proven good and right,
"My yoke is easy," saith Thy Word
In truth: "my burden, light!"

5 From bondage of my sin set free
Thy yoke of grace I wear
To keep Thy Word in love to Thee—
This burden light I bear.

6 Redeemed by Thy most precious Blood
O rule me all my days,
Until I see Thee, Lord and God,
And sing Thine endless praise.

7 Then Thine elect shall enter rest
For all eternity
With Father, Son and Spirit blest,
Our God, the One in Three.

C.M.

Preparatory Reading: Old Testament: Proverbs 14;
New Testament: Hebrews 13 Psalm: 119:33–48

1 Timothy 6:3–5

3If any man teach otherwise, and consent not to wholesome words, *even* the words of our Lord Jesus Christ, and to the doctrine which is according to godliness; 4He is proud, knowing nothing, but doting about questions and strifes of words, whereof cometh envy, strife, railings, evil surmisings, 5Perverse disputings of men of corrupt minds, and destitute of the truth, supposing that gain is godliness: from such withdraw thyself.

From such withdraw thyself: Paul spent much time in Ephesus, as he told the church's elders, giving out warnings—"Therefore watch, and remember that by the space of three years I ceased not to warn every one night and day with tears" (Acts 20:31).

And most of Paul's warnings call us to withdraw or separate from error and evil: "Mark them . . . and avoid them" (Rom 16:17–18), "note that man, and have nothing to do with him" (2 Thess. 3:14), "come ye out from among them, and be ye separate" (2 Cor 6:14–18), "mark them which walk so as ye have us for an ensample. For many walk, of whom I have told you often, and now tell you even weeping, that they are the enemies of the cross of Christ" (Phil. 3:17–18).

He has already given Timothy several such warnings in throughout this Epistle (1:3–4; 4:7; 5:11, 20, 22; 6:11, 20). Here he points out a pillar of salt standing amid the overthrow of the wicked, as surely as our Master Christ Jesus bade us, "Remember Lot's wife" (Gen 19:26; Luke 17:32). *From such withdraw thyself.* No consideration of person or past friendship may mitigate the mandate: *If any man teach otherwise . . . from such withdraw thyself.* Deficiency of truth is as bad as departure from truth, in the Apostle's view: *If any man teach otherwise, and consent not to wholesome words. . . from such withdraw thyself.*

In truth, either we know nothing but Christ crucified (1 Cor 2:2) or we know nothing at all—*knowing nothing.* From start to end, Paul will tolerate "no other doctrine" except *the doctrine which is according to godliness* (cf. 1:3). There is no fidelity to the Bible and its saving Gospel than what is total, single and exclusive (2 John 9–10).

The tree is known by its fruits (Matt 12:37, 7:16–21). This warning earmarks the error of the wicked by its corrupt fruits—its destructive impact on the lives of those who heed it. What the apostle declares *otherwise* will subvert ethics as well as doctrine, and bring dishonor, despite and disservice. Do I watch the impact of what I teach? (Cf. 1 Cor 15:33–34; Gal 5:4). This terrible monument ought never to leave my sight, and must needs cry out, "Be not high minded, but fear" (Rom 11:20). If I would "keep myself pure" and not "be partaker of other men's sins" (5:22), I must heed the command, *From such withdraw thyself.*

122. Christ is risen from the dead!

1 Through the darkness and the dawning
See the women sad and mourning
Come, the first day of the week
Hearts and hands with sorrow wringing
To the tomb sweet spices bringing
They the Master's body seek.

2 Ointments for the dead they made Him
To anoint Him where they laid Him:
At the breaking of the day,
At the tomb they view the wonder:
Pilate's seal is torn asunder,
And the stone is rolled away!

3 Entering the tomb, there meet them
Angels shining bright who greet them,
Filling all their souls with dread:
"Fear not! Ye the place see plainly,
Here ye seek for Jesus vainly—
Christ is risen from the dead!"

4 Now before Him let us gather,
High exalted by the Father
Reigning to eternity;
Jesus, Lord of all proclaiming
By His resurrection gaining
Over death the victory

5 Saints, rejoice, for ye inherit
Through the Savior's Blood and merit
Life and immortality
Let each heart and voice declare it
"Father, Son and Holy Spirit,
Triune God all praise to Thee!"

8.8.7.8.8.7

The House of God

Preparatory Reading: Old Testament: Proverbs 15
New Testament: 1 John 1 Psalm: 119:49–64

1 Timothy 6:3–5

3 If any man teach otherwise, and consent not to wholesome words, *even* the words of our Lord Jesus Christ, and to the doctrine which is according to godliness; 4 He is proud, knowing nothing, but doting about questions and strifes of words, whereof cometh envy, strife, railings, evil surmisings, 5 Perverse disputings of men of corrupt minds, and destitute of the truth, supposing that gain is godliness: from such withdraw thyself.

If any man teach otherwise and consent not to wholesome words: any deviation from the truth, any divergence from "the faith once delivered to the saints" (Jude 3) is departure from the faith, and "doctrine of devils" (cf. 4:1–2). Only the Holy Scriptures provide the *wholesome words* by which we must live (Deut 8:3; Matt 4:4). "The law of the wise is a fountain of life, to depart form the snares of death" (Prov 13:14). "Lord, to whom shall we go? Thou hast the words of eternal life, and we believe and are sure that Thou art that Christ, the Son of the living God" John 6:68–69). *Not* to *consent* to these is to *teach otherwise*. These *wholesome words* are our holdfast (2 Tim. 1:13).

These *wholesome words* are *even the words of our Lord Jesus Christ.* In the broadest sense all inspired Scripture is "the word of Christ" (Col. 3:16). Paul's teaching in all this Epistle does echo the Lord's own words at many points. Consider these comparisons:

Epistle Passage	Topic	Gospel Passage
1:5	The End of the Law	Matt 22:34–40
1:9	The Law and Sin	Mark 10:17–19
2:4	The Divine Will to Save	John 10:16, 12:32
2:5	The One Mediator	John 14:6
2:6	The Ransom	Mark 10:45
2:8	Prayer without Wrath or Doubt	Mark 11:22–26
3:16	The Mystery of Godliness	Luke 24:46–48
4:4	All Foods Clean by Creation	Matt 15:10–20
5:5	The Devout Widow	Luke 18:1–8
5:18	The Workman's Hire	Luke 10:7
5:19	Two or Three Witnesses	Matt 18:16
6:7–10	Food, Raiment and Love of Money	Matt 6:24, 28
6:13	Christ's Confession to Pilate	John 18:37
6:18–19	Lay up Treasure in Heaven	Matt 6:19–21

And the specific principle of honorable work accords with Paul's desire to "remember the words of the Lord Jesus" (Acts 20:35). Paul writes the commands of the Lord, and follows Christ (1 Cor 11:1; 7:10, 25, 40; 14;37). Do I follow him in following Christ?

123. God forbid that I should glory

1 God forbid that I should glory
Save in our Lord Jesus Christ
By whose cross the world is to me
Crucified, and I to it.

2 In Christ Jesus our salvation
Outward rites are nothing worth
We are made a new creation
By the Spirit's second birth.

3 On as many walk according
To this Gospel rule be peace,
God, His mercy still affording,
His true Israel shall increase.

> Based on Galatians 6:14–16
> 8.7.8.7.
> Tune: Stainer

The House of God

Preparatory Reading: Old Testament: Proverbs 16;
New Testament: 1 John 2 Psalm: 119:65–80

1 Timothy 6:3–5

3If any man teach otherwise, and consent not to wholesome words, *even* the words of our Lord Jesus Christ, and to the doctrine which is according to godliness; 4He is proud, knowing nothing, but doting about questions and strifes of words, whereof cometh envy, strife, railings, evil surmisings, 5Perverse disputings of men of corrupt minds, and destitute of the truth, supposing that gain is godliness: from such withdraw thyself.

The Scripture's authority rests on being *the words of our Lord Jesus Christ* ; its efficacy on being *wholesome words* ; and its content on being *the doctrine which is according to godliness.* Faith and life are inseparable; truth and love, integral; Law and Gospel, indivisible. This is Paul's trademark for the Gospel (cf. 2:10, 3:16, 4:4–6, 6:1).

The Holy Spirit once more directs the Apostle to lay down, with no equivocation, the divine verdict on *any man* who should *teach otherwise and consent not* to this Gospel found in the *wholesome words* of Holy Scripture. He diagnoses the MOTIVES, the COMPETENCE, the EMPHASIS, the CHARACTER, and the IMPACT of such a man. He pinpoints the radical DELUSION behind all this man's career—behind all his defects of truth and all his departure from truth. The Apostle plainly does not spare the rod (1 Cor 4:21; 2 Cor 13:2), just as John unmasks Diotrephes (3 John 9–10). *Any man* who teaches *otherwise* is this man—and *from such,* says Paul, *withdraw thyself.*

What are his MOTIVES? God, who searches the heart and tries the reins (Jer 17:9–10), whose Word discerns the thoughts and intents of the heart (Heb. 4:12) has one sole answer—*he is proud:* pride puffs us up to be "wise" above what is written (1 Cor 4:6). Pride provokes contention and stirs strife (Prov 13:10; 28:25). Nothing could set us so in conflict with God than pride (1 John 2:16). He hates it (Prov 6:17), abominates it (Prov 16:5) resists it (Prov 3:34; Jas. 4:6; 1 Pet. 5:5), holds it at arm's length (Ps 138:6), brings it low even to destruction (Prov 29:23). *Any man* who may *teach otherwise* than God's Word cannot but desire to exalt himself—and such God will abase (Dan 4:37; Luke 18:14). "To this man will I look" says the LORD God, "even to him that is poor and of a contrite spirit and trembleth at My Word" (Isa 55:2).

Is pride poisoning my ministry? Leading me away from the *wholesome words* of *the doctrine according to godliness*? "Everyone that is proud in heart is an abomination to the LORD" (Prov 16:5).

124. May I not trust Thee, Jesus?

1 May I not trust Thee, Jesus,
To save me from my sin—
To heal all my diseases,
To cleanse my heart within?
Might I not trust Thy mercy,
Thy love, Thy truth and grace,
Who on the Cross of Calv'ry
Once suffered in my place?

2 Can I not trust Thee freely
My Savior, God and Lord?
Is not Thy saving promise
Recorded in Thy Word?
Dare I not trust Thee fully?
What greater love could be,
Than that which paid my ransom,
And shed Thy Blood for me?

3 Must I not trust Thee solely?
None other Name is given
To pardon, cleanse and save us,
Than Thine, from under heaven!
Should I not trust Thee wholly,
My Prophet, Priest and King?
Thy grace is all-sufficient
To heav'n my soul to bring!

4 Will I not trust Thee only?
Lord Jesus, hear my plea—
No man can to Thy Father
E'er come, except by Thee!
Do I not trust Thee truly?
Oh let Thy Spirit place
A heart of faith within me,
To cling to Thee always!

7.6.7.6.D

The House of God

Preparatory Reading: Old Testament: Proverbs 17;
New Testament: 1 John 3 Psalm: 119:81–96

1 Timothy 6:3–5

3If any man teach otherwise, and consent not to wholesome words, *even* the words of our Lord Jesus Christ, and to the doctrine which is according to godliness; 4He is proud, knowing nothing, but doting about questions and strifes of words, whereof cometh envy, strife, railings, evil surmisings, 5Perverse disputings of men of corrupt minds, and destitute of the truth, supposing that gain is godliness: from such withdraw thyself.

When any man *teach otherwise, and consent not to . . . the doctrine . . . according to godliness* what real COMPETENCE does he have? God, whose folly exceeds all the world's wisdom, and whose wisdom ordained the foolishness of preaching (1 Cor 1:21, 25), declares such a teacher to be utterly ignorant—*knowing nothing*. To reject the love of the truth in faith is not to embrace reason, but ignorance and deceit (Prov 3:5–7; 2 Thess. 1:8–12). The unregenerate live in ignorance (Acts 17:30, Eph 4:13); as believers we are to abandon that ignorance (1 Pet. 1:14). But the unlearned and unstable wrest the Scriptures through ignorance (2 Pet. 3:15, Matt 22:29) and the pride of knowledge brings ignorance (Rom 1:21–22, 1 Cor 8:2). Without the love of God, our knowledge is vain (1 Cor 13:2–3 cf. Ps 14:1).

Let me be a fool to this world to be wise to God (1 Cor 3:18–20). Let me esteem nothing above the knowledge of God through His written Word—the Holy Scriptures which are able to make us wise to salvation through faith in Christ Jesus (2 Tim. 3:15). What is such a teacher's EMPHASIS? What is the trademark, the signature of any man who may *consent not to wholesome words . . . of our Lord Jesus Christ?* Nothing of worth—*knowing nothing, but doting about questions and strifes of words:* God's Word has no praise for mere intellectual acuity that serves no end to safeguard the truth of the Gospel. Paul disdains "philosophy and vain deceit, after the tradition of men . . . not after Christ" (Col. 2:8) as the fevered appetite of a sickened mind for noise. Paul over and again pleads with Timothy to keep himself and the congregation clear of such dazzling deceits; he castigates them in catalogue: "fables, endless genealogies, questions" (1:4) "vain jangling" (1:6) "doctrines of devils" (4:1) "profane and old wives' tales" (4:8) "profane and vain babblings" "science falsely so called" (6:20). *Any man* who departs from *the doctrine according to godliness* plays with trifles. Will I waste my powers of mind and voice, my short, fleeting days of life, my heart and soul to mere *questions and strifes of words?* Look long over the burdened shelves of libraries and see in all the tomes tainted with rationalism, superstition; a cemetery of tombstones to men who spent their lives *doting about questions and strifes of words.* Well spoke Solomon, "Buy the truth and sell it not!" (Prov 23:23).

125. Rise, My Soul, Awake and Bless

1 Rise, my soul, awake and bless
God the LORD, whose holiness,
Wisdom, justice, truth and grace
Merits all thy powers of praise!

2 Glory give the King of kings,
Faithful Maker of all things—
Righteous Judge, who rules o'er all:
Storm, or sea, or sparrow's fall!

3 Praise His love who freely gave
His own Son to seek and save
Sinful man from all our loss
By His Blood shed on the Cross!

4 Lengths, and depths, and breadths, and heights—
Praise the God of love and light
Ever one LORD—God of hosts:
Father, Son and Holy Ghost!

7.7.7.7.

The House of God

Preparatory Reading: Old Testament: Proverbs 18;
New Testament: 1 John 4 Psalm: 119:97–112

1 Timothy 6:3–5

3If any man teach otherwise, and consent not to wholesome words, *even* the words of our Lord Jesus Christ, and to the doctrine which is according to godliness; 4He is proud, knowing nothing, but doting about questions and strifes of words, whereof cometh envy, strife, railings, evil surmisings, 5Perverse disputings of men of corrupt minds, and destitute of the truth, supposing that gain is godliness: from such withdraw thyself.

When any man teach otherwise, *and consent not to . . . the doctrine . . . according to godliness* what real CHARACTER does he have? What IMPACT does he make on his hearers? From these strifes of words come envy, strife, railings, evil surmisings, perverse disputings of men of corrupt minds and destitute of the truth. False teaching always produces the works of the flesh, never the fruits of the Spirit. It spawns men of corrupt minds and destitute of the truth. If men may handle the truth itself with deceit to corrupt ends (2 Cor 2:17, 4:1–2); if men can preach the Gospel itself "from envy and strife" (Phil. 1:15–18), how much more evil will come of error in their hands? False teaching poisons the soul as surely as arsenic poisons the body. The symptoms never change.

There is *envy*: what else is *envy* but pride crossed, pride of heart hungry for vainglory, pride breeding the sins of "hatred, variance, emulation, wrath, heresies . . . murders . . . and such like" (Gal 5:20–21)? How can anyone "saved by the washing of regeneration and renewing of the Holy Ghost, which God hath shed abundantly on us by Jesus Christ our Saviour" continue to live "in malice and envy, hateful and hating" others? (Titus 3:3, 5–6). There is *strife*: *strife* rises from *envy*, and signals the heart of *envy*, the *corrupt mind destitute of the truth*. Paul repeats this warning in his last Epistle of all: "Strive not about words to no profit . . . the servant of the Lord must not strive" (2 Tim. 2:14, 24). Christ did not strive; why should we? (Matt 12:16–21). *Railings* erupt as the mouth speaks from the fullness of the heart (Matt 12:34). *Railings* place us beyond communion with the saints, and into the company of fornicators, drunkards and extortioners (1 Cor 5:11). This odious trio are the defensive gestures of pride as it dotes about strifes of words.

The aggressive gestures of this pride are *evil surmisings* and *perverse disputings*: misunderstanding willfully, misjudging rashly, misspeaking stupidly the views of others not in search of truth but of victory. How we treat others and their words reveals more about ourselves than our opponents.

Like the carrier of a deadly pox, a man so possessed of *corrupt mind and destitute of truth, proud, knowing nothing but doting about strifes of words* will bear and spread all this. Beware.

126. A Wretched Man Am I

1 A wretched man am I—
No good thing is in me!
Out of the body of this death
Who shall my soul set free?
I humbly thank my God!
Believing in His Word,
He justifies me by the Blood
Of Jesus Christ our Lord.

2 Most holy, just and good
All God's commandments are:
Yet with the good work that I would
My sinful flesh makes war:
My inward man delights
To do His will, but sin
Against my mind contends and fights
My members from within.

3 No condemnation now
From sin and death is ours:
All in Christ Jesus have the law
Of life, the Spirit's power:
The flesh we mortify,
And in the Spirit live—
The righteous Law we fructify
In grace the Savior gives.

4 All things shall work to us
For good, our God who love,
Foreknown, predestined by His grace
To reign with Christ above:
Now called, and justified,
In likeness to His Son
We shall be raised and glorified
When Jesus soon shall come!

D.S.M.

The House of God

> Preparatory Reading: Old Testament: Proverbs 19;
>   New Testament: 1 John 5 Psalm: 119:113–128

1 Timothy 6:3–5

3 If any man teach otherwise, and consent not to wholesome words, *even* the words of our Lord Jesus Christ, and to the doctrine which is according to godliness; 4 He is proud, knowing nothing, but doting about questions and strifes of words, whereof cometh envy, strife, railings, evil surmisings, 5 Perverse disputings of men of corrupt minds, and destitute of the truth, supposing that gain is godliness: from such withdraw thyself.

When any man *teach otherwise, and consent not to . . . wholesome words, even the words of our Lord Jesus Christ,* what PREMISE or rather DELUSION can be directing his pride and ignorance to work such disruption and destruction upon "the church of the living God?" What can be his object or goal in hazarding the dread sanctions which Scripture has against such a course? It is no trifle to wreak such havoc: "These six things doth the LORD hate; yea, seven are an abomination unto Him . . . He that soweth discord among brethren" (Prov 6:16–19). "If any man defile the temple of God, him shall God destroy; for the temple of God is holy, which temple ye are" (1 Cor 3:17). Once more, the Apostle in words taught by the Holy Ghost makes bare the secrets of the heart in writing of such a man, *supposing that gain is godliness.*

Hardly any heretic or false prophet has ever spoken that did not sell himself to evil with a hireling heart. All who "have forsaken the right way . . . are gone astray, following the way of Balaam the son of Bosor, who loved the wages of unrighteousness" (2 Pet. 2:15). The Sanhedrin which rejected our Lord Jesus was dominated by Pharisees "who were covetous" (Luke 16:14 cf. Mark 12:38–40); their greatest fear of Christ was this: "If we let Him thus alone, all men will believe on Him: and the Romans shall come and take away our place and nation" John 11:48). Both at Philippi and Ephesus, Paul's bitterest foes feared "the hope of their gains was gone" (Acts 16:19, 19:23–28).

Mammon is no measure of God's work or workers. To see *gain* as the measure of *godliness,* or *godliness* as a means to *gain,* or *gain* as the meaning of *godliness* is to "make merchandise of souls through covetousness with feigned words" (2 Pet. 2:3), to "corrupt the Word of God" (2 Cor 2:17)—it is to preach idolatry, and not truth (Eph 5:5; Col. 3:5). The elders who rule well must be "counted worthy of double honour" 5:17), yes; "they that preach the Gospel should live of the Gospel" (1 Cor 9:14), yes; "let him that is taught in the Word communicate unto him that teacheth in all good things" (Gal 6:6), yes. But "having food and raiment, let us be therewith content," for "godliness with contentment is great gain" (6:6, 8). *Supposing that gain is godliness* has no place in any believer's life, far less in any elder's life; *from such withdraw thyself.*

127. I praise and bless Thy Name!

1 O Father God, to me draw near
And listen to my prayer:
In all my need bow down Thine ear:
On Thee I cast my care!

Refrain:
According to Thy faithful Word,
I praise and bless Thy Name
For all Thy truth and mercy, Lord,
From age to age the same!

2 Lord Jesus, blessed Son of God,
For Thy sake do I pray,
Now wash me in Thy precious Blood
And take my sins away.

3 O Holy Ghost, within my heart
Now shed abroad the love,
Our Father showed and will impart
By His dear Son above.

4 All good things Thou to me hast given,
On earth: My thanks I raise;
And for the blessed hope of heaven
Thy Name I'll ever praise!

5 To Father, Son and Holy Ghost
Our God the One in Three,
I'll sing with all the angel hosts
To all eternity!

Tune: "God Sees the Little Sparrow Fall"
C.M. (with refrain).

Preparatory Reading: Old Testament: Proverbs 20;
New Testament: Acts 1 Psalm: 119:129–144

1 Timothy 6:6–8

⁶But godliness with contentment is great gain. ⁷For we brought nothing into *this world, and it is* certain we can carry nothing out. ⁸And having food and raiment let us be therewith content.

Paul now sets forth, as from his own experience, the divine standard of life which applies to pastor and people, teacher and taught alike (Phil. 4:11–13). Timothy's own conduct must demonstrate what he would "teach and exhort" those who are "under the yoke" of servitude (6:1–3). Every believer's body and soul can be, and should be, satisfied to have *godliness with contentment*. "If any man teach otherwise . . . supposing that gain is godliness," he will neither help himself or his hearers. If I on this practical point "take heed unto" myself "and the doctrine," I shall both save myself and my hearers (4:16).

Godliness is the grand end of redemption (Titus 2:11–14); the sum of the believer's lifestyle (1 Tim. 4:7–8, 6:11); the true fruit of sound doctrine (1 Tim. 3:16, 6:3, Titus 1:1). The genuine Christian is "godly" (Ps 4:3; 2 Pet. 2:9), and lives "godly in Christ Jesus" (2 Tim. 3:12). His soul is fulfilled with "meat indeed . . . and drink indeed" (Ps 63:5, John 6:53–57, 63); he is "rich toward God" (Luke 15–21) and has laid up "treasure in heaven"—there is his heart (Matt 6:20–21). *Contentment* finds the body's peace and rest in God's provision at any given time by the sufficiency of Christ's grace (Phil. 4:12–13). God's abiding presence and help undergirds that rest (Heb. 13:5–6). The true Christian's body is fulfilled, come what may (Rom 8:31–39). *Godliness with contentment* fits us to pursue heaven on earth; to seek the eternal amid the temporal, to find joy in God whether we are rich or of low degree, hungry or full (Gal 3:1–2, 23–24; 2 Cor 4:16–18; James 1:9–11).

Godliness with contentment is great gain. There is no real *contentment* without *godliness*: "For what shall it profit a man, if he shall gain the whole world, and lose his own soul?" (Mark 8:36). There is no *godliness* which does not create *contentment*: "Although the fig tree shall not blossom, and the be no herd in the stalls; yet I will rejoice in the Lord, I will joy in the God of my salvation" (Hab 3:17–19). "For me to live is Christ, and to die is gain" (Phil. 1:21). "My flesh and my heart faileth, but God is the strength of my heart, and my portion forever" (Ps 73:26). So every saint, poor, rich, teacher, taught, slave, free can find fulfillment of body and soul (Ps 128:1–2). *Godliness with contentment is great gain*. Paul attests this fact from two facts in Old and New Testaments—the shortness of life, and the simplicity of life. Job's trials prove the vanity of possessions in so short a life; and Solomon's wisdom confirms it (Job 1:21; Eccl 5:13–20). *We brought nothing into this world, and it is certain we can carry nothing out*. The Lord Jesus' "wholesome words" furnish a pattern for simple living (Matt 6:24–34; Luke 12:23). *Having food and raiment, let us be therewith content*. Savior, grant me each day sufficient grace, my daily bread, and Thyself. Amen.

128. If Thou wilt, Thou Canst make me Whole!

1 Under the curse of sin depraved,
A vile diseased and leprous soul
I come, Lord Jesus, to be saved:
"If Thou wilt, Thou canst make me whole!"

2 My friends and lovers stand apart,
From my uncleannesses they flee:
I know the plague within my heart—
I have no other help but Thee!

3 My every power and member fails,
To death they all decay, dissolve:
Thy Name upon me now prevails
To seek Thee as my last resolve.

4 Stretch forth Thy hand, and hold me fast,
Set not my sins before Thy face!
My all upon Thee now I cast—
I wait Thy words of truth and grace!

5 Thy heart and hand compassion show
As from Thee virtue flows unseen:
Thy word of promise now I know—
Thou say'st, "I will: O be thou clean!"

6 I feel Thy power to cleanse my soul
At once! I haste to blaze abroad
The Man who spoke and made me whole,
The praises of my Savior God!

7 O come to me, ye who God fear:
What He has done to save my soul
I'll tell, till all who pass shall hear
This news: "Christ Jesus makes me whole!"

8 My need He met, my prayer He heard;
I needs must speak what I have seen—
Believe His love, and plead His Word:
"If Thou wilt, Thou canst make me clean!"

L.M.

The House of God

Preparatory Reading: Old Testament: Proverbs 21;
   New Testament: Acts 2 Psalm: 119:145–160

1 Timothy 6:9–10

9But they that will be rich fall into temptation and a snare, and *into* many foolish and hurtful lusts, which drown men in destruction and perdition. 10For the love of money is the root of all evil: which while some coveted after, they have erred from the faith, and pierced themselves through with many sorrows.

The only safety which pastors and people have in a world given to Mammon is "godliness with contentment"—this alone is "great gain." Depart from this, and we fall into *the love of money* which is *the root of all evil*. Not all *evil* comes directly from the love of money, but there is no *evil* which *the love of money* cannot root, and nourish.

Paul understood this danger well. In closing his farewell to the elders at Ephesus he avows, "I have coveted no man's gold or silver or apparel" (Acts 20:33). He demands that elders be "not greedy of filthy lucre" (1 Tim. 3:3). So he once more warns Timothy, the Church, all elders, all Churches, and me (Exod 18:19–23).

They that will be rich are led by *the love of money*. And this *root of all evil* brings dangers to our souls, both direct and indirect. *The love of money* in itself directly brings *temptation and a snare* whereby those who *fall* into it *have erred from the faith*. *The love of money* also indirectly occasions *many foolish and hurtful lusts* into which those who *fall have pierced themselves through with many sorrows*, and shall *drown in destruction and perdition*.

The *temptation* before those *that will be rich* is essentially to "trust in uncertain riches" rather than in "the living God, who giveth us richly all things to enjoy" (6:17). This false confidence sets sinful man against God in pride (Ezek 28:5) and undermines faith (Ps 52:7; 62:10), barring us from the kingdom of heaven (Mark 10:25, Luke 19:23–24), and placing us under bondage (Matt 6:24).

Both the false security (Hab 2:9) and anxiety of men over riches (Eccl 5:12) choke the Word of grace in men's hearts (Mark 4:19, Luke 8:14). Our only glory must be in the Lord (Jer 9:23). This is the *snare* in *the love of money* which leads men to *err from the faith* (Ezek 33:30–33).

It is with God alone to grant any and all good in this world, and *they that will be rich* seek that good without His will or blessing (Deut 8:17–18; 1 Sam 2:7; 1 Ch. 29:12; Rev. 5:12). It is a cardinal symptom of an evil heart (Mark 7:21–23). The direct danger which *the love of money* poses so many—*the temptation and snare*—is not the sole threat to us. *They that will be rich fall into many foolish and hurtful lusts . . . some have coveted after money have pierced themselves through with many sorrows*.

129. I cry to Thee!

1 My soul in darkness cries to Thee:
Father of mercies hear my plea!
Upon Thee let me learn to lean,
And trust Thee on the path unseen.

2 My heart in pain cries out to Thee:
Lord Jesus, hear, and pity me!
O make Thy Word a balm to ease
My heartache with Thy promised peace.

3 My flesh both faints and longs for Thee:
Blest Holy Ghost, I thirst to see
Fresh streams of living water rise
To cleanse, restore, renew, revive.

4 O Triune God, draw near and bless
Uproot all sin and bitterness
By Christ's own Blood now set me free;
O answer, as I cry to Thee!

L.M.

The House of God

Preparatory Reading: Old Testament: Proverbs 22;
   New Testament: Acts 3 Psalm: 119:161-176

1 Timothy 6:9-10

9But they that will be rich fall into temptation and a snare, and *into* many foolish and hurtful lusts, which drown men in destruction and perdition. 10For the love of money is the root of all evil: which while some coveted after, they have erred from the faith, and pierced themselves through with many sorrows.

What contrary and opposite *lusts* does *the love of money* inspire in men's hearts! Excess and riot in the prodigal son, or the rich man in hell (Luke 15:11-19, 16:19); avarice and hoarding in others who are rich (Eccl 5:10-17). One ends life in dissipated poverty (Prov 23:19-21); another never enjoys what he has gathered (Ps 39:6, Eccl 6:2). All are *foolish*, all are *hurtful* (Prov 28:22 cf. Jer 17:11), sure to pass (Jas. 1:10-11; 1 Cor 7:31; 1 Tim. 2:9; 1 John 2:15-17).

What *sorrows* possess those *that will be rich*, and *pierce them through!* Riches are uncertain to acquire (Prov 23:4-5). Riches do not endure (Matt 6:19-21, James 5:1-2), and are hard to retain (Prov 27:24).

In time these *foolish and hurtful lusts drown men in destruction* in this world, and in *perdition* in the world to come. For riches will neither deliver (Prov 11:4) nor redeem (Ps 49:6-7, 16-17). Those "rich in this world" who are "not rich toward God" face woe, death, and hell, wrath and judgment (Luke 6:24, 12:16-21, 16:19-31; Eph 5:3-5, 1 Cor 5:10-11; Rev. 6:15, 18:17).

Nothing therefore can so brand a false teacher as a wolf in sheep's clothing as evidence of *the love of money* and the *will to be rich*.

Father of mercies! For the sake of Jesus Christ, Thy dear Son, who for our sakes became poor that we through His poverty might be made rich toward Thee, grant me the godliness with contentment which is great gain. Save me from the love of money, its temptations, snares, lusts, destruction and perdition by the Holy Ghost.

Let my heart be sound in Thy statutes, and Thy statutes my song in the house of my pilgrimage as I sing these truths (Ps 119:54):

> I have rejoiced in the way of Thy testimonies
> as much as in all riches ; (14)
> Incline my heart unto Thy testimonies and not to covetousness; (36)
> The law of Thy mouth is better unto me
> than thousands of gold and silver (72)
> Thy testimonies have I taken as a heritage forever:
> For they are the rejoicing of my heart (111)
> Therefore I love Thy commandments above gold;
> yea, above fine gold: (127)
> I rejoice at Thy word as one that findeth great spoil. (162)
> Hear me, O God Triune: let Thine eye be upon me, and Thine ear open to my cry, for the Lord Jesu's sake. Amen.

130. "Pay what thou owest!" God demands

1 "Pay what thou owest!" God demands:
Ye who despise His just commands
On pain of hell and endless wrath
Shall learn "Sin's wages are but death"

2 In future hope ye to amend?
'Tis not enough your guilt to end!
The record of your sins will last,
For 'God requireth what is past!'

3 Ye cannot for one sin atone—
Neither for others', nor your own—
No promise, penance, prayer or pain
Could e'er a mite of merit gain.

4 One saving Name alone is given
Among mankind from under heaven
The way, the truth, the life alone
By which we to the Father come.

5 This name is our Lord Jesus Christ
Our only Prophet, King and Priest
In person one, both God and man
Who can fulfill the Law's demand.

6 Behold the holy Lamb of God
Who on the Cross once shed His Blood
And in His Body on the Tree
Was bruised for our iniquity!

7 "Now it is finished!" hear Him cry,
As at the end He comes to die:
Our every sin on Him is laid
Sin's wages has He fully paid!

8 This finished work has paid the price
For us to enter Paradise:
With contrite heart His grace receive—
O come, on Jesus Christ believe!

L.M.

The House of God

Preparatory Reading: Old Testament: Proverbs 23;
   New Testament: Acts 4 Psalm: 120–121

1 Timothy 6:11-12

11But thou, O man of God, flee these things; and follow after righteousness, godliness, faith, love, patience, meekness. 12Fight the good fight of faith, lay hold on eternal life, whereunto thou art also called, and hast professed a good profession before many witnesses.

But thou, O man of God: Paul sees his beloved son of the faith, Timothy, and all who follow in his train down to me, neither in light of the current scene, nor in light of any personal infirmities—but in the eternal light of God's calling and gifts. Never can Timothy join with such nor mimic such—Paul says not "and thou," rather *but thou.* Paul appeals to him not personally, as later, "O Timothy" (6:20), but formally: *O man of God.*

The true pastor must and will stand apart from all around him—certainly, and utterly distinct form false teachers (6:3–5) in motive (1:3–11), emphasis (1:18–20), character (4:1–6). He will stand apart from the run of men in dealing with "the love of money" (6:6–10), not least for the sake of those "under the yoke" who need his example and well as his exhortation "that the Name of God and His doctrine be not blasphemed" (6:1, 3). Let society decay as it may, let the wicked prosper for their little day, let the false teacher make merchandise of souls, "deceiving and being deceived" (2 Pet. 2:1–3; 2 Tim. 3:13)—*but thou, O man of God,* must differ.

Of any honor or title the Bible bestows upon a pastor, *man of God* is the most profound and pre-requisite. To the people I am "preacher, teacher," "bishop," "elder" (2:7, 3:2, 5:17). To the Savior Jesus I stand as "the servant of the Lord," seeking to be "a good minister of Jesus Christ" (4:6, 2 Tim. 2:24). But to be these, I must be, first, last, ever, only a *man of God* (6:11, 2 Tim. 3:16–17).

Man of God: this term denotes who I am, whose I am, why I am, and what I am. *Man of God:* this places me in a long line of men given to proclaim the Word of God—Moses (Deut 33:1; 1 Chr 30:16, Ps 90 title), Samuel (1 Sam 9:6), Shemaiah (1 Kgs 12:22), David (2 Chr 8:14; Neh 12:24, Elijah 1 Kgs 17:24, 2 Kgs 1:9–10, Elisha 2 Kgs 4:7, 5:8; 7:17)—"the prophets who came before" the apostles (Matt 5:12), on both of whose inspired Scriptures we are built in the holy faith (Eph 2:20, 2 Pet. 3:1–2, Jude 17, 20–21). I am His entirely, for life and service—a *man of God,* bound to His glorious Gospel, His Word, His house, His Name and His doctrine (1:11, 3:12, 4:5, 6:1).

In Gospel privilege in the kingdom of God, all saints are greater than John the Baptist (Matt 11:11); yet as a *man of God,* I could desire no better record than his: "There was a man sent from God, whose name was John. The same came for a witness to bear witness of the Light that all men through him might believe. He was not that Light, but was sent to bear witness of that Light . . . John did no miracle, but all things that John spake of this Man were true" (John 1:6–8, 10:41).

131. Lord Jesus Christ! What Treasures In that blest Name I Find

1 Lord Jesus Christ! What treasures
In that blest Name I find: (Col. 2, Phil. 4)
From Thy right hand its pleasures (Ps 16)
Fill heart, and soul, and mind. (Deut 6)
None have I, none desire
In heaven or on earth,
Beside Thee, God my Savior— (Ps 73, Tit. 2)
Lamb of matchless worth! (Rev. 5)

2 *Jesus!* Name of salvation, (Matt 1)
 That ravishes mine *ear*, (1 Cor 2)
Let every tribe and nation (Rev. 5)
Its *joyful sound* now *hear*! (Ps 89)
Above all names in glory (Eph 1, Phil. 2)
It speaks of peace with God,
For sinners once far from Thee
Brought nigh now by Thy Blood! (Eph 2)

3 What rich and sweet communion
Is mine, Thou Son of God,
To feed in mystic union
Upon Thy flesh and blood! (John 6)
I *taste* and see Thy goodness, (Ps 34, 1 Pet 2)
In all words of Thy *mouth*: (Ps, Ct)
Exceeding honey's sweetness, (Ps 19, 119)
So full of grace and truth! (John 1, Luke 4)

4 Thou camest, Lord, in weakness
My sins and griefs to bear:
In lowliness and meekness
Thou dost my burdens share. (Matt 11)
I *touch* the nail-prints driven (John 20)
When on me Thou dost place
Thy *hands,* all pierced and riven.
And in Thy love embrace! (Mark 1, Matt 17)

5 How fragrant is the *savor*
The knowledge of Thy grace
Sheds forth, my faithful Savior,
Abroad in every place! (1 Cor 2)
With pungent myrrh and aloes, (Ps 45)
Spikenard and cassia rare, (John 12)

The House of God

As spice that from a tree flows,   (Ct)
Thy garments do I wear.   (Is. 62, Ps 45)

6 What glowing light and *beauty*
Which once from out Thee shone
Transfigured, now adorns Thee   (Luke 9, Mark 9)
The LAMB upon the Throne!
When Thou shalt come and gather,
From every clime and race,
Thy Bride before Thy Father,
I'll see Thee, face to face!   (1 Cor 13, 1 John 3)

7 Awakened, in Thy likeness
Shall I be satisfied
To see Thee in Thy brightness,
LORD JESUS, glorified!   (Ps 17, Ro. 8)
With CHRIST I all inherit: (Rom. 8)
Mine eyes shall look upon   (Job 19, Is. 25, Matt 5)
The Father, Son and Spirit—
My God, the Three in One!

                                                            7.6.7.6.D

The House of God

Preparatory Reading: Old Testament: Proverbs 24;
  New Testament: Acts 5 Psalm: 122–123

1 Timothy 6:11–12

11But thou, O man of God, flee these things; and follow after righteousness, godliness, faith, love, patience, meekness. 12Fight the good fight of faith, lay hold on eternal life, whereunto thou art also called, and hast professed a good profession before many witnesses.

Such a *man of God* as I am, has a "charge" and "commandment" (6:13–14) to *flee all these things* the Apostle has been addressing: **flee the love of money*, its *temptation and snare*, its *many foolish and hurtful lusts* *flee the falsehood that *gain is godliness* *flee and *withdraw* from *any man* who may *teach otherwise, and consent not* to Holy Scripture's *wholesome words and the doctrine according to godliness* **flee questions and strifes of words* with their evil fruits *of envy, strife, railing, evil surmisings and disputings*. Where the world craves the wisdom of scribe and disputer (1 Cor 1:20); where the godless defer to riches, and the pagan see luxury as due devotion (Acts 19:23–28), the *man of God* must *flee these things*. As much as I must "flee the wrath to come" to be saved by faith in the Lord Jesus (Matt 3:7); as much as I must "flee idolatry" and "flee fornication" for my soul's safety as a believer (1 Cor 6:18, 10:14); as much as I must "flee youthful lusts" (2 Tim. 2:22) to which I am vulnerable as "the servant of the Lord" (2 Tim. 2:24)—I must *flee these things*. The safest way to *flee* is to *follow after*—pursue, hunt down—the graces and fruits of the Holy Ghost which ensure "godliness with contentment" (6:6). Paul readily numbers these comprehensively in the six terms which follow. *Righteousness* and *godliness* sum the OUTWARD LIFE of true holiness of character before man and God—duty and devotion, life and piety (1 Tim. 4:7–8, 2 Tim. 3:16–17). *Faith, love, patience, meekness* sum up the INWARD LIFE of true holiness, setting out the three eternal graces which abide (1 Cor 13:13)—*faith, love* and *hope*, expressed as *patience* in the face of adversity (2 Tim. 3:10) and as *meekness* in the face of adversaries (2 Tim. 2:22, cf. 1 Thess. 1:3, Titus 2:2). Together these six express the mature life in Christ for which all saints are redeemed to live "soberly, righteously, and godly in this present world" (Titus 2:11–14). Above all others the *man of God* must strive to "follow peace with all men and holiness without which no man shall see the Lord" (Heb. 12:14 cf. 2 Tim. 2:22). In *righteousness* he will fulfill all lawful duty to neighbor and shun filthy lucre (3:3). In *godliness*, he will pursue a peaceable life in all honesty, and shun the idolatry of covetousness (2:2, 6:6). Walking by *faith*, he will trust God's faithful supply (6:17). *Love* will fill us with thanksgiving (Eph 5:1–4); *patience* will weather any want (Ps 37:18–19), *meekness* will endure the evildoer without envy (Ps 37:7–11). *But thou, O man of God, flee . . . follow!*

132. Come, Lord Jesus, Quickly Come!

1 Come, Lord Jesus, quickly come!
How we long to see Thy face,
Shining brighter than the sun
With the glory of Thy grace!
Keep the promise, gracious Lord,
At Thy Table which we claim
As we keep Thy holy Word:
"Fear not: I will come again!"

2 Savior, hasten Thy return!
End the reign of death and sin:
All Thy ransomed people yearn
For Thy kingdom to come in!
Over all the nations, reign
As the wondrous Prince of peace!
Then shall famine, war, and pain,
Sorrow, tears forever cease.

3 Rise, O Bright and Morning Star!
Sun of righteousness, shine forth!
Gather us from near and far
As Thy Bride from all the earth!
Soon shall we Thy glory see
Near th'eternal Father's heart:
So forever let us be
Like Thee, with Thee where Thou art!

7.7.7.7.D

The House of God

Preparatory Reading: Old Testament: Proverbs 25;
  New Testament: Acts 6 Psalm: 124–125

1 Timothy 6:11–12

11But thou, O man of God, flee these things; and follow after righteousness, godliness, faith, love, patience, meekness. 12Fight the good fight of faith, lay hold on eternal life, whereunto thou art also called, and hast professed a good profession before many witnesses.

To FLEE AND TO FOLLOW is to *fight: fight the good fight of faith* and *lay hold on eternal life*. For the first duty of a pastor as a man of God is this: "save thyself and them that hear thee" (4:16), keeping this caution, "lest, having preached to others, I myself be found a castaway" (1 Cor 9:27). The success of our ministry turns upon this *good fight of faith* (cf. 2 Tim. 4:7) for by "holding faith and a good conscience" we "war a good warfare" in defending, confirming and advancing the Gospel (1:18–19) against the world the flesh, and the devil cf. (Eph 6:10–20, 1 John 5:4–5, Rom 8:12–13).

"A good conscience" verifies and sustains the *good profession* of the *eternal life* to which the Gospel calls us outwardly, and the Spirit draws us inwardly (2 Thess. 2:13–14). As every believer has *professed a good profession before many witnesses* in baptism, so the pastor, elder, teacher, preacher as *a good minister of Jesus Christ* must by "a good conscience" confirm his own *good profession. Many witnesses* have seen it, just as the laying on of the hands of the presbytery has attested our gift (4:14).

Paul exults in this as his victory at the end of life cf. (2 Tim. 4:6–7). He rests his entire labor upon this "good conscience" cf. (2 Cor 1:12; Acts 23:1, 24:14–16). He submits it before believers as a claim to their confidence and prayers (Heb. 13:18).

Conscience lost, all is lost; that is the warning Paul gives against those who "in latter days depart from the faith . . . Having their conscience seared with a hot iron" (4:2), "Holding faith and a good conscience" I also shall withstand all in the evil day, and having done all, yet stand (Eph 6:13). I too may rejoice that my name is written in heaven (Luke 10:20). And my hearers will also have "a good conscience" through the impact of my ministry (cf. 1:5; 4:16).

My people must follow me as I follow Christ (1 Cor 11:1). What I have by believing in the Lord Jesus (John 3:36, 1 John 5:12), I must show by appropriating its sanctifying benefits and exhibiting them in my life cf. (2 John 8; Phil. 3:8–14). In this way am I to *lay hold of eternal life*.

Lord Jesus, let me finish my course with joy and the ministry I have received of Thee, to testify the Gospel of the grace of God. Let me rejoice in this, that my name also is written in heaven. Let me *lay hold of eternal life* and honor the *good profession* I made *before many witnesses* at my baptism. So may I fight the good fight of faith under Thee, the Captain of my salvation. Amen.

The House of God

133. Lord Christ, the King of Israel

1 Lord Christ, the King of Israel
Among the nations, we would tell
Thy glory; and from day to day
Salvation for Thy people pray.

2 King of the Jews, by wise men sought
Who myrrh and gold and incense brought
And worshipped Thee in Bethlehem,
Thee only do we seek, like them.

3 To Thee we raise our hands and songs
As did Jerusalem's Paschal throngs:
"Hosanna! Blest be David's Son,
Who in Jehovah's Name has come!"

4 "Behold your King!" to all we cry
But not in Pilate's mockery;
In torment once, in triumph now
"Hail, King of Jews!" men say and bow.

5 Upon the Cross Thy claim they read,
"This is the King of the Jews" who bled
And died; on Thee we fix our eyes—
Heal, save, and bring to Paradise!

6 Now lifted up, all men now draw
To trust Thee, praise and serve with awe:
To kings of earth, Thy Word proclaims:
"Another King, one JESUS, reigns!"

7 O King of kings, and Lord of lords,
We worship Thee, th'eternal Word,
With Father and with Holy Ghost,
One God, Jehovah, Lord of hosts!

L.M.

The House of God

Preparatory Reading: Old Testament: Proverbs 26;
   New Testament: Acts 7 Psalm: 126–127

1 Timothy 6:13–16

¹³I give thee charge in the sight of God, who quickeneth all things, and *before* Christ Jesus, who before Pontius Pilate witnessed a good confession; ¹⁴That thou keep *this* commandment without spot, unrebukeable, until the appearing of our Lord Jesus Christ: ¹⁵Which in his times he shall shew, *who is* the blessed and only Potentate, the King of kings, and Lord of lords; ¹⁶Who only hath immortality, dwelling in the light which no man can approach unto; whom no man hath seen, nor can see: to whom *be* honour and power everlasting. Amen.

The sum of man's duty toward God, both as creature and sinner; the sum of all the effects of his experience of God's grace in the soul is embodied in these words, when Paul gives to Timothy the *charge* to "lay hold of eternal life"—*keep this commandment.*

Solomon in all his wisdom declares: "Let us hear the conclusion of the whole matter: Fear God, and keep His commandments; for this is the whole duty of man" (Eccl 12:13–14). Greater than Solomon, in whom all the treasures of knowledge and wisdom are hid, the Lord Jesus says, "If ye love me, keep My commandments" (Matt 12:42; Col. 2:3, John 14:15).

To this the beloved disciple of Jesus, His cousin the Apostle John bears witness over and again: "This is His commandment, that we should believe on the name of His Son Jesus Christ, and love one another, as He gave us commandment" "Here is the patience of the saints: here are they that keep the commandments of God, and the faith of Jesus" "Blessed are they that do His commandments, that they may have right to the tree of life, and may enter in through the gates into the city" (1 John 3:23–24; Rev. 14:12, 22:14).

Throughout the ages, the Lord of hosts declares, "This thing commanded I them, saying, Obey My voice, and I will be your God, and ye shall be My people: and walk ye in all the ways that I have commanded you, that it maybe well with you" (Jer 7:22).

Because an elder's piety must be exemplary, Paul says, *Keep this commandment without spot, unrebukable* (cf. 3:2).

I give thee charge... that thou keep this commandment, writes Paul—the fourth of five charges laid upon Timothy as a minister of the Gospel: integrity of doctrine (1:3), edification in ministry (1:18), impartiality of discipline (5:21), godliness of life (6:13), and, at the last, fidelity of preaching (2 Tim. 4:1–5). How well do I grasp, how seriously do I take, how fully do I bear these solemn obligations? How often do I recall, heed and pay my ordination vows?

134. Gleams of the Morning

1 Gleams of the morning, shades of the night
Herald His glory, wisdom and might:
Winter and autumn, summer and spring,
All to our God their praises shall bring!

2 Meadow and mountain, forest and field,
Beauty and bounty, all of them yield
Mercies to man through all of his days,
And to Jehovah honor and praise!

3 Trickling streams from glacier snows
Lost where the river murmuring flows
Roar as the rapids tumble and fall:
Hail to the Lord and Maker of all!

4 Stillness of wind and whispering breeze,
Blast in the surging gales of the seas
Out of the earthquake, flood and the flame
God shall His righteous kingdom proclaim

5 Father of mercies, well-beloved Son,
Spirit of grace, the Three in the One—
Glory and honor, riches and power
Give to the Lord our God evermore!

9.9.9.9.
Tune: "John Dunbar" Theme of Film "Dances With Wolves"

The House of God

Preparatory Reading: Old Testament: Proverbs 27;
  New Testament: Acts 8 Psalm: 128

1 Timothy 6:13–16

¹³I give thee charge in the sight of God, who quickeneth all things, and *before* Christ Jesus, who before Pontius Pilate witnessed a good confession; ¹⁴That thou keep *this* commandment without spot, unrebukeable, until the appearing of our Lord Jesus Christ: ¹⁵Which in his times he shall shew, *who is* the blessed and only Potentate, the King of kings, and Lord of lords; ¹⁶Who only hath immortality, dwelling in the light which no man can approach unto; whom no man hath seen, nor can see: to whom *be* honour and power everlasting. Amen.

I give thee charge: Paul lays upon me a direct, personal responsibility for my ministry and all its consequent influence (cf. 1:2–3, 3:14–15, 4:6, 11–16, 5:21, 6:3, 11). *This commandment* I receive as my own legacy from the forbears of my Churches and their ministry, indeed from all the holy, catholic, apostolic Church which is one in her King and Head—*I give thee charge.* Paul has passed the torch he bore to Timothy, to faithful men able to teach others also, and to me (2 Tim. 2:2, 3:10, 14, 4:2). As I read the "form of sound words" here which I must "hold fast, with faith and love in Christ Jesus," I am hearing Paul say to me, *I give thee charge* cf. (2 Tim. 1:13, 1 Pet. 5:1–5).

This *charge* gives me no scope for "off the record" remarks or "off-duty" conduct—for Paul says, *I give thee charge in the sight of God* (cf. 5:21). All the life, speech, conduct and work of a "man of God" must be *in the sight of God*. Like the Apostle, my whole life and doctrine must be transparent (Rom 1:9, 9:1; 2 Cor 2:17, 4:2, 5:11; 1 Thess. 2:1–6; Phil. 1:8)

All the more because He is *God who quickeneth all things*—"See now that I, even I am He, and there is no god with Me; I kill and I make alive: I wound and I heal: neither is there any that can deliver out of My hand. For I lift up My hand to heaven, and say, I live forever" (Deut 32:39–40). "In Him we live, and move, and have our being" "the God in whose hand thy breath is, and whose are all thy ways" (Acts 7:24–28, Dan 5:23). *God who quickeneth all things* holds my body and soul in His hand: how mad then to trifle with, neglect or defy Him!

Said our Savior Jesus "unto His disciples first of all, Beware ye . . . of hypocrisy . . . And I say unto you My friends, Be not afraid of them that kill the body, and after that have no more that they can do. But I will forewarn you whom ye shall fear. Fear Him, which after He hath killed hath power to cast into hell; yea, I say unto you, fear Him!" (Luke 12:1–9). *I give thee charge in the sight of God who quickeneth all things.*

135. What Evil hath He done?

1 "What evil hath He done?"
The Savior Jesus stands
Condemned as God's eternal Son
Betrayed to wicked hands.

2 "What evil hath He done?"
So Pilate in surprise
Demands an answer and finds none
Among the people's cries.

3 "What evil hath He done?"
His words, and works, and ways
Of righteousness blaze like the sun
With God's own truth and grace.

4 "What evil hath He done?"
Yet Christ the Crucified
Has life eternal for us won,
Has suffered, bled and died.

5 "What evil hath He done?"
Behold, in light He stands
Before the Father's glorious throne
The once-slain, risen Lamb!

6 To God, the Father, Son,
And Spirit—One in Three,
The Church through endless ages on
Shall sing triumphantly!

S.M.

Preparatory Reading: Old Testament: Proverbs 28;
   New Testament: Acts 9 Psalm: 129

1 Timothy 6:13–16

¹³I give thee charge in the sight of God, who quickeneth all things, and *before* Christ Jesus, who before Pontius Pilate witnessed a good confession; ¹⁴That thou keep *this* commandment without spot, unrebukeable, until the appearing of our Lord Jesus Christ: ¹⁵Which in his times he shall shew, *who is* the blessed and only Potentate, the King of kings, and Lord of lords; ¹⁶Who only hath immortality, dwelling in the light which no man can approach unto; whom no man hath seen, nor can see: to whom *be* honour and power everlasting. Amen.

I give thee charge in the sight of God . . . and before Christ Jesus: Father and Son alike as one God are Alpha and Omega, quickening and judging—"for as the Father raiseth up the dead and quickeneth them, even so the Son quickeneth whom He will. For the Father . . . hath committed all judgment unto the Son: that all men should honour the Son even as they honour the Father" (John 5:21–23; cf. Rev. 1:8; 21:6). Every pastor must labor to enter the eternal rest by faith (Heb. 4:11), to make his own calling and election sure (2 Pet. 1:10–11), to "fight the good fight of faith, lay hold of eternal life" which he has "professed a good profession before many witnesses" (6:12), not only that the Son may confess him before the Father (Luke 12:8–9), but because *Christ Jesus . . . before Pontius Pilate witnessed a good confession,* once for all on our behalf. He is now the "True and Faithful Witness" to our talk and walk (Rev. 3:14–19) because He Himself *witnessed a good confession.* Our "good profession" (6:12) must match His *good confession.*

What can we learn about the Savior's *good confession before Pontius Pilate?* All we may know of the contact between *Christ Jesus* and *Pontius Pilate* comes from these Old and New Testament Scriptures: Ps 2:1–2; Isa 49:5–10, 52:13–15, 53:7–9; Matt 27:1–2, 11–26, 57–66; Mark 15:1–15, 42–47; Luke 23:1–25, 50–56; John 18:28–19:22; Acts 3:13–15, 4:24–28, 13:35–39. Reflecting on all the events of the Savior's passion and resurrection as they touched Pilate, we may say the Lord Jesus *witnessed a good confession* to His person, mission and work.

This confession was PLAIN—forthrightly answering the governor's impatient questions with the truth; SCRIPTURAL—submitting to the purpose of the Father, and the words of the prophets, He "answered nothing" to His accusers; STEDFAST—He stood by His claim and title in face of the Sanhedrin's hostility and the mob's rejection; COMPELLING—His bearing and majesty shook Pilate into washing his hands; CONFIRMED—by Pilate's wife, Joseph and Nicodemus, by the very fears of the rulers; and COSTLY—taking Him to the cross. Is my confession like His? Shall He confess me, as I confess Him?

The House of God

136. Lo, On Mount Zion Stands the Lamb

1 Lo, on Mount Zion stands the Lamb
Amid those myriad souls
Redeemed from earth, who follow Him
Whithersoe'er He goes!

2 With all its charms this world could not
Their virgin-souls defile;
They stand before the throne of God
Their mouth found free of guile.

3 Before that throne without a fault
They harp and sing new songs;
Unknown to elder, angel, beast
That round about Him throngs.

4 Here is the patience of the saints:
They all keep God's commands,
None in the faith of Jesus faints,
By grace alone each stands.

5 The voice from heav'n now bids us "Write,"
And all the truth record:
"Blest are the faithful dead henceforth,
Who shall die in the Lord!"

6 "Yea," saith the Spirit, "they shall find rest,
From all their labors sore;
Their works shall follow them and blest,
Their pains shall all be o'er!"

7 By faith we take our pilgrim path
To enter heaven's rest,
Where Father, Son and Spirit reign
One God forever blest!

C.M.
Tune: Crediton

The House of God

Preparatory Reading: Old Testament: Proverbs 29;
   New Testament: Acts 10 Psalm: 130

1 Timothy 6:13–16

¹³I give thee charge in the sight of God, who quickeneth all things, and *before* Christ Jesus, who before Pontius Pilate witnessed a good confession; ¹⁴That thou keep *this* commandment without spot, unrebukeable, until the appearing of our Lord Jesus Christ: ¹⁵Which in his times he shall shew, *who is* the blessed and only Potentate, the King of kings, and Lord of lords; ¹⁶Who only hath immortality, dwelling in the light which no man can approach unto; whom no man hath seen, nor can see: to whom *be* honour and power everlasting. Amen.

Keep this commandment . . . until the appearing of our Lord Jesus Christ, which in His own times He shall shew: In every age, in every land, believers keep their watch "till He come." Whatever our talents or task, the Master calls, "Occupy till I come" (Luke 19:13). "In due time," the Savior gave His life a ransom for all and died for the ungodly (cf. 2:6; Rom 5:6). *In His own times He will shew* His *appearing.* "Blessed are those servants, whom the Lord when He cometh shall find watching" (Luke 12:37, Matt 24:46). Should I not look for "the glorious appearing of the great God and our Saviour Jesus Christ?" (Tit. 2:13). Should I not "love His appearing?" (2 Tim. 4:8). Let the trial of my faith, more precious than gold tried with fire, be found to praise, honor and glory at the appearing of Jesus Christ (1 Pe.1:6-7). For *our Lord Jesus Christ* is worthy of *honor and power everlasting.* His is SUPREME SOVEREIGNTY, ABSOLUTE ASEITY, PERFECT PURITY, DREADFUL DEITY. He has the SUPREME SOVEREIGNTY as *the blessed and only Potentate,* as much as God the Father, to be praised as "the King eternal" (1:17) in His divinity; in His incarnate, glorified, triumphant humanity exalted to be King of kings and Lord of lords (Rev. 17:14, 19:11-16). His is the ABSOLUTE ASEITY of Jehovah who declares "I AM THAT I AM" (Exod 3:14, 6:3), for He *only hath immortality* like as the Father, "the King eternal, immortal" (1:17). "As the Father hath life in Himself, so hath He given the Son to have life in Himself" (John 5:20). His is also the PERFECT PURITY of the Holy One, who is "Light, in whom is no darkness at all" (Isa 6:3, 57:15; 1 John 1:5), *dwelling in the light which no man can approach unto.* The three pillar apostles were "eyewitnesses of His majesty . . . in the holy mount" (Matt 17:1-12; John 1:14; 2 Pet. 1:16-18). John the Apostle beheld His glory as the exalted Son of man (Rev. 1:13-18, 16). Paul himself, born out of due time as an apostle, saw Christ Jesus in His glory (1 Cor 9:1, 15:8; Acts 22:6-11, 26:13-18). His is the DREAD DEITY of "the invisible God"—the Son, as image of the Father who is "the King . . . invisible" (1:17; cf. Col. 1:15, Heb. 1:3) *whom no man hath seen nor can see* apart from the Incarnation (cf. John 1:18, Exod 34; 23). We shall appear with Him, and shine like Him (Col. 3:4; Matt 13:43). *Keep this commandment!*

137. Himself He Cannot Save

1 "Himself He cannot save!"
Upon the cursed Tree,
The Savior Jesus bears reproach
For us at Calvary.

2 "Himself He cannot save!"
The scribes in taunting prate,
Among themselves the chief priests mock,
With hardened hearts of hate.

3 "Himself He cannot save!"
The passers-by all rail,
With wagging heads, "Come, save thyself!"
Their lips His heart assail.

4 "Himself He cannot save!"
The soldiers toast the King
And offer Him their soured wine
Him from the cross to bring.

5 "Himself He cannot save!"
One thief dies in despair,
And yet, the other thief believes
His glory, grace and care.

6 "Himself He cannot save!"
Ah no! Upon that Cross
"He others saved" by dying there—
He came to seek the lost!

7 "Himself He cannot save!"
He must redeem by Blood,
The souls on whom He set His love,
And bring them back to God.

8 "Himself He cannot save!"
Nor would, till He had won
The victory over death and hell,
God's risen, reigning Son!

9 "Himself He cannot save!"
He saves me! Ever more
The Father, Son and Holy Ghost
My Savior God adore!

                                                                                    S.M.

The House of God

Preparatory Reading: Old Testament: Proverbs 30;
   New Testament: Acts 11 Psalm: 131

1 Timothy 6:17-19

17Charge them that are rich in this world, that they be not high-minded, nor trust in uncertain riches, but in the living God, who giveth us richly all things to enjoy; 18That they do good, that they be rich in good works, ready to distribute, willing to communicate; 19Laying up in store for themselves a good foundation against the time to come, that they may lay hold on eternal life.

Paul has shaped the future course of Timothy's life, of mine, of every biblical pastor and elder with five solemn charges—as to doctrine (1:3), ministry (1:18), discipline (5:21), life (6:13) and preaching (2 Tim. 4:1–5). Each pastor in turn must charge his people to integrity of faith and life. Twice this charge turns upon doctrine (1 Tim. 1:3; 2 Tim. 2:14) and once, here, his charge aims at believers' use of worldly wealth (6:17). The very poorest of the saints, who as slaves are "servants . . . under the yoke" carry a special responsibility to adorn the Gospel "that the Name of God and of His doctrine be not blasphemed" (6:1). These saints, *that are rich in this world* are more directed to salvage their own souls *that they may lay hold on eternal life,* and so prove the "good profession" they have made "before many witnesses" (6:12, 17, 19). This confirms the Savior's own teaching, "the words of our Lord Jesus Christ" how He said, "How hardly shall they that have riches enter the kingdom of God!" (Mark 10:23). "They that will be rich" (6:9) have a very distinct "temptation" and "snare" from *them that are rich in this world*. To seek what God has denied is a sin distinct from abusing what God has given. While God has chosen the poor in this world to be rich in faith and heirs of His kingdom (Jas. 2:5), yet His elect include *them that are rich in this world*. And God is the source of their wealth (Deut 8:17–18; 1 Sam 2:7; Prov 10:22). The annals both of Old and New Testaments reveal several rich believers. The fathers of the faith all acknowledged and trusted themselves to the Lord as their inheritance, and their exceeding great reward—so ABRAHAM (Gen 13:2, 14:22, 15:1), ISAAC (GEN 26:12–23), and JACOB (Gen 32:9–10). JOB (Job 1:1–3, 42:10–25, Jas. 5:11) and SOLOMON (2 Chr 1) also possessed great wealth from God's hand at His Word with His blessing. The New Testament also reveals an honored roll of believers *rich in this world*. NICODEMUS and JOSEPH OF ARIMATHEA provided the "King of the Jews" a royal burial (John 19:33–42 cf. Isa 53:9). JOANNA as wife of Herod's steward Chuza supported the Master's ministry (Luke 8:3), while Herod's companion MANAEAN is later found among Antioch's "teachers and prophets" (Acts 13:1). SERGIUS PAULUS (Acts 13:6–12), the ETHIOPIAN EUNUCH of Candace (Acts 8:27–40), and ERASTUS the chamberlain of Corinth (Rom 16:22) rank high in government. Nor should we forget John's Ephesian host GAIUS (3 John 1, 5–8). Yes, Jesus seeks and saves both Bartimaeus and Zaccheus (Luke 19).

138. Lord Jesus, Thou hast prayed for me!

1 Lord Jesus, Thou hast prayed for me—
Now let Thy prayer prevail!
Return my contrite heart to Thee,
Forbid my faith should fail!

2 Behold how Satan hath desired
Thy saints to sift as wheat!
For every trial Thou hast required,
O purge and make me meet!

3 Thus, chastened, humbled 'neath Thy hand
And once again restored,
Grant me to help my brethren stand
According to Thy Word!

4 Faint as my love and faith may be
Appoint me yet to keep,
To feed, to tend as unto Thee
Thy flock, Thy lambs, Thy sheep!

5 When Thou, Chief Shepherd, shalt appear
That great and dreadful day
May I a crown of glory wear
That fadeth not away.

C.M.
Based on Luke 22:31–32; John 21:15–19; 1 Peter 5:1–4.

The House of God

Preparatory Reading: Old Testament: Proverbs 31;
New Testament: Acts 12 Psalm: 132

1 Timothy 6:17–19

17Charge them that are rich in this world, that they be not highminded, nor trust in uncertain riches, but in the living God, who giveth us richly all things to enjoy; 18That they do good, that they be rich in good works, ready to distribute, willing to communicate; 19Laying up in store for themselves a good foundation against the time to come, that they may lay hold on eternal life.

Just as Paul had learned in whatsoever state he was, to be content; so he also was sure, "My God shall supply all your need from His riches of glory by Christ Jesus" (Phil. 4:11, 19). God has His servants among *them that are rich in this world* to be rich in His work and cause (Luke 16:9–13). Paul's counsels to *them that are rich in this world* carry a serious and practical *charge* covering the heart (17) and the life (18–19), viewed both here (17–18) and hereafter (19), both manward (17–18) and Godward (17, 19).

The heart of *them that are rich in this world* must be purified by faith in Christ Jesus through the Spirit toward God and life. They are to *be not high-minded, nor trust in uncertain riches, but in the living God*. With humility they are to acknowledge *all things* which *God gives us richly to enjoy*. The *rich* tend to be *high-minded* because money occasions self-conceit (Prov 28:11), arrogance (Prov 18:23), the flattery of fair-weather friends (Prov 14:20), and false security (Prov 10:15). This diverts their *trust* from *God* who gives riches to the *riches* themselves. Yet *riches* are *uncertain* not least because our capacity to use them is uncertain (Mark 10:24; Eccl 6:1–2; Luke 12:15–21). The *living God,* unlike the idols of the heathen, is by creation and providence alike the Fount of life, who *giveth us all things richly to enjoy* (Acts 17:25; Ps 115:3–9, 36:5–9). The modest enjoyment of life's blessings in the fear of God is the highest affluence and greatest security to which anyone can truly aspire and in which the heart can rest (Acts 14:15–17; Ps 128; Eccl 2:24, 3:12–13, 22, 5:18). Our Father will surely care for His children (Matt 5:40–45; Luke 6:20–38). Here is every Christian's contentment, and mine.

What service does God ask of *them that are rich in this world?* They are to be stewards of their wealth in the service of God and neighbor through time to eternity; they invest here for the Master's "Well done" hereafter (Matt 24:42–25:30). *Be rich in good works*; we save for heaven what we spend for others on earth (Luke 12:21). Saved by grace without works, and created in Christ Jesus for good works (Eph 2:7–10) to all and especially the household of faith (Gal 6:10), we thus prove our faith and bear fruit (Titus 3:8–11).

139. Christ is our All

1 *Christ is our peace*; He shed His precious Blood
To reconcile and bring us nigh to God.

2 *Christ is our hope*; abolished, death and night!
Life's immortality now comes to light!

3 *Christ is our life*, now raised to God's right hand;
We lift our hearts where we shall with Him stand

4 *Christ is our all*; according to His Word,
"Let him that glorieth, glory in the Lord!"

5 Wisdom and righteousness in Christ have we—
Sanctification, and redemption free!

6 Strength everlasting, fullest grace on grace,
Is ours in Jesus—to His Name be praise!

10.10. or 10.10.10.10.

The House of God

Preparatory Reading: Old Testament: Isaiah 49–50;
New Testament: Acts 13 Psalm: 133

1 Timothy 6:17-19

17Charge them that are rich in this world, that they be not highminded, nor trust in uncertain riches, but in the living God, who giveth us richly all things to enjoy; 18That they do good, that they be rich in good works, ready to distribute, willing to communicate; 19Laying up in store for themselves a good foundation against the time to come, that they may lay hold on eternal life.

What I do for Jesus is what I do for His own—the least, lowest and last (Matt 20; 25:40). As Dorcas' legacy was her coats for the poor (Acts 9:36, 39), so we must be *ready to distribute* cf. (Eph 4:28), generous in imparting good to others. No less vital is denying the use of our own for others. We walk the second mile when we are *willing to communicate* (Luke 3:11; Matt 5:40-42). Such *good works in this world* enrich us for *the time to come laying in store a good foundation* with treasures in heaven (Matt 6:19-21; 19:21). Christ Jesus has made us rich toward God by His poverty (2 Cor 8:9), and granted us His unsearchable riches (Eph 3:8). Our obedient faith makes our calling and election sure (2 Pet. 1:3-11; Rev. 3:18), and grounds us for eternity (Matt 7:24-25) in the proven, felt possession of these riches *against the time to come* (1 Pe.1:3-9). "Where your treasure is, there will your heart be also", and so with our hearts set upon Christ in heaven, we *lay hold of eternal life* (cf. Col. 3:1-4, 23-24).

Our Lord Jesus came that we might have life more abundant; but that life does not consist of the abundance of our possessions (John 10:10; Luke 12:15). We do not live by bread alone, but by every word proceeding out of His mouth (Deut 8:13; Matt (4:14). My people need to see and hear, and receive from me these truths (Phil. 4:9), as I *charge them that are rich in this world* so to live.

Living God, loving Father, who givest me richly all things to enjoy, put my heart's trust in Thee; teach me to do good; make me rich in good works, ready to distribute, willing to communicate. Give me grace to charge the saints that are rich in this world to go and do likewise, laying in store a good foundation against the time to come, that they may lay hold on eternal life through Thy beloved Son Jesus Christ. Grant me Thy Holy Spirit, and all good things with Christ, even for His Name's sake. Amen.

140. Souls of the Blest

1 Souls of the blest, beloved
Of Jesus Christ our Lord,
Which out of tribulation great,
Have come to Heav'n's reward!
Souls of the blest, redeemed
And washed in precious Blood,
Without a fault or stain ye stand,
Before the Throne of God!

2 Souls of the blest, in light
Arrayed, in glory crowned,
Walking in God's full countenance,
Hearing the joyful sound!
Souls of the blest, in song
Full surging like the sea,
The praise of seraphim ye swell
Proclaiming victory!

3 Souls of the blest, at peace,
Your toils and sorrows done;
How paltry all earth's wealth or ease,
Beside the prize now won!
Souls of the blest, ye yearn
For resurrection day,
When God our Savior shall return,
To bear His Bride away:

4 Souls of the blest, by faith,
Not sight, we still must walk:
We still the cross must preach and bear,
As foes still hate and mock.
Souls of the blest, who throng
Beneath the altar high,
The plaint ye raise, "O Lord, how long?"
From earth we also sigh!

5 Souls of the blest, with you,
The Bridegroom we await,
Who promised, "I shall come again"
Howe'er He tarry late:
Souls of the blest, our cries,

The House of God

"Lord Jesus, come!" are heard:
Together shall we fill the skies,
Forever with the Lord!

6 Souls of the blest, ye just
Made perfect all and pure,
Like you by grace we faith hold fast,
And to the end endure.:
With heaven's glorious host,
The one true God we praise,
The Father, Son, and Holy Ghost,
Now and through endless days!

D.S.M.
Tune: Ich Halte Treulich Still

Preparatory Reading: Old Testament: Isaiah 51–52;
    New Testament: Acts 14 Psalm: 134

1 Timothy 6:20-21

²⁰O Timothy, keep that which is committed to thy trust, avoiding profane *and* vain babblings, and oppositions of science falsely so called: ²¹Which some professing have erred concerning the faith. Grace *be* with thee. Amen.

O Timothy . . . grace be with thee: Paul's First Epistle to Timothy is at once both systematic and specific, intensely personal in address and intently planned in argument. His Second Epistle to Timothy, his last before gaining the martyr's crown, is in many ways a final, hurried dispatch bearing his precious "last words" both to Timothy and the Churches. It closes with several notices of varied laborers in the Gospel under the Apostle's care, and ends with farewells to Timothy and others: "The Lord Jesus Christ be with THY SPIRIT. Grace be with YOU. Amen." (2 Tim. 4:22). The Epistle to Titus is rather more like an 'open letter" backing up a younger man in a turbulent area with apostolic authority for his commission. It ends fairly corporately, as do the Prison Epistles—Ephesians, Philippians, Colossians: "All that are with me salute THEE. Greet them that love US in the faith. Grace be with YOU ALL" (Titus 3:15). The Holy Spirit inspired this First Epistle both as a personal brief and a customized pastoral manual for the first generation and all generations of the Churches founded on apostolic lines under the New Testament (1 Cor 3:16-17; Eph 2:20; 1 Tim. 3:14-15). So in this last, loving farewell, the Holy Ghost moves Paul to pen both a personal appeal and assurance, and an abiding precept and promise. Fully knowing all his infirmities and susceptible weakness, Paul boldly applies his final words directly, inseparably to his dear son in the faith—*O Timothy.* Yet the Spirit of God who prompts him to write the Lord's commandments (1 Cor 14:36-37), enables him so to write that we may readily supply our own names. This personal touch pervades the first and final sections of the Epistle (1:18, 6:20). *O Timothy . . . keep . . . Grace be with thee:* Promise attends precept; the Spirit animates and writes upon the heart the commandment in the covenant of grace (1 Thess. 5:24; Ezek 36:26-27; Jer 31:33; Heb. 8:10). So Timothy may also testify as Paul did; and I may testify as Timothy—"not that we are sufficient of ourselves to think anything as of ourselves; but our sufficiency is of God, who hath also made us able ministers of the New Testament; not of the letter, but of the Spirit, for the letter killeth but the Spirit giveth life" (2 Cor 3:5-6). *O Timothy, keep . . . avoiding:* to the last Paul entreats Timothy, and me, to an exclusive and entire commitment to the Word, to "doctrine according to godliness," to "the glorious Gospel of the blessed God" *committed to thy trust* (1:11, 6:2; cf. 2 Tim. 4:2). There is no "both . . . and" with Paul; all is "either . . . or"—"no other doctrine," "godly edifying" or "vain jangling," "the faith in a pure conscience" or "lies . . . with a conscience seared;" "fables" or "good doctrine," "wholesome words" or "strifes of words" (1:8; 1:4, 6; 3:9, 4:4; 4:6-7; 6:3-4).

The House of God

141. Lift up your heads, ye Saints who mourn

1 Lift up your heads, ye saints who mourn:
The Christ of God, who died to save,
Has all your sins and sorrows borne,
And risen in triumph o'er the grave.

2 Your Prince of life on high now reigns,
Your great High Priest now pleads for grace:
Your Prophet soon shall come again,
From heaven whence He prepares your place.

3 Our long, sad night of death and fear
Full soon shall end in glorious day:
The dawn shall break, the morn appear,
And all the shadows flee away.

4 No sorrow, pain, nor bitter sigh
Nor sting of death for us shall stay:
For every tear from every eye
Shall God our Savior wipe away.

5 Once more shall we each other greet
Who now are gone, or yet remain:
The saints with joy shall surely meet
And never, never part again.

6 As without hope no more despair,
Nor let your hearts still troubled be:
Lord Jesus, come! And in the air
We all shall gather unto Thee!

L.M.
Tune: Niagara

Preparatory Reading: Old Testament: Isaiah 53–54;
   New Testament: Acts 15 Psalm: 135

1 Timothy 6:20–21

²⁰O Timothy, keep that which is committed to thy trust, avoiding profane *and* vain babblings, and oppositions of science falsely so called: ²¹Which some professing have erred concerning the faith. Grace *be* with thee. Amen.

Keep that which is committed to thy trust: just as you would guard your soul in the love of God (Jude 14) and from idols (1 John 5:21), guard the Word of God (Luke 11:28, Acts 16:4) keep that faith once delivered (2 Tim. 1:12–14; Jude 3) as a precious treasure of unsearchable riches (Eph 3:8, Acts 19:35), knowing He is able also to keep that which we have committed to Him (2 Tim. 1:12). Keep it all your own life, and commit it to others to keep it on through coming generations (2 Tim. 2:2). Keep it whole, pure, undefiled, delivering to others what you yourself received as from the Lord, of His Gospel and its ordinances (1 Cor, 11:2, 23; 15:1). How I shall behave in "the Church of the living God, which is the ground and pillar of truth" will serve to *keep that which is committed to* my *trust,* even the "mystery of godliness" (3:14–16). *That which is committed to* my *trust* I must *keep,* because it ever lies under threat of being polluted, diminished, neglected, distorted, or displaced in whole or part by heathen religion or heathen philosophy (Col. 2:6–8). I can only *keep* it by *avoiding* these influences. Heathen religion supplies the fruitless talk rooted in its legends—*profane and vain babblings* cf. (2 Tim. 2:16). From heathen philosophy come the *oppositions of science falsely so called*—conflicting speculations of secular thought which claim knowledge unproven and unrevealed. Nothing—nothing—of good can ever come from these at all. People *professing* such things have undermined the "good profession" which believers have made "before many witnesses" (6:12). *Some professing* these *have erred concerning the faith*. To me Christ Jesus, the Wisdom of God (1 Cor 1:30–31) calls yet: "Trust in the Lord with all thine heart, and lean not unto thine own understanding" "Be not wise in thine own eyes; fear the Lord, and depart from evil;" "Cease, my son, to hear the instruction that causeth to err from the worlds of knowledge" (Prov 3:5, 7, 19:27). *Grace be with thee:* Paul will not be with Timothy soon, perhaps never (cf. 3:14–15); but the Apostle can commend him, with all Ephesus' elders to God and the Word of His grace (Acts 20:32). The grace which has abounded to Paul and to all saints "with faith and love in Christ Jesus" never will forsake us from first to last (1:2, 14–16, 6:20). Grace given in eternal election (2 Tim. 1:9), secured by redemption (Tit. 2:11–14), sealed in salvation, all-sufficient in our weakness, for our service (2 Cor 3:5–6, 12:9–10) and our strength (2 Tim. 2:1)—grace is with us all (2 Tim. 4:22) and *with thee.* Now let me embrace and ratify every faithful saying and charge by faith in my faithful Savior Jesus Christ; and let me say with heart and lip. *Amen!*

142. See! Serve! Go! Tell!

1 Far away in the isles,
Over many thousand miles,
Distant tribes have not heard
God's own gracious written Word:
How He loved us, and gave
His own Son the world to save,
So that all who believe
Shall eternal life receive.

Refrain:
They are lost—but who will see?
Who will serve—and who will go?
Who will tell of Calvary
Of the Christ who loves them so?

2 Through the shanties and slums,
Foraging for scraps and crumbs,
Teem the poor of the earth—
Without hope or sense of worth:
While our Savior, who bled
With no place to lay His head,
Calls them all to be blest
As they come to Him for rest!

3 In the streets, in the malls,
Through the campuses and halls
Stream the world's growing youth,
Asking blindly "What is truth?"
While ignoring the Word
Given by our blessed Lord:
"By My Word, knowing Me,
"All the truth shall set you free."

4 In the shadows and lights
Of the cities through the nights,
Countless souls are enslaved
To the vices which they crave:
Yet our Savior and Prince
Came to save them from their sins,
And can give them release,
Filling them with joy and peace!

The House of God

5 As our Lord Jesus stands,
Stretching forth His pierced hands,
Still He welcomes us all,
Still for sinners does He call:
Can you see with His eyes
All the need that round you lies?
Will you serve? Will you go?
Live for Christ who loves you so!

Final Refrain
I was lost—but now I see!
Let me serve, Lord—I will go!
Let me tell of Calvary,
Of the Christ who loves us so!

6.7.6.7. D + Refrain

The House of God

Preparatory Reading: Old Testament: Isaiah 55–56;
New Testament: Acts 16 Psalm: 136

1 Timothy: Reading over Chapter 6

The final chapter of this First Epistle to Timothy confronts me with the prevalent problem of money—"servants . . . under the yoke" in their poverty, and "they that will be rich," along with "them that are rich in this world" all must resist in their own way "the love of money which is the root of all evil." Nor am I beyond the lure of "filthy lucre". "Supposing that gain is godliness," many "consent not . . . to the doctrine which is according to godliness." As I read over this chapter, let me surrender my purse to my Prince and Savior; let me pray neither for poverty nor riches, but for godliness with contentment, and be true to my trust.

Prayer for the Witness of the Church

God be merciful unto us and bless us
And cause His face to shine upon us
That Thy way may be known upon earth,
Thy saving health among all nations.
Let the people praise Thee, O God,
Let all the people praise Thee:
O let the nations be glad and sing for joy
For Thou shalt judge the people righteously
And govern the nations upon earth.

We have seen, O Lord, Thy salvation
Prepared before the face of all people
The Light to lighten the Gentiles, the Glory of Israel:
We have seen and do testify that the Father sent the Son
To be the Savior of the world.
And we have known and believed the love that God hath to us.
We having the same Spirit of faith we also believe and therefore speak:
Knowing the terror of the Lord we persuade men.

We continue steadfastly in prayer with one accord:
We tarry to be endued with power from on high.
Lord Jesus, grant us the promise of the Father!
Let the Holy Ghost come upon us with power
That we may be witnesses to Christ Jesus
To the uttermost part of the earth:
Fill us with the Holy Ghost to speak Thy Word with all boldness
Holy Father, Thou hast set Thy dear Son JESUS CHRIST

The House of God

A Light to the Gentiles, the Light of the world,
Thy salvation to the ends of the earth:
Work in us to will and to do Thy good pleasure
That we may be blameless and harmless,
Sons of God without rebuke,
Shining as lights of the world
Holding forth the Word of life:
Let our light so shine before men
That they may see our good works
and glorify the Father in heaven.

Thou hast sent, O Father, Thy blessed Son,
Thy Holy Child Jesus
Into the world to save sinners,
To bless us in turning everyone of us away from our iniquities
To seek and to save the lost:
Thou hast loved Him and given Him the sheep of Thy hand
The people of Thy pasture
As the Good, true, chief, great Shepherd of the sheep.

Other sheep has He, which are not of this fold
Them He must also bring
That there be one fold and one Shepherd
Multitudes He sees, and He is moved with compassion
Because they are scattered and faint
As sheep having no shepherd:

As they hear us, let them hear Thee
Let them hear Thy voice and follow Thee
Let no man pluck them out of Thy hand.

Open to us the door of utterance
To speak the mystery of Christ:
Open our mouths boldly
To make known the mystery of the Gospel
To speak boldly as we ought to speak.
Sanctify the Lord Christ in our hearts
And make us ready to give an answer to every man that asks
A reason of the hope in us
With meekness and fear
Teach us to walk in wisdom to all that are without
Season our speech with the salt of grace
That we may known how to answer and redeem the time.

The House of God

Make us servants to all, giving none offence in any thing
Pleasing all men in all things
Seeking their profit not our own
That they may be saved.
Forbid that we should offend or despise the least little child
To come to Jesus.

Create in us a clean heart, O God,
and renew a right spirit within us
Cast us not away from Thy presence
And take not Thy Holy Spirit from us.
Restore unto us the joy of our salvation
And uphold us with Thy free Spirit;
Then will we teach transgressors Thy ways,
and sinner shall be converted unto Thee
Then shall a soul be saved from death,
And a multitude of sins hid.

Do good in Thy good pleasure to Zion:
Gather the outcast,
Heal the brokenhearted and bind their wounds
Let the whole earth be filled with Thy glory
Let the earth be full of the knowledge of the Lord
As the waters cover the sea.

O Lord Jesus, lifted up from the earth,
Draw all men unto Thee!
Gather together in one all the children of God scattered abroad
That they all may be one, as the Father is in Thee,
And Thou art in Him
That the world may believe.

We ask all, O Father, in the Name of JESUS CHRIST
Thy beloved Son
Praying in Thy Holy Ghost, that Thou be glorified in Him.
Amen.

143. Lord Jesus Christ, To Whom Now Shall We Go?

1. Lord Jesus Christ, to whom now shall we go?
To us Thou say'st "I AM" and Thou art so:
Thou hast the words of life, and we believe
And know, because Thou livest, that we live.

2 Thou art *Messiah*: prophets long had shown
How Thou should' st come into the world unknown;
How to Thine own Thou camest, unreceived:
How only children, born of God, believed.

3 Thou camest down, *the Bread of Life* from heaven,
All who partake of Thee in faith are given
Life everlasting by Thy flesh and Blood,
Dwelling in Thee, by Thee indwelt of God.

4 *Light of the world*, God's glory in Thy face,
Out of our darkness, shines to every place.
Walking with Thee, we have the light of life,
Freed from the night of sorrow, sin and strife.

5 Thou *the Good Shepherd* art, who freely gave
Thy life a ransom, all Thy sheep to save;
We hear Thy voice, and follow Thy commands,
Safe in Thy Father's and Thy pierced hands.

6 Thou art *the Door*: by Thee we enter in
Called each by name, delivered from our sin,
Life more abundant in Thy folds to know,
Finding green pastures in and out to go.

7 Thou art *the Resurrection and the Life*:
Death Thou hast conquered, dying in the strife:
With us Thou weepest; and, at Judgment Day,
All from the graves Thy voice shall call away.

8 We Thy poor servants—*Lord and Master*, Thou,
Holding the towel and basin showest how
Love for each other makes all service sweet:
All things possessing, dost Thou wash our feet?

The House of God

9 Thou *the True Vine*—in Thee we would abide,
Cleansed by Thy Word, from all our sin and pride
Purged by Thy Father, loving Thine and Thee,
Knowing, "Ye can do naught apart from Me."

10 Blest Son of God—the Life, the Truth, the Way,
Thou know'st we love Thee, Thee would we obey—
Thou, *First and Last*—we follow at Thy call:
Alpha, Omega—Thou art all in all!

10.10.10.10.

Preparatory Reading: Old Testament: Isaiah 57–58;
   New Testament: Acts 17 Psalm: 137

"Sound Doctrine" (1:10)

Meditation on the Teaching of 1 Timothy

"Thou hast fully known my doctrine." Paul will tell Timothy this in his final Epistle, facing death (2 Tim. 3:10, 14–17). He had told the elders of the Church at Ephesus as much when he gave his farewell address at Miletus: "I have not shunned to declare unto you all the counsel of God" (Acts 20:27). Have I met this apostolic standard in my own ministry? Does my preaching, writing, counsel and prayer resonate with "sound doctrine?" Is mine a Christ-exalting ministry filled "from all the Scriptures" with "the things concerning Himself?" (Luke 24:27, 32, 45–48).

A thoughtful reading of this short Epistle of only six chapters demonstrates the truth of Paul's claims, for the entire span of Bible truth is mentioned or alluded to. Consider this catalogue, compiled by a simple, cursory survey—

ONE GOD—2:5

LIVING GOD—3:13, 4:7, 6:17

TRIUNE GOD—Father 1:1; Son 1:1, 123, 14–15; 4:6, 6:13–14; Holy Ghost 4:1, 12

GLORY of GOD—blessed 1:11; glory 1:17; honor 1:17, 6:16

ATTRIBUTES of GOD—eternal, only wise 1:17; immortal, invisible 1:17, 6:16; power 6:16; quickens all 6:13; longsuffering 1:16; gracious 1:14; sovereign 1:17, 6:12, 15; in light unapproachable 6:16

CREATION—all things good 4:3–5; Adam and Eve 2:13–14; bodily life 4:8

ANGELS—elect 5:21

SATAN and DEVILS—1:20, 2:14, 3:6–7, 4:1, 5:15

HOLY SCRIPTURES as WORD of GOD—1:3–5, 2:4, 3:9, 4:1, 5–6, 13, 16; 5:17–18; 6:1.3

FALL, DEPRAVITY, SIN of MAN—1:9–10, 13, 15, 20; 2:13–14; 3:3, 6, 8, 11; 4:1–2; 5:6, 8, 11, 13, 20–22, 24–25; 6:4–5, 9–10

PERSON and WORK of JESUS CHRIST—1:1 our Hope 1:15 came to save sinners 2:5 one Mediator 2:6 the ransom 3:16 God manifest in flesh, justified in the Spirit, received into glory 6:2 wholesome words 6:13 confession before Pilate 6:14–15 second appearing, King of kings, Lord of lords

THE GOSPEL—1:11, 14–16; 2:3, 7; 3:9, 13, 16; 4:9

THE MORAL LAW, GOOD WORKS, RIGHTEOUSNESS and HOLINESS—1:5 sum

The House of God

of the Law 1:8–11 lawful use of the Law; First Table (ungodly, unholy 1:9, godliness 2:2); Second Table (sinners 1:9, honesty 2:2)

The Commandments—

I: unholy 1:7; love of money 6:10; pride 3:6, 6:17; doubt 2:8
II: doctrines of devils 4:1–2, error 6:1, usurp authority 2:12
III: profane 1:9; blasphemer 1:13; perjurer 1:10
IV: idle 5:13
V: hospitality 3:2; rule house 3:3; piety at home 5:1–2, 4; duty to superiors 6:1–2
VI: murder, manslaughter 1:9; Wrath 2:8; brawler, striker 3:3
VII: one wife 3:2; given to wine 3:3; false celibacy 4:3; wantonness 5:11
VIII: menstealers 1:10
IX: liars, perjured 1:10, 2:7; good report 3:7; double-tongued 3:8; slander 3:11
X: greedy, covetous 3:3; contentment, covetousness 6:6, 10–11

SOCIAL RELATIONS—men and women 2:11–12; family and marriage 3:4, 12, 4:32, 5:3–10; work and class 6:1–19; state 2:1–3

THE CHURCH—the entire Epistle is given to the doctrine, worship, offices, fellowship and witness of the local Church. Only Baptism (possibly alluded to in 6:12) and the Lord's Supper are not addressed.

Lord Jesus! Grant me in my own soul, and in all my service to Thy cause, as a brother, a teacher, an elder or a pastor, to continue in Thy Word, and know Thy truth that sets free. Amen.

144. In His Steps Let Me Go

1 Christ has suffered for us: He was threatened and reviled,
Who Himself did no sin, in whose mouth was found no guile;
We were sheep gone astray, but the Shepherd of our souls
Has returned us to the shelter of His fold.

2 His own self bare our sins in His body on the Tree;
By those stripes we were healed, which He bore in agony:
Being dead to our sins, we now live to righteousness—
His example we must follow in His steps!

Refrain:
*In His steps let me follow, in His steps let me go
As I live to the Son of God who loved me so
As He gave Himself for me on the cross of shame,
Let me serve Him, though I suffer, in His Name.*

3 In His steps we must go, when we suffer wrongfully;
Doing well, suffering wrong, as we take it patiently,
Threatening not, we submit: God will judge us righteously
Grief enduring, we will find it thankworthy.

4 To us all Jesus said, "Take the cross and follow Me,
Self deny day by day; none shall of Me worthy be,
Who loves kindred or wealth or his life above My name,
Or who of My words shall ever be ashamed."

Refrain:
*In His steps let me follow, in His steps let me go
As I live to the Son of God who loved me so
As He gave Himself for me on the cross of shame,
Let me serve Him, though I suffer, in His Name.*

5 Jesus promised this too: "Let my servant follow Me,
And wherever I am, there my servant too will be;
Holy Father, I will that my own should be with Me,
That My glory in Thy presence they may see!"

Irregular.

The House of God

Preparatory Reading: Old Testament: Isaiah 59–60;
  New Testament: Acts 18 Psalm: 138

"No Other Doctrine" (1:3)

Meditation on the Background of 1 Timothy

THE SCRIPTURES provide us a fairly full background to this First Epistle of Timothy, inasmuch as Paul writes to him as he serves the Church at Ephesus. We are thus able to draw upon the inspired narratives of Acts, the entire Epistle to the Ephesians, and the Savior's letter to the Church through the Apostle John in Revelation 1–2 to profile the Church's history; as well as the scattered notices to Timothy himself found in Acts and Paul's other Epistles. We might also note the Apostle John's attachment to Ephesus in his Gospel and Epistles.

ACTS—From the outset the Gospel faced varied challenges to its claims and threats to its integrity as it entered Ephesus. We may notice these first from the account of (Acts 18:18–20:38). Though the Apostle's first passing visit found some receptive to the truth (18:19–21), and a nucleus for the Church soon emerged around Aquila and Priscilla (18:19, 26–27), Paul faced both the *defective views* of disciples of John Baptist (18:25, 19:1–7) and the outright *rejection* of Christ by the synagogue's leaders (19:8–9). His farewell remarks about "the lying in wait of the Jews" suggests the sort of quarrelsome encounters our Savior had in His own life (Luke 11:54).

With the separation of the Church from the synagogue, and its extended outreach to the wider region (10:8–10) a new danger to the Gospel appeared in the hold of the *occult* upon local people, Jewish, Gentile, unbelievers and even believers (19:10–20). At length the inroads of the Gospel among the pagan population evoked "no small stir" of opposition from the silversmiths and the townspeople in favor of their world-renowned temple and cult to *Diana of the Ephesians* (19:22–41). Paul's farewell warned the Church's elders both of "grievous wolves" as *outside* and "perverse disciples" as *inside* dangers lying ahead (20:28–30).

EPHESIANS—In this Epistle, the Apostle's primary concern is on *outside* threats to the truth, as he urges the saints to separate from their pagan past (2:1–3, 4:17–19, 5:3–6, 11) and realize their fully equal standing with Jewish believers in the New Testament Church, in the face perhaps of the synagogue's exclusion (2:11–12, 19). They must discern the deceit of cunning, false teachers (4:11) and resist the influences of spiritual wickedness (6:10–13).

1 TIMOTHY—In our Epistle, the *inside* influence of "perverse disciples" seems to alarm the apostle. He repeatedly mentions those who have deviated and departed from the faith, whether under Jewish (1:4–7) or pagan (1:4, 4:1–7) influence. The hold of vain sophistry and philosophy is felt here (1:4–6, 6:45, 20). The chief threat comes from decay within the membership of the Church itself in doctrine (1:19–20; 2:11–12; 4:1–3; 6:3–5, 20–21) or morals (4:7; 5:6, 8, 11–12, 15; 6:5, 10).

REVELATION—This final book of Scripture affords our last glance at the Church of Ephesus in the short letters sent by the glorified Savior to the seven leading congregations of Asia Minor through John the Apostle. Ephesus is first addressed among them (2:1–7).

Christ Jesus commends them for their zeal in keeping the truth. They have shown this by active service, persevering endurance, discerning contention against error, and vigilant moral discipline (2:2–3, 6). But the Lord lays a serious censure against the Church demanding radical repentance and the restoration of their "first love" for Himself (2:4–5, 7). In this, the Church, without losing its orthodoxy or morality, compromised its spirituality and missed the goal which Paul set before Timothy in his labors there: "charity out of a pure heart, and of a good conscience, and of faith unfeigned" (1 Tim. 1:5).

Orthodoxy, morality and spirituality—these are the basic "tests of life" which the Apostle John lays before us in his First Epistle. By these we measure both our own souls and our ministry to other souls. Orthodoxy of doctrine, morality of duty, spirituality of devotion—may my faithful Savior Jesus Christ by His Holy Spirit preserve these vital signs of newness of life in my soul, and through my service in His Church, to the praise of the glory of the grace of God the Father. Amen.

The House of God

145. Now let us all depart in Peace

1 O God, salvation have we seen
In Jesus Christ our Lord:
Now let us all depart in peace
According to Thy Word.

2 Shine forth, O Savior, through the night
In which the nations dwell,
To all the Gentiles, Life and Light,
Glory of Israel!

3 Spirit of God, Thy truth set forth—
The Scriptures now unseal,
As preached and read throughout the earth
Salvation they reveal!

4 O Father, Son, and Holy Ghost,
In peace now keep our hearts,
Till gathered with Thy ransomed host
We never more shall part!

C.M.

The House of God

Preparatory Reading: Old Testament: Isaiah 61–62;
   New Testament: Acts 19 Psalm: 139

1 Timothy: A Final Reading

We have read over this portion of Holy Scripture now for a considerable time, that we might gain knowledge, skill, and above all grace to serve "the house of God, which is the Church of the living God, the ground and pillar of the truth." We have sought to enter into the will of "God our Saviour, who would have all men to be saved, and come to the knowledge of the truth." We have sought to listen attentively and submissively to the Apostle Paul both our pattern as a believer, and our mentor as "a preacher, an apostle . . . a teacher of the Gentiles in faith and verity." As we take a final reading of the whole of this grand Epistle, let me call on my faithful, covenant God Triune, to confirm all these words of life to me by the grace of the Lord Jesus, the love of the Father and the communion of the Holy Ghost.

A Prayer of Consecration

The Law of the Lord is perfect, converting the soul:
The testimonies of the Lord is sure, making wise the simple;
The statutes of the Lord are right, rejoicing the heart:
The commandment of the Lord is pure, enlightening the eyes,
The fear of the Lord is clean, enduring forever:
The judgments of the Lord are true and righteous altogether.
More to be desired are they than gold, yea, than much fine gold:
Sweeter also than honey and the honeycomb.
Moreover by them is thy servant warned,
And in keeping them there is great reward.

Who can understand his errors?
Cleanse Thou me from secret faults:
Keep back Thy servant also from presumptuous sins,
Let them not have dominion over me.
Then shall I be upright,
and I shall be innocent of the great transgression.
Let the words of my mouth, and the meditations of my heart
Be acceptable in Thy sight
O Lord
My strength and my Redeemer.

Thy words were found, and I did eat them
And Thy Word was unto me the joy and rejoicing of mine heart:
For I am called by Thy Name, O Lord God of hosts.

The House of God

Let not this Book of the Law depart from my mouth
Day and night teach me to meditate in it,
and observe to do all that is written therein:
grant me strength and good courage
make my way prosperous, be with me withersoever I go
with Thy good success.

Let the Word of Christ dwell in me richly with all wisdom
And open my understanding to understand the Scriptures
and all that is written concerning Christ.

Let the Holy Ghost, the Comforter, sent of the Father and of the Son
To teach me all things,
Bring to my remembrance whatsoever my Savior has said
Lead me into all truth, and glorify Jesus as Lord.

And so accept the reasonable service of my spiritual worship
O blessed God
My body a living sacrifice
My broken, contrite heart a sacrifice
The fruit of my lips giving service of praise a sacrifice

That I might know how to behave myself
In the house of God
As a man of God
Adorning the doctrine of God.

Now unto the one, true living God
Jehovah
Father, Son and Holy Ghost
Be glory, honor, riches, power, dominion and praise
Now and ever
Through Jesus Christ

Amen.

From My Bible

A Selection of Devotional Thoughts
   On Varied Texts and Topics

146. Lord Jesus, purge my soul, I pray

1 Lord Jesus, purge my soul, I pray,
From error, sin and self today:
Make me a vessel Thou dost choose,
Both fit and clean for Thee to use.

2 O separate me to Thy Name;
My heart, my mind, my lips all claim,
And teach me by Thy truthful Word
To tell the glory of the Lord.

3 O wash and cleanse me by Thy Blood,
Till as a holy man of God
My heart, my life, my conduct show
The Savior whom I love and know.

4 O search and know my heart within,
And mortify my every sin:
Purge by Thy Holy Spirit's fire
All selfish pride, all vain desire.

5 Grant in my soul that Thou increase,
While error, sin and self decrease,
Till at Thy throne my soul shall fall
And sing forever, "Christ is All!"

L.M.

Preparatory Reading: Old Testament: Jonah 1;
   New Testament: Acts 20 Psalm: 140

"Lord, help me!" (Matthew 15:25)

This is one of the great prayers of the Bible. Not long; not eloquent. But these three little words take the measure of the infinite compassion, wisdom and power of our faithful High Priest and Advocate Jesus Christ.

This prayer tells us *no one is beyond prayer*. It is the anguished plea of a "Greek, a Syrophenician by nation"—"a woman of Canaan" with alien speech and pagan culture. She certainly had no claim to be good or respectable. She well knew she approached the Savior as the "Son of David" "sent to the lost sheep of the house of Israel." Yet she cried, "Lord, help *me*"

This prayer tells us *no need is beyond prayer*. The woman's daughter had "an unclean spirit" and was "grievously vexed with a devil." Her condition could hardly be more deadly or desperate. Frantic with fear, she pestered the Master till the disciples pleaded, "Send her away for she crieth after us." But she persisted, "Lord, *help* me."

This prayer tells us *no impediment is beyond prayer*. The Lord Jesus, with infinite wisdom, tried and tested the woman's faith in Him. He at first was silent to her cry. He then reminded her His mission lay elsewhere. And at last, He pointed out she had no claims on Him: "It is not meet to take the children's bread, and to cast it to dogs." Yet even this rebuff she eagerly seized to find reason for hope: "Truth, Lord: yet the dogs eat of the crumbs which fall from their masters' table." Without covenant or promise, knowledge or merit, she wholly cast herself at the mercy of Christ: "*Lord,* help me."

Without God, without hope in the world; a stranger to God's people and promises; refused and rebuffed; this most untaught, unclean and unworthy of sinners found hope and help *through simple faith in Jesus Christ alone*: "Lord, help me!"

The Savior heeds her: "O woman, great is thy faith: be it unto thee even as thou wilt." The Savior helps her: "And when she was come to her house, she found the devil gone out, and her daughter laid upon the bed."

Christ Jesus will not rebuff or refuse you now. You can claim far more than crumbs under His table today. "If any man sin, we have an Advocate with the Father, Jesus Christ the Righteous: and He is the propitiation for our sins, and not for ours only, but also for the sins of the whole world." He says, "In My Name, ask, and receive."

In your sin and need, call on Jesus now: "Lord, help me!"

147. As round the depths of Darkness fall

1 As round the depths of *darkness* fall
Lord Jesus, on Thy Name I call:
O bright and Morning Star, shine forth
In glory, and return to earth!

2 As tears of *sorrow* well mine eyes,
Thou Sun of Righteousness arise,
With wings of healing, bring the Day
When former things shall pass away.

3 Where is thy victory, O grave?
The Savior who my ransom gave,
In brightness comes, with His own breath
Destroying last the reign of *death*!

4 My God in Christ a ransom found
Whose grace o'er *sin* might so abound
That, from its guilt and power set free.
I might forever holy be.

5 Sin, sorrow, suffering, darkness, death
Shall all be put His feet beneath:
Our Father, let Thy kingdom come—
And manifest Thine only Son!

6 Then shall I see Him face to face,
And in the fullness of His grace
Be like Him, with Him where He is,
Forever mine—forever His!

L.M.

Preparatory Reading: Old Testament: Jonah 2;
  New Testament: Acts 21 Psalm: 141

"Even So, Come, Lord Jesus!" (Revelation 22:20)

The Bible's first recorded prayer is the bewildered cry of Abram, "Lord GOD, what wilt Thou give me?" The Bible's last recorded prayer gives the answer in the Apostle John's brief call: "Even so, come, Lord Jesus!"

This five-word petition is as splendid as it is short. It seeks for the ultimate end of all evil, and the ultimate glory of God. It sums up the final realization of every petition in the Lord's Prayer. It absolutely agrees with the supreme supplication of our Savior's own High Priestly Prayer.

As often as we close the Book, at home or church, in private study or public service, we ought to repeat this request: "Even so, come, Lord Jesus!"

This prayer claims the Bible's last promise: "He which testifieth these things saith, '*Surely I come quickly*.'" Though God forbears long with His elect who cry to Him day and night, yet He will "avenge them speedily." He is not willing that any of them should perish, but all come to repentance.

This prayer strengthens us to endure to the end: "The time is at hand . . . He that is holy, let him be holy still. And *behold, I come quickly*; and my reward is with Me, to give every man according as his work shall be."

This prayer moves us to give out the message of the Gospel: "The Spirit and the Bride say, Come. And let him that heareth say, Come. And let him that is athirst come. And whosoever will, let him take the water of life freely." God now commands all everywhere to repent as He has appointed that day in which He shall judge the world by the Man Christ Jesus whom He raised from the dead.

The Last Day will be either the best day of your existence, or the worst: "If any man love not the Lord Jesus Christ, let him be Anathema—Maranatha." *Are you ready? Can you pray, "Even so, come Lord Jesus?"*

148. As the Sabbath Morn We Greet

1 As the Sabbath morn we greet,
With God's people here we meet,
Thus to learn His holy Word
Telling us of Jesus Christ our Lord
How the Son of God in love
Came to earth from heaven above
Seeking, saving sinners in His mercy

2 Tell a world of sinners lost,
How the Savior on the Cross
Suffering shed His precious Blood
Once for all to make our peace with God:
Tell how, risen from the grave
He is able now to save
To the uttermost in all His mercy!

3 Let our voices rend the air
Till the sound of praise and prayer
Blends with saints and angels' cries,
"Glory, glory be to God on high!
Peace on earth, good-will to men!"
All His people from their sin
Jesus Christ has saved in boundless mercy!

4 Come, O Savior, quickly come!
Then shall heaven and earth be one
Perfect in the new creation
Praising Thee, the King of our salvation:
To the glory of Thy grace,
We shall see Thee, face to face!
We shall taste the fullness of Thy mercy!

Irregular.

The House of God

Preparatory Reading: Old Testament: Jonah 3;
New Testament: Acts 22 Psalm: 142

Your Heart

As you enter this House of Prayer today and sit in this congregation, you are in the special manifest presence of God.

The Bible promises us that God the Father dwells the praises of His people; that God the Son speaks from His Word in their midst, that God the Holy Spirit fills their souls as His temple (Ps 89:7, 22:3; Matt 18:20; Eph 2:22).

God Triune, Most High and Holy—God is here, unseen, seeing all.

God sees you and knows you perfectly. He is not impressed with how fashionably you dress, what position you hold at work, how much you earn or put in the collection plate, how glibly you can talk or sing, or what you think you know.

Man looks on the outward appearance; God looks on your heart.
(1 Sam 16:7) His Word discerns its every thought and intent (Heb 4:12–13).
Man's heart is sinful, deceitful, evil (Gen 6:5; Jer 17:9; Mark 7:21–23).

Is your heart right with God? (Acts 8:21)

God desires those who come to Him to have broken heart, contrite hearts, confessing honestly and forsaking truly their sin in His sight. (Isa 57:15, 66:2; Ps 34:18, 51:17) He looks for a true heart, trusting the Lord Jesus wholly and solely to pardon and cleanse from sin (Acts 15:8–9, 11; Heb. 10:19–22). He reveals Himself to the pure heart, set upon Him with single-minded sincerity (Matt 5:8; Ps 86:11; 2 Tim. 2:22).

His call to you in this place, in this hour is plain: "Give me your heart!" (Prov 3:5–7, 4:23, 23:26).

149. O Come to Me, My Savior

1 O come to me, my Savior,
For far spent is the day,
Open to me the Scriptures,
Walk with me in the way.

2 Come, manifest Thyself, Lord,
And dwell within my heart:
That I may keep to Thy Word
Thy Spirit now impart.

3 O leave me not an orphan
In pain or sorrow's hour:
Come to me by Thy Spirit
In all Thy ris'n power.

4 In death itself, come to me:
Good Shepherd, bid me rise
To heaven, and be with Thee
This day in Paradise.

5 Lord Jesus, come—come quickly,
To claim Thy chosen Bride:
Then all shall see Thy glory,
And every tear be dried.

7.6.7.6.

Preparatory Reading: Old Testament: Jonah 4;
   New Testament: Acts 23 Psalm: 143

Two At Prayer

Of all the questions and requests the disciples ever put to our Savior during the days of His flesh, this was the wisest: "Lord, teach us to pray."

We do well to ask it ourselves, for we can ask none better. *As our High Priest,* Jesus the Son of God has passed into the heavens to appear at the throne of grace in our behalf, claiming the blessings of redemption His own Blood has bought, interceding for us by the power of an endless life. *As our King,* Jesus Christ is Lord of all, with all power in heaven and earth to grant us whatever we ask of the Father in His Name, and in His will. *As our Prophet,* the Savior has both furnished us with His all-sufficient Word, and left us an example that we might follow in His steps.

In Luke 18, Christ Jesus gave two most memorable parables to teach us to pray. The second parable startles us with an unforgettable contrast (vv. 9–14). "Two men went up into the temple to pray: the one a Pharisee, and the other a publican."

Both men had the same need for acceptance with God. *Both men had the same means* of access to God in the Temple with its Most Holy and Holy Places, its altars and priests, its offerings and incense. The Pharisee had *great privileges* in his strict upbringing, knowledge of the Law, vocation to religious life. The publican had *great problems* as a traitor to his people, an outcast from society, with a life of ignorance and sin.

Yet while both men went up to pray, *the Pharisee didn't pray at all.* Christ declares that "the Pharisee stood and prayed thus *with himself.*" He really worshipped himself, not God! For a show, his long prayer was designed to be "seen of men." Parroting his lack of scandal and his works of devotion, he clearly stood with those "which trusted in themselves that they were righteous, and despised others." He had no sense of guilt, need, repentance, hope in atoning Blood, or humility. His words were but mere whistling in the dark. *Is this how you "say your prayers?"*

Once in the courts of the Temple, *the publican truly prayed.* Seized with his guilt, "he stood afar off," feeling his sin separated him from God. In his humility, "he would not lift up so much as his eyes unto heaven." With godly sorrow to repentance, "he smote upon his breast." From a heart of need he cried again and again, "God be merciful to me a sinner." Before God "he humbled himself" and by faith called for God to be propitiated toward him by the Blood shed for sin at the altar. Of him Jesus said, "I tell you, this man went down to his house justified rather than the other."

Today, God has set forth His Son a propitiation through faith in His Blood to redeem us from all sin. By Christ we may have access to the Father by one Spirit. With heartfelt sense of guilt and repentance, with humble hope in Christ's precious Blood, *you too may pray. You will be heard.* Call on Him now: "God be merciful to me a sinner!"

150. Worn and Weary by the Well

1 Worn and weary by the well,
'Neath the burning sun to dwell,
Thou didst sit, Lord Jesus Christ,
Seeking still to save the lost.
Kindly, Thou didst never shun,
Jew, nor yet Samaritan,
Male or female, bond or free:
Thy compassion all doth see!

2 Meek and lowly, all our pride
Thou in love dost lay aside:
Yet our deepest sins all lie
Open to Thy searching eye.
Living water Thou shalt give
All who in Thy Name believe:
Like a river peace shall roll,
Springing up within the soul.

3 Now, Messiah, dost Thou show
Every truth we do not know:
Of the Jews Salvation's King,
Thou dost teach to us all things.
Tasting love and pardon, we
Bid all men to "Come and see—
This indeed is Christ the Lord,
Jesus—Savior of the world!"

4 Lift our eyes the fields upon,
Master, who the seed hast sown:
In the harvest, white with wheat,
Bid us enter now to reap!
Let true worshippers be brought
To the Father, who them sought,
By the Truth who is the Son,
With the Spirit—Three in One!

7.7.7.7D

Preparatory Reading: Old Testament: Habakkuk 1;
  New Testament: Acts 24 Psalm: 144

"Worship in Spirit and in Truth" (John 4:24)

She was a Samaritan from Sychar.

She went out to the well at noon to get her water and evade the village gossips.

She hadn't been looking for Him, but He was looking for her.

Step by step the Man Christ Jesus kindly revealed Himself to her—and revealed her to herself. The weary Stranger, the suspect Jew, the eccentric Rabbi, suddenly showed He knew her heart—her sordid past—her sad present all too well. He had the divine knowledge of a prophet.

She really wasn't that interested; she was only looking to escape her embarrassment. So she asked a "religious question" to get the conversation away from herself, distract Him, perhaps entangle Him in talk. "Where should we worship—our temple or yours?"

The reply was far more stunning than she expected: "Neither!" "*God is a Spirit: and they that worship Him must worship in spirit and in truth*" (John 4:24). Through this she came to learn that He was in reality the Messiah—Christ, the Savior of the world.

As you join us in this House of Prayer, you may be expecting to meet old friends, to find solace in familiar ritual, to listen to the singing, to hear a good joke or word of wit from the preacher. You may enjoy all these, and completely miss the point of today's gathering.

We are here because God is here. He is looking for us, seeking "worshippers in spirit and in truth." He encounters and engages us here through *His truth,* as His Word, the Bible, is read and preached; for *He speaks to us through His Word.* We encounter and engage Him through *His Spirit*, as the Holy Ghost awakens and enables us to offer Him praise and prayer; *for we speak to Him through His Spirit.* We know He hears us, and we hear Him, because we worship through the mediation of His Son, Jesus Christ, alone.

Often He exposes the secrets of our hearts by His Word with painful clarity; often we feel His love shed abroad in our hearts by the Spirit. (1 Cor 14: 24–25; Hebrews 4:12; Romans 5:5). For the Savior keeps His promise: "*Where two or three are gathered in My Name, there I am in the midst.*" (Matt 18:20).

You are here today because He is seeking you. Today you may experience the wellspring of joy and hope which that lonely, bitter woman tasted so long ago: "Come see a Man which told me all things that ever I did: is not this the Christ?" "We have heard Him ourselves, and know that this indeed is Christ, the Savior of the world." (John 4:29, 42).

151. What in all the Richest Beauty

1 What in all the richest beauty
That abounds this vast world o'er
Can compare with my Lord Jesus—
Christ, the Savior I adore?
Not the Lily of the Valley,
Not the Rose of Sharon rare,
Not the Cedars spreading Leb'non—
None with Jesus can compare!

2 Though no beauty to desire Him,
Men see in the Crucified,
Yet to me is Jesus precious,
And on earth there's none beside!
For to save me He has suffered,
Died and shed His precious Blood
To redeem from all transgressions—
Worthy, worthy Lamb of God!

3 All ye ransomed—tell the story!
All the realms of heav'n and earth,
Join to sing His grace and glory—
All acclaim His matchless worth!
Hallelujah to the Father!
Hallelujah to the Son!
Hallelujah to the Spirit!
Praise Jehovah—Three in One!

8.7.8.7D
Tune: 'Tis the Last Rose of Summer.

Preparatory Reading: Old Testament: Habakkuk 2;
   New Testament: Acts 25 Psalm: 145

"Thy Will be Done " (Matthew 6:10)

"Thy will be done." Fewer prayers are simpler to say and harder to mean. Yet this prayer forms the pinnacle of the Lord's Prayer which the Savior taught every believing disciple as the pattern of all prayer (Matt 6:10). And this prayer on His own lips in Gethsemane was pivotal to His redeeming work (Matt 26:42; Heb 5:7–10).

Christ's sufferings for us were both expiatory and exemplary. They put down a pattern for our grateful service while they paid the price for our eternal salvation. In living union with Him by the Holy Spirit, we thus trace the pattern of His suffering and glory—saved only, wholly by His cross, yet called to serve by bearing ours (Luke 9:18–26; 1 Pet. 2:21–25; 2 Tim. 2:8–13).

This prayer patterns our supplications. We watch with Simon Peter and the sons of Zebedee as Christ Jesus offers it in His sinless, perfect humanity. Here is *confiding prayer*: "Abba Father." Here is *believing prayer*: "all things are possible unto Thee". Here is *honest prayer*: "take away this cup from me." Here is *submissive prayer*: "nevertheless, not what I will, but what thou wilt" (Mark 14:36). Here is *persevering prayer*: "And again He went away, and prayed, and spake the same words" (Mark 14:39). Here is *earnest prayer*: "And being in an agony, He prayed more earnestly: and His sweat was as it were great drops of blood falling down to the ground." (Luke 22:44). Here is *committed prayer*: "O my Father, if this cup may not pass away from me, except I drink it, thy will be done." (Matt 26:42). Peter never forgot the lesson his Savior taught by practice and precept that night: "Watch and pray" (1 Peter 4:7; cf. Matt 26:40–41).

This prayer paid for our salvation. Our Lord Jesus had come into the world only for this, to do the will of His Father in heaven (Psalm 40: 6–10; Hebrews 10:5–9). As a Boy of Twelve, He was anxious to "be about His Father's business" (Luke 2:49). During His public ministry, He sustained His soul by that will despite hunger and thirst (John 4:34) . In praying "Thy will be done," the Savior consecrated Himself to offer His perfect life to merit our acceptance with the Father, and to offer His precious Blood to gain our access to the Father (Hebrews 9:14, 10:10; cf. John 17:2, 17–19; 19:30; Eph 2:13–18; Romans 5:8–10, 19). Of this prayer it is written:

In the days of His flesh, when He had offered up prayers and supplications with strong crying and tears unto him that was able to save him from death, and was heard in that he feared; Though he were a Son, yet learned he obedience by the things which he suffered; And being made perfect, he became the author of eternal salvation unto all them that obey him (Heb 5:7–9).

No works of ours can ever merit or fit us to receive salvation. Yet even as we receive salvation freely by grace alone through faith alone in Christ alone, so our lives should be yielded to live to His will who loved us and gave Himself for us. Let us who trust in Christ Jesus render to Him this thank-offering of praise and obedience, heeding the Apostle Paul:

The House of God

I beseech you therefore, brethren, by the mercies of God, that ye present your bodies a living sacrifice, holy, acceptable unto God, which is your reasonable service. And be not conformed to this world: but be ye transformed by the renewing of your mind, that ye may prove what is that good, and acceptable, and perfect, will of God. (Rom 12:1–2).

"Thy will be done."

152. Daily, Gladly, let me sing

1 Daily, gladly, let me sing
Of my Savior, Christ the King!
Ready to obey His will
On His Word I ponder still:
Teach me how to spend my days
Holy Ghost, to Jesu's praise!

2 Yet this one thing would I seek:
Hear me, Father! Make me meek,
Always patient, bearing loss
Zealous to proclaim the Cross;
Ever by my life to show
Love for Christ who loved me so!

3 By the Blood of Christ my Lord
Overcoming by His Word
Dangers of besting sin
Now around, without, within
Endless life O let me gain
Reigning with my Savior slain!

7.7.7.7.7.7.

The House of God

Preparatory Reading: Old Testament: Habakkuk 3;
 New Testament: Acts 26 Psalm: 146

Day by Day (part i)

"O<small>NE</small> D<small>AY AT A TIME</small>" is a very popular adage in our hurried age. We grow accustomed to a daily dose of vitamins, a daily routine of work, a daily regimen of exercise. Much of life becomes manageable on the bite-size of a "daily basis."

Have you ever considered what Holy Writ tells us about *our daily walk with God?* I was drawn to this fascinating study as I prepared to minister to work-worn and world-weary members of my own local Church.

In this first part, let me just outline to you *God's daily covenant promises* to each of His children redeemed by Christ's Blood and born of the Holy Spirit:

- His gifts as our faithful Creator (Genesis 8:22)
- His grace in the blessings of the Gospel (Acts 2:18, 3:24–26, Mic 7:20–21, 2 Corinthians 6:2)
- His loving-kindness (Lamentations 3:21–41, Psalm 36:10). His goodness and mercy (Psalm 23:6, 90:13–17) and benefits (Psalm 68:19).
- His renewing grace (2 Corinthians 4:16, Lamentations 5:21)
- His provisions of food, clothing, shelter (Matt 6:11,33; Hebrews 13:5–6) and the gift of life itself (Deuteronomy 30:20)
- Sufficient strength for each day's trouble (Matt 6:34; Nah 1:7; Prov 23:17–18).
- His special presence by the Holy Ghost (Ex 13:22, 1 Peter 4:14, Matt 28:20, Ps 73:23).
- His watch-care (Ps 37:18, 121:6) and protection (Deuteronomy 33:12, 26)
- His comfort with freedom from fear (Isa 51:11–13)
- His guidance (Genesis 48:15, Isaiah 58:11) and blessing (Hag 2:19)

Have we not ample grounds to pray these words each morning?

Now as the new-born day begins,
Lord Jesus, save me from my sins:
Unto Thy glory let me live
By all the grace which Thou dost give.

O Savior, let me clearer see
Thy glory; to me dearer be,
Walk with me nearer in Thy way,
That I may love Thee day by day.

153. Raise unto the Lamb of God

1 Raise unto the Lamb of God
Every saint, redeemed by Blood,
Voices high, to bless and praise
Jesus Christ, the King of grace:
Over all exalted now,
Heaven and earth to Him must bow!

2 Never could lost sinners find
Peace of conscience, heart or mind:
Everlasting hell was ours,
Till the Savior's darkened hours
Ended at the Cross our strife,
Raised from death to endless life!

3 Be His glory lifted high
Over earth, through sea and sky:
Daily let His kingdom claim
Nations for His worthy Name:
Ever bless the Lamb whose Blood
Reconciled our souls to God!

7.7.7.7.7.7.

The House of God

Preparatory Reading: Old Testament: Haggai 1;
    New Testament: Acts 27 Ps: 147

Day by Day (part ii)

DAY BY DAY our gracious Triune God cares for all the needs of His people redeemed by Christ's Blood and renewed by the Holy Spirit. Daily, then, every true child of God owes a debt of love and duty. Duty is not a four-letter word to the Christian; duty is simply love in its work-clothes.

In this second part, allow me to sketch for you *God's daily covenant precepts* to His children that we may enjoy His favor and fellowship. To this He calls each of us each and every day:

- To abide in the Lord Jesus by His Word and Spirit (John 15:1–17), continuing in the faith (Acts 2:41–46,14:22), and keeping our vows (Psalm 61:8).

- To offer worship (Psalm 145:2), thanksgiving (Psalm 34:1, Hebrews 13:15), and praise (Psalm 72:15), to the Father and the Son by the Spirit (Ephesians 5:18–20).

- To continue in (John 8:31); read (Deuteronomy 17:9); search (Acts 17:11); meditate on (Joshua 1:8 and Psalm 1, 119:97); enquire of (2 Chronicles 18:4 and Proverbs 8:34); and obey (Deuteronomy 6:2 and Ps 119:44); God's written Word.

- To pray constantly (Ps 86:3, Neh 1:6, Dan 6:10, 2 Tim 1:3; Col 4:2, 1 Thess. 5:17, Luke 11:1–13,18:7) and fast statedly (Mark 2:20; Matt 6:1–18)

- To love the brethren (Heb 13:1) and exhort one another against sin (Hebrews 3:13) seeking peace and holiness (Ps 34:12).

- To enjoy God's blessings in marriage (Ecclesiastes 9:9), family (Ephesians 6:4–5), work and leisure (Eccl 5:18), with a cheerful heart (Prov 15:15).

- To keep watch against the flesh (Deuteronomy 4:9–10, 1 Corinthians 15:31) the world (Ephesians 5:12–16) the ungodly (2 Peter 2:8) and the devil (1 Peter 5:8–10, Ephesians 6:13) remembering life is short (Ecclesiastes 12).

- To live without fear (Psalm 91:5) anxious care (Philippians 4:4–6) trusting our way to God (James 4:15).

- To wait patiently upon God (Psalm 25:5, 1 Chronicles 16:11, Proverbs 23:17–18, Hosea 12:6) applying ourselves to our daily work (2 Thessalonians 3:12–13, John 9:4, 11:9) and honoring His Day of Rest and Worship (Exodus 20:8–11, Hebrews 10:25).

- To look, pray for and love the Savior's return (Luke 12:32–33, Hebrews 9:27–28, 2 Timothy 4:6–8,18; Revelation 22:20).

154. Doxology

1 Father, Son and Holy Spirit,
Boundless riches we inherit
Of Thy grace and mercy free;
From the FATHER's love eternal
Through the LAMB's shed Blood supernal
To the SPIRIT's liberty.

2 Glory, honor, riches, power
Wisdom, blessing, hour and hour
Heaven and earth ascribe to Thee:
Let the saints, their voices raising,
Join them, THREE in ONE, in praising
Thee—High, Holy TRINITY!

8.8.7.D

The House of God

Preparatory Reading: Old Testament: Haggai 2;
   New Testament: Acts 28 Psalm: 148

Peace Now

"Peace on earth, goodwill toward men." That song of angels to shepherds seems as distant as heaven from earth to so many—and as empty as "Have a nice day."

International conflict. Tensions at home between poor and rich, labor and management, government and opposition—where's the peace? At a personal level, the age of "excellence" breeds overwork, anxiety, stress and depression. Families feud; neighbors spat. Peace?????

Many want peace—but find only fleeting escape: in the gym, at the bar, on vacation. Money can't buy it; nothing you smoke, snort or swallow will bring it.

What the angels were singing about lies at the bottom of any real hope for peace we can have here or hereafter—peace with God. Until we are reconciled and restored to God, there can be no peace (Isaiah 57:19–21).

That's why the Bible proclaims "Christ is our peace" (Eph 2:11–18). Here and now, the Lord Jesus has purchased our peace (Rom 5:1–11); He imparts that peace (John 14:1, 27); He can keep us in that peace (Phil. 4:4–9), better than any 24/7 security system (Ps 4:6–8). The "blood of His cross" achieved that peace (Col. 1:12–23); the "fruit of the Spirit" applies that peace (Gal 5:22–25).

You may experience peace with God in heaven, and the peace of God in your heart. Peace now: trusting Jesus Christ. Trust yourself to Him now; "He is our peace."

155. Behold the Lamb of God

1 "Behold the Lamb of God!"
We hear the Baptist cry:
He comes to shed His precious Blood,
And for our sins to die.

2 The Lamb long fore-ordained
In these last days appears,
Before the world's foundation slain
To bear our guilt and fears.

3 The Lamb who knew no guile,
No blemish, spot, or stain,
Most holy, harmless, undefiled—
By wicked hands is slain!

4 All we like sheep had strayed
Each turned to his own way;
Upon the Lamb the Lord has laid
Our sin to take away.

5 For all who shall believe
He stands to take their place;
So that we all may now receive
His fullness, grace on grace

6 With all the saints we praise
The Lamb upon the throne.
And glory give through endless days
To God Triune alone!

S.M.

The House of God

> Preparatory Reading: Old Testament: Malachi 1–2;
>   New Testament: 2 Timothy 1–2 Psalm: 149

When He Comes

The Gulf War in Kuwait was about to erupt. The Iraqi dictator Saddam Hussein was predicting "the mother of all battles" would consume the forces of the international Coalition.

A Christian with a keen interest in prophecy stopped me to ask, "Well, what do *you* think is going to unfold—*prophetically speaking*?" My answer was accurate: "*Prophetically speaking*, I foresee a huge spike in the sales of books on prophecy!"

Too often Christians find prophecy much like the weather. It is a subject all too easy to talk about without doing anything. But the Bible plainly teaches the most certain truths about the Savior's return for very practical ends.

The Lord Jesus promised, "I will come again" (John 14:2). We spread the Communion Table "till He come" (1 Cor 11). *What can we expect when He comes?*

- *When He comes,* Christ Jesus will appear physically and visibly, just as He ascended to heaven. (Luke 17; Acts 1; Rev. 1). Do you look for and love His appearing? (Heb. 9; 2 Tim 4).

- *When He comes,* the Savior will raise the dead. (John 5; 1 Thess. 5), and end all sorrow (Rev. 22). Are you living for time or eternity? laying up treasure for heaven, or earth?

- *When He comes,* our Lord will claim His Bride (Eph 5; Titus 2; Rev. 19) and gather His people (Matt 24, 1 Thess. 4). Are you His? Are you ready?

- *When He comes,* the Master will reward His servants (Luke 12; Matt 25). Are you living to please and serve Him?

- *When He comes,* believers will see God's dear Son "face to face," with Him, like Him, where He is (John 17; 1 John 3). Are you purifying yourself for that day?

- *When He comes,* all who are lost, wicked, and unbelieving shall be condemned to everlasting punishment (1 Thess. 1; 2 Thess. 1; Matt 25; Rev. 22). Have you fled for refuge from the wrath to come to Jesus Christ?

Are you watching, working, walking, waiting, witnessing to hasten that Day *when He comes*?

156. Lord Jesus, let me follow Thee

1 Lord Jesus, let me follow Thee
My Master, Lord and God!
Thy loving voice yet calls to me
To go where Thou hast trod.

2 Let me repent and die to sin
Deny myself each day
And through the strait gate enter in
Upon Thy narrow way.

3 Let me confess Thy saving Name
Each day take up the cross
Hold fast Thy truth, and without shame
Endure reproach and loss.

4 Let me, believing in Thy Word,
Keep Thy commands in love
Be Thou my Shield and great Reward
In earth and heaven above.

5 Lord Jesus, once-slain, risen Lamb
Fulfill Thy Word to me
"Serve, follow, that wher'er I am,
There shall My servant be!"

6 Till to the glory of Thy grace
I hear Thee say, "Well done!"
And stand before Thee, face to face
My God, my Shield and Sun!

C.M.

The House of God

Preparatory Reading: Old Testament: Malachi 3–4;
New Testament: 2 Timothy 3–4 Psalm: 150

"Watch!"

Shaded by the olive trees near Gethsemane, the Lord Jesus sat down with His four closest disciples. Across from them they could take in the vista of old Jerusalem, its walls glistening with marbles, its Temple gleaming with gold. The Master had just left the Temple courts for the last time, "a house desolate" (Matt 23:38). He had shocked them with a prediction—"there shall not be left one stone upon another, that shall not be thrown down" (Mark 13:2–3). Privately, they now pressed but two key questions, "When?" and "What signs?" (13:4).

Answering in reverse order, the Master outlined "what signs" would mark the *course* (13:5–13), the *commencement* (13:14–23) and the *close* (13:24–31) of the present age. These signs signal to us the need to "endure to the end" (13:13) and "publish the gospel to all nations" (13:10).

But answering the question "When," our Savior emphasized "of that day and that hour knoweth no man" (13:32).

Hence every true believer, every faithful disciple, every true Church must "watch"—*watch and wait* (33) as we patiently "take heed" to the times; *watch and pray* (33) to remain alert and active; *watch and work* (34) in whatever role or task He has appointed us in the 'household of faith' (Eph 2:11–22), *watch and wake* (35–36) at all hours and conditions of crisis or lull as they roll on; and *watch as one* (37) as heirs together of "the common salvation" (Jude 1–2) in Christ. Are you watching, "till He come?"

Let us draw near with a true heart in full assurance of faith, having our hearts sprinkled from an evil conscience, and our bodies washed with pure water. 23*Let us hold fast the profession of our faith without wavering; (for he is faithful that promised;)* 24*And let us consider one another to provoke unto love and to good works:* 25*Not forsaking the assembling of ourselves together, as the manner of some is; but exhorting one another: and so much the more, as ye see the day approaching (Hebrews 10:22–25).*

157. Father of Jesus Christ our Lord

1 Father of Jesus Christ our Lord,
To Thee the knee we bow
To plead the promise of Thy Word—
Hear our petitions now!

2 Of Thee through all of earth and heaven
The house of faith is named:
One family Thou hast freely given
To Christ, in Christ reclaimed.

3 The riches of Thy glory grant:
Thy Spirit's might impart
To strengthen all the inner man,
As Christ indwells the heart.

4 O root and ground Thy saints in love,
That all may comprehend
Its depths below, its heights above,
Its breadth and length's full end!

5 Grant us the love of Christ to know
Surpassing knowledge all
Till God's own fullness overflow
And fill us in Thy thrall.

6 Now to our God, whose boundless power
Is able to achieve
Exceedingly, abundantly
Above all we conceive;

7 To Him who in His church is known
Be glory without end
To all the world and ages shown
By Jesus Christ, Amen!

Based on Ephesians 3:14–21
C.M.

"For This Cause"

For this cause I bow my knees unto the Father of our Lord Jesus Christ, 15Of whom the whole family in heaven and earth is named, 16That he would grant you, according to the riches of his glory, to be strengthened with might by his Spirit in the inner man; 17That Christ may dwell in your hearts by faith; that ye, being rooted and grounded in love, 18May be able to comprehend with all saints what is the breadth, and length, and depth, and height; 19And to know the love of Christ, which passeth knowledge, that ye might be filled with all the fulness of God. 20Now unto him that is able to do exceeding abundantly above all that we ask or think, according to the power that worketh in us, 21Unto him be glory in the church by Christ Jesus throughout all ages, world without end. Amen.

Ephesians 3:14–21

"Prayer is the language of a needy heart."

These words of E. M. Bounds, himself a man of prayer, lay a plumb-line to judgment on so much that we think is prayer. Let us for but a moment stop, cease from all of our talking about God, all of our talking at God. Let us pause, consider, reflect: *What is it we pray for, from our hearts?*

The words we read here from the Apostle Paul express the prayer of a large, clean, pure heart. We could well say of Paul what James wrote of Elijah the prophet: "He prayed earnestly," literally, "he prayed in his prayer" (Jas. 5:17). We can do much else in prayer—preach, snipe, rhapsodize, self-congratulate. Our Savior laid this damning indictment on such prayer: "The Pharisee stood and prayed thus *with himself*" (Luke 18:11).

Paul's fervor comes through in his posture: "I bow my knees" (14). True, a physical pose cannot create the soul's emotions. Yet the inward must affect the outward. Our standing should express reverence, our sitting humble penitence, our kneeling the beggary of need. The last sight the elders of Ephesus had of Paul was on his knees (Acts 20: 36). *What drives us to our knees?*

As Paul prays for his beloved converts, his aspirations soar to encompass the entire Church of God throughout all ages, in all places (21). We can truly say he prays for us here. And as he prays, so should we pray for ourselves, for each other, for all the saints (6:18). "After this manner therefore pray ye," said our Lord Jesus (Matt 6:9). "Hitherto ye have asked nothing in My Name: ask, and receive, that your joy may be full" (John 16:24). Paul's prayer follows and unfolds the Divine pattern of the Lord's Prayer.

His preface claims our adoption as God's children by the Savior, both in our access to the Father, and in our fellowship with all the election of grace (14–15 cf. 2:19–21). His plea seeks all good only from God as "the Father of our Lord Jesus Christ," whose redeeming Blood alone has purchased for us "the riches of His glory" (15–16 cf. 1:3–7, 18). His petitions long for the Holy Ghost to strengthen and enlarge our souls (16); for the Savior to make our hearts entirely His home (17). His purposes grasp at tip-toe and finger-tip for the infinite. It will take all God's children to span the immeasurable dimensions of Christ's love—a breadth to embrace peoples of all the world; a length in seeking and saving the lost; its depths in reaching even "the chief of sinners" himself; its height in raising us to sit and reign in heaven (17–19). It will take the whole Church, fitly framed together as a living temple of the Spirit, to "be filled with all the fullness of God." (19). Thus all the Body of Christ shall become "the fullness of Him that filleth all in all" (1:22–23). How else will our Father's Name be hallowed, His kingdom come, His will be done?

Paul's faith is as large as his requests. His doxology of praise strains and stretches grammar to the breaking-point. He piles phrase upon phrase, coins new terms in double-superlative as he declares his confidence that God is hearing and answering prayer (20–21). See for yourself as you read it. Think of *all you ever asked*; add to it all you dared to *think* of asking. *Above* all, *abundantly* above all, *exceeding* abundantly above all we ask or think, God is well able to effect by the resurrection power of His Son even now at work in us by His Spirit. Infinity, eternity, omnipotence set the expectations of prayer, because in prayer we lay hold on God.

Paul's "Amen" affirms and appropriates all (21). Dare we say "Amen" as well?

Do we pray? Do we pray in prayer? What is it we pray for, from our hearts?" For this cause" may our Triune God drive us to our knees!

www.ingramcontent.com/pod-product-compliance
Lightning Source LLC
Chambersburg PA
CBHW080406300426
44113CB00015B/2413